MW01193207

Message to Our Folks

MESSAGE TO OUR FOLKS

The Art Ensemble of Chicago

Paul Steinbeck

The University of Chicago Press
Chicago and London

The University of Chicago Press, Chicago 60637
The University of Chicago Press, Ltd., London
© 2017 by The University of Chicago
All rights reserved. Published 2017.
Printed in the United States of America

26 25 24 23 22 21 20 19 18 17   1 2 3 4 5

ISBN-13: 978-0-226-37596-0 (cloth)
ISBN-13: 978-0-226-37601-1 (e-book)
DOI: 10.7208/chicago/9780226376011.001.0001

Library of Congress Cataloging-in-Publication Data

Names: Steinbeck, Paul, author.
Title: Message to our folks : the Art Ensemble of Chicago / Paul Steinbeck.
Description: Chicago ; London : The University of Chicago Press, 2017. | Includes
    bibliographical references and index.
Identifiers: LCCN 2016028219| ISBN 9780226375960 (cloth : alk. paper) | ISBN
    9780226376011 (e-book)
Subjects: LCSH: Art Ensemble of Chicago—History. | Jazz—Illinois—Chicago—
    History and criticism. | African Americans—Illinois—Chicago—Music—History
    and criticism.
Classification: LCC ML28.C4 A774 2017 | DDC 784.4/165—dc23 LC record
    available at https://lccn.loc.gov/2016028219

♾ This paper meets the requirements of ANSI/NISO Z39.48–1992 (Permanence of
Paper).

Malachi said to me, "We're preaching FREEDOM, whether we like it or not." and i understood exactly what he meant.

—**JOSEPH JARMAN**, *Black Case*

Contents

Acknowledgments

First I want to express my gratitude to Lester Bowie, Malachi Favors Maghostut, Shaku Joseph Jarman, Roscoe Mitchell, and Famoudou Don Moye for their amazing, life-changing music.

My introduction to the Art Ensemble came from Mwata Bowden, a former president of the Association for the Advancement of Creative Musicians (AACM) and the longtime director of the Jazz X-tet at the University of Chicago. I went to college at UChicago, and as a sophomore I auditioned for the X-tet. Mr. Bowden accepted me into the ensemble on the condition that I switch from electric bass to double bass, an instrument better suited for the X-tet's repertoire. Learning to play a new instrument was a struggle at first, especially because I could not hear myself in rehearsals. The double bass I borrowed from the Department of Music did not have a pickup, and as a novice I was unable to project my sound without amplification. During one Wednesday-night rehearsal, I complained to Mr. Bowden, hoping for sympathy (and the use of a microphone). Instead, he told me to study the technique of Art Ensemble bassist Malachi Favors, who for decades refused to play with an amplifier, preferring an entirely acoustic tone. That weekend I bought several Art Ensemble recordings from the old Jazz Record Mart in downtown Chicago, and immediately I was hooked. I've been listening to the

Art Ensemble ever since—long enough, it turns out, to write a book about the group.

Besides Mr. Bowden, I am grateful to my other teachers at the University of Chicago, including Lawrence Zbikowski, Thomas Christensen, and Richard Cohn, who taught me everything I know about music theory and analysis. I continued my education at Columbia University, where I studied with George E. Lewis, Joseph Dubiel, and Christopher Washburne. Special thanks are due to Prof. Lewis, a brilliant improviser, composer, and scholar whose research is a model for my own work. I also want to acknowledge Marion Guck (University of Michigan), Jerome Tharaud (Brandeis University), and Travis Jackson and Steven Rings (both of the University of Chicago), all of whom offered valuable advice as I began my research.

I conducted research for *Message to Our Folks* in every city that the Art Ensemble called home: Chicago, Paris, New York, and St. Louis. My thanks to the archivists and librarians at the Chicago History Museum, the Chicago Public Library, Columbia College's Center for Black Music Research, the University of Chicago's Special Collections Research Center, the Bibliothèque nationale in Paris, the New York Public Library for the Performing Arts, the Institute of Jazz Studies at Rutgers University–Newark, and the Gaylord Music Library at Washington University in St. Louis. A big thank-you to Jason Yonover, who spent a summer helping me dig into Chicago's many archives. In addition to my archival research, I conducted more than fifty interviews for this book, and I am obliged to those who took the time to share their perspectives on the Art Ensemble: Martin "Sparx" Alexander, Malba Allen, Fred Anderson, Kevin Beauchamp, Jacques Bisceglia, Larayne Black, Jodie Christian, Philip Kelan Cohran, Velena Daniels, Thulani Davis, Alex Dutilh, George Favors, Bobby Few, Alvin Fielder, Lawrence Kart, Marty Khan, Gabriele Kleinschmidt, John Litweiler, Howard Mandel, Terry Martin, Francesco Martinelli, Jacques Michelou, Douglas Mitchell, Kunle Mwanga, Rosetta Rimmer, Jordan Sandke, Shirley Scott, Jaribu Shahid, Charles "Bobo" Shaw, Rasul Siddik, Thomas Stöwsand, Rev. Edwin Walker, Richard Wang, Martin Wieland—and most of all, Joseph Jarman, Roscoe Mitchell, and Don Moye. Further insights into the Art Ensemble came from the photographers who contributed their images to this book: Jacques Bisceglia, Lauren Deutsch, Enid Farber, Hans Harzheim, Leonard Jones, Jacky Lepage, and Roberto Masotti.

Message to Our Folks was written at Washington University in St. Louis, where I have taught since 2012. I could not have completed the book without a series of grants from Washington University's Center for the Humanities and the Faculty of Arts and Sciences. Thanks to all who made these grants possible, in particular Jean Allman, Gerald Early, Bill Maxwell, Erin Mc-Glothlin, Keith Sawyer, Barbara Schaal, and Rebecca Wanzo. Additionally, I am indebted to my wonderful colleagues in the Department of Music. Pat Burke, Todd Decker, Dolores Pesce, and Peter Schmelz helped me apply for the grants mentioned above. Ben Duane, Denise Elif Gill, and Alex Stefaniak read almost every word of the book manuscript, while Craig Monson and Robert Snarrenberg—two expert writers—worked miracles on the thorniest passages. The department's outstanding administrators, Kim Daniels and Pat Orf, made my job easier every day. Another member of the Department of Music, PhD student Dan Viggers, turned my Art Ensemble transcriptions into elegant musical examples.

I feel fortunate to have found a home for my book at the University of Chicago Press. My editor, Douglas Mitchell, is the best in the business: ask any of his authors, who positively revere him. Moreover, he's the only editor I know to have performed with John Cage and the Art Ensemble's Joseph Jarman . . . in the same concert. When I started writing *Message to Our Folks*, I hoped that Mr. Mitchell would take it on, and now with the moment of publication upon us, I'm astounded by all that he did to make the book better. Several other individuals from the Press played critical roles in bringing this book to publication, including Kyle Wagner, who worked tirelessly on the photographs and musical examples; Marianne Tatom, whose careful copyediting made the text easier to read; Ryan Li, who designed the book's jacket and pages; Jenni Fry and Joan Davies, who shepherded the book through the production process; and Ashley Pierce, whose publicity efforts helped *Message to Our Folks* reach readers around the world. Thanks also to the Press's reviewers, especially Nick Gebhardt.

Last but certainly not least, I want to say how much I appreciate my family and friends from Nebraska to Tennessee, Chicago to Tokyo, Brooklyn to Birmingham, whose encouragement kept me writing for the better part of three years. If you're reading *Message to Our Folks*, you care about the Art Ensemble or you care about me—maybe both—and I am thankful for your support. No one gave more to this project than my wife, Candice Ivory, and I lovingly dedicate this book to her.

Paul Steinbeck
St. Louis, Missouri

Introduction

Thus we unite, say AACM
GREAT BLACK MUSIC POWER
and we act; To make our dreams
realities.[1]

The 1972 Ann Arbor Blues & Jazz Festival took place near the University of Michigan in a field named for bluesman Otis Spann. This was the third edition of the festival, which had grown from a small on-campus concert into a major musical event that drew audiences numbering in the tens of thousands. The first two festivals exclusively featured blues bands, but in 1972, the concert lineup expanded to include performers from the world of contemporary jazz. This programming scheme yielded a remarkable series of musical pairings: Miles Davis and Otis Rush, Sun Ra and Howlin' Wolf, and on the cloudless afternoon of 9 September, the Art Ensemble of Chicago and Muddy Waters.[2] The members of the Art Ensemble had already been in Ann Arbor for a few weeks, rehearsing each day at the precise hour when their festival set was slated to begin, and their meticulous preparation helped them deliver an explosive, briskly paced performance.[3] They opened with "N'Famoudou-Boudougou," a percussion piece dedicated to the Guinean master drummer Famoudou Konaté, then immediately transitioned to the startling theatrical sketch "Immm," in which the musicians broke into a collective coughing fit before singing an ecological lament:

> The air, you is a-killing me
> I can't feed my children in the sea
> And the flowers, they cry all day

While the Art Ensemble moved about the stage, ringing bells and chanting, the audience marveled at the band members' costumes: the tuxedo jacket and train conductor's cap sported by Lester Bowie; Malachi Favors and Don Moye's face paint and African attire; the East Asian martial-arts kit worn by Joseph Jarman; and Roscoe Mitchell's priestly white robe. After "Immm," the Art Ensemble tore through three instrumental compositions, including the climactic "Ohnedaruth," played at a breakneck tempo approaching four hundred beats per minute. The performance concluded with the group's theme song, "Odwalla"—at first bluesy, then swinging, sparse, and ultimately silent, as one musician after another laid down his instrument and walked off the bandstand.[4]

This spectacular performance earned the Art Ensemble a standing ovation. Some of the festivalgoers shouted so joyfully that Malachi Favors felt as if he and his bandmates had "baptiz[ed]" all of Ann Arbor.[5] Muddy Waters, whose set followed the Art Ensemble's, was waiting backstage to congratulate his fellow Chicagoans. "I don't know what y'all was doing," he told Favors, "but y'all was *doing* it."[6]

Muddy Waters's fascination with the musicians' virtuosic playing and audacious showmanship led him to attend several more Art Ensemble concerts after the Ann Arbor performance.[7] He wanted to gain a deeper understanding of what the Art Ensemble was "doing," and a single performance could not satisfy his curiosity. Of course, nothing could have prepared Waters for what he experienced that day in September 1972, because he had never heard—or seen—a band like the Art Ensemble. During their concerts, the five group members played hundreds of instruments, creating a vast array of sounds and musical forms. They also recited poetry and performed theatrical sketches, all while wearing face paint and masks, laboratory coats, and traditional dress from Africa and Asia. Their music could be alternately tranquil and raucous, mythic and political, humorous and intense. As Lester Bowie used to say, the Art Ensemble's performances were "serious fun."[8]

This book, *Message to Our Folks*, is the first history of the Art Ensemble as well as the first in-depth study of the group's music. The Art Ensemble's story begins—where else?—in Chicago. The members of the Art Ensemble belonged to the Association for the Advancement of Creative Musicians (AACM), an African American community organization on Chicago's South Side. After its formation in 1965, the AACM became the most influential artists' collective in jazz and experimental music. Roscoe Mitchell founded the Art Ensemble one year later, and soon his band was setting the pace for the entire Association. At the end of the 1960s, the Art Ensemble left Chicago for Paris, becoming the first AACM group to reach a "world audience."[9] In the 1970s, the band started recording for major labels, paving the way for AACM colleagues such as Anthony Braxton. Moreover, the Art Ensemble stayed together longer than any other AACM group, continuing to perform for more than forty years. Because of these achievements, many considered the Art Ensemble to be the "flagship" AACM band, the Association's ambassador to the globe.[10]

The Art Ensemble's distinctive model of social relations, adapted from the AACM, made all of these accomplishments possible. Although AACM musicians composed and performed in many different styles, they were bound together by a shared commitment to supporting one another's creative explorations. Drawing on the Association's example, the members of the Art Ensemble established their own social model based on the principles of cooperation and personal autonomy. As George E. Lewis wrote in his AACM history, *A Power Stronger Than Itself*: "The Art Ensemble of Chicago . . . radically exemplified the collective conception of the AACM as a whole."[11]

The Art Ensemble's revolutionary musical practices were also rooted in the early discoveries of the Association. In the 1960s, AACM members devised new means of integrating improvisation and composition, "hybrid" modes of music-making not previously envisioned by jazz players or experimentalist composers.[12] The Art Ensemble took AACM-style hybridity to a new level, developing a unique performance practice that combined group improvisation with intermedia (poetry, theater, costumes, movement) and a large repertoire of written compositions.

A note on intermedia: I have adapted this term from Dick Higgins, who employed it to describe fusions of multiple media forms into experimental artworks that are much more than the sum of their parts. For Higgins, the prime example of intermedia was the postwar "happening"—"an uncharted land," in his description, "that lies between collage, music, and the theater."[13] The intermedia happenings of the 1950s and 1960s were a major influence on the Art Ensemble, whose performances integrated musical sound with text, gesture, and image in unprecedented ways. Crucially, no two Art Ensemble performances were alike: one concert might be particularly theatrical, while another might emphasize the visuals created by the group onstage. Of course, the band members were musicians first, and in their performances, the most meaningful intermedia relationships always brought other art forms into dialogue with music. Accordingly, I use *intermedia* (rather than related terms like *multimedia* and *mixed media*) when referring generally to all the elements of the group's performances that reached beyond music into other artistic realms. In the band's concerts and recordings, dramatic scenarios, visual imagery, physical gestures, and poetry recitations were never presented in isolation. Instead, these intermedia elements always emerged from—and remained integrated with—the sounds that the Art Ensemble played.

The Art Ensemble's musical and social practices are the core themes of *Message to Our Folks*. I show how the group's social model and musical techniques evolved from the 1960s into the twenty-first century, while staying true to the founding ideals of the AACM. Additionally, I examine the social implications of the band's performances, in which the musicians transformed their social practices of cooperation and autonomy into strategies for group improvisation.

I could not have done justice to any of these topics without the participation of the Art Ensemble. When I began my research, Don Moye granted me access to the group's archives, where I found musical scores, compositional sketches, and documents not available in any library. I also conducted dozens of interviews with the musicians as well as their families, friends, collaborators, and business associates. On a few unforgettable occasions, I listened to Art Ensemble recordings with the band members, who offered valuable insights on everything that shaped the performances: their rehearsal procedures, the stories behind their compositions, the in-the-moment decisions they made while improvising, and the cultural contexts in which their concerts and re-cording sessions took place. The Art Ensemble's contributions were absolutely essential to this book, which I see as the product of a "collaborative mode of writing history," much like *A Power Stronger Than Itself*, Lewis's collective autobiography of the AACM.[14]

Indeed, there are many connections between this book and *A Power Stronger Than Itself*. The Art Ensemble members played major roles in the Association, and every chapter of *Message to Our Folks* is in dialogue with Lewis's archival research and authoritative oral histories. *Message to Our Folks* is also informed by three other important texts: Lincoln T. Beauchamp's *Art Ensemble of Chicago*, a self-published collection of interviews with the band; Ronald M. Radano's *New Musical Figurations*, a biography of AACM composer

Anthony Braxton; and Benjamin Looker's *"Point from Which Creation Begins,"* a history of the Black Artists' Group (BAG), a St. Louis collective organization modeled on the AACM.[15] For many readers, *Message to Our Folks* will be a companion to the groundbreaking work of Lewis, Beauchamp, Radano, and Looker.

Unlike these books, however, *Message to Our Folks* combines historical inquiry with musical analysis. History and analysis, two very different methods of musicological research, rarely come together in books on jazz and improvisation.[16] *Message to Our Folks* includes both, using history and analysis to provide a comprehensive view of the Art Ensemble's social and musical practices. The band's social model can best be understood in historical terms, as a set of practices initially influenced by the AACM and subsequently revised as the musicians traveled the world. The Art Ensemble's musical practices, on the other hand, can be comprehended only through analytical episodes that show how the group members make music together in real time.

Message to Our Folks is organized chronologically. Six of the book's nine chapters are historical in nature, as is the brief conclusion that follows chapter 9. In the other three chapters, I pause the historical narrative so that I can closely analyze exceptional performances by the Art Ensemble, all of which represent key moments in the group's history. Chapter 4 is devoted to *A Jackson in Your House*, a 1969 studio album recorded just weeks after the band arrived in Paris.[17] Chapter 7 centers on *Live at Mandel Hall*, a recording of a 1972 concert in Chicago, the musicians' biggest hometown performance since their return from Europe in 1971.[18] And chapter 9 examines the concert video *Live from the Jazz Showcase*, taped in 1981, when the group's popularity was at its peak.[19] All three recordings are widely available, and I recommend playing the audio (or video) while reading chapters 4, 7, and 9. When read in this way, *Message to Our Folks* becomes a guidebook to the Art Ensemble's music, a real-time accompaniment to performances already rich with meaning.

Chapter 1 offers a prehistory of the Art Ensemble. Malachi Favors, Joseph Jarman, and Roscoe Mitchell came of age in postwar Chicago, a city remade by African American migrants from the southern United States. They encountered music at home, in churches and schools, and across the South Side's busy entertainment district. All three served in the army during the 1950s, then returned home to Chicago, intent on performance careers. By the 1960s, however, there was very little work on the South Side for black musicians. The young saxophonists Mitchell and Jarman found an outlet in the Experimental Band, a workshop ensemble led by Richard Abrams. The Experimental Band created a constituency for new music on the South Side, and in 1965, Abrams and three colleagues founded the AACM to organize this emerging community.

Chapter 2 chronicles the early years of the AACM. Favors, Jarman, and Mitchell joined the Association at its founding in 1965, enlisting in a nationwide movement of African American organizations working to achieve social change through the arts. By 1966, the preeminent bands in the AACM were Jarman's quartet and Mitchell's Art Ensemble, which featured Favors on bass and a new arrival from St. Louis, trumpeter Lester Bowie. The two groups were developing distinct yet compatible approaches to improvisation, composition, intermedia, and instrumentation, and the members of the Art Ensemble started inviting Jarman to collaborate with them. He joined the Art Ensemble in 1969, just as the group was planning a voyage to Paris.

Chapter 3 focuses on the Art Ensemble's Paris debut in the summer of 1969. The Chicagoans were an overnight success, rapidly finding performance opportunities, recording contracts, and enthusiastic audiences. Paris-based critics also embraced the Art Ensemble, although their reviews often emphasized the actual and imagined political content of the band's music, reflecting concurrent debates on colonialism and Vietnam, as well as enduring misrepresentations of black performance in France. During this pivotal period, the musicians began practicing cooperative economics, sharing all earnings and expenses, a practice that became the foundation of their social model. Cooperation helped the group members thrive in their new surroundings, and they commemorated the partnership by renaming their band the Art Ensemble of Chicago.

Chapter 4 examines *A Jackson in Your House*, the first of fifteen albums the group recorded in Europe. *A Jackson in Your House* brilliantly illustrates the band's innovations in intermedia performance. On the album's A-side, the musicians use verbal commentary and dramatic scenarios to address a number of political and cultural issues—notably the reception of black experimental music, including their own. However, on the B-side, they take a different approach, blending music with poetry and theater to create the kinds of vibrant soundscapes that Paris audiences found so compelling.

Chapter 5 narrates the final year and a half of the group's European sojourn. By the fall of 1969, word of the Art Ensemble had spread throughout the continent, and the band began venturing outside France to perform. They maintained a home base near Paris until 1970, long enough to recruit a fifth group member: percussionist Don Moye, an American who had relocated to Europe in the late 1960s, like the Chicagoans. Soon after Moye came aboard, the musicians' radical political reputation caught up with them, and local authorities forced them to leave the Paris suburbs. So they hit the road, playing concerts across France and Western Europe until the spring of 1971, when they were ready to return to the United States.

Chapter 6 centers on the Art Ensemble's activities during the 1970s. Back home in America, the musicians worked to build a larger domestic audience, a task that became easier after they signed with Atlantic Records. They also formalized the cooperative practices that they first implemented in France, establishing Art Ensemble of Chicago Operations (AECO), a corporation held equally by the five members of the group. But the most significant change to their social model was a new ethic of personal autonomy. The musicians set up separate residences and launched independent side projects that could generate supplemental income when the Art Ensemble was on hiatus. This arrangement allowed them to reinvest even more of the band's earnings, which increased throughout the 1970s as the Art Ensemble toured the United States, Europe, and Japan.

Chapter 7 explores the concert recording *Live at Mandel Hall*. Unlike the other performances analyzed in this book, *Live at Mandel Hall* contains relatively few intermedia elements. Instead, this stunning seventy-six-minute concert shows the Art Ensemble's social practices in action, with autonomy and cooperation functioning as improvisational techniques. The concert be-gins and ends with preselected compositions, but the hour-long stretch in between is structured entirely through improvisation. The musicians impro-vise independently at first, then work together to build a thrilling series of frameworks for group improvisation.

Chapter 8 addresses the group's tenure at ECM Records, when the Art Ensemble achieved international renown and critical acclaim. By the 1980s, the band was touring more widely than ever, both abroad and at home. In the United States, the musicians' mastery of intermedia allowed them to break into the performing-arts scene, while the success of their ECM albums earned them a prominent place in the jazz community, which was contending with the rise of a powerful traditionalist movement headed by Wynton Marsalis. This movement attracted many opponents, including the members of the Art Ensemble, who resisted traditionalism by proposing an alternative aesthetic, expressed in their evocative slogan "Great Black Music, Ancient to the Future."

Chapter 9 concentrates on *Live from the Jazz Showcase*, a video recording that captures all the sounds and sights of an Art Ensemble performance. In this concert, the band plays pieces inspired by the African diaspora, from Nigeria, Mali, and Morocco to New Orleans and New York. As the music unfolds, the group members' onstage movements turn the performance into an immersive intermedia experience. *Live from the Jazz Showcase* is a ritual, a community celebration, and a captivating sonic and visual narrative about the meaning of Great Black Music.

Message to Our Folks concludes with a survey of the band's final decades, from the 1980s into the twenty-first century. In the late 1980s, the musicians began touring and recording with collaborators from around the world, sharing their musical and social practices with a global network of performers. As their collaborators would discover, the Art Ensemble's social model was so strong that it could keep the group together even in the most trying circumstances. Jarman took a lengthy sabbatical, Bowie passed away in 1999, and Favors died in 2004. But Mitchell and Moye soldiered on until 2010, bringing Jarman back into the fold and delivering their resonant message to all with ears to hear.

1 The South Side Scene

We realized that we all had this vital thing in common, which was the spirit of searching.[1]

Sweet Home Chicago

For over forty years, the members of the Art Ensemble carried their city's name with pride, declaring to the whole world that there was no place like Chicago. Indeed, the Art Ensemble could not have emerged anywhere else. During the middle of the twentieth century, Chicago was widely regarded as the "capital of black America."[2] It was home to more African Americans than any metropolitan area but New York. The South Side of Chicago, in fact, had a larger black population than Harlem.[3] Many of the nation's most influential African American politicians, business leaders, writers, and artists were based in Chicago. And the city's music scene was second to none. The spirited performances of South Side church musicians like Mahalia Jackson and Thomas Dorsey made gospel music a national phenomenon.[4] After World War II, the local circuit of nightclubs and recording studios drew the best blues singers from the Mississippi Delta to Chicago.[5] Jazz, too, was an integral part of the Chicago music scene. At midcentury, the South Side boasted some seventy-five jazz venues, even more than in the Roaring Twenties, when a young Louis Armstrong was Chicago's brightest star.[6] In the 1960s, Chicago became a crucial staging ground for the Black Arts Movement, as African American organizations across the country worked to achieve social change through the arts.[7] The Art Ensemble emerged from one of Chicago's foremost black arts organizations, the Association for the Advancement of Creative Musicians (AACM). From the AACM, the members of the Art Ensemble learned not only musical techniques but also the social practices that sustained them from the 1960s into the twenty-first century. In other words: without Chicago, the South Side music scene, and the AACM, there would have been no Art Ensemble.

Likewise, the community that gave rise to the Art Ensemble could not have come to be without the Great Migration. From the early twentieth century to the 1970s, six million African Americans left the South and resettled elsewhere in the United States. Some moved to the West Coast, but most traveled northward, and the greatest number of migrants headed to the booming cities of the industrial North.[8] No northern city was affected more by the Great Migration than Chicago. In 1900, there were only thirty thousand African Americans in Chicago, less than two percent of the city's population.[9] Over the next three decades, nearly two hundred thousand black Southerners came to Chicago, with the majority arriving during World War I and the 1920s.[10] The rate of migration slowed in the 1930s, as the Depression made it difficult for newcomers to find work.[11] When the United States entered World War II, the economy began to grow again, setting off a second wave of mass migration from the South. In the three decades that followed, another five hundred thousand African American migrants entered Chicago, and the local black community swelled to more than a million, one-third of the city's population.[12]

Prior to the Great Migration, most black Chicagoans lived along the State Street corridor, a narrow strip of land extending southward from 22nd Street. When migrants from the South began to stream into Chicago, the city's black residential area expanded, though not fast enough to keep pace with the ever-increasing population. By 1930, a few isolated enclaves had developed elsewhere in Chicago, but the vast majority of African Americans resided in the South Side "black belt"—still centered on State Street, now a little more than a mile wide from west to east (Wentworth Avenue to Cottage Grove Avenue), and five miles long from north to south (22nd Street to 63rd Street).[13] This territorial expansion was not achieved without a struggle. White realtors and property owners used restrictive covenants to prevent African Americans from purchasing or leasing homes in certain neighborhoods. With the housing supply artificially constricted, the black belt became overcrowded and overpriced.[14] In Chicago, the boundary lines between white and black spaces were sharply drawn, and stepping across a border could be dangerous, even deadly. During the summer of 1919, the city erupted in a weeklong race riot after a black teenager was killed for swimming too close to a whites-only beach.[15] Racial violence also broke out in the neighborhoods, especially those adjacent to the black belt. White gangs guarded their turf against all trespassers.[16] And when black families managed to buy or rent property in districts dominated by whites, their new neighbors resisted fiercely. From the 1910s to the 1950s, African Americans who moved into contested areas saw their homes mobbed, firebombed, and burned to the ground.[17]

The African American community countered segregation and intimidation by building vibrant institutions across the South Side: social clubs, churches, top-notch public schools, and businesses of all kinds.[18] To its residents, the black belt seemed like "a city within a city," a world unto itself.[19] And life in the place they called Bronzeville could be wondrous, particularly for those who had a few dollars to spare. Recent arrivals from the South were able to establish themselves quickly, often with the assistance of family and friends from back home who had preceded them to Chicago.[20] In some ways, it was as if African American migrants had never left the South. Instead, they brought southern culture to the North.[21] On any Saturday night in Bronzeville, black Chicagoans could dine at restaurants that served southern food or socialize at nightclubs that featured down-home music.[22] Then, on Sunday morning, they could attend churches where the style of worship—and sometimes the minister and whole congregation—had been imported directly from the South.[23]

Bronzeville offered much more than northern echoes of southern folkways. By midcentury, the black belt had a larger population than "all but eighteen . . . cities of the United States," and its citizens had access to every amenity and attraction of a modern metropolis.[24] The *Chicago Defender*, Bronzeville's renowned African American newspaper, was read throughout the nation.[25] South Side residents could attend professional sporting events, shop at well-appointed department stores, and watch the latest Hollywood features at cinemas that seated thousands.[26] In the nighttime, the action shifted to the broad sidewalks of "the Stroll," a bustling commercial district initially centered at 35th Street, and subsequently at 47th Street.[27] Many of the businesses along the Stroll were open around the clock, drawing crowds in which locals rubbed shoulders with visitors "from all over the world. . . . just like Times Square."[28]

The sheer visual spectacle was part of the Stroll's appeal, but the main event was live music. According to Malachi Favors, a proud Bronzeville native and a future member of the Art Ensemble, "Chicago had the greatest entertainment section in the world, right there on the South Side."[29] During the early years of the Great Migration, the premier nightclubs were located near 35th and State, the heart of the Stroll.[30] As Bronzeville expanded, a number of new venues opened to the south, where the population was growing the fastest. In the late 1920s, when the Stroll moved to 47th Street and South Parkway (later Martin Luther King Jr. Drive), it was anchored by the three-thousand-seat Regal Theater and the mammoth six-thousand-seat Savoy Ballroom.[31] After World War II, African Americans gained entry to residential neighborhoods on the periphery of the black belt: Englewood and Greater Grand Crossing to the south and west, as well as Oakland, Kenwood, Hyde Park, and Woodlawn, which lay east of Cottage Grove Avenue.[32] By the 1950s, this flourishing area had become the hub of the Bronzeville music scene. The intersection of 63rd Street and Cottage Grove was encircled by more than a dozen nightclubs.[33] As one South Sider remembered, 63rd and Cottage was a "mecca for musicians": "You didn't need to go in a joint to hear some music . . . you could [listen] just walking up and down the street."[34]

In the 1960s, with little warning, the South Side scene would change dramatically, a development that led to the formation of the AACM. However, for Malachi Favors, Joseph Jarman, and Roscoe Mitchell—young musicians who came of age in the 1940s and 1950s—Bronzeville was an ideal place to grow up. The tradition that they came to call "Great Black Music" was taking shape right in their neighborhoods. And all they had to do was open up their front doors and walk out into the night.

Malachi Favors

Rev. Isaac Favors and his wife, Maggie Mayfield Favors, came to Chicago from Lexington, Mississippi.[35] An ambitious young couple, they had much in common with their fellow migrants. Both were born and raised in Mississippi, which sent more African Americans to Chicago than any other state.[36] Additionally, like many migrants from the South, they were following a trail blazed by a close relative—Rev. Favors's uncle, Elder P. R. Favors, who settled in Chicago during the 1910s.[37] On 22 August 1927, not long after Rev. and Mrs. Favors moved to Chicago, they had a son, the first of their ten children.[38] Instead of naming their oldest son for his father, Isaac, they chose a name belonging to a different Old Testament figure: Malachi, the "messenger" of the Lord.[39]

The Favors and Mayfield families were among the earliest members of the Church of God in Christ (COGIC), a Protestant denomination founded in

Lexington, Mississippi, by Charles Harrison Mason.[40] In the 1890s, Mason and several other Baptist ministers from the Mississippi Delta became involved with the Holiness movement, an outgrowth of Civil War–era Methodism. According to Holiness teaching, believers could receive the Holy Spirit in their souls and become sanctified—set apart from the world and delivered from sin. The doctrine of sanctification led Mason and his associates to split with the Baptists and form their own denomination.[41] They also began studying the relationship between African American religious practices and the ecstatic worship of the first-century Christian church.[42] These investigations brought Mason to the famous Azusa Street Revival in Los Angeles, where in 1907 he spoke in tongues and experienced the baptism of the Holy Spirit, like the apostles at Pentecost. When Mason returned from the Azusa Street Revival, he reorganized the Church of God in Christ as a Pentecostal assembly and moved its headquarters to Memphis, Tennessee. After the move to Memphis, Mason's denomination took off. Thousands of converts joined the church, and Mason sent out evangelists to establish new congregations throughout the country.[43] Elder P. R. Favors, who had served as a deacon at the "mother church" in Lexington, was dispatched to Chicago, where he started one of the city's first COGIC congregations.[44] In the next decade, the South Side became home to twenty more COGIC churches, including Friendly Temple, founded by Rev. Isaac Favors upon his arrival in Chicago.[45]

Music played an essential role in the church where Malachi Favors was raised. All COGIC church members were expected to sing, and at a testimony service, anyone might be called to lead the entire congregation in a song. Those who demonstrated special talents were given additional opportunities to develop their voices, from singing solos during worship services to performing at revival meetings.[46] The singing culture of the Church of God in Christ would produce some of the most celebrated vocalists of the twentieth century, beginning with the first gospel singer to cross over into popular music, Sister Rosetta Tharpe, a frequent visitor at Elder P. R. Favors's congregation.[47] The instrumentalists in COGIC churches were just as innovative as the singers, introducing new performance practices that transformed the sound of African American religious music.[48] As Malachi Favors observed: "The Church of God in Christ brought with it in its praise the use of all musical instruments: tambourine, guitar, you name it. . . . They completely turned around praise in this hemisphere."[49] Sister Rosetta Tharpe, for instance, was known as much for her brilliant guitar playing as for her singing voice. However, young Malachi preferred another COGIC singer-guitarist, the itinerant evangelist Utah Smith:[50]

The first musical instrument that I ever heard played was the guitar, [by] Elder Utah Smith. He was my first idol. Everybody that picked up a guitar in the Church tried to sound like Elder Utah. The man was powerful. He could sing. He had a big baritone voice and he didn't need a microphone.[51]

A typical preacher's kid, Favors spent every Sunday and most weeknights at his family's church. Outside the walls of Friendly Temple, though, he faced the same issues confronting every other working-class child in Chicago, from family finances to juvenile gangs. Favors grew up near 41st Street and Langley Avenue in the Grand Boulevard neighborhood, where "[y]ou got your reputation by dealing with your fists. I wasn't all that good at first, but I got ran home from school a couple of times, and one time a little short guy came to my rescue. He was pretty bad, so I started running with him."[52] Favors's fighting days did not last long, but his toughness served him well when he entered Wendell Phillips High School, the first African American high school in the city. High school football was big in 1940s Chicago, and he joined the Phillips team, playing lineman despite being undersized for the position (at five-foot-six and a hundred and fifty pounds).[53] In addition to sports, Favors was also into music. He and three classmates formed a "street corner doo-wop group" that debuted at the high school's annual Spring Festival.[54] Unfortunately, the Spring Festival was also the group's last performance. A doo-wop quartet was only as good as its lead singer, and the group members never found a reliable tenor. They even auditioned Sam Cooke—*the* Sam Cooke, a fellow student at Phillips High—but he didn't make the cut. As Favors recalled:

> It looked like the group was going to disband because the tenor William Green, he fell in love with every girl that he knew, and so that interfered with the rehearsal of the group. He would never show up because it was a new girl, so we tried to get somebody else. We tried Sam Cooke, and Sam Cooke couldn't quite measure up to Green, so the group eventually broke up.[55]

After Favors graduated from Wendell Phillips High School, he found a job in the mail room of a firm in the Loop, Chicago's downtown business district. Because he was still living with his family, he had few expenses, and his eight-to-five job gave him plenty of pocket money.[56] So Favors became a "nighthawk," spending his evenings listening to music at Bronzeville's theaters and nightclubs.[57] He developed a keen interest in all styles of jazz, from small-group bebop to the big-band music of Count Basie, Duke Ellington, and Earl Hines.[58] And no matter who was performing, Favors always paid close attention to the double bass. He heard Ellington's mid-1940s orchestra at the Regal Theater, and was captivated by the bass playing of Junior Raglin. Some months later, when the Ellington band returned to the Regal Theater, Favors was upset when he discovered that Raglin had been replaced by another bassist, Oscar Pettiford:

> [W]hen these bands came to the Regal, they would list their personnel. This one time when I went to the Regal, I saw Oscar Pettiford and I was totally discouraged. . . . I started not to go. I said, "Man, Junior Raglin is not playing," but I went on in and Duke Ellington was playing and Oscar Pettiford came to the mic and took a solo and that was it. I couldn't get over that.[59]

Week by week, Favors was growing more interested in music and less committed to his day job. His coworker Louis Blackwell, a friend from Phillips High, already had one foot out the door, having taken up guitar with the aim of becoming a professional musician. He urged Favors to do the same, saying, "Man, you better get you something to do. You know you don't like working down here."[60] After hours, the two friends listened to records and plotted their next move. "We'd get together at night and listen to Charlie Parker and all the great jazz players," Favors remembered. "I would just be listening to the bass and I would strum like I'm playing the bass."[61]

One day, he finally decided to follow Blackwell's advice. Favors was walking along Wabash Avenue when he came upon a shop with a double bass for sale: "I was working, so I went in there, paid down on it, and bought the bass."[62] This purchase would change his life, not just his career path, and to him it felt almost like a religious experience. As Favors put it, "[t]he Spirit of the music has always been a part of my being, but did not manifest itself until I was in my late teen years. Then I awakened to GREAT BLACK MUSIC!"[63]

Favors left the Wabash Avenue shop and brought the bass home. When he walked through the door, his father questioned him immediately:

> "What are you going to do with that thing, boy?"
> I said, "I'm going to play it."[64]

This reaction did not take Favors by surprise. Certain musical instruments, including Utah Smith and Rosetta Tharpe's electric guitars, were welcome in COGIC churches. But the bass Favors carried into his parents' apartment was associated with secular entertainment, and in the COGIC tradition, believers were taught to avoid playing or listening to "the Devil's music."[65] Rev. and Mrs. Favors did not want their son to come into conflict with the church's teachings, and at first they tried to persuade him to quit. After a few months, however, they finally relented. Malachi's musical pursuits did not affect his religious devotion, and he impressed his parents by diligently practicing his new instrument. If he continued to apply himself, they reasoned, he could experience greater success as a musician than as a mail-room clerk.[66] "I guess," Favors mused, "they were happy to see me do something."[67]

With his parents' blessing, Favors began making his way onto the South Side music scene. At a nightclub on 43rd Street, he befriended Wilbur Ware, "the most famous bass player in Chicago."[68] Ware volunteered to serve as Favors's teacher, but his unorthodox bass technique was difficult for a novice to emulate. And because Ware played exclusively by ear, he couldn't help Favors learn how to read musical notation or interpret chord symbols.[69] Eventually Favors found another instructor: Roscoe "Bali" Beach, an accomplished bassist who taught music at DuSable High, Chicago's second African American high school.[70] But by the time he started taking bass lessons from Beach, Favors had already become a full-fledged professional musician. He had hoped to study music intensively before venturing into the professional world. However, there was a "shortage of bass players" in Bronzeville, and he did not want to turn down gigs.[71] So he learned on the job, rapidly acquiring the skills he needed to get by on the bandstand. Just one year after he began playing, Favors was working so much that he had to join Local 208, the African American musicians' union:[72]

> I remember the guys walked me over to the union, which was on 39th and State, to get me to join the union, because the union representative would come around to the gigs, and if you weren't in the union you were in trouble. I was playing when I really didn't know what I was doing, because they called me: "Are you working?" I'd say "No." "You want a gig?" "Yeah." So I was out there, it was something. I think back, I don't know how I made it.[73]

In February 1951, after playing bass professionally for some four years, Favors enlisted in the U.S. Army.[74] At the time, the Korean War was at its height, and many American servicemen were sent to the 38th Parallel, including Favors's younger brother Isaac Jr.[75] In contrast, Malachi's tour of duty took place much closer to home. He was assigned to a support unit at Camp Atterbury, Indiana, an infantry installation located two hundred miles south of Chicago.[76] By all accounts, Favors's military career was rather uneventful. He was able to visit Chicago almost every weekend.[77] While at Camp Atterbury, he kept up his musical skills by practicing on a cello that he brought from Bronzeville: "I had a cello that I took with me, and I tuned it like a bass. All the time I was [soldiering], after I'd come back off of the field, I would go get my cello."[78] Favors's experience with the cello helped him develop a virtuosic technique uncommon among bassists of his generation. When his two-year stint in the army came to an end, he returned to Chicago as one of the most proficient bass players in the city.[79]

Favors lost no time in resuming his performance career. By the summer of 1953, soon after his discharge from the army, he was playing a regular gig with saxophonist Paul Bascomb at the Strand Show Lounge near 63rd Street and Cottage Grove Avenue. His rhythm-section partner in the Bascomb group was Vernel Fournier, who later worked the 63rd Street nightclub circuit with Ahmad Jamal. In August 1953, Favors made his recording debut with Bascomb's band, backing up the singer Dinah Washington, a fellow alumnus of Wendell Phillips High School. He continued to perform and record with Bascomb until the end of 1953.[80] Favors worked as a freelance musician through the fall of 1955, when he joined trumpeter King Kolax, a veteran bandleader whose past sidemen included a young John Coltrane.[81] Favors's association with Kolax lasted a little more than a year.[82] Then he was hired by the pianist Andrew Hill, a rising star on the Bronzeville jazz scene. Favors stayed with Hill from 1956 to 1959, tracking a number of 45- and 78-rpm records as well as the LP *So in Love*, the pianist's first album as a leader.[83] Equally adept at timekeeping and playing countermelodies, Favors was the perfect bassist for a piano trio. After Hill's trio dissolved, Favors found his way into another popular piano trio, led by King Fleming. In 1962, he appeared on Fleming's album *Stand By*, recorded for the Arco label, a subsidiary of Chess Records.[84] The Fleming trio performed primarily on the South Side, like every group that had hired Favors in the previous ten years. By the mid-1960s, though, gigs were harder to come by, and Fleming's sidemen had to look elsewhere for work.[85] Favors was engaged by the pianist Reno Tondelli, who played jazz standards in the lounge of the O'Hare Airport Holiday Inn. For the first time in his career, Favors had to leave the South Side to earn a living.[86] However, African American musicians born a decade after Favors never even had the chance to perform regularly in Bronzeville. Like their parents, who migrated from the South to

Chicago in search of better lives, the members of this generation would have to make their own opportunities.

Joseph Jarman

On 14 September 1937, in Pine Bluff, Arkansas, Eva Robinson had her first and only child. She named the boy Joseph Jarman, after his father.[87] Mr. Jarman did not stay with the family following the birth of his son, and Ms. Robinson, who was still a teenager, had to raise Joseph herself.[88] Pine Bluff was mired in the Depression, and like most people in her hometown, Ms. Robinson did not have much money. So she set her sights on Chicago.[89] When World War II broke out, the U.S. government rushed to build several defense plants in Chicago, and hundreds more local manufacturers turned to war production, seemingly overnight. Faced with a labor shortage, the city's factories opened their doors to African American women, including Ms. Robinson, who found a defense-industry job soon after migrating to Chicago.[90]

Joseph Jarman was just a toddler when he came to Chicago with his mother. They were joined by her younger sister, Joseph's aunt Mary.[91] The family moved into a modest residence at 720 West Scott Street in the Near North Side neighborhood.[92] Located several miles north of Bronzeville, the Near North Side was one of the only integrated areas in the entire city.[93] When Jarman entered Schiller Elementary School, a block east of the family home, his class included both white and black students. Things changed during Jarman's early adolescence. His family briefly relocated to Grand Boulevard, the South Side neighborhood where Malachi Favors grew up, and Jarman started getting into fights.[94] When he returned to the Near North Side, he clashed with his old classmates at Schiller Elementary and was labeled a "bad boy."[95] Jarman overcame his disciplinary problems by throwing himself into extracurricular activities such as the Boy Scouts. He also signed up for Junior ROTC, a program designed to prepare high school students for service in the Armed Forces. In the spring of 1952, Jarman was awarded a medal for his performance as a first-year ROTC cadet at Waller High School (later Lincoln Park High), which he attended after graduating from Schiller Elementary.[96] Later that year, his family moved to the South Side for good, and at DuSable High, his new school, he continued to excel in Junior ROTC, winning additional medals in 1953 and 1954.[97]

When Jarman arrived at DuSable High, he was especially excited about the music program, which offered the finest training of any Chicago public school.[98] He had loved music all his life, thanks to his upbringing in the Robinson clan. As Jarman recalled:

> I first started becoming aware of music crawling around the living room floor. I'm very fortunate that I had this tradition in the family. Mother in the [Baptist] church singing gospel in the choir, uncle a great jazz buff telling me all about Lester Young, Charlie Parker. My aunt madly in love with people like Billy Eckstine, Paul Quinichette. And being taken out to the nightclubs and bars while these people were all playing.[99]

The family's first South Side residence was near 48th Street and St. Lawrence Avenue, only three blocks from the 47th Street Stroll.[100] One year, in celebration of Jarman's birthday, his uncle brought him to the Regal Theater to hear the saxophonist and blues singer Eddie "Cleanhead" Vinson, an event he never forgot: "They had big elaborate shows at that time with dancing girls, and they would have a film, and then the stage show. . . . It was such a spectacle."[101] By the time Jarman entered DuSable, the family lived at 46th Street and Woodlawn Avenue, still close to the Stroll but also within walking distance of the jazz clubs on East 55th Street. He and his friend James Johnson would "break the rules and come all the way to 55th, where the Beehive Lounge was."[102] Without a chaperone, they couldn't get into the nightclub, so they stood outside and gazed at the window, hoping to catch a glimpse of the jazz musicians onstage: "We think we saw Charlie Parker. . . . whether it's myth or reality, we don't care, because it was so important to us."[103]

James Johnson played bassoon in the DuSable High School band, and Jarman became determined to join.[104] He wanted to take up trumpet or alto saxophone, but those instruments cost too much.[105] He could, however, afford to play the snare drum: DuSable High owned several snare drums, and for just six dollars, he could buy two drumsticks and a practice pad for working on rudiments at home.[106] With this small expenditure, Jarman started his percussion studies under "the incredible guidance of Captain Walter Dyett," the director of DuSable's music program.[107] Capt. Dyett earned his officer's rank while directing the 8th Army Band. Then he became an educator who "applied military rigor to the art of training young musicians," a method that transformed talented students into polished professionals.[108] Capt. Dyett taught in Chicago public schools for more than thirty years, primarily at DuSable High, where his pupils included Gene Ammons, Dorothy Donegan, and Johnny Hartman.[109] In 1939, then-student Red Sanford—better known as Redd Foxx—was the star of the DuSable *Hi-Jinks*, the annual musical written and directed by Capt. Dyett.[110] Another prominent alumnus, Nat "King" Cole, left a lasting impression on the DuSable music program, according to Jarman: "[T]he thing I remember most in the music room is that Nat 'King' Cole had carved his name into one of the desks."[111] In Jarman's view, Capt. Dyett's famous protégés owed their success to his "extraordinary example":

> He was just an extraordinary man, also an extraordinary musician and extraordinary teacher. . . . [A]ll these very young students from this kind of rough city-life background, he had the capacity to instill in them the idea of self-realization, of self-esteem, of self-purpose. . . . And music was his vehicle to instill these qualities into his students.[112]

Jarman studied music with Capt. Dyett until 1955, the end of his junior year. Then he put his education on hold, dropping out of DuSable High School to enlist in the army.[113] He needed to help support his family, and military service promised a steady paycheck.[114] Moreover, the knowledge Jarman had gained through ROTC would enable him to quickly advance through the ranks, increasing his army salary. In basic training, he performed brilliantly, finishing second in his company, though he felt that he should have placed ahead of the white recruit who finished first. The newly integrated Armed Forces did not always treat African American soldiers equally, and according to Jarman, his drill sergeants "wouldn't accept a black as number one."[115] After basic training, he volunteered for additional training at Fort Benning, Georgia. There, he completed paratrooper training at Airborne School and proceeded directly into Ranger School for rigorous instruction in small-unit combat tactics.[116] Once his training ended, Jarman joined a Pathfinder platoon belonging to the 11th Airborne Division. In 1956, his platoon was deployed in Southeast Asia to aid in the incipient war against communist North Vietnam. Jarman was wounded in combat, but after he recuperated, he was given the opportunity to choose his next assignment.[117] He asked to be transferred to the 11th Airborne Division Band.[118]

Jarman's army band was stationed in Augsburg, West Germany, not far from Munich.[119] When his transfer went through, he had just started playing alto saxophone, the instrument he originally wanted to study back in high school. The 11th Airborne Band director, in true military fashion, was willing to take on a new recruit, provided he could keep pace with the other soldiers.[120] Jarman had to learn the band's core repertoire in just two months:

[T]he band director gave me sixty days to be able to play the basic marches. So the musicians in there, all of these men, from seven in the morning until midnight, would be on my case, and that was the greatest time, because I didn't have but sixty days to get my stuff together. The band director knew I couldn't play when I got there, so I had to learn. Otherwise, he was going to throw me out. So I made it. At the end of the sixty days, I was able to read the music and play the marches and stuff.[121]

On the weekends, Jarman developed his improvisation skills by playing in jazz jam sessions held in nearby Munich. By his own admission, he was "not very good": "At least I had the audacity and nerve to get up there."[122] However, trial and error proved to be effective teachers. Before long, he was sufficiently skilled to earn a temporary duty assignment with a jazz trio that traveled as far as Frankfurt, West Germany, to perform at American officers' clubs.[123]

In the summer of 1958, Jarman received his discharge from the army.[124] He was anxious to return to civilian life. Military service had given him a way to stay engaged with music and learn the alto saxophone, which would become his primary instrument. But ultimately Jarman was not cut out for the army. To be an effective soldier, particularly in combat settings, Jarman had to adopt a "military attitude" that clashed with his innate "humanism."[125] After three years in the army, he was suffering from what he described as "emotional [and] psychological problems."[126] When he made it back to Chicago, he tried to self-medicate with alcohol and drugs, to no avail. At one point, the stress became too much to bear, and he lost his ability to speak. "The vocal apparatus wouldn't work," Jarman recalled. "I had internalized all of the anguish and frustration."[127] For more than a year, he would be completely mute.[128]

Jarman began to doubt that he could get well while living in Chicago. In 1959, he set out on a cross-country odyssey, roaming from New York City to California, the Great Lakes to the Rio Grande, in search of experiences that would help him speak again.[129] One fateful night, he found himself in El Paso, a border town where he heard a saxophonist playing "really powerful, heavy alto, Texas blues."[130] Jarman captured this pivotal encounter in a poem:

El Paso - spring 1959 - i arrive on
the hot summer Greyhound from the East, full
of dust and silence. High off - pills, smack,
other deadly joys, mute, silent and noiseless.
Moving through on the Texas side/niggers played jazz, blues,

drunken songs in empty sweaty bars, i
remember the alto player, clean like Lou
Donaldson and Bird, singing magic through
the metal tube; mexican girls, nigger,yea
"poor white" women sucking vamp threads
from the stripes on his pants. and the U.S. Army has
a missle school at El Paso, friend in khaki
invite me to the barracks; (to rest, sleep, get
myself together) the smack inside me feelin
the texas Sun. like lizards crawling through
my face while i pee, wetness in the desert
sunlight, sand and sheep dung in my hair.

At first i wandered into the white distract
soon (as i read the signs) big loud police
"nigger, where you thank you going"
"don't you hear us boy!"
i write on my pad "MUTE" "I CANNOT SPEAK"
bang, against my chest, night stick,
"nigger this ain't where you want to be,
now about three block thata way is the
nigger-wetback place; understand me
boy"-
bang, night stick on my head
bang, leg-bang-chest again-

i move away - The Texas air sweet fire
knowledge between the crack of my ass,
laughter follows, i run slowly into the
neon pleasure of America' biggest border
town, full of lust, and sin and smack.
growing "pains" to self, he said, "realization".[131]

Jarman's account of his El Paso experience was his first attempt at poetry.[132] In the years to come, he would write enough poems to fill an entire
book.[133] But the most important thing he took away from that night in West
Texas was a renewed interest in music, which had faded when he was struck
mute. The "empty sweaty bars" of El Paso were far less glamorous than venues
like Bronzeville's Regal Theater, yet he was captivated by the sounds of the

anonymous saxophonist who "[sang] magic through the metal tube."[134] As Jarman remembered, his 1959 visit to El Paso "sort of BOOM, opened me up. It was a signal that [music] was the thing for me to do."[135]

Jarman left El Paso and headed to Tucson, Arizona. He wanted to obtain psychiatric treatment at the local Veterans Administration hospital, the same facility where his uncle Theodore Robinson had convalesced after serving in World War II.[136] While in Tucson, Jarman spent much of his time at a local public library. He formed a friendship with one of the librarians, who thought that studying Buddhism could aid him in his recovery.[137] Although Jarman was brought up Baptist, he was intrigued by what he was hearing about Buddhism.[138] The librarian gave him a little volume entitled *The Teachings of the Buddha*, and Jarman found that reading the book helped him accept what he went through in the army.[139] "That's what Buddhism teaches you," he explained. "You're OK. If you want to be cool, be cool. If you want to be crazy, be crazy. There's no gods, no demons to blame for your condition. Nobody controls your life but you."[140]

After several months in Tucson, Jarman returned to the Midwest.[141] He stopped in Chicago for a short while, then moved to Milwaukee, Wisconsin, arriving in 1960 and living there for a year. "Milwaukee," according to Jarman, "is where I really began to come back around."[142] He rented a room at the YMCA, practiced his saxophone, and "learned to refocus [his] energy into positive, concrete directions."[143] He also went back to school, taking courses in philosophy at the Milwaukee Institute of Technology (later Milwaukee Area Technical College). While in Milwaukee, Jarman continued the course of psychiatric treatment that he had begun in Tucson, and at long last his speech was restored.[144] As he recalled: "They got me to be able to talk again, and I haven't shut my mouth since."[145] By 1961, Jarman felt healthy enough to come home to Chicago. He returned to the South Side and enrolled in the music program at Woodrow Wilson Junior College, where he would meet Malachi Favors and another promising saxophonist in his early twenties, Roscoe Mitchell.[146]

Roscoe Mitchell

Ida Carter and her husband, Roscoe Mitchell Sr., had a son on 3 August 1940. He was the second of their two children but their first son, and they named him Roscoe Jr. for his father. Roscoe Mitchell Jr. was born in Chicago, his parents' hometown, and he grew up near 60th and State Street, just west of Washington Park, one of the largest public parks on the South Side.[147] At the time of Mitchell's birth, the Washington Park neighborhood formed the southern boundary of the old black belt. In the 1940s and 1950s, African Americans moved into new neighborhoods to the east, south, and west of Washington Park, and the area where Mitchell was raised became the geographic center of an expanded Bronzeville.[148] During daylight hours, black Chicagoans gathered in Washington Park for sporting events and other diversions, and at dusk, they headed a few blocks south of the park to listen to live music at the nightclubs surrounding 63rd Street and Cottage Grove.[149] Both destinations were only minutes away from Mitchell's childhood home—everything offered by midcentury Bronzeville was at his fingertips.

Young Roscoe had a number of artistic interests: movies, other strains of popular culture, even painting.[150] But his first love was music. Indeed, Mitchell "always wanted to be a musician," and he found inspirational figures all around, in his neighborhood as well as in the family home.[151] Mitchell's parents were regular churchgoers, and each week they brought him to the South Side church pastored by his uncle, Rev. Charles Commodore Carter, an ordained minister in the Spiritualist denomination.[152] Worship services at Rev. Carter's church were full of music, and Mitchell was fascinated by the choral selections and vocal solos performed by the members of the congregation. He also appreciated the musical qualities of his uncle's sermons, which blended elements of speech and song.[153] "The music in the church," Mitchell recalled, "really had the most profound initial influence on me."[154]

At home, Mitchell's parents exposed him to a wide variety of music, which proved crucial to his development as a musician.[155] His father enjoyed listening to jazz singers, and was something of a vocalist himself, according to Mitchell: "I guess you could group him into the [category] of singers that they call crooners. He also used to do a thing where he would imitate instruments with his voice."[156] Roscoe Sr. hoped that his son would learn to sing, and he encouraged him to emulate the vocal styles of famous artists such as Louis Armstrong, Billie Holiday, and Nat "King" Cole.[157] Mitchell's listening regimen, of course, was not limited to vocal music. The family radio was often tuned to the broadcasts of Al Benson and McKie Fitzhugh, pioneering African American DJs known for diverse playlists that included rhythm-and-blues songs, jazz records, and Top 40 hits.[158] Moreover, many of the recording artists promoted on these broadcasts could be found performing at the lounges and nightclubs around 63rd and Cottage, a mile east of the Mitchell residence. "[W]hen I grew up in Chicago," Mitchell remembered, "not only did I listen to the same music that my parents listened to, I could go right outside of my house and go down the street, and they'd be playing there."[159] Washington Park was another important site for musical learning. Many of the musicians in Mitchell's neighborhood liked to practice their instruments in the park, and he would spend long hours with them, observing their practice routines and picking up tricks of the trade.[160]

Mitchell began his formal music studies around the age of twelve.[161] The family moved to Milwaukee temporarily, and his brother Norman Mainie came along, bringing with him an impressive collection of jazz records.[162] "[H]e would get me to sit down and listen to them," Mitchell recalled.[163] Saxophone players were well represented in Norman's record collection, from swing stalwarts like Coleman Hawkins and Lester Young to bebop innovators like James Moody and Charlie Parker.[164] Norman was also a close friend of the South Side saxophone prodigy Nicky Hill, who was making a name for himself in the clubs at 63rd and Cottage, and he thought that his brother had the same kind of musical potential.[165] With Norman's support, Mitchell decided to "actually pursue an instrument."[166] At West Division High School in Milwaukee, he began playing the clarinet, a typical starter instrument for students interested in woodwinds.[167] Mitchell and his family soon returned to their old neighborhood in Chicago, and he continued his musical education at the city's third African American high school, Englewood.[168] In the course of his studies at Englewood High, he learned to play two additional woodwind instruments. The school's dance band needed a baritone saxophonist, and Mitchell volunteered, getting his introduction to the saxophone family. By his senior year, he was ready for another challenge, so he borrowed a fellow student's alto saxophone.[169] He took to this instrument immediately. "[T]he alto," Mitchell affirmed, "was the saxophone that really caught my interest."[170] Like any musician learning a new instrument, Mitchell was looking for a role model, and he found one in his Englewood High classmate Donald Myrick, a talented saxophonist who some years later joined Earth, Wind & Fire.[171] According to Mitchell, "Donald Myrick was an excellent musician when I met him in Chicago, and he was a big motivation for me."[172] He continued: "I was fortunate to meet him at that time, because he was already playing the instrument in high school, and he . . . took me under his wing."[173]

In 1958, Mitchell graduated from Englewood High School and enlisted in the army.[174] Unlike Malachi Favors and Joseph Jarman, who joined the military intending to be soldiers, Mitchell's plan from the beginning was to become an army musician. He had only been playing saxophone for a short time, but he was proficient enough to pass his audition for the prestigious U.S. Army Europe Band, one of the best service bands on the continent. Mitchell would spend almost three years with this band, which was based at the army's European headquarters in Heidelberg, West Germany.[175] When he arrived in

Heidelberg, he discovered that the lifestyle of an Armed Forces specialist was much different than that of a high school music student. By his own admission, Mitchell "wasn't really serious" about music before the army: "I played . . . but I also hung out with all my friends."[176] In contrast, the army band offered a "full musical environment": "[W]e'd have breakfast . . . and then there's rehearsal until lunch time, and then after that there was another rehearsal, and if there wasn't a gig, like going out and playing a parade or something, then there'd be caring and cleaning of instruments and individual practice."[177]

During his time in Germany, Mitchell took every opportunity to advance his musical knowledge. In the U.S. Army Europe Band, he played both alto and baritone saxophone. He also developed his clarinet skills by taking lessons from the principal clarinetist of the Heidelberg Philharmonic.[178] Additionally, Mitchell frequented the jam sessions held at the Heidelberg jazz club Cave 54, where he performed with American servicemen and met standout German musicians like Karl Berger and Albert Mangelsdorff.[179] On a few occasions, Mitchell's army band visited West Berlin to play in parades alongside two other Armed Forces ensembles, the West Berlin–based 298th Army Band and the 76th Army Band from Orleans, France. When their parade duties ended, the musicians who were interested in jazz would gather for after-hours jam sessions. The free-jazz saxophonist Albert Ayler, then a member of the 76th Army Band, was a regular participant in these sessions.[180] Before Mitchell met Ayler, he had only encountered "freer form music" by listening to Ornette Coleman's recordings with his army colleagues.[181] At the time, Mitchell and his bandmates were "conventional" players who did not welcome Coleman's musical experiments: "As a matter of fact, a bunch of buddies of mine, we'd make fun of Ornette's music."[182] They reacted in much the same way to Ayler's improvisations at the jam sessions in West Berlin. According to Mitchell, "I remember everyone was putting him down, because we were all so obsessed with playing correctly":

> But at this one session, Albert led off with three or four choruses of the blues and then went off into his own thing, with that awesome sound he had, and everything became clear to me. I had already heard Ornette Coleman on records and couldn't quite grasp what he was doing. But hearing Albert live was an enlightening experience.[183]

The sounds Mitchell heard that evening would stay with him for years. As he recalled: "That was my first real awakening to [the fact that] there may be another way of doing things."[184]

In 1961, Mitchell received his army discharge and returned to Chicago.[185]

He had decided to pursue music as his civilian career, but first he wanted to further his education. So he enrolled at Woodrow Wilson Junior College (later Kennedy–King College), a Chicago city college with a dynamic music program. Then located at West 71st Street and South Stewart Avenue, just three blocks from Englewood High School, Wilson Junior College attracted music students from all over the South Side. Joseph Jarman was there, as were several other young woodwind players who would become key AACM members: Anthony Braxton, Richard "Ari" Brown, and Henry Threadgill.[186] The music program also pulled in established professionals like Malachi Favors, who came to Wilson Junior College for the opportunity to play in the orchestra and concert band.[187]

Part of the college's appeal was its low cost of attendance, especially for military veterans, whose educational expenses were subsidized by the G.I. Bill.[188] But the main draw was Dr. Richard Wang, a music professor who directed the college's ensembles and also taught courses in music theory. Like DuSable High School's Capt. Dyett, Dr. Wang had a background as a jazz performer, which helped him devise a unique music curriculum that was decades ahead of its time.[189] At most colleges and universities, professors exclusively used the European classical repertoire to teach music theory, but Dr. Wang found ways to integrate jazz and modernist composition into the Wilson Junior College curriculum. In harmony classes, his students analyzed Duke Ellington pieces like "East St. Louis Toodle-Oo" as well as the operas of Richard Wagner. And in Dr. Wang's composition classes, students learned how to construct melodies by examining Charlie Parker's saxophone solos alongside scores by Arnold Schoenberg.[190]

Mitchell and Jarman met for the first time in one of Dr. Wang's music-theory classes.[191] Jarman was one of the "most assiduous" theory students at Wilson Junior College, according to Dr. Wang.[192] Many of Mitchell's important educational experiences, however, took place outside the theory classroom. Music students had a free period on Mondays, and Mitchell would summon his classmates to a practice room to play jazz.[193] He tried to recruit Malachi Favors for these practice sessions, but initially the bassist turned him down. As Jarman remembered, "Malachi didn't even speak to us, because he was in the union."[194] Soon, however, Favors was playing in small groups with both Jarman and Mitchell.[195] The two saxophonists also participated in the Friday-afternoon jam sessions held at the college. At these sessions, Dr. Wang's students performed with a rotating cast of guests that included some of Bronzeville's best professional musicians: pianists Andrew Hill and Charles Stepney, saxophonist Eddie Harris, and drummer Steve McCall.[196]

After each Friday jam session, the Wilson Junior College music department would close its doors until the following Monday, but Mitchell and Jarman did not take weekends off. They formed a jazz combo that rehearsed at Mitchell's residence every Saturday, from mid-morning to the early evening. Mitchell and Jarman's group played a few paid engagements at community centers and 43rd Street nightclubs, but it was primarily a rehearsal band dedicated to exploring the repertoire of Art Blakey's early 1960s sextet.[197] In addition to playing Blakey-style hard bop, the group investigated recent developments in modal jazz and free jazz. The musicians built study breaks into their rehearsals, during which they listened to and discussed the latest jazz albums. On one Saturday morning, according to Jarman, the drummer showed up with three "weird records":

> One was called *The Shape of Jazz to Come*, by this funny guy named Ornette Coleman, the other was by this guy named Eric Dolphy, and the other was by John Coltrane, but we knew he was OK because he played with Miles Davis. See, we would start playing at nine o'clock, take a break in the afternoon, then we would go back 'til six or seven at night. . . . During the break they played these three records. . . . [E]verybody was so taken by these records that when we went back and played "All the Things You Are" it had changed completely.[198]

This new music may have seemed peculiar to most of the group members, but in Mitchell's recollection, the influence of free jazz was already evident in Jarman's saxophone playing. When Mitchell was in the army, listening to Albert Ayler helped him come to terms with the advances of Ornette Coleman. A few years later, at Wilson Junior College, Jarman gave Mitchell his "second stimulation toward freer form music":[199] "Joseph Jarman . . . always played really strange to me, in a bebop-ish strange way. . . . I think he was a very good influence on me at that time."[200]

Experiments

Malachi Favors, Joseph Jarman, and Roscoe Mitchell had a lot in common when their paths converged at Wilson Junior College. Although they were born in three different decades and grew up in different parts of Chicago, their musical journeys were remarkably alike. They first encountered music in their churches and at other vital neighborhood institutions. Their upbringings gave them an appreciation for the full spectrum of African American music, but when they discovered jazz, it was love at first sound. As Mitchell remembered, "after I started listening to jazz I didn't want to listen to anything else anymore."[201] They began playing instruments during their adolescent years, and continued to study jazz while serving in the Armed Forces. In 1961, the year they met at Wilson Junior College, Favors had considerably more professional experience than Jarman and Mitchell, whose musical careers had just begun. But all three were united in searching for something that they had not been able to find in the Bronzeville music scene.

Jarman and Mitchell's first forays into experimental music took place in a South Side workshop ensemble. Founded in 1961 by Eddie Harris and several other seasoned bebop players, the ensemble rehearsed weekly, first at the C&C Lounge at 63rd Street and Cottage Grove, and later at the Abraham Lincoln Center at Oakwood Boulevard and Langley Avenue. Playing in the workshop ensemble gave participants an opportunity to test out new ideas and develop skills like leading a horn section, reading unfamiliar charts, and composing adventurous music—none of which were emphasized in the nightclubs where most South Side musicians were employed.[202] The group stayed intact until 1963, when a disagreement emerged between two of its cofounders.[203] Trumpeter Johnny Hines wanted to remake the ensemble into a money-making venture, with the goal of becoming the house band at the Regal Theater. In contrast, pianist Richard Abrams hoped that the group would remain committed to musical experimentation, without any commercial pressures.[204] Hines and most of the original members left the ensemble, and Abrams took over as bandleader. He was one of the group's most prolific composers, and he had already brought a number of young South Side musicians into the ensemble, more than enough to sustain it after the departure of Hines's clique. Now under Abrams's direction, the workshop ensemble continued under a new name: the Experimental Band.[205] This name would prove to be prophetic. In just a few short years, the members of the Experimental Band would transform both jazz and experimental music—not just in the city of Chicago, but around the world.

Many of the younger musicians in the Experimental Band came from Wilson Junior College. The drummer Jack DeJohnette, then a student at the college, introduced Abrams to Roscoe Mitchell, who promptly joined the Experimental Band.[206] In addition to attending the band's regular rehearsals, Mitchell started visiting Abrams at his home near 63rd and Cottage to discuss musical composition, painting, and philosophy.[207] Before long, Mitchell's college classmates Joseph Jarman and Henry Threadgill followed him into the Experimental Band.[208] As Jarman remembered, "Roscoe said, you oughta come, there's this guy who's got a rehearsal band":

So I went down there and there was [Abrams], and he greets you like you were his brother or something. He said, welcome, and there were all these people in there, and I had to step back, because some of them were like famous people—local Chicago musicians, Jack DeJohnette, Scotty Holt, Steve McCall. And then this guy gave me an invitation whenever I felt like it to come by his house and get music lessons. He'd offer you herb tea and it would be so *good* . . . . He was into herbology, astrology, painting, all this mystical stuff that I had dreamed of. It was like I had found a teacher.[209]

Mitchell and Jarman had never encountered a teacher like Abrams. Each afternoon, they left the Wilson Junior College campus and headed straight for Abrams's residence, where they spent hours studying music and a variety of other subjects. During Experimental Band rehearsals, their performance skills were stretched to the limit as they navigated Abrams's complex scores.[210] "The first rule of the band," according to Abrams, "was that all music had to be original material," and he brought a new composition to the ensemble virtually every week.[211] He also asked the group members to write pieces for the Experimental Band, even though most had little to no experience as composers. Jarman, Mitchell, and their bandmates were up for the challenge, and with Abrams's guidance, they gradually developed their own distinctive approaches to composition.

Crucially, the compositional practices that emerged from the Experimental Band did not preclude improvisation. All of the ensemble members were capable jazz improvisers, and just as in mainstream jazz, the compositions played by the Experimental Band were often conceived as platforms for improvisation. However, Abrams's insistence on constant experimentation kept the group from relying exclusively on techniques inherited from jazz or any other style.[212] The music Abrams wrote for the ensemble drew on the compositional method invented by Joseph Schillinger, which offered composers a way of organizing musical materials according to mathematical relationships, not stylistic conventions.[213] (At midcentury, the Schillinger system attracted adherents across the country, from composers working in commercial music, concert music, and jazz to Lawrence Berk, founder of the Berklee College of Music.[214]) In addition to studying the Schillinger system, Abrams and the other group members paid close attention to trends in contemporary experimental music. In Europe and the United States, experimentalist composers were using graphic scores to depict unconventional sounds and prompt performers to improvise—concepts that aligned precisely with the aims of the Experimental Band. The members of the Experimental Band wanted to break down the barrier between composition and improvisation, and graphic notation became an indispensable resource in this critical endeavor.[215] The ensemble's research into new forms of musical notation led to further discoveries in the realm of conducting. As the Experimental Band delved deeper into graphic notation, Abrams devised a novel system of conducting gestures that enabled him to direct every section of a piece, from fully scored passages to open-ended improvisations.[216] For Jarman and Mitchell, playing in Abrams's Experimental Band was like studying at a first-rate conservatory. In Mitchell's estimation, "I learned more from my sessions and discussions with [Abrams] than I learned from school."[217]

The Experimental Band also served as a refuge during a turbulent period in the Bronzeville music scene. Since the earliest days of the Great Migration, residents of the South Side had been surrounded by live music. In the 1960s, though, everything changed. The city of Chicago began requiring nightclubs to pay an exorbitant licensing fee in order to host performances by four or more musicians.[218] Some South Side establishments could only afford to employ smaller ensembles, while others had to hire disc jockeys, who would spin hit records all night for less than the price of a live band. The DJ format also provided a better fit with popular tastes, which were tilting away from jazz in favor of rock music and soul.[219] Many jazz musicians lost their jobs, but for nightclub owners, this was the least of their worries. During the past five decades, the South Side entertainment industry had benefited from a continuously expanding customer base, courtesy of the Great Migration. Now this customer base was shrinking. Urban-renewal efforts decimated entire neighborhoods, and the once-mighty Bronzeville economy contracted rapidly. Countless businesses closed their doors, including most music venues and virtually every jazz club.[220] Of course, jazz did not simply vanish from Chicago. Like Malachi Favors, who landed a gig at the O'Hare Airport Holiday Inn, some African American musicians were able to work in the suburbs or on the predominantly white North Side.[221] Meanwhile, on the South Side, jazz went underground, surfacing only at late-night jam sessions and during the weekly rehearsals of the Experimental Band.[222]

Early in 1965, Richard Abrams and three of his musician colleagues decided to found an organization that could bring music back to the South Side. All four cofounders were experienced professionals in their mid-thirties, and three were linked to the Experimental Band: Abrams directed the group, Steve McCall was its drummer, and pianist Jodie Christian had played in the workshop ensemble from which the Experimental Band emerged.[223] The other cofounder, trumpeter Philip Cohran, did not belong to the Experimental Band, but he had spent two years working with another forward-looking ensemble,

Sun Ra's Arkestra, which was based in Chicago until 1960.[224] Moreover, like his colleague Abrams, Cohran was a self-made intellectual and respected teacher who freely shared his discoveries with younger musicians.[225] The involvement of Abrams and Cohran ensured that interest in the nascent organization would be high. By May 1965, Abrams, Christian, Cohran, and McCall were ready to launch their organization. They mailed postcard announcements to many of the leading African American musicians in Chicago, and dozens showed up for the organization's first meeting, held at Cohran's residence near 75th Street and Cottage Grove.[226]

There were fourteen items on the agenda for the inaugural meeting, but one item—"original music"—inspired more discussion than all the others combined.[227] The musicians who attended the meeting were employed by nightclubs and lounges where they played the standard jazz repertoire, not their own compositions. Club dates could be tiresome even when they paid well, and the sudden decline of the South Side had made lucrative gigs harder to find than ever before. For many musicians, playing the same standard tunes night after night felt like driving down a dead-end street, and now the road was falling into disrepair. Instead of trying to fix this decaying infrastructure, Abrams and his colleagues wanted to replace it entirely. The solution they envisioned was a musicians' collective that could provide an alternative to the nightclub scene. In this collective organization, members would work together to produce concerts of music they composed themselves. Presenting original compositions in a concert setting was an opportunity rarely granted to African American musicians, and those present at the meeting knew that they could achieve this goal only through collective effort.[228]

As the meeting continued, the attendees began to develop a broader understanding of original music, one that would become essential to the organization's self-conception.[229] Mere originality, they concluded, was not enough. At the most basic level, writing an original composition could be as simple as crafting a new melody to fit an existing chord progression—something these musicians did every time they played a solo over a jazz standard. From their perspective, musical creativity was far more important than originality. Indeed, some original music could be rather ordinary, but the compositions and improvisations of "creative musicians" came from personal engagement with a source of spiritual inspiration.[230] As saxophonist Gene Easton asserted, "creative music can only be original anyway, in a true creative sense."[231] Certain musicians at the meeting found inspiration by delving into cutting-edge experimental music, while others explored ancestral forms, styles of music once played in the southern United States or even in Africa. More than a few of those present that day in May 1965 had already been changed by their studies of creative music. By the meeting's end, it was clear that no one in the room would ever be the same.

Enthusiasm ran high after the first meeting, and before long the organization was up and running. In a few weeks' time, the members had elected Abrams as president and chosen eleven more officers and directors, many of whom belonged to the Experimental Band. They also gave the organization a name: the Association for the Advancement of Creative Musicians (AACM). One of the most urgent issues facing the AACM's new leadership was financing. The AACM needed money to present concerts, and the cofounders debated whether they should solicit funds from local businesses and other institutions. However, they ultimately settled on a self-financing model in which the Association would pay for its operations with member dues and concert ticket sales. The members wanted to create a space for experimentation in an industry that was indifferent at best to noncommercial black music, and they were wary of being co-opted by funders with other agendas.[232]

For similar reasons, they agreed that only African Americans would be permitted to join the AACM.[233] In Chicago and throughout the country, social tensions related to the civil rights struggle were making it difficult for white and black Americans to collaborate, even on matters of shared interest. This was no less true for musicians. The New York–based Jazz Composers Guild, an interracial musicians' collective founded a few months before the AACM, had already fragmented due to mistrust between its black and white members.[234] Yet another racial conflict was unfolding closer to home. For more than sixty years, Chicago had two musicians' unions, both affiliated with the American Federation of Musicians: white performers belonged to Local 10, and black performers belonged to Local 208.[235] The Civil Rights Act of 1964 outlawed segregation in trade unions, and the two locals were ordered to merge. As many members of Local 208 predicted, the merger was largely ineffective in helping African American musicians secure gigs that had been off-limits during the era of segregation.[236] Moreover, once the merger was complete, the integrated Local 10–208 enriched itself by selling Local 208's South Side headquarters, erasing the union's connection to the black community.[237] These cautionary examples were fresh in the minds of the AACM's leaders when they decided to limit membership eligibility to African Americans. In their view, a racially restrictive membership policy seemed to be a prudent strategy, the best way to achieve the Association's goal of empowering black musicians. The AACM, according to Abrams, was not interested in "fighting a racial fight": "We're promoting ourselves and helping ourselves up to the point where we can participate in the universal aspect of things, which includes all people."[238]

The state of Illinois accepted the AACM's application to become a registered nonprofit corporation in August 1965, just three months after the musicians held their first meeting.[239] As part of their application, Abrams and his fellow cofounders submitted a soon-to-be-famous list of nine purposes, the aims that would guide all of the Association's future activities:

1. To cultivate young musicians and to create music of a high artistic level for the general public through the presentation of programs designed to magnify the importance of creative music.
2. To create an atmosphere conducive to artistic endeavors for the artistically inclined by maintaining a workshop for the express purpose of bringing talented musicians together.
3. To conduct a free training program for young aspirant musicians.
4. To contribute financially to the programs of the Abraham Lincoln Center, 700 E. Oakwood Blvd., Chicago, Ill., and other charitable organizations.
5. To provide a source of employment for worthy creative musicians.
6. To set an example of high moral standards for musicians and to uplift the public image of creative musicians.
7. To increase mutual respect between creative artists and musical tradesmen (booking agents, managers, promoters and instrument manufacturers, etc.).
8. To uphold the tradition of cultured musicians handed down from the past.
9. To stimulate spiritual growth in creative artists through recitals, concerts, etc., through participation in programs.[240]

A few of the nine purposes were directly related to the members' needs: the AACM would produce concerts, sponsor a musical workshop (the Experimental Band), and encourage creative pursuits that aided the members' "spiritual growth." Most of the purposes, however, spoke not to the membership but to the African American community on the South Side—the AACM's family, friends, and neighbors. The members of the Association were deeply rooted in Bronzeville, and they realized that they could not advance creative music without contributing to the community from which it arose. With these nine purposes, the AACM declared that it was going to be much more than a musicians' collective. AACM members saw themselves as community organizers, charged with transforming society through the power of creative music.

2 Two Art Ensembles

Roscoe, Lester, Malachi and Phillip had a group. And Joseph
and Thurman and Charlie and Christopher had a group. And
lots of other people had groups as well. But those two groups
had something special about them.[1]

Presenting Creative Music

The Association for the Advancement of Creative Musicians staged
its first three concerts in August 1965.[2] On the South Side and
across the United States, there was no precedent for a concert series featuring experimental music by African American composers,
and the AACM needed to make a positive first impression. The
members concentrated their promotional efforts on the local black
community, distributing flyers in African American neighborhoods
and publishing announcements in the *Chicago Defender*.[3] As stated
in one *Defender* announcement, the members of the Association
intended to "provid[e] a concert showcase for original contemporary music," and they modeled AACM events after classical
performances, not jazz gigs.[4] Like classical performances, AACM
concerts took place in the early evening, often on Monday nights,
when many jazz clubs were closed. The concerts were held in rented
halls rather than nightclubs or taverns, and the AACM sold advance

tickets so that audience members could reserve their seats. When patrons arrived at the concert venue, they were greeted by AACM members and given printed programs listing the names of the musicians and the compositions to be performed.[5] According to AACM president Richard Abrams, the members wanted their concerts to be both "serious" and "spontaneous," as well as "unique to our heritage."[6] In order to "create [this] atmosphere," the Association had to move beyond the cultural conventions of jazz performance.[7] Indeed, at most AACM events, the only visible connections to the jazz tradition were the saxophones and drum sets played by the musicians onstage.

The inaugural concert series featured the AACM's best ensembles, including groups led by Joseph Jarman and Roscoe Mitchell. Strong performances by well-rehearsed bands would help the AACM cultivate a loyal audience of repeat ticket-buyers that it needed to fund future events.[8] Another important consideration was the Association's "original music" rule.[9] Performers at AACM concerts had to play their own original compositions, but in August 1965, some AACM groups did not have enough material to fill a two-hour concert.[10] The ensembles that were selected to play the earliest events all had multiple composers, and they were able to construct compelling concert programs that demonstrated how diverse the AACM's music could be.

Joseph Jarman led a quintet at the very first AACM concert, which was held on 16 August 1965 at the South Shore Ballroom on East 79th Street. Jarman played alto saxophone and contributed some of his compositions, as did two other band members, tenor saxophonist Fred Anderson and trumpeter Bill Brimfield. (The quintet was rounded out by bassist Charles Clark and drummer Arthur Reed.[11]) Anderson and Brimfield were perhaps the only AACM members living outside the Chicago city limits: both resided in the northern suburb of Evanston, Illinois.[12] On occasion, Anderson ventured into the city to participate in jam sessions at sites like the West Side lounge Fifth Jack's, where he met Abrams and Mitchell.[13] But most of Anderson's musical activities took place at his house on Dewey Avenue in Evanston. For a number of aspiring musicians, the Anderson home was a suburban counterpart to Abrams's South Side apartment, a gathering place for the saxophonist's many talented protégés.[14] By 1963 or so, Jarman had become part of Anderson's circle. Every week, Jarman would take an hour-long train ride from the South Side to Evanston "just to play with him and Billy [Brimfield]."[15] Soon Jarman formed a quintet with Anderson and Brimfield, and it was this band that played the first concert sponsored by the AACM.[16]

Philip Cohran's Artistic Heritage Ensemble performed at the second AACM concert, on 23 August 1965. One week later, on 30 August, the featured group was the Roscoe Mitchell Quartet with Fred Berry on trumpet, Malachi Favors on double bass, and Alvin Fielder on drum set.[17] Mitchell's career as a leader began shortly after he joined the Experimental Band. Like Jarman's group with Anderson and Brimfield, Mitchell's quartet was modeled after the influential piano-less ensembles of Ornette Coleman. The earliest version of the Mitchell quartet included Berry on trumpet, Scotty Holt on bass, and Jack DeJohnette on drums—all members of the Experimental Band.[18] It took some time for Mitchell to find a steady bass-and-drums team. In addition to Holt and DeJohnette, bassist Wilbur Ware and drummer Steve McCall played in the group for brief periods. Mitchell's quartet finally coalesced around 1963, when he found a new rhythm section: Malachi Favors and Alvin Fielder.[19] A native of Meridian, Mississippi, Fielder was a pharmacist by day and a drummer by night. He became a professional musician while still in his teens. During his college years at Texas Southern University in Houston, he worked with several local bands, including Eddie "Cleanhead" Vinson's group. When Fielder moved to Chicago to pursue a master's degree in pharmacy, he continued performing professionally, often in ensembles that played rhythm and blues as well as jazz. He also developed an interest in free jazz, thanks to an unexpected encounter with Roscoe Mitchell.[20] In the 1960s, Mitchell would spend long nights going from club to club, looking for opportunities to sit in with other bands. One evening he went onstage with John Coltrane at the Plugged Nickel, and the two saxophonists proceeded to "[blow] up a hurricane."[21] On another occasion, Mitchell turned up at a West Side nightclub where Fielder's band was playing a hard-bop rendition of the jam-session standard "Cherokee." Fielder was astounded at what happened when Mitchell approached the bandstand and took a saxophone solo: "[T]he music just loosened up so much. I think that was the first time I had played really, really loose music. He made me play that way."[22] Some months later, Fielder was rehearsing at Richard Abrams's residence when Mitchell appeared in the doorway. The saxophonist listened intently for a while, then approached Fielder and asked:

"Can you play free music?"
    "Yeah, I can play free music."
    "Come to my rehearsal next Thursday."[23]

Fielder showed up for the rehearsal and was pleasantly surprised to see Malachi Favors there. The two musicians had worked together a few years before, in a short-lived dance band that featured Gene Ammons on tenor saxophone and Sun Ra on piano.[24] At Mitchell's rehearsal, Favors and Fielder were able to pick up right where they left off. "It was like being in heaven," Fielder remembered, "because everything clicked":

> The front line was playing very loose and out, and the rhythm section was playing more or less post-bebop, like the Billy Higgins, [Ed] Blackwell thing. Mal was mainly playing a 4/4 pulse. Think of the first Ornette Coleman group. That's how it was.[25]

Fielder was glad to be working with Favors again, but Mitchell was ecstatic. He had been trying to recruit Favors ever since they met at Wilson Junior College. When Mitchell first asked Favors to join his quartet, the bassist declined because he had too many responsibilities: "I was [studying] at the college and I was working with Reno Tondelli. . . . I was just loaded."[26] But Mitchell was persistent, and Favors finally agreed:

> We had a class together and one day after class he asked me, "Man, why don't you come on and go with me and let's just jam a little bit?" They had basses up there. So I went up there and jammed a little. He said, "Really, man, I want you to be with the group." Roscoe kept after me and said, "Man, we're having a rehearsal. Can you make it?" But anyway, he convinced me, so I made the rehearsal.[27]

The Roscoe Mitchell Quartet stayed together for two years, until late 1965. Fred Berry was preparing to enter graduate school at Stanford University, and the AACM concert on 30 August 1965 would be one of the band's last public performances.[28] After Berry's departure, Mitchell continued playing with Favors and Fielder for another year, sometimes bringing in guest musicians from the AACM, such as saxophonist Gene Dinwiddie, violinist Leroy Jenkins, and saxophonist Maurice McIntyre.[29] It seemed that Mitchell could make any lineup work, as long as Favors was holding down the low end. "Malachi was sort of the glue," Mitchell explained. "He had enormous ears."[30] Mitchell wanted to find a new trumpeter eventually, but because his musical rapport with Favors was so extraordinary, he could afford to wait until the perfect candidate emerged. Finally, in the summer of 1966, Mitchell told Favors, "I think I have a trumpet player for our group."[31]

Lester Bowie

William Lester Bowie Jr. was born on 11 October 1941 in Frederick, Maryland.[32] His mother, Earxie Willingham Bowie, was a college graduate, and his father, Lester Bowie Sr., held bachelor's and master's degrees in music.[33] The Bowie family was highly musical. Columbus Bowie, father of Lester Sr., played trombone, and all of his sons became brass players.[34] Several members of the Bowie clan belonged to the Bartonsville Cornet Band, a marching band that performed at community functions in and around Frederick.[35] Lester Sr. played in the band too, although he was more interested in concert music than the marching repertoire. According to his eldest son, Lester Jr., "he wanted to be a classical trumpeter, but they wouldn't open that up to black cats."[36] So he became an educator, like many classically trained African American musicians before and since. In the late 1930s, Mr. Bowie served as the band director at Paul Laurence Dunbar High School in Little Rock, Arkansas. After his first son was born, he returned to his job at Dunbar High.[37] Then, in 1943, he moved his family to St. Louis, Missouri, where he became the band director at Booker T. Washington Technical High School, a position he would hold for decades.[38]

Mr. Bowie taught hundreds of young musicians at Washington Technical, but his prize students were at home. The Bowies had two more children in St. Louis, Byron and Joseph, and all three Bowie boys studied music with their father.[39] In the Bowie household, music lessons were mandatory. As Lester Jr. remembered, "I took lessons from my father, and it was not by choice, it was by complete force."[40] Lester Jr. started on the trumpet, his father's instrument, when he was just five years old.[41] Soon he was advanced enough to study with a trumpeter from the St. Louis Symphony.[42] Byron and Joseph Bowie followed suit, taking up the saxophone and trombone, respectively.[43] Back in Frederick, Maryland, the Bowies were the leading musicians in town as well as one of the area's most prominent African American families. Now the three newest Bowies were poised to make their mark in St. Louis, with Lester Jr. taking the lead.

Lester Bowie Jr. attended Charles Sumner High School in St. Louis. Founded during the Reconstruction period, Sumner was the first high school for African American students west of the Mississippi River.[44] Like DuSable High School in Chicago, Sumner High was nationally known for producing successful musicians and entertainers. Chuck Berry, Grace Bumbry, and Dick Gregory preceded Bowie at Sumner, and his classmates included Tina Turner (then Anna Mae Bullock).[45] During his years at Sumner High, Bowie took full advantage of the instrumental-music program, which was directed by Clarence Wilson. "In high school," Bowie recalled, "my whole life was band." "I spent more time in the band room than in any school room. I learned how to kiss in the band room."[46] A standout trumpeter, Bowie played in every one of Sumner High's ensembles. He also participated in "the All-City Band, the

All-City Orchestra, the All-City Swing Band, [and the] All-City Marching Band"—audition-only groups for the best music students in the St. Louis city schools.[47] And on the weekends, he could be found playing at churches and community centers in the Ville, the neighborhood that was home to the Bowie family and most other black St. Louisans.[48]

Bowie started performing professionally when he was still in high school. By the age of fifteen, he was already a member of Local 197, the black musicians' union in St. Louis.[49] He started out as a sideman, backing up performers like rock-and-roll pioneer Chuck Berry and blues singer Sonny Boy Williamson.[50] Bowie also formed his own group, a five-piece outfit called the Continentals. The band's repertoire was truly eclectic: the Continentals played Dixieland tunes, doo-wop hits like "The Great Pretender," boogie-woogie numbers, and even a polka or two when performing for white audiences.[51] According to Bowie, the Continentals "worked a lot," but the music students at Sumner High were not impressed.[52] With an instrumentation of trumpet, alto saxophone, piano, sousaphone, and drums, the group seemed more like a clone of Louis Armstrong's late 1920s Hot Five than a modern jazz ensemble. "It was just a real weird-looking band," Bowie explained.[53] His classmates at Sumner High, pianist John Hicks and drummer Phillip Wilson, took it upon themselves to expand his musical horizons. Hicks and Wilson were already skilled bebop players, and they introduced Bowie to the music of Charlie Parker.[54] Once Bowie discovered Bird, the next step was studying the late saxophonist's disciple Miles Davis, who grew up near St. Louis. So Bowie took trumpet lessons from Davis's childhood friend Bobby Danzig, who gave him pointers on his embouchure. With Danzig's coaching, Bowie learned how to produce "that soulful sound with a little bit more air in it," just like Miles.[55]

In 1959, Bowie graduated from Sumner High School and enlisted in the air force.[56] He had lived in St. Louis nearly all his life, and he hoped that military service would give him a chance to see the world. Unfortunately, the world would have to wait. After basic training, Bowie was sent to Amarillo Air Force Base in northern Texas, which became his home for the next three and a half years.[57] "I joined the service to travel," he recalled, "and ended up spending all my time in Amarillo."[58] Still, Bowie was happy to be out on his own: "I wanted to get away from home. My choices were getting a job, go to college, or join the military. . . . For me, the military was adventure. . . . I learned all the things in life that you be reading about but you don't get to do as a kid."[59] Bowie was a young airman with money to burn, and most nights he could be found in town, drinking and carousing in Amarillo's many watering holes. He also joined a blues band that performed at local clubs. Bowie wanted to play in an air force band too, but at Amarillo AFB, the only ensemble with a vacant trumpet chair was the Drum and Bugle Corps. This did not interest him in the least, so he chose another assignment, the Strategic Air Command (SAC) police:[60]

> At that time I couldn't stand bugle corps. I thought that was beneath me because I had played in a concert band, solo cornet. So I wasn't gonna play no one-valve bugle. That was for simpletons. . . . I [would] rather be with the police force and play with them guns.[61]

When Bowie started serving on the SAC Air Patrol, he was a firm believer in the military's reputation as a meritocracy. However, he eventually realized that white airmen were the only ones climbing the ranks. After two long years in Amarillo, he was still waiting for his first promotion. "It was southern racism," he remembered. "That's when I turned crook."[62] Bowie became a rogue cop, supplementing his air force salary by directing a gambling operation and smuggling whiskey onto the base. One afternoon the authorities finally caught up with Bowie, though it was not his sideline vice business that attracted their scrutiny.[63] Instead, he was court-martialed for firing his handgun in the barracks:

> It wasn't malicious or anything really, but this white boy from Tennessee took my seat in the TV room. So when I asked him about it he came out of his southern bag: "Yeah I took your seat, so what," he says. Well, I ain't never been afraid of white folks. A lot of people got that fear built in, but I don't. So I grabbed him by the collar, pulled him down, pulled [out] my gun, and fired off four or five shots right next to his head and said: "M— f—, if you ever think about saying some s— to me like this again, I'll blow your head off." This cat was begging. "Lester, please don't kill me."[64]

For this offense, Bowie was sentenced to six months in the Amarillo AFB prison.[65] His punishment included two weeks in solitary confinement, an unlit room known as the "black box."[66] This experience could have broken Bowie, but it ended up turning his life around: "I thought to myself, whatever I'm doing must not be that hip because it's led to that black box. . . . Everything I thought I must have wanted to do was a mistake. So I decided to get serious and be a full-time pro in music."[67]

Bowie was discharged from the air force once his sentence was complete.[68] Before his stint in prison, he had been listening closely to the recordings of hard-bop trumpeter Kenny Dorman, who was becoming one of his favorite musicians. "He sounded so hip that I said, 'I [want] to be like Kenny Dorham, just a really hip trumpet player.'"[69] If Bowie was going to have a career like Dorham's, though, he needed to practice harder than ever before. As he explained, "I didn't really play that well to be a pro. I wanted to be a jazz musician and I knew I didn't know enough songs."[70] Bowie escaped Amarillo and headed to Jefferson City, Missouri, the home of historically black Lincoln University. Two friends from Sumner High, John Hicks and saxophonist Oliver Lake, were studying at the university, as was his childhood neighbor Fontella Bass.[71] Bowie enrolled as a music major so he could learn from Marshall Penn, an expert brass player who directed the Lincoln University band: "The only reason I went was to take lessons from him. . . . So I never went to classes, I never bought a book. I just went to my trumpet lesson and practiced twelve, fourteen hours a day."[72]

While at Lincoln University, Bowie paid his bills by performing with Jack Harris and the Arabians, a Jefferson City blues band.[73] This caused him to clash with the music department's conservative chairman, who did not want his respectable institution to be associated with down-home revelry. Bowie was already on thin ice for skipping classes—all of them—and for daring to play jazz in the university's practice rooms, which was grounds for suspension.[74] To Bowie, the department chairman's disdain for African American music seemed deeply hypocritical: "I think these kind of people have done a lot to thwart the advancement of blacks because they are anti-cultural. . . . [Y]ou take your own creation and say it ain't s— in lieu of some m—f— that's playing Mozart."[75] In search of a school that would embrace black music, Bowie left Lincoln University after one year and transferred to North Texas State University (later the University of North Texas).[76] Located in Denton, Texas, not far from Dallas, North Texas was the first university to offer a degree in jazz, and Bowie "figured they were as slick as scientists."[77] Unfortunately, his new college was plagued by another form of cultural hypocrisy. North Texas welcomed African American music but was much less hospitable to black students like Bowie: "[T]hey got nerve enough to be racist down there, and they studying black music. They see the benefits of it, but they still want to dog us."[78] Bowie decided to stay at the university for just a year, when he expected to be "good enough to go on the road."[79] By the end of his time at North Texas, he was playing with the top jazz groups in the Dallas area, including bands led by saxophonists James Clay and David "Fathead" Newman.[80] Now ready to turn professional, he quit school for good and returned to St. Louis, five years after he first left home.

Back in St. Louis, Bowie quickly found all the gigs he could handle. With his high school classmate Phillip Wilson, he joined a band that backed up touring rhythm-and-blues artists such as Jerry Butler, Gene "The Duke of Earl" Chandler, and Jackie Wilson.[81] Bowie also worked on the blues circuit, performing with Albert King and Little Milton.[82] There was a familiar face in Little Milton's band: pianist Fontella Bass, whom Bowie had not seen since his year at Lincoln University. In addition to playing piano, Bass was an electrifying vocalist, and when Milton began featuring her songs in his concerts, she became a star in her own right. Bass left Milton's group and joined a new soul revue led by veteran saxophonist Oliver Sain.[83] Bowie followed Bass into the Sain band, and soon the two young musicians were married.[84]

In January 1965, Bass signed a recording contract with the Chicago label Chess Records.[85] Her first two singles performed well enough, earning her a place on the national rhythm-and-blues charts.[86] But her solo career took off in September, when Chess released "Rescue Me," her third single.[87] "Rescue Me" was a major hit, topping the rhythm-and-blues charts and crossing over into the pop market—in Great Britain as well as the United States.[88] By December 1965, "Rescue Me" had sold a million copies, and Bass was the biggest name on the Chess label's roster.[89] Bass and Bowie wanted to get "close to the cash," so they packed up and moved from St. Louis to Chicago.[90] The newlyweds' decision paid off immediately. Bass was able to record new material for Chess, and she performed regularly at theaters and nightclubs across the city. She even served as a paid endorser for soft-drink companies, appearing in radio spots and print advertisements for Coca-Cola ("Things Go Better with Coke") and Nehi ("Fontella Bass says, 'If You Like a Lot of Flavor, Buy Nehi'").[91] Meanwhile, Bowie became Bass's musical director as well as a first-call sideman. He played on a number of record dates and jingle sessions at Chess, and he joined George Hunter's big band, the house band at the Regal Theater.[92] After just two years as a professional trumpet player, Bowie seemed to be living the dream. He had "plenty of bread. . . . a '51 classic Bentley, a motorcycle, [and] a hip apartment in Chicago."[93]

By all appearances, Bowie was a success, but he was beginning to feel "bored."[94] Studio sessions and rhythm-and-blues gigs could be lucrative, but they did not offer him the creative outlet that he desired. "I had always wanted to be a jazz player," Bowie affirmed. "I never wanted to be a director of a rock show or anything like that."[95] So he asked saxophonist Delbert Hill, a fellow session player at Chess Records, to show him around Chicago and introduce him to some new musicians. Hill was a member of Richard Abrams's Experimental Band, and one day in the summer of 1966 he brought Bowie to a rehearsal.[96] By the time Bowie had taken his trumpet out of its case, he knew that he belonged. As he recalled, "I had never seen so many weird m—f—s in my life":

> I said this is home here. As a musician there's always a couple of dudes you hang with. But here was thirty or forty crazy m—f—s all in one spot. I mean Roscoe Mitchell, Anthony Braxton, and Abrams, eccentric-type cats.[97]

The musicians in the Experimental Band welcomed Bowie with open arms. "I just sat right down," he remembered, "and then we played":

> Richard had me take a solo, and as soon as we finished everybody came over. Roscoe and Joseph gave me their numbers, right away, and that same night Roscoe called and wanted me to do a concert with him. It was like, *bam!* There it was.[98]

The Roscoe Mitchell Art Ensemble

For Roscoe Mitchell's group, 1966 was a banner year. In the span of a few months, Mitchell and his bandmates recorded their debut album, gave their ensemble a new name, and started exploring a number of unusual instruments that would transform the way they made music together. Even more momentous was the arrival of Lester Bowie, who became (along with Malachi Favors) one of the most dedicated members of Mitchell's group. The week after Bowie's first rehearsal with the Experimental Band, he and Fontella Bass came to a South Side jam session to meet with Mitchell and Favors.[99] Once Bowie had taken his turn on the bandstand, Mitchell revealed to Favors that the trumpeter was going to take part in their next concert. Favors liked Bowie's sound, but he doubted that someone with a thriving career in popular music would actually join Mitchell's band: "I was skeptical because of the success that he and his wife were having, and wondered if he would be a committed member to a group of nobodies."[100] For Bowie, however, playing rhythm and blues was simply a means to an end. As he explained, "I was doing pretty good with what I was doing. So, I didn't really need the bread: I could do what I wanted to do. You know, my old lady had a hit record out and I was working. S—, I was paying myself a salary."[101] With a steady source of income, Bowie could afford to take a risk, and he chose to devote himself to Roscoe Mitchell's group: "That was what I had been looking for, an opportunity to really deal into the music."[102]

Bowie was not the only new addition to the Mitchell ensemble. He joined at a time when the group members were beginning to venture into the realm of "little instruments," a musical concept that Favors brought to the band.[103] Favors's inspiration was a performance by Les Ballets Africains, the national dance company of Guinea. Back in 1959, he was in the audience for one of the company's first concerts in Chicago.[104] "[T]hey started with a procession," he recalled, "and [the] drums started raining, and I thought, 'Man, what is this here,' and the musicians would go from one instrument to another."[105] The percussionists of Les Ballets Africains were especially versatile, playing large drums like the djembe and dunun as well as smaller bells and rattles. At the time, Favors was working alongside the South Side conga drummer Pepe Brown in Andrew Hill's trio, and he began experimenting with small percussion instruments that could blend with Brown's congas.[106] On Hill's 1959 album *So in Love*, Favors played castanets and finger cymbals as well as double bass.[107] After he left the Hill trio, he set his percussion instruments aside for several years, until the day of a Roscoe Mitchell performance at the Abraham Lincoln Center.[108] As Favors remembered, "I brought a bunch of them to one of our concerts, and Roscoe's first reaction was 'What are you going to do with those?' I just said, 'Play them,' and we've had the little instruments ever since."[109]

Favors's little instruments caught on quickly. After the Lincoln Center concert, many AACM members started acquiring their own collections of small percussion instruments and other unconventional "sound tools."[110] Composing and improvising with little instruments eventually became a trademark of the Association, although no two AACM ensembles used their instrument arsenals in the same way.[111] The Mitchell group was at the forefront of this movement, and it was not long before little instruments became essential to the band's music. In the mid-1960s, Mitchell's performances were characterized by an incredible variety of musical textures and instrument combinations. The musicians might play a composed theme and then fall silent, or proceed from a dense group improvisation into a spacious texture built from just one or two instruments. Once Favors introduced little instruments into the ensemble, the band members could create even more unique sonic structures that had never been heard before—or even imagined.

Little instruments are prominently featured on Mitchell's 1966 debut album *Sound*, the first commercial recording by an AACM band.[112] (Mitchell recorded *Sound* for the Chicago independent label Delmark, which went on to produce a series of albums by other AACM groups.) The six musicians on *Sound* play almost two dozen instruments, and Mitchell encouraged them to "make any sound they think will do, any sound that they hear at a particular time."[113] The album's first track is "Ornette," Mitchell's tribute to Ornette Coleman. In between statements of the theme, the musicians move through four distinct textures: solos by Mitchell on alto saxophone, Bowie on trumpet, and Maurice McIntyre on tenor saxophone, then a dazzling trio improvisation by Lester Lashley on cello, Favors on bass, and Alvin Fielder on drum set. During the remaining two tracks, the ensemble's instrument palette significantly expands. "The Little Suite" opens with Bowie on harmonica, Mitchell on recorder and guiro, and Lashley on cello, supported by the bass-and-drums team of Favors and Fielder. As the suite unfolds, Bowie moves to trumpet, then flugelhorn; McIntyre plays tambourine and tenor saxophone; and Mitchell alternates between alto saxophone, clarinet, whistle, maracas, and other small percussion instruments. The twenty-one-minute title track, "Sound," begins with Lashley playing trombone rather than cello, and later in the piece, many of the instruments from "The Little Suite" reappear. "Sound" had been in the group's repertoire for some time, and in concert settings, the piece could last as long as forty minutes.[114] The two takes that Mitchell's sextet recorded for Delmark were much shorter, but the best take was still too lengthy to fit on the album's B-side. To Mitchell, presenting all sections of his composition in sequence was more important than preserving a single unedited take. So he worked with Delmark's staff to assemble a composite performance of "Sound" that incorporated material from both takes, and it was this version that appeared on the LP.[115]

Recorded in August 1966 and released later that year, *Sound* helped Mitchell become a critical success. *Down Beat*, the premier American jazz magazine, awarded *Sound* the maximum five stars, an exceptional showing for a debut album.[116] Mitchell's concerts were also well received, garnering uniformly positive reviews in *Down Beat* as well as in international forums like the British journal *Jazz Monthly* and the Canadian outlet *Coda*. Most of these reviews were written by a circle of Chicago-based writers—Jamil Figi, Lawrence Kart, John Litweiler, Terry Martin, Chuck Nessa, and Pete Welding—who hailed Mitchell as the next big thing in jazz and experimental music. According to these critics, Mitchell was a virtuosic saxophonist, a visionary composer, and the leader of one of the best bands in Chicago (or anywhere else). Soon, they predicted, he would overtake Ornette Coleman as the most influential figure in avant-garde jazz. In a review of a 16 October 1966 performance at the Happening in Chicago, John Litweiler described Mitchell as "[a] man with an Ornette Coleman-like imagination":

Like other Chicago avant-gardists, Mitchell attempts to find ways to make solo and collective improvisations, composed sections, in- and out-of-tempo playing, shifting rhythms, and all the other material of contemporary jazz into a controlled, unified whole. His special contribution is his attention to the uses of sounds as such. Hence at this concert the musicians could be heard, at various times, playing harmonicas, zithers, tambourines, bells, a mouth accordion, whistle, scratchers, and various other exotic percussion devices. . . . [A]ll sections of [the performance], composed and improvised, seemed exactly right, neither unfulfilled nor overdone. . . . Mitchell, Bowie & Co., five accomplished, sensitive players, managed to reveal much about themselves this Sunday evening—and to point out a possible road for tomorrow's jazz as well.[117]

Besides the core of Mitchell, Bowie, and Favors, the quintet at the Happening included AACM violinist Leroy Jenkins and a new collaborator, St. Louis drummer Leonard Smith. After Mitchell recorded *Sound*, he became interested in creating denser percussion textures, and he decided to bring additional drummers into the group. Smith was passing through Chicago, and he played a few concerts with the ensemble, as did another percussionist recently arrived from St. Louis, Bowie's old friend Phillip Wilson.[118] Alvin Fielder did not like working with other drummers, so he left the band, and before long Smith had to return home to St. Louis. By late 1966, only Wilson remained.[119]

Phillip Wilson was a natural fit for Mitchell's band. Like Bowie, he had paid his dues on the St. Louis rhythm-and-blues scene, and when he moved to Chicago he supported himself by performing with bluesman Otis Rush.[120] Mitchell appreciated the "melodic concept" that informed Wilson's playing, whether on drum set or on the many other percussion instruments he picked up after joining the group.[121] According to Favors, Wilson was always eager to rehearse—and then hit the late-night jam sessions with his new bandmates: "[W]hen Phillip came, that was it. . . . the guys would hate to see us coming to the jam sessions. We sort of hung together."[122] Wilson was dedicated to the music, and in Bowie's view, this was just what Mitchell's ensemble needed:

At first the AACM was like, guys that did things on the weekend. Once a week they would get together, have a meeting. Roscoe's band was like that too. Roscoe worked in a factory that made adding machines. All the guys had jobs on the side. Malachi and I were the only full-time professionals. . . . I wanted to start doing music all the time. We had to rehearse and play all the time, all day, all night, every day.[123]

With both Wilson and Bowie on board, Mitchell decided that his group was ready for a new name. Favors had been with Mitchell from the beginning, in the ensemble with Fred Berry and Alvin Fielder. The members of that band called themselves the Roscoe Mitchell Quartet, a fitting name for a group whose music was firmly rooted in jazz.[124] However, by the end of 1966, Mitchell and his bandmates were moving beyond old musical models into a new sound-world that was entirely their own. On 3 December 1966, Bowie, Favors, Mitchell, and Wilson played a midnight concert at the Harper Theater on East 53rd Street. For this performance, Mitchell billed his group as the Roscoe Mitchell Art Ensemble, suggesting to the audience that the performance would transcend jazz—and every other known style of music.[125] Finally, Mitchell's band had a name equal to its aspirations.

The Roscoe Mitchell Art Ensemble presented several concerts in late 1966 and early 1967. Most of these performances took place in Chicago, with a few in nearby cities like St. Louis and Detroit.[126] By springtime, the group members "wanted to expand [their] horizons" beyond the Midwest.[127] So Mitchell reached out to his friend Nick Gravenites, whom he knew from the underground jazz and blues scene in Hyde Park, the South Side neighborhood surrounding the University of Chicago. A few years earlier, Gravenites had hired Mitchell to play saxophone on an obscure 45-rpm recording entitled "Whole Lotta Soul."[128] Since then, Gravenites had relocated to the Bay Area, where he was working with Big Brother and the Holding Company, Janis Joplin's band. Gravenites had a rented house in Mill Valley, California, just north of the Golden Gate Bridge, and he offered it to Mitchell's group.[129] Favors couldn't make the trip, but Bowie, Mitchell, and Wilson were game. They loaded "a couple of cartons of the LP *Sound* . . . [into] Bowie's metallic emerald green Bentley" and headed west.[130] Upon arriving in California, they were able to arrange a few impromptu performances at local schools and theaters.[131] But the musicians spent most of their time rehearsing at Gravenites's house in Mill Valley. They resided there for several weeks, until another Chicagoan came calling. Guitarist Mike Bloomfield was forming a new rock band, the Electric Flag, and he asked Gravenites to be the lead singer. Gravenites said yes, and when the members of the Electric Flag showed up on his doorstep, the Roscoe Mitchell Art Ensemble had to go.[132]

Bowie, Mitchell, and Wilson drove home to Chicago and reunited with Favors. The four musicians were rehearsing every day, as they had done before the California expedition, and they rapidly developed into a "powerful group," as Favors put it.[133] Critic Terry Martin, reviewing a July 1967 performance at the University of Chicago, acclaimed the Roscoe Mitchell Art Ensemble as a group without peer:

> [I]t is my opinion that Mitchell's liberation of jazz form is the most import-ant development since [Ornette] Coleman's discoveries and that the quartet is now the most creative *ensemble* in jazz. . . . Music of such sensitivity, richness, and vigor is too rare to be ignored. It's just possible that this is only a beginning.[134]

Unfortunately for Mitchell's quartet, the concert at the University of Chicago turned out to be an ending, not a beginning. In the summer of 1967, the group was rehearsing at the same Hyde Park house as the Paul Butterfield Blues Band, a successful touring act that had until recently featured Mike Bloomfield on guitar.[135] When Bloomfield moved to California to establish the Electric Flag, Butterfield decided to revamp his band. Butterfield wanted a new drummer, and he chose Phillip Wilson, who had just lost his regular gig with Otis Rush. Desperate for cash, Wilson left the Roscoe Mitchell Art Ensemble and went on the road with Butterfield.[136]

Wilson's former bandmates were deeply disappointed by his sudden exit. According to Favors, "Phil Wilson promised us that he'd be back in a couple of weeks, that he was going to bring us a boatload of money because he knew that we were broke. And he never came back. So we were very hurt."[137] Bowie, Favors, and Mitchell soon realized that Wilson would not return, and they resolved to forge ahead without him. "In the next concert," Bowie recalled, "we had a bit where the telephone rang and we answered and said, 'Phillip's not here.'"[138] At subsequent concerts and recording sessions, the Roscoe Mitchell Art Ensemble occasionally hired guest performers for pieces that required a fourth musician. When they wanted an additional woodwind specialist, they brought in Joseph Jarman, and if they needed someone to play drum set, they might call Thurman Barker, Robert Crowder, or Alvin Fielder—or even summon Leonard Smith from St. Louis.[139] But in the majority of their perfor-mances, they played as a drummer-less trio. This led to significant changes in the band's performance practice. As Mitchell explained, "we wanted to have percussion in the music, but we hadn't actually decided on who was actually going to be doing that."[140] He continued, "[T]his is when we started to add more percussion through the coaching of Malachi Favors."[141] The group mem-bers scoured the city in search of novel percussion instruments, and indeed new instruments of all kinds. By the spring of 1968, Favors was playing bells, banjo, electric bass, and kazoo; Mitchell had acquired two new saxophones (soprano and bass) as well as several bicycle horns, cowbells, and a xylophone; and Bowie was the proud owner of a bass drum, cymbals, wood blocks, and two curious wind instruments—a steer's horn and a "kelp horn" fashioned out of seaweed.[142]

The year after Wilson's departure would be just as pivotal for Mitchell's group as 1966 had been. Losing Wilson, according to Mitchell, was "a good thing and a bad thing," a blessing in disguise.[143] Bowie, Favors, and Mitchell were upset at first, but during the year that followed, they learned that their bond was unbreakable. They had stuck together through thick and thin, and they were increasingly confident that their hard work would be rewarded. During this period, the band made two more albums, both for an independent label founded by Chuck Nessa.[144] In August 1967, a few weeks after Wilson left Chicago, they recorded *Numbers 1 & 2* under Bowie's name, and in March 1968, they tracked *Congliptious*.[145] Moreover, by 1968 the group members were no longer just "little instrument" specialists: they had become true multi-instrumentalists, able to perform fluently on every instrument in their arsenal, from gongs and gourds to brass, strings, and woodwinds. In the summer of 1968, when the Roscoe Mitchell Art Ensemble made a return visit to the Bay Area, the musicians' instrument collection had grown so large that they had to drive two vehicles.[146] Bowie led the procession with his BSA Thunderbolt motorcycle, while Favors drove his Volkswagen van, with Mitchell in the passenger seat and the instruments in back.[147] At summer's end, the musicians were reenergized and eager to come back to Chicago. Their musical accomplishments over the past few years had made them the most respected group in the AACM. Now the members of the Roscoe Mitchell Art Ensemble were ready to take on a larger role in the Association and guide it into the next decade.

Black Art

Richard Abrams served as the AACM's president until September 1968.[148] The members of the Association wanted their next president to be an outstanding musician and motivator, just like Abrams. They chose Bowie, who was universally regarded as a natural leader.[149] Since 1966, when Bowie joined Mitchell's group, their ensemble had made great strides, recording three albums and traveling farther than any other AACM band. The first album he made with Mitchell and Favors, *Sound*, convinced Delmark Records to offer contracts to other AACM members, including Abrams, Anthony Braxton, Joseph Jarman, and Maurice McIntyre.[150] Bowie had an entrepreneurial spirit, and he worked tirelessly to find paying gigs for the Roscoe Mitchell Art Ensemble.[151] He also evangelized on behalf of the AACM, spreading the Association's message of creativity and self-determination to musicians back home in St. Louis. Bowie's exhortations proved to be persuasive. In the summer of 1968, not long before Bowie was elected as the AACM's second president, his St. Louis colleagues founded the Black Artists' Group (BAG), a collective organization modeled after the AACM.[152] (See chapter 6 for more on Bowie's involvement with BAG.)

BAG was one of many African American arts organizations inspired by the AACM. After the formation of the AACM in 1965, a number of similar groups set up shop in Chicago, intent on bringing socially conscious, unapologetically black literature, theater, and visual art to the local African American community. Indeed, 1965 was a watershed year for the Black Arts Movement that swept the nation during the 1960s and 1970s. The Black Arts Repertory Theatre/School was founded in Harlem that year, concurrently with Broadside Press in Detroit and the Watts Writers' Workshop in Los Angeles.[153] Each of these crucial institutions provided a close-at-hand organizational model that would be emulated by other African American artists in that city. The same process unfolded in Chicago, with the AACM as the catalyst that encouraged fellow black artists to organize. By the late 1960s, the South Side was home to several new cultural organizations that had ties to the AACM.[154] In 1967, AACM cofounder Philip Cohran opened the Affro-Arts Theater, which sponsored educational programs, musical performances, and political assemblies.[155] The Organization of Black American Culture (OBAC), also established in 1967, presented an equally wide-ranging slate of events, including concerts by AACM bands.[156] Additionally, AACM members worked as actors and musical accompanists in plays produced by the Kuumba Theatre, founded in 1968 by Val Gray Ward.[157]

Theorists of the Black Arts Movement argued that artists should "[speak] directly to the needs and aspirations of black America."[158] One way to achieve this goal was to revolutionize the creative process itself, so that art-making became a community-centered event rather than a private pursuit. In the summer of 1967, a team of visual artists from Chicago's OBAC painted the *Wall of Respect*, a massive mural depicting key figures in African American history, from political and religious leaders to athletes, musicians, and writers. The mural site, an exterior wall of a South Side tavern, became an important community nexus that summer, and after the *Wall of Respect* was complete, new mural projects were launched in African American neighborhoods across the country.[159] Likewise, the members of the AACM worked to develop innovative programs that would engage black Chicagoans who had not attended the Association's regular concerts. When Bowie began his term as president in 1968, the AACM had just moved its headquarters from the Abraham Lincoln Center to the Parkway Community Center, located at 500 East 67th Street in the Woodlawn neighborhood.[160] As his first act in office, Bowie staged an epic four-day concert at the Parkway's theater-in-the-round. Woodlawn residents could enter the theater at any time of day (or night) to meet their new neighbors, who performed around the clock for ninety-six hours straight. As AACM saxophonist Henry Threadgill remembered, he and the other musicians were "sleeping in the theater and getting up to play in shifts."[161]

The AACM community project with the greatest impact was the weekend music school. AACM members started offering free music lessons to South Side youth in the fall of 1967. By 1968, the AACM School of Music was in full swing, enrolling dozens of students in Saturday-morning classes at the Parkway Community Center. Roscoe Mitchell served as the school's dean and also taught woodwinds (as did Joseph Jarman). Lester Bowie gave brass lessons, while Anthony Braxton taught harmony and Richard Abrams taught composition.[162] Significantly, students at the AACM School were not required to compose or perform in the styles favored by their teachers. Instead, the students' lessons were designed to help them excel in any musical setting. As Bowie explained, "when you go to an AACM school, you don't have any particular dogma forced on you, where you gotta play free or you gotta play this way or that way. . . . The thing that was really taught was individualism."[163] In essence, students at the School of Music benefited from the same kind of supportive mentoring that their teachers had received from Abrams during the early days of the Experimental Band. According to Jarman, "in these formative years . . . everyone had support from everyone else":

> [W]e were all told it was okay to try whatever you'd like to try—see, if it's a little bit different, that's okay, do it if it feels good. So it was in this atmosphere that . . . all of us from the "Chicago School," if you will, formulated our own individual ways. But there's commonness, if you look at the whole spectrum, and this commonness is the idea of continuous searching.[164]

During the late 1960s, the members of the Association were fearless explorers. In addition to experimenting with new modes of composition and improvisation, many AACM members started venturing into other art forms. These artistic experiments, in turn, transformed how they presented their music. Mitchell and Abrams taught themselves how to paint, and they became brilliant visual artists.[165] One of Mitchell's paintings appeared on the album cover of *Numbers 1 & 2*, and Abrams provided the cover art for *Levels and Degrees of Light*, his Delmark Records debut.[166] In 1967, the year Abrams recorded *Levels and Degrees of Light*, he took the name Muhal. After he became Muhal Richard Abrams, several other AACM musicians also adopted new names, often to express the connection they felt to African cultural traditions.[167] While Abrams and Mitchell were painting on canvas, Malachi Favors was investigating another form of painting. By 1967, Favors was wearing face paint for performances, in emulation of the dancers and drummers of Les Ballets Africains.[168] Soon Joseph Jarman was painting his face too, using designs inspired by Asia as well as Africa. Jarman had studied drama at the Art Institute of Chicago and Second City (the Chicago-based improvisational theater company), and he began incorporating a number of theatrical elements into his concerts.[169] Besides face paint, Jarman's performances often involved scripted dialogue, poetry recitations, and vivid stage designs.[170] Jarman was also a top-notch saxophonist, recognized for his lyricism and his command of extended techniques like overblowing and altissimo playing. He had always been a leading figure in the Association, ever since his appearance at the very first AACM concert. In the years that followed, he grew into one of the Association's most creative personalities—and his quartet became the Roscoe Mitchell Art Ensemble's only rival for the title of best band in the AACM.

Joseph Jarman and Company

Joseph Jarman formed his quartet in 1966, the same year as the Roscoe Mitchell Art Ensemble.[171] Prior to 1966, Jarman had been working with two different bands. One was his quintet with Fred Anderson, the ensemble that played the inaugural AACM concert in August 1965. The other was a semi-professional group best known for its November 1965 performance with the experimentalist composer John Cage. Jarman's 1965 group came together at the University of Chicago. At the time, Jarman was sharing an apartment near the university with a student named John Gilmore, who was an avid supporter of the AACM.[172] Gilmore wanted to bring the AACM to campus, so he founded a student organization called the Contemporary Music Society that sponsored concerts by Jarman and other AACM musicians. Jarman and Gilmore also organized a series of Friday-night jam sessions held at the Reynolds Club, the student union building at the corner of East 57th Street and South University Avenue.[173] At one of the Reynolds Club sessions, Jarman got to know Douglas Mitchell, a drummer and University of Chicago student. The two musicians shared a Fred Anderson connection (Mitchell played with Anderson during his high school years) as well as an interest in all kinds of avant-garde music, from Arnold Schoenberg and Anton Webern to Ornette Coleman. Mitchell and Jarman became fast friends, and they decided to start an "Ornette-style" quartet with two other university students, trumpeter Pete Bishop and bassist Bob Hodge.[174]

According to Jarman, the "sole purpose" of the 1965 group was to "[carry] his musical concepts further, into the areas of contemporary music and music theater."[175] Jarman was soon presented with a unique opportunity to advance his art by collaborating with John Cage, the most prominent experimentalist in the United States. Cage and Jarman were already acquainted, having met in Ann Arbor, Michigan, at the ONCE Festival of New Music.[176] In November 1965, not long after the ONCE Festival, Cage came to Chicago with the Merce Cunningham Dance Company for a series of performances at the Harper Theater. Upon Jarman's request, Cage agreed to join the Jarman group for a special midnight concert (also at the Harper Theater) on Thanksgiving weekend.[177] The program began with a set by Jarman's quintet and concluded with a few pieces by the Bishop-Hodge-Jarman-Mitchell quartet. In between was the quartet's collaboration with Cage, which Jarman entitled *Imperfections in a Given Space*.[178] The title Jarman chose was prescient, for the musicians used every corner of the "given space" during the twenty-three-minute performance. Mitchell moved from drum set to piano, playing chords and striking the inside of the instrument with mallets, while Hodge dragged a bamboo pole across the stage. Jarman and Bishop wandered up to the theater's balcony as they played their horns, dialoguing with Cage, who was seated at a table just in front of the stage. On Cage's table were several microphones and amplifiers, which he used to fill the theater with sounds usually heard only at close range, or not at all: erasers on paper, clicking latches on his briefcase, and even the swallowing noises that came from his throat as he drank a glass of water.[179]

The reception of the concert was mixed. Reviewers praised both of Jarman's ensembles but were less enthusiastic about *Imperfections in a Given Space*.[180] According to one critic, *Down Beat* writer Pete Welding, the Jarman quartet offered "very little in the way of actual interaction with what Cage was generating."[181] This unusual performance strategy, however, was exactly what Jarman and Cage were aiming for. Instead of trying to produce a tightly interactive improvisation, they wanted to create unexpected sonic combinations, relying on the theater's natural echo to help the quartet's acoustic instruments blend with Cage's electronics.[182] From Jarman's perspective, the experiment had succeeded, and the concert was both a professional and a personal triumph. For years leading up to the performance, he had studied Cage's music and writings, including the book *Silence*, and he felt "really honored" to work with someone who had influenced his development as a composer.[183] Significantly, *Imperfections in a Given Space* was Jarman's first collaboration with a major figure in contemporary concert music—as well as Cage's first performance with a jazz group.[184] After participating in such a historic event, it was easy for Jarman to brush off criticism, even when it came from his biggest fan, Ms. Eva Robinson. As he recalled: "My mother was at the concert, and she said, 'I don't care what you do, I hope you never play with that guy again.' Which is the sort of commentary Cage would like."[185]

For Jarman, the Cage concert was a turning point. *Imperfections in a Given Space* had shown him that bodily movements and spatial relationships could change how listeners experienced music. This revelation led to a new series of experimental performances in which he combined music with a range of art forms. "What we are trying to do," Jarman explained, "is present a total expression that an audience has to approach with greater involvement than merely listening."[186] At his next concert, *Winter Playground* (held on the University of Chicago campus at the end of 1965), Jarman's group accompanied a poetry recitation by AACM member David Moore.[187] Months later, in May 1966, Jarman presented *Tribute to the Hard Core*, the first of several ambitious "theater pieces" where his ensembles played alongside dancers, singers, and other performing artists.[188] At these events, Jarman was joined by two new musicians: drummer Thurman Barker and pianist Christopher Gaddy. Barker, a teenage percussion prodigy, played in the Experimental Band, and Gaddy was a close friend of Charles Clark, the bassist in Jarman's quintet.[189] Gaddy and Clark lived just a few blocks from Jarman, and before long the three musicians were rehearsing constantly. "It was like triplets," Jarman remembered. "We were that close. It was like one unit. We would play every day."[190] Soon they added Barker to the mix, and Jarman had a brand-new quartet, replacing the group that had played on *Imperfections in a Given Space*. Jarman's long-standing quintet with Fred Anderson would stay together for another year, until 1967.[191] But with Barker, Clark, and Gaddy, Jarman had finally found his band.

Jarman's two groups joined forces on his debut album, *Song For*.[192] Recorded in the fall of 1966, shortly after Roscoe Mitchell's *Sound*, *Song For* was the second entry in Delmark's AACM series.[193] And much like Mitchell's first album, the music on *Song For* captured where Jarman had come from—and where he was headed. Two of the four compositions on the LP, Fred Anderson's "Little Fox Run" and Bill Brimfield's "Adam's Rib," were in the repertoire of Jarman's quintet. For these compositions, he brought together all of the musicians from both of his ensembles: Anderson, Brimfield, and Steve McCall from the quintet; Barker and Gaddy from the new quartet; and of course Jarman himself and Clark, who belonged to both groups. The same seven players appear on the title track, "Song For," an extended work that Jarman composed expressly for the album. The fourth composition, "Non-Cognitive Aspects of the City," features only the quartet. "Non-Cognitive Aspects of the City" is a poetry piece, a musical setting of a poem by Jarman.[194] The poem is divided into three sections, and in each section, Barker, Clark, and Gaddy create a distinct texture that emphasizes key aspects of Jarman's recitation. The first section portrays a haunting cityscape—"where no one is more alone than any other"—and the musicians respond with a chaotic texture that leads into an explosive drum solo.[195] In contrast, the second section begins quietly, then grows denser as Jarman repeats the same few lines with increasing emotional intensity. During the third section, the poem turns away from the urban landscape to depict the "homeliness," "hopeless[ness]," and "callousness" of the city dwellers.[196] Here, Barker and Clark yield to Gaddy, who accompanies Jarman's recitation with a poignant piano lament.

In addition to reciting the text, Jarman also plays alto saxophone on "Non-Cognitive Aspects of the City," during brief instrumental interludes that frame each section of the poem. But the most remarkable moments are the three poetic sections, where Barker, Clark, and Gaddy help Jarman bring the text to life. Indeed, like all great intermedia performances, the quartet's version of "Non-Cognitive Aspects of the City" uncovered layers of meaning in the poem that even Jarman did not anticipate. A few months after the *Song For* sessions, Jarman presented a richer, thoroughly theatrical interpretation of the piece at the Abraham Lincoln Center. In this performance, witnessed by *Down Beat* critic Bill Quinn, "[j]azz, poetry, drama, and graphic art were the media combined by Jarman and crew":

> Sound effects came from behind the curtain to begin Jarman's "Non-Cognitive Aspects of the City"—curious knocking, whistling effects, and birdlike sounds from Jarman's flute. Jarman and Clark rushed from the curtains reading poetry in counterpoint and ringing bells. The curtains parted to reveal a psychedelic setting: variously hued lights flashed, junk was piled like Rauschenberg sculpture, clothes were strewn everywhere,

giant pop-poster canvases of Ku Klux Klansmen and Alabama sheriffs hung high at stage rear. . . . Stage lights went on. A couple strolled onstage, drinking from paper cups, and the music came laced with phonic imagery. Lights flashed on and off. There was a murder, and the body, fallen amid the junk on the floor, was hauled away. Anderson came to center stage and began a blues line. There were angry shouts from the rear of the auditorium by some of the musicians. Jarman walked onstage and picked up his horn to join the fray. Barker glided from meter to meter, waltzing and grinding straight ahead.[197]

Jarman's innovative concerts attracted attention outside Chicago, notably in Detroit. During the late 1960s, he frequently visited the Motor City to perform with his quartet and also in ensembles led by Detroit trumpeter Charles Moore.[198] Many of these events took place at the Artists Workshop, the hub of Detroit's underground arts scene. Jarman relished his visits to the Artists Workshop. He would arrive in Detroit several days before the concert date "just [to] hang out," and for each performance at the Artists Workshop he earned as much as fifty dollars, "which was a lot of money in those days."[199] In addition to hosting concerts, the Artists Workshop produced arts publications like the music journal *CHANGE*, which in 1966 printed a report by Jarman on his summer visit to New York City.[200] At a 1967 benefit for the Artists Workshop, Jarman's quartet accompanied a reading by the Beat poet Diane di Prima.[201] Back home in Chicago, Jarman was finding an audience for his own poetry. He gave a number of solo poetry performances during this period, reading his poems and punctuating the text with sounds from his little instruments: whistles, bells, and rattles.[202]

Jarman's poetry was central to many of his theater pieces. From 1966 to 1969, Jarman presented large-scale intermedia events at sites across Chicago, including every major university in the city.[203] At these spectacular happenings, Jarman integrated live music, literary texts, and movement in unexpected, even surreal ways. His most creative production may have been *Bridge Piece*, held at the University of Chicago's Ida Noyes Hall on 9 and 13 February 1968. When audience members arrived at the performance, they were "directed into areas where they would have to sit down or stand up."[204] Some had to put sacks over their heads, and others were draped with tinfoil. There were strobe lights, video projections, a smoke machine, and performing artists who circulated amid the audience: a juggler, a tumbler, and someone carrying a portable radio tuned to a Top 40 station. Jarman and his bandmates moved throughout the room as well, playing along with a tape recording of the *Bridge Piece* music.[205] As Jarman recalled, "[t]he variation came in the mistakes that the musicians made playing the composition. After the notated parts, those spaces where improvisation occurred were different. It sounded like two of the same person playing a solo."[206] For those in attendance at Ida Noyes Hall, *Bridge Piece* offered more than a rich intermedia experience. Jarman also used the event to advance a subtle critique of hippie-era college culture—by means of a strictly enforced dress code. The performers wore casual clothing on the first night, and overdressed audience members were asked to leave. But on the second night, Jarman remembered, "[t]he band was in complete tuxes, and you could not get in if you were not formally dressed":

> [A] lot of people were turned away. That turning away was as much a part of the performance as attendance. Most of the people enjoyed . . . the first environment because that was a part of their immediate culture that they could dig—a big wild party. But the demand for formal conformity in the sense of attire turned a lot of people off. Women could not get in unless they had skirts and dresses on. Some people actually went home and changed in order to participate.[207]

In March 1968, one month after *Bridge Piece* was performed, Jarman's group suffered a heartbreaking loss. Christopher Gaddy's health had been declining for years. He contracted kidney disease as a young man, during a stint in the Armed Forces, and at the end of his term of service, he underwent a lengthy course of treatment at the Walter Reed Army Medical Center in Washington, D.C.[208] When he returned home to Chicago in the mid-1960s, he was on dialysis, but he did not let his illness stop him from practicing, performing, and composing.[209] Gaddy's last project, a composition for chamber ensemble, was left unfinished when he passed away on 12 March 1968. Jarman took it upon himself to complete the piece as a tribute to his late bandmate.[210] The result was "Song for Christopher," an extended work for ten musicians. In the summer of 1968, Jarman recorded a twenty-minute version of "Song for Christopher," and this track became the B-side of his second Delmark album, *As If It Were the Seasons*.[211]

Jarman continued to work with Charles Clark and Thurman Barker for several months after Gaddy's death. At a spring 1968 concert sponsored by the University of Chicago's Contemporary Music Society, the trio performed with Pamela Hunt and Jeanne Nüchtern, two dancers from Martha Graham's company.[212] In the audience that evening was Larayne Black, a student of the Chicago dancer-choreographer Kim On Wong. Black went to the concert to see Hunt and Nüchtern, but she ended up focusing her attention on the music played by Jarman's trio. After the performance, Jarman introduced himself to Black, and she became a friend to Jarman as well as a major booster of the AACM. Black was a devout Buddhist, and with her encouragement Jarman began studying the Jodo Shinshu tradition with her teacher, Rev. Gyoko Saito. Soon, Jarman was a regular at the religious community headed by Rev. Saito, the Buddhist Temple of Chicago (then located in Hyde Park, not far from Jarman's apartment). In late 1968 and early 1969, Jarman presented several concerts at Rev. Saito's temple, many of which combined music and dance.[213] Jarman also collaborated with Kim On Wong, providing the music for a December 1968 dance performance based on *The Tibetan Book of the Dead*.[214]

At the performance of *The Tibetan Book of the Dead*, Jarman was joined by three new sidemen: Lester Bowie, Malachi Favors, and Roscoe Mitchell.[215] Jarman and Mitchell had been close since their time at Wilson Junior College, and they found opportunities to make music together even after forming their own groups. These collaborations became more frequent after Christopher Gaddy's death, which affected Jarman profoundly.[216] Indeed, Jarman believed that Bowie, Favors, and Mitchell brought him into their circle out of concern for his emotional well-being. "[T]hey called me to help me," Jarman asserted, "because they sure didn't need me. I mean they were SMOKING." He continued, "[T]hey invited me to play a concert with them. And then very rapidly, if I did a concert I would ask them to play. If Lester did a concert, he would ask me to play. The same with Roscoe."[217]

The emotional support offered by Bowie, Favors, and Mitchell gave Jarman hope when he experienced yet another tragedy. In the spring of 1969, Charles Clark was accepted into the Chicago Civic Orchestra on the recommendation of his teacher Joseph Guastafeste, principal bassist of the Chicago Symphony. On 15 April 1969, after one of Clark's first rehearsals with the Civic Orchestra, he walked from Symphony Center to the Illinois Central train station on Randolph Street, intending to catch a ride back to the South Side. While waiting at the train station, Clark was struck with a cerebral hemorrhage, and he died instantly. He was only twenty-four, the same age Gaddy had been at his death, but unlike Gaddy, Clark seemed to be in perfect health.[218] No one expected him to die young, least of all Jarman, who was "devastated" by the terrible news.[219] In the span of fourteen months, Jarman had lost two of his bandmates, and he fell into a deep depression. But Bowie, Favors, and Mitchell intervened, and with their help Jarman began to recover:

> [T]hose guys pulled me out of the great dark despair, and they did it . . . through the wonder of music. They said, "You have to come over here and play now," you know? They understood my pain and my hurt, but that I still had to play. So they invited me once. Then they invited me again, and then they invited me again, and again, and again.[220]

3 The Art Ensemble of Paris

Everything that we had thought and projected started happening in Paris.[1]

Paris Calling

By the spring of 1969, Lester Bowie was "becoming quite restless" in Chicago.[2] He told his partners in the Roscoe Mitchell Art Ensemble that he and his family were planning to "pack up, buy a trailer, and take the music on the road cross-country."[3] After three years of participating in the AACM's activities and traveling as far as California to practice and perform, Bowie sensed that the Art Ensemble had "come to an impasse":

> We were working in the States maybe four times a year. . . . but we were rehearsing every day, and we had really come upon something that we felt we could dedicate our lives to. I mean, I couldn't dedicate my life to being an R&B trumpeter. Malachi didn't want to just work at the Holiday Inn for the rest of his life. And we had a group that we knew had a unique sound, a language of our own, and we knew we had something to contribute to the music, and we wanted to do that exclusively. . . . That was impossible for us in the States.[4]

As Bowie saw it, the Art Ensemble's rigorous rehearsal schedule was akin to a full-time job, but despite all of their efforts, he and his bandmates were not earning nearly enough to "sustain ourselves and our families."[5] Malachi Favors and Bowie made their living from commercial music gigs, while Mitchell supported himself by working at the Victor Comptometer factory, "making calculators or something."[6] They could fully devote themselves to their music if the Art Ensemble was performing four times a week, even four times a month, just not four times a year—but this seemed out of reach in Chicago and everywhere else they had ventured. In order for the Art Ensemble to survive and ultimately thrive, they had to leave America behind.

For Bowie and the Art Ensemble, the most promising destination was Paris. The city had welcomed African American performers for more than fifty years. The Harlem Hellfighters regimental band, led by composer James Reese Europe, toured France during World War I and made a lasting impression on French musical culture, while Josephine Baker, the Southern Syncopated Orchestra, Ada "Bricktop" Smith, and jazz drummer Louis Mitchell entertained Parisians during the interwar period.[7] Decades later, Sidney Bechet, Kenny Clarke, and Bill Coleman joined the Paris jazz community, newly reconstituted in the wake of World War II.[8] Paris also became home to numerous African American painters, sculptors, and writers—so many that even a partial listing of black essayists, novelists, and poets in Paris reads like a history of twentieth-century African American literature (James Baldwin, Chester Himes, Langston Hughes, Ted Joans, Claude McKay, Richard Wright . . .).[9] For these musicians and artists, the appeal of Paris was twofold. Life in Paris and other European cities offered black Americans a degree of social mobility that was elusive back home in a country riven by segregation, whether *de jure* or *de facto*. The continent's reputation for tolerance was widespread throughout the African American community, due to the experiences of several hundred thousand black servicemen during both world wars and to the laudatory accounts of European life that appeared in the African American press: for instance, the *Chicago Defender*'s "Across the Pond" column, which reported on the successes of black entertainers overseas.[10] Additionally, it was often possible for black musicians and artists to earn more money and live more economically in Paris than in American metropolises with comparable entertainment and media industries, such as Chicago and New York. "Europe is known as a haven for Black artists," Bowie affirmed, "[a]nd for the New."[11]

Bowie's interest in Paris was validated by his readings of music magazines like *Down Beat* and *Jazz Monthly*, which published dispatches from Western Europe alongside their reviews of stateside jazz events and Art Ensemble concerts. These reports conveyed images of Paris and other European cities as fertile ground with ample working opportunities for adventurous African American musicians.[12] Paris seemed uniquely receptive to the jazz avant-garde: Don Cherry, Ornette Coleman, and Steve Lacy performed there in 1965, as did Albert Ayler and Cecil Taylor the following year.[13] Further encouragement was provided by two drummers: Steve McCall and Claude Delcloo. McCall, one of the four cofounders of the AACM, had moved to Europe in 1967, not long after participating in the recording of Joseph Jarman's album *Song For*.[14] Initially, McCall and his family settled near Amsterdam, where he worked with Don Byas and Dexter Gordon.[15] Then McCall relocated to Paris, Delcloo's hometown.

Delcloo was an important figure on the burgeoning Paris free-jazz scene, not just for his abilities as an instrumentalist and bandleader but also because of his talent for brokering connections between French musicians and immigrants like McCall. These skills were evident in the two groups Delcloo led during the late 1960s, a big band and the midsized Full Moon Ensemble, both of which featured American musicians: McCall himself played drums in the big band's rhythm section. Through McCall, Delcloo heard the groundbreaking Delmark and Nessa albums recorded by McCall's colleagues back in Chicago, and he took it upon himself to contact the AACM.[16] By 1968, Delcloo was corresponding with the Association's president, Muhal Richard Abrams.[17] Delcloo wanted to link the AACM with experimentalists in Paris and several other cities — Berne, Brussels, Copenhagen, Hamburg, New York, Philadelphia, and Rome — forming a global "federation of free musicians."[18]

In addition to his performance and organizational activities, Delcloo was the artistic director for BYG, a small record label based in Paris, as well as the founder and editor of *Actuel* magazine, which debuted in October 1968.[19] *Actuel's* ambit was "jazz and contemporary arts," including poetry and experimental theater: in other words, the very same musical and intermedia territories that the Art Ensemble and much of the AACM were exploring.[20] An article about the AACM appeared in an early issue of *Actuel*, and following its publication Delcloo wrote a letter to Abrams, proposing a closer relationship between *Actuel* magazine, the BYG label, and the members of the Association. Delcloo offered to publish AACM members' writings in *Actuel*, to serve as the distributor in France for AACM albums, and to set up paying gigs for AACM groups.[21] Abrams shared the letter with the rest of the Association, and Lester Bowie chose to reprint it in the 16 December 1968 issue of the *New Regime*, the house journal that he edited after succeeding Abrams as AACM president.[22]

Viewed in retrospect, the appearance of Delcloo's letter in the *New Regime* would seem to directly prefigure what happened a few months later, when the Art Ensemble accepted Delcloo's proposal and set out for Paris. However, the Art Ensemble's decision was far from inevitable. In early 1969, another AACM group—the trio of Anthony Braxton, Leroy Jenkins, and Leo Smith—announced their intentions to abandon Chicago for Europe. Bowie tried to discourage them, saying the AACM needed "black power . . . [and] solidarity," and that by leaving, Braxton, Jenkins, and Smith would "mess up the whole organization."[23] Both Braxton and Jenkins suspected Bowie of being less than forthright. As they saw it, Bowie wanted the Art Ensemble to be the first AACM band to travel overseas. By asking the trio to reconsider, Bowie and the Art Ensemble could buy themselves some time, formulate their own plans, and get to Europe ahead of Braxton's group.[24] This explanation, though, does not take into account Bowie's leadership role in the AACM. The Association was only three years old when Bowie assumed its presidency, and many of the ideas that he put into action as president were aimed at securing the AACM's future on the South Side of Chicago. None of these initiatives, unfortunately, could improve the economic fortunes of the Art Ensemble or the Braxton-Jenkins-Smith trio. The Art Ensemble performed too infrequently, while Braxton would "give concerts, work all week or two weeks to get the music right, then maybe get three people [to] turn up."[25] Furthermore, some in the AACM felt as if they were facing an existential threat that went beyond mere financial need. Joseph Jarman was "absolutely crushed" by the April 1969 death of Charles Clark, his closest musical collaborator.[26] For Braxton, "it made no sense to stay in Chicago": "I was determined not to die in Chicago, I could die in Paris."[27]

Bowie's own take on the situation departed from the tragic narrative supplied by Braxton. For Bowie, the Art Ensemble was a promising investment opportunity, and he was in a position to provide start-up capital. He and Fontella Bass had prospered from their rhythm-and-blues careers, and by liquidating much of their property, they could finance a journey from Chicago to Paris. "I had a Bentley and a house full of fabulous furniture and everything that went with that whole scene in the 60s," Bowie recalled. "I figured if I sold all of that, I'd have enough to take the [Art Ensemble] to Europe."[28] Roscoe Mitchell credited Bowie for having the courage and creativity to invest in the Art Ensemble: "He knew we had to go to Europe, so he said, 'I'll sell out.' Next day there was an ad in the paper, 'Musician Sells Out!' And he did—all his furniture and everything in his apartment."[29] Bowie's scheme must have been daunting to Bass. She would be uprooting her two children, moving them overseas, and also putting her own career on hold (although none of her records after 1965 had approached the popularity of "Rescue Me").[30] Whether due to Bowie's persuasiveness or her own experiences in the rhythm-and-blues industry, Bass felt that "it was time . . . to make a sacrifice for her husband and for the music," and she agreed to accompany Bowie to France.[31] If Bass's decision was based in part on Bowie's resolve, he attributed the depth of his conviction to the bond that he shared with the Art Ensemble:

> I didn't go to Paris and put up all this cash unless I knew what was going to be happening. . . . I had been a pro in music for a long time when I met the Art Ensemble cats. It was not like we were youngsters, 17 or 18; cats were grown. I had been on the road since the 50s. So, I knew exactly what we were doing. I knew we had something different and unique, not only in terms of music, but in terms of a vision.[32]

Now Bowie had to convince the others to come along. Mitchell, who had invited Bowie into the Art Ensemble, was "tired of working" his day job, and just as "ready" as Bowie to set out for Europe.[33] Bowie also extended an offer to Joseph Jarman, who had been "perform[ing] almost exclusively" with the Art Ensemble since the fall of 1968.[34] With Charles Clark gone, Jarman was adrift in Chicago, and he bought into the plan almost immediately, with an assist from Bowie's charismatic salesmanship:

> One day Lester, who had been interim AACM president at that time, pulled out a bunch of 100 dollar bills and said, "You wanna go to Europe with us?" Lester is a funny guy, so he had to make it dramatic. I was alone. I didn't have anything to lose. I was struggling to survive. The next day I said yes.[35]

And so Jarman formally joined the Art Ensemble. Significantly, what Bowie gave Jarman and his bandmates were loans, not gifts, in whatever amounts they individually required to pay for their passage to France. What could have been a financial power play, though, instead became the first step toward the cooperative ethic that henceforth defined the Art Ensemble, in music and in the social realm. Jarman and the others simply made a commitment to repay Bowie out of their future earnings, after which they would become full and equal partners in the business of the Art Ensemble—just as Mitchell, Bowie, and Malachi Favors were already equal contributors in shaping the group's music.[36]

The Art Ensemble's emerging social practices would demand unanimity on matters of such importance, and initially Favors was unwilling to leave Chicago, where he had lived his entire life. He felt that "the music should stay where it is, and people should come and check out the music where it originates." Of course, this had been a goal for the AACM since 1965, and four years later the Association's labors had still not generated a substantial audience for creative music on the South Side. Favors himself conceded that this objective "never really would have happened because of the poor interest in our community." Eventually Bowie, Jarman, and Mitchell were able to move Favors past his reluctance. "The cats had to coax me into going," Favors explained.[37] In contrast to Favors, Bowie was brimming with optimism. Once the members of the Art Ensemble escaped Chicago, Bowie believed, they were certain to succeed:

> It wasn't like taking a chance or anything. Anytime you take a band intact anywhere you're going to work. You can take an intact band to the jungle or Siberia. They're gonna say, "Give them a gig." A Black band especially— anywhere in the world you can work.[38]

On 24 May 1969 the Art Ensemble played a "farewell" concert at the Blue Gargoyle near the University of Chicago. The performance was Jarman's first as an official member of the group, an event that he commemorated by giving an interview to the university's student newspaper and by inscribing on the concert poster a John Cage quotation: "They told me to continue what I was doing and to spread joy and revolution."[39] In the pages of *Jazz Monthly*, John Litweiler described the concert as featuring "almost continuous Bowie trumpet, complex percussion moods on ringing objects, [and] a sudden, perfect silence that lasted several minutes in the midst of the performance." Litweiler had been one of the Art Ensemble's biggest boosters among the community of Chicago music critics, and for him the evening at the Blue Gargoyle was a "sentimental occasion."[40] Surely others present felt the same; still, sentimentality was not the only mood on display. Bowie, for one, was triumphant, asserting that "the AACM was becoming a world-wide organization" that would "carry [its] music everywhere."[41] The farewell performance also included plenty of the musicians' typically wry humor. At the end of the concert, the audience members were told "America is in your hands now." Jarman supplied the punch line by walking the aisles and handing out miniature American flags.[42] This being the University of Chicago in 1969, one of the attendees "predictably . . . set fire to his flag, to merry cheers; unpredictably, there was no *Chicago Tribune* aghast story-plus-kill the Commie editorial about it the next day."[43]

Entering the City

Four days after the farewell concert, the Bowie family, Favors, Jarman, and Mitchell left Chicago, bound for France by way of New York City. In New York they boarded the *SS United States*, an immense ocean liner, on one of its final transatlantic voyages.[44] Their cargo included a dog, Favors's Volkswagen van, Bowie's prized BSA Thunderbolt motorcycle,[45] and "an arsenal of nonviolent weapons, several hundred musical instruments that weighed over two tons."[46] As the musicians set sail, Favors remembered that, just a year earlier, "my horoscope said that I was going to be on a ship and I was going somewhere way away. I said they ain't talking about me. Man, in a year's time I was on a ship going overseas."[47] The speedy *United States* made the eastbound crossing to Normandy in only a few days. On 2 June 1969 the ship landed at the port of Le Havre, where the Chicagoans were greeted by Claude Delcloo and the photographer Jacques Bisceglia, Delcloo's colleague at BYG Records and *Actuel* magazine.[48] Two hundred kilometers later, the Art Ensemble reached Paris. "We went over there," Mitchell declared, "and carried the banner of the AACM."[49]

The Art Ensemble and the Bowies found temporary lodging in a "little hotel that's not there anymore" bordering Place Saint-Michel, just across the Seine from the Île de la Cité.[50] Jarman was already familiar with the Left Bank, having visited the area on a thirty-day leave during his European tour of duty with the army. Back then, he roamed the Saint-Germain-des-Prés district, "trying to find a saxophone for me to play," and met Kenny Clarke as well as the French saxophonist Barney Wilen. Jarman also encountered some of the Beat writers then residing in the Latin Quarter—"the people I was supposed to be hanging out with, because I was a jazz musician"—including William S. Burroughs, Gregory Corso, and Allen Ginsberg, who gave him a copy of *Howl and Other Poems*.[51] Jarman was drawn to what he termed the "nihilistic concept of being" in Ginsberg's work, and he credited the Beats for inspiring his subsequent development as a poet. He was also impressed by the "fantastic" lifestyle of the "Left Bank bohemians": "smoking dope right on the street, and feeling up girls right on the street."[52] During those thirty days in midcentury Paris, Jarman felt a rare sense of belonging, and his return to the Left Bank in 1969 must have seemed like a homecoming. For the rest of the Art Ensemble, though, the City of Light was an entirely new experience. Favors, who had at first opposed the venture to France, "found Paris to be pretty interesting and exciting." He laughed at motorists "trying to maneuver in two directions down those narrow streets," and he immersed himself in the jazz scene, crossing paths with "a bunch of cats that I had just heard of or read about."[53]

Many of the Art Ensemble's early meetings with other expatriate musicians took place at the Bar Le Chat qui Pêche on rue de la Huchette, a moment's stroll from their Place Saint-Michel hotel. For more than a decade, the Chat qui Pêche had been an important site for performances by African American bebop players.[54] By the mid-1960s, the Chat qui Pêche was also staging concerts by free-jazz musicians, beginning with Don Cherry, who was in residence there for much of June 1965.[55] One night in December 1967, Stokely Carmichael visited the club to hear a set by Archie Shepp's quintet, which he found much more compelling than the political rally he would participate in several days later at the Maison de la Mutualité. As Carmichael told the poet Ted Joans, "the only revolutionaries that I saw in Paris, I met at a jazz *cave*, the Chat qui Pêche!"[56] During the summer of 1969, the Chat qui Pêche was the main hangout for a rapidly growing contingent of avant-garde musicians who had recently arrived from New York—some at the invitation of Claude Delcloo, like the Art Ensemble.[57] Favors got to know both Shepp and Philly Joe Jones at the Chat qui Pêche, and subsequently recorded with them.[58] This kind of intergenerational contact, not always evident on the American scene, was the order of the day in Paris, perhaps because of the expatriate experience shared by black musicians regardless of age or aesthetic inclination. Mitchell deeply appreciated the exchanges he witnessed among the bebop elder statesmen who had permanently settled in and around Paris (Don Byas, Johnny Griffin, Arthur Taylor, et al.) and ambassadors of the New Thing, from Ornette Coleman to Grachan Moncur III.[59] The camaraderie usually found at the Chat qui Pêche, however, occasionally transformed into something more pugilistic, as Favors recalled: "Man, there were rough cats hanging out down there: Philly Joe, Sunny Murray, Reverend Frank Wright; and you know he was rough. They was Joe Louis, Muhammad Ali, anything you wanted to call. You couldn't step out of line."[60]

Besides the Chat qui Pêche, the Chicagoans also frequented the American Center for Students and Artists, located at 261 boulevard Raspail, two kilometers south of Place Saint-Michel in the Montparnasse district. Founded in the 1930s to promote "social vocation, philanthropy, and anti-communism" among Americans living in Paris,[61] the American Center gradually evolved into a "vibrant, multidisciplinary hub" for avant-garde artists.[62] During the late 1960s, the Center hosted visual art exhibits, dance performances, intermedia happenings, political meetings, theater productions, and concerts of classical music, experimental music, and jazz.[63] Visiting artists were also provided rooms where they could rehearse, store their supplies and musical instruments, and sleep. These services were invaluable for African Americans and members of other minority groups, who faced difficulties in securing studio space or rental housing in the byzantine and frequently discriminatory Paris real estate market.[64]

On 12 June 1969, ten days after arriving in France, the members of the Art Ensemble made their Paris debut at the Théâtre du Lucernaire. Sited at 18 rue d'Odessa in Montparnasse (not far from the American Center), the Lucernaire had recently begun presenting concerts of "nouveau jazz" in partnership with *Jazz Hot*, one of France's leading periodicals dedicated to the music.[65] The band performing at the Lucernaire in June was the Free Action Music Orchestra, a sextet that included two foreign-born saxophonists, Ronnie Beer of South Africa and Kenneth Terroade of Jamaica, along with four French musicians: trumpeter Bernard Vitet, pianist François Tusques, bassist Beb Guérin, and the omnipresent Claude Delcloo on drums. Some weeks before, Sunny Murray and Alan Silva had worked with the Orchestra at Delcloo's behest, and now Delcloo was offering the Lucernaire gig to the Art Ensemble—not as guest performers with Free Action Music, but as the headlining artists on a double bill. For Delcloo, this was a chance to make good on his promise to Muhal Richard Abrams, and also to benefit by association with the first-rate reputation that had preceded the Chicagoans to Paris. After all, the Art Ensemble wasn't just any jazz band: Bowie, Favors, Jarman, and Mitchell were "four prestigious members of the AACM," in the glowing phrase employed by *Jazz Hot* critic Daniel Caux, who published the first review of the Art Ensemble's Lucernaire concerts less than a week after their 12 June premiere.[66]

Caux had already introduced his readers to the Delmark and Nessa albums recorded by the Art Ensemble and other AACM musicians.[67] For Caux, the AACM's name was a mark of quality as well as the signifier of a "multifaceted music whose feeling is so different from New York [free jazz]."[68] The hard work that the Association had put into the South Side was finally paying off—in France, of all places. Caux's perspective would quickly become dominant among Paris-based critics, and was one of several crucial factors that made the Art Ensemble an "immediate sensation" at the Lucernaire.[69] To investigate this matter in more detail, it will be helpful to quote Caux at length:

When the quartet from Chicago appears, the stage of this curious 140-seat theater is nearly overrun by a multitude of instruments: xylophones, bassoon, sarrusophone, various saxophones, clarinets, banjo, cymbals, gongs, bells, bass drum, balafon, rattles, etc. On the first night, the audience was quite surprised to see Joseph Jarman, bare-chested and face painted, passing slowly through the aisles murmuring a poem, while bassist Malachi Favors, his face a mask of horror, shouted curses at Lester Bowie, and Roscoe Mitchell played [bicycle] horns. Obviously, the spectacle is integral to their expression: they truly take possession of the space, and consequently the hall seems to be specially designed for them.[70]

Caux further praised the Chicagoans for forging "new relationships between the visual and auditory," and for the virtuosic technique they demonstrated on every instrument they touched. He heard in their music an "impeccable *formal precision*": the Art Ensemble had "perfectly assimilated" the "language of the New Thing" and could use it as a "springboard for other ventures," other musical styles, other atmospheres. Finally, Caux was astonished by the sheer unpredictability of the Art Ensemble's performances, which ranged from "discretion and restraint" to "devastating and often caustic humor," from "serious and profound music" to an "ambiguous and violent Black Power psychodrama."[71]

Virtually all of these observations—the last one excepted—had previously appeared in reviews of the Art Ensemble's American concerts, an indication that there was substantial continuity between how the band sounded (and looked) in Chicago and their first performances in Paris. Yet at the Lucernaire the Art Ensemble was finding, seemingly overnight, a sizeable audience that had eluded them back home in the United States. Why? For Mitchell, the explanation was straightforward: "We were received with open arms, once people heard our music. Not many people were doing anything like what we were doing in Europe when we went there in 1969."[72] Additionally, even before the Art Ensemble traveled to Paris, the AACM brand was strong there, at least among the readership of *Actuel* and *Jazz Hot*. And then one must also consider the final, discordant note in Caux's influential review: the specter of revolutionary black nationalism.

For more than a few French critics and listeners, the Art Ensemble's music was radical in the most literal sense. Only a select number refrained from this interpretation, notably Francis Hofstein, who reviewed several Art Ensemble performances for *Présence Africaine*, the venerable pan-Africanist journal of politics and culture. In his review of a 15 June concert at the Musée d'Art Moderne, Hofstein acknowledged that the Art Ensemble's music had political implications: "The four men do not separate ethics and aesthetics, art and ideology." But the group's politics, Hofstein wrote, were about "sovereign individuality" rather than groupthink, an adroit analysis of the social philosophy that the Art Ensemble inherited from the AACM.[73] For each Francis Hofstein, however, there were many other critics who struggled to see the members of the Art Ensemble as anything but *les damnés de la terre*, the musical avatars of an imminent black nationalist rebellion—though it was never made clear why Bowie, Favors, Jarman, and Mitchell were playing experimental music in Paris instead of building a weapons cache in Chicago. Philippe Adler, writing in the national newsweekly *L'Express*, was fixated on the "AACM Great Black Music" bumper sticker glued to Bowie's bass drum:

> All four of them are black, young, from Chicago, and members of the AACM. . . . [T]he AACM is a resistance movement that unites young musicians and applies Black Power principles to the world of music. [No] more white intermediaries; jazz should be exclusively the province of blacks. The music of the '69 Chicagoans is a reflection of their ideas: violent and revolutionary.[74]

Adler's interpretation was echoed by Paul Alessandrini of *Jazz Magazine*, who heard the Art Ensemble on 28 June at the American Center. The performance was part of the Premier Festival de Free-jazz et de Nouvelle Musique, one of several musical events organized by *Actuel* during the summer of 1969.[75] Steve McCall played with the Art Ensemble that day, as did Anthony Braxton, who had arrived in Paris about two weeks earlier.[76] Alessandrini began his concert review by comparing the Chicagoans' stage setup to "altars of torture and sacrifice," a primitivist metaphor that was outmoded even then. After this statement, he retreated to the familiar nexus of music and politics. In Alessandrini's account, the performance was so riotous that to describe it in musical terms, rather than as a political act, was impossible:

> To speak of the Chicago musicians is to always use the same expressions: *black music, black power, aggression, political and musical happening*. The critic feels overwhelmed because, musically, the explosion paralyzes his words; only his aggravated, ringing ears can bear witness.[77]

Black Exotica: French Culture and Black Performance

The Art Ensemble was not the only group of African American musicians to experience this kind of reaction in Paris, and the practice of viewing black performance through a highly politicized lens was not restricted to the late 1960s.

Anthony Braxton, whose encounters with this phenomenon largely paralleled the Art Ensemble's, called it "black exotica"—a memorable description for the many ways in which French intellectuals have used the cultural products of the African diaspora to theorize racial difference.[78] The roots of black exotica in France can be traced as far back as the 1830s, when Eugène Delacroix was painting North African subjects and Alexis de Tocqueville was studying the social and political import of race (among other topics) in antebellum America.[79] Beginning in the 1870s, French impresarios installed a series of infamous *villages nègres* at the Jardin d'Acclimatation, the Paris zoo. These *villages nègres* were populated by African men, women, and children, brought all the way to Europe to serve as human exhibits for the entertainment of Parisians.[80] By the dawn of the twentieth century, black exotica was firmly entrenched in French culture, particularly the Paris art world. Visitors to the Musée Ethnographique des Missions Scientifiques, and later the Musée de l'Homme, could view hundreds of African artworks and handicrafts that had been collected by French ethnographers, evangelists, and explorers.[81] The precondition to this virtual contact between cultures, of course, was the colonial enterprise. Indeed, the operative ideologies of colonialism were inseparable from the earliest strains of black exotica. According to the colonizers, Africans were the polar opposites of Europeans: not civilized, but primitive; and not diverse, but essentially alike.[82] Back in the metropole, primitivism and essentialism reemerged as the two fundamental claims made by interpreters of so-called *art nègre*. African masks and sculptures merely represented "the origins of human creativity" and had little intrinsic value, except as raw material for anthropological research or imaginative reworkings by European artists like Pablo Picasso.[83] Furthermore, these African objects were perceived to be undifferentiated outpourings of the *âme nègre*, the "soul" that supposedly governed all people of African descent irrespective of their individual identities.[84]

The black exotica phenomenon evolved throughout the twentieth century in response to new cultural stimuli and a series of landmark historical events, but its colonialist presuppositions were never far from the surface.[85] World War I and the golden era of transatlantic travel brought African American music and dance to European shores, and the 1920s would become the Jazz Age, the *années folles*. Despite the mass popularity of African American performance in France during the interwar period, it rarely gained acceptance on its own terms. One widely held belief equated jazz with "rhythm and the instruments used to make it," namely the drum set.[86] The rhythmic principles of the music, however, were assumed to be esoteric or non-existent: jazz percussion was nothing more than "unruly noise," and jazz dance was an involuntary, atavistic reaction to the provocative sounds of the drum set and other instruments.[87] These perceptions could scarcely be distinguished from the centuries-old accounts of African music and dance written by European and Arab travelers, who saw these performance practices as the physical manifestation of "erotic compulsion or demonic possession."[88] French listeners also heard jazz as "music of liberation," due to the legacy of James Reese Europe and the continued American presence in France after the armistice.[89] This interpretation of jazz did not long remain confined to the political domain, and the music's liberatory connotations were quickly extrapolated into the moral universe that had been shattered during World War I. Parisians desired "a lush, naive sensuality and spirituality that cold, rational Europeans had lost," and they found it in an imagined Africa, now exemplified by African American popular music and iconic performers such as Josephine Baker, star of *La Revue Nègre*.[90] As the historian Tyler Stovall wrote, "[w]hen the French looked at black Americans, they saw a new version of the sensuous, spontaneous African."[91] In the Jazz Age, primitivism and essentialism were alive and well. Like turn-of-the-century *art nègre*, jazz was *musique nègre*, "from origins unknown . . . a disembodied elsewhere, an exotic world."[92]

World War II transformed French politics, society, and culture, including notions of black exotica. Primitivist stereotypes began to recede, and racial essentialism was replaced by political essentialism, the conviction that African American expressive culture was necessarily and exclusively political. To their credit, French critics and listeners gave serious consideration to the assertions of agency made by African American bebop musicians as well as other black artists who demanded equal treatment in the cultural landscape.[93] In France, "being a jazz fan assumed a moral dimension," even though the audience gathered to hear Sidney Bechet at Le Caveau de la Huchette could do little to aid the African American civil rights movement.[94] This shift in attitudes was not solely motivated by the urgency of the civil rights struggle or the aesthetic qualities of black music. France's declining prestige in the postwar international order, coupled with disagreements over U.S. foreign policy during the Cold War, created an atmosphere of fierce anti-Americanism in midcentury Paris. This stance was especially prevalent among members of the political left, who "regarded black Americans as a symbol of ideological consciousness, not good times."[95] In these circles, to appreciate jazz was to strike a blow against Jim Crow—and, by extension, Uncle Sam.[96]

The Art Ensemble arrived in Paris at a time when French perceptions of African Americans had grown even more politicized, in response to the global anti-colonial struggle, the events of May 1968, and developments in the United States. During the sixteen-year period from 1946 to 1962, France fought and lost colonial wars in both Vietnam and Algeria—two protracted conflicts that exhausted the nation, inspired domestic anti-war movements, and contributed to the dissolution of the Fourth Republic, France's government since the end of World War II.[97] Anti-war activists, already sympathetic to Marxist perspectives, began studying Frantz Fanon and a number of like-minded Francophone writers who were under the sway of Mao and his *Little Red Book*.[98] By 1968, the ascendant ideology on the French left was Third Worldism, which transposed the old Marxist concept of class struggle onto the efforts of developing countries to gain political and economic independence from Western colonial powers. In France, would-be revolutionaries concluded that they could support the Third World by critiquing Western imperialism and mobilizing against capitalism.[99] These imperatives led directly to the events of May 1968: protests by radical students, sympathy strikes by millions of union workers, and chaotic mass demonstrations in central Paris that (for a few weeks at least) threatened to forcibly end Charles de Gaulle's presidency.[100] Although the May uprising failed to achieve its political goals, it had a broad impact in the cultural realm. Dozens of periodicals were launched in Paris after the events, including Claude Delcloo's *Actuel* magazine. French youth also developed a strong interest in art forms associated with the British and American countercultures, from rock music to free jazz.[101]

For a variety of reasons, African American free-jazz musicians were perfectly positioned to appeal to the sensibilities of post-May French critics and listeners. The 1968 generation viewed African Americans as revolutionaries in their own image, whose long struggle against racial oppression in the United States paralleled their own anti-imperialist and anti-capitalist actions on the streets of Paris.[102] Similarly, free jazz—more so than any other musical style identified with black America—was seen as the sonic equivalent of the May movement, which attempted to remake French culture while upending the political order. "[F]ree jazz appeared . . . to be a symbol of political rebellion as well as a cultural critique," according to the historian Ludovic Tournès, "and thus it was aligned with one of the essential characteristics of the '68 spirit."[103] Additionally, the music's spontaneity seemed to represent the bottom-up, non-hierarchical quality of the May protests. By 1970, these themes would be taken up by the sociologist Alfred Willener in his book *The Action-Image of Society: On Cultural Politicization*.[104]

The pervasive identification of the New Thing with radicalism could be partially attributed to the activities of French free-jazz musicians, who as early as 1966 were staging politically oriented concerts at the Mutualité, the Paris hall known for hosting speeches by Malcolm X and Stokely Carmichael.[105] But the most significant influence on the music's politicized reception was the arrival of a new generation of critics, installed by 1968 at both *Jazz Hot* and *Jazz Magazine*, and also at mass-market publications like *L'Express*, *Le Nouvel Observateur*, and *Paris Match*.[106] These critics brought to France the ideas of Archie Shepp, Frank Kofsky, and above all Amiri Baraka, Americans who regarded free jazz as a cultural arm of the nascent Black Power movement.[107] Two *Jazz Magazine* writers, Philippe Carles and Jean-Louis Comolli, would go on to author the book *Free Jazz/Black Power*, in which they synthesized Third Worldism with Amiri Baraka's ideas on African American music.[108]

The connection between Black Power and African American experimental music (including free jazz) was more than rhetorical. Stokely Carmichael, writing with the political scientist Charles V. Hamilton, defined the movement's aims as "black self-determination and black self-identity," a phrase that could also be read as a summary of what the AACM was doing in Chicago.[109] However, the meaning of Black Power became distorted as it crossed the Atlantic—as happened all too often in the stateside media. Many in France's 1968 generation were convinced that "all Afro-Americans were becoming Black Panthers," a scenario that would have required an increase in the party's membership by three orders of magnitude.[110] Perhaps because of this illusion, *Jazz Hot* sent journalist Annette Lena to the United States to report on black nationalism, and routinely published articles on the Black Panther Party.[111] Furthermore, certain French critics made a habit of portraying African American musicians as violent militants, in thought if not in deed. This was black exotica in the wake of May 1968: still politically essentialist, and once again primitivist. The "sensuous, spontaneous African" of the interwar period was now a freedom fighter, taking up arms against the imperialist West.[112]

The black exotica phenomenon both helped and hindered the members of the Art Ensemble during their first summer in Paris. Critics and listeners alike were fascinated by their ties to the AACM, an organization whose purported revolutionary stance lent the Art Ensemble a considerable amount of radical-chic allure. And of course the band's repertoire did include a few pieces with political content (to be examined in chapter 4). There is also a convincing argument, advanced by the saxophonist Steve Lehman, that racial essentialism continued to shape how some French critics assessed black music, as revealed in their reactions to particular aspects of the Art Ensemble's performances:

> The group's dramatic use of costumes, face paint, humor, and collective improvisation, as well as the especially prominent role which they gave to

percussion, was intended to evoke and pay homage to the great diversity of pan-African musical traditions; however, many French jazz critics wrongly understood the Art Ensemble's performance practice as reinforcing their own narrow views of African music. . . . that all Africans, and more specifically, all African musicians have "natural rhythm" on which their music is founded. . . . For [Philippe] Carles and other French jazz journalists of this period, the Art Ensemble's apparent confirmation of such notions . . . was one of the most compelling qualities of this music.[113]

The members of the Art Ensemble quickly learned how to rebut the most common misconceptions of their work. In a major interview with three critics from *Jazz Hot*, the Chicagoans were asked whether their music bore any relationship to "traditional" African American musics such as the blues. Jarman's explanation, which would become a standard reply to questions of this nature, quite deliberately emphasized that the band's musical compass extended far beyond the critically policed borders of African American culture:

> We play the blues, we play jazz, rock; Spanish, Gypsy, and African music; classical music, contemporary European music, voodoo. Everything, really—because, ultimately, we play "music." We create sounds, period.[114]

During the same interview, one of the critics inquired if the AACM was allied with the Black Panther Party. The answers given by the musicians—first Bowie, then Jarman—demonstrate two complementary strategies that the Art Ensemble employed when faced with journalists who "sought to elicit statements of political commitment":[115]

> *Jazz Hot*: In the States, are you connected with any political organizations such as, for example, the Black Panthers?
> Bowie: We are in contact with all of the black organizations.
> Jarman: We are not affiliated with any political association; that would be contrary to the designs of the AACM. Of course, we have relationships and friendships in those movements, but strictly on a personal level. We intend to stick to the concepts of the AACM, and besides, the AACM's purposes explain our political and social beliefs. What we're interested in, above all, is sharing our music, and the power of our music. The music is a response to these problems, meaning that when people listen to it, they hear a reaction to these problems. Because of the music, they can in turn become more active and more responsible.[116]

Fortunately, the Art Ensemble's experiences in Paris were not completely determined by French political and racial ideologies. The band's performances were well received by the community of American artists in Paris. Jarman was especially encouraged by the respect and recognition that the Art Ensemble garnered from another South Side musician, the blues pianist Memphis Slim:

> The line of Americans that were coming in had all been conditioned by the changes on the American scene. So they were game to go all the way out. There were blues guys there, jazz guys there, painters, writers, poets. Everybody welcomed us. And Memphis Slim with his Rolls-Royce. . . . He would come up to me: "Hello Joe," very dignified, but warm like a brother. He was such a royal guy. You just dug the recognition from him, a master like that. In America, the famous never spoke to us. They would put us down as a matter of fact: "You guys ain't playing s—." There, in Paris, Memphis Slim came to several Art Ensemble concerts, and he would say: "Um hum, yes!" He would never say thumbs down. And for him to give us his OK, we felt like, wow! We are doing something![117]

Memphis Slim was one of the highest-paid African American musicians in Paris at the time, and that famous Rolls-Royce made his stature all the more conspicuous.[118] Seeing "Memphis" out and about on the Left Bank, Favors recalled a conversation they had back in Chicago during the early 1960s—prior to the decline of Bronzeville, and just before the pianist moved to Paris:

> I was standing out in front of McKie's nightclub down on 63rd and Cottage Grove in Chicago. Memphis Slim was standing there. . . . saying: "I'm getting ready to go to Europe. I'm moving to Europe." I said to myself, why would he want to go to Europe? At that time, Chicago had the greatest entertainment section in the world, right there on the South Side. When I first started playing, it was ten years before I ever really went off the South Side working. . . . And this is the reason I couldn't understand Memphis Slim making that statement. But when I got to Europe and checked out Memphis Slim in his Rolls-Royce, I never would have thought it.[119]

Saint-Leu-la-Forêt

The members of the Art Ensemble were not yet earning Rolls-Royce money in June 1969. The concerts they played three or four nights per week at the

Théâtre du Lucernaire were far from lucrative: Mitchell remembered that "sometimes we'd have enough at the end of the gig to go get ourselves a cheese sandwich and a beer."[120] After a few weeks of paying hotel bills and buying meals, their cash reserve had become seriously depleted. Seemingly just in time, the musicians met Dr. Jean-Paul Rondepierre, a free-jazz trumpeter in Delcloo's circle. Dr. Rondepierre was a psychiatrist who worked at the Maison Blanche, a hospital located in a suburb east of Paris.[121] He invited the Art Ensemble and the Bowie family to stay in the doctors' quarters, an offer that a few other American experimentalists had capitalized on, including bassist Alan Silva and flutist Becky Friend.[122] At the Maison Blanche, the Chicagoans were provided room and board as well as practice space: before and after meals, the musicians would rehearse in the dining hall, squeezing their instruments into the spaces between the tables. The visitors did not remain at the Maison Blanche for long. Their rooms were in the portion of the facility reserved for female patients, where four "strange men" were not especially welcome. Furthermore, some of the staff felt uncomfortable among African Americans, and expressed their displeasure to the hospital director.[123] The Chicagoans were equally uncomfortable in the psychiatric hospital setting. "We were like patients too," Jarman stated.[124] Only too ready to leave, they departed the Maison Blanche and checked into another Left Bank hotel, in the Saint-Germain-des-Prés area west of Place Saint-Michel.[125]

Staying at the Maison Blanche helped the musicians save their earnings, and their return to hotel life convinced them of the need for an economical, permanent residence.[126] As Bowie recalled, they soon "found a real estate agent, dropped a couple of thousand-dollar bills on him, and boom, we was in business. 'Yes monsieur, whatever you want.'"[127] The Art Ensemble and the Bowie family arranged to rent a six-bedroom farmhouse in Saint-Leu-la-Forêt, a verdant community located twenty kilometers north of the Paris urban center.[128] Steve McCall helpfully offered to "guide" the Chicagoans on their first drive to Saint-Leu, but "he didn't know where he was going" and had trouble asking for directions, according to Jarman: "We went in a circle. He was talking about he was speaking French. All he could say was *bonjour*, and stuff like that."[129]

The house in Saint-Leu-la-Forêt transformed the Art Ensemble's European existence. After spending almost a month shuttling between cramped hotels and the Maison Blanche, the musicians finally had sufficient space for their vast instrument collection.[130] With six bedrooms, they could even accommodate houseguests, namely Anthony Braxton, Leroy Jenkins, and Leo

Smith. Jenkins and Smith left Chicago in late June, sailed to France like the
Art Ensemble, headed straight for the American Center, met McCall, and
with his assistance located their bandmate Braxton, who was staying with his
AACM colleagues in Saint-Leu.[131] At the farmhouse, the members of the Art
Ensemble were able to rehearse from morning to afternoon, as they had done
in Chicago. After rehearsals and before nighttime concerts, they would "sit
down and have a home-cooked meal in a home environment with the kids
and the dog running around."[132] Bowie relished this family-oriented, bucolic
lifestyle, which was "completely unique" when compared to the tedious urban
routine endured by many of their fellow American musicians:

> [M]ost cats were in the regular jazz thing; you come, you get a hotel room,
> and that's it; but we had children, a dog . . . Most jazz cats were sitting
> around Paris, and we had a big country estate, cherry trees and apple
> trees.[133]

Saint-Leu-la-Forêt also represented the next stage in the Art Ensemble's
evolution toward the cooperative social model. Shortly after arriving at the
farmhouse, the musicians called a meeting to consider giving the band a new
name. They had been billing themselves as the Art Ensemble—not the Roscoe
Mitchell Art Ensemble—since May, when Jarman joined the group.[134] Until
then, Jarman had been a bandleader in his own right, and Bowie, Favors, and
Mitchell perhaps felt that his addition merited a different name that would
suggest a "collective . . . conception" for the group, rather than leadership
by one individual.[135] In France, however, the press used "Art Ensemble" and
"Roscoe Mitchell Art Ensemble" interchangeably, along with generic terms
such as "A.a.c.m." and "le quartette de Chicago." Jarman tells the story of how
he and his bandmates became the Art Ensemble of Chicago:

> When we got out there . . . the decision was made to refer to the group
> as the Art Ensemble of Chicago, because we were from Chicago, and we
> were an Art Ensemble. . . . I believe it was Lester who said, "Chicago." It
> was just like in the movies. We were sitting around having a discussion,
> and we agreed. Everybody raised up their glasses of wine and saluted: ART
> ENSEMBLE OF CHICAGO FOREVER! That was . . . camaraderie and
> commitment.[136]

More significantly, the musicians began to implement at Saint-Leu the
financial partnership that Bowie had envisioned back on the South Side.

Although their individual incomes were marginal, the members of the Art Ensemble discovered that they could prosper through "cooperative economics," by earning and consuming as a unit.[137] This awareness promoted the exercise of good judgment during the business meetings that were convened whenever decisions affecting the group needed to be made.[138] Typically, the musicians chose to reinvest their earnings into the Art Ensemble's operations, following the pattern that Bowie established in funding their voyage to Paris. As he explained:

> Instead of squandering our money, we would collectively get together and buy things that the group needed—instruments and equipment. We had the Volkswagen, and we bought two more trucks over there. No other group over there had any kind of mobility. We could travel everywhere. . . . We could be hired to come to Germany; all we had to do was put our stuff in the truck and come.[139]

The band members would generate additional income by renting out their trucks, two German-built Ford Transits.[140] As the musicians' finances began to improve, Mitchell credited the AACM for teaching them the value of cooperation and consensus decision-making:

> I saw Johnny Griffin, who to me is one of the giants of the music. He's over there [in Europe], and I don't know if he even has his own band. . . . Whereas, the Art Ensemble went over there as a unit. When we had a gig, we sat down and figured out what we could get paid out of this and what we needed to do. We went over there as a strong unit. We had our own house. We had several trucks. . . . That's what comes of staying together. I don't know why people don't really learn that. I think that people think that "oh, I'm the chosen one" . . . It's not even about that. That's one of the best things I got out of the AACM.[141]

For the Art Ensemble, cooperation was not just smart business; it was the achievement of a goal, the realization of a dream. According to Bowie, "[e]verything that we had thought and projected started happening":

> In Paris we really practiced what we preached. That was the first time we actually were the Art Ensemble and functioning as such, that music was our life blood. . . . We did learn how to survive as the Art Ensemble playing the music that we play.[142]

4 *A Jackson in Your House*

In the songs we sing there is love, and life.[1]

On 23 June 1969, the Art Ensemble visited Studio Saravah in Paris to record the album *A Jackson in Your House*.[2] The session, which was produced by Claude Delcloo for BYG Records, took place a mere twenty-one days after the band's arrival in France. Later that week, on 26 June, the Art Ensemble would record two more LPs for the Freedom label, *The Spiritual* and *Tutankhamun*.[3] In no time at all, the group's discography had doubled in size, and with the advance payments for these albums, the Chicagoans could afford to rent their house in Saint-Leu-la-Forêt.[4]

The Art Ensemble's *A Jackson in Your House* was one of the first entries in the Actuel series of recordings, a "major effort" initiated by Delcloo and BYG Records principal Jean Georgakarakos.[5] The BYG label was founded in April 1968 by Georgakarakos and two co-investors, Fernand Boruso and Jean-Luc Young. Georgakarakos hoped that BYG could break down the "barriers between differ- ent forms of contemporary music," an agenda that also appealed to Delcloo, who launched *Actuel* magazine six months after the formation of BYG.[6] Indeed, *Actuel* was read by the same con- sumers that BYG was targeting—members of the 1968 generation with a taste for experimentalism. Georgakarakos saw fit to give

Delcloo "carte blanche" as BYG's artistic director, with the authority to record whomever and whenever he wanted.[7] At first, the BYG/Actuel series grew incrementally: only a few albums were recorded in June and July 1969. By August, the recording process had greatly accelerated, with over a dozen LPs tracked that month alone and several more added to the label's catalog by the end of the year.[8] The August 1969 Actuel sessions yielded two more Art Ensemble albums, *Message to Our Folks* and *Reese and the Smooth Ones*, as well as LPs by Don Cherry, Sunny Murray, Archie Shepp, Alan Silva, and other New Thing figures.[9] The Art Ensemble's AACM colleagues also recorded for BYG—Braxton, Jenkins, and Smith having joined forces with McCall to form a quartet known as the Creative Construction Company. And in accordance with Georgakarakos's boundary-crossing ambitions, the BYG/Actuel series would include recordings by a few white American experimental musicians (Terry Riley, Musica Elettronica Viva) along with the psychedelic rock band Gong.[10]

More than any other Art Ensemble album from 1969, *A Jackson in Your House* represents all of the central characteristics of the group's music during their first months in Paris. We hear a remarkable variety of sounds, musical styles, and compositional structures—everything that captivated French critics and listeners when they encountered the Chicagoans. We also hear many of the intermedia elements that define the band's performance practice: verbal commentary, vocal sounds, theatrical scenarios, and poetry. On the first two tracks of the album, the musicians employ intermedia in humorous, playful, and critical ways, addressing a number of cultural and political matters that confronted them in their new surroundings. In contrast, on the album's B-side they use intermedia not to advance cultural and political critiques, but instead to create vivid imagery. Because these intermedia elements are present throughout the album, listening to *A Jackson in Your House* can be a thoroughly visual experience, despite the limitations of the audio-only medium. *A Jackson in Your House* also possesses an emotional range that the musicians rarely explored on their Paris albums, with the exception of their astonishing disc *People in Sorrow*, recorded for the Pathé label.[11] The pieces that make up *A Jackson in Your House* are funny, shocking, intense, wry, and passionate: fittingly so, for an album that the Art Ensemble dedicated to "the honor and memory of the beautiful spirit known to us as CHARLES CLARK."[12]

"A Jackson in Your House"

The album begins with "A Jackson in Your House," the title track. Like every other composition on the LP, it had been in the Art Ensemble's repertoire for a

introduction	0:00-0:14
percussion interlude	0:14-1:35
theme statement 1	1:35-2:16
theme statement 2	2:16-3:04
theme statement 3	3:04-3:36
swing vamp	3:36-4:34
first swing strain	4:34-4:47
second swing strain	4:47-5:10
first swing strain (return)	5:10-5:45

EXAMPLE 4.1 "A Jackson in Your House": formal diagram

year or more; all but Jarman's "Erika" were composed by Mitchell.[13] "A Jackson in Your House" is both expansive and fast-paced. In less than six minutes, the musicians play an epigrammatic introduction, a moody percussion interlude, three contrasting versions of the main theme, and an extended ending passage with two new melodic strains (see example 4.1). The various sections of the piece allude to distinct musical styles, ordered both successively and simultaneously. As the composition unfolds, this stylistic counterpoint creates numerous instances of "intermusical[ity]," Ingrid Monson's term for "aurally perceptible musical relationships that are heard in the context of particular musical traditions."[14] Considered together, the intermusical relationships in "A Jackson in Your House" constitute an intricate text that riffs on the history of jazz. Additional levels of meaning arise from the intermedia components of the piece: vocal interjections and spontaneous verbal commentary. Throughout the performance, the members of the Art Ensemble dialogue with the music they are playing, an aspect of "A Jackson in Your House" that was not part of Mitchell's original compositional design but developed in Paris during the rehearsals that preceded the recording session.[15] Indeed, the intermedia elements function as specific responses to the Parisian setting of the performance. On the surface, the vocal sounds and verbal commentary are humorous, and seem to signify on the intermusical relationships embedded in the composition. Further analysis reveals that the musicians' vocal and verbal contributions also communicate several subtextual messages. These subtexts form a pointed cultural critique of multiple issues related to the jazz-history

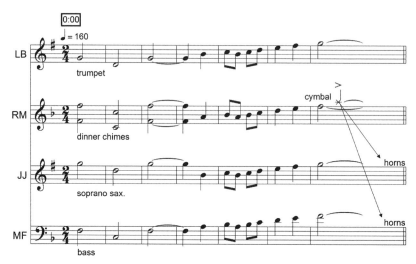

EXAMPLE 4.2 "A Jackson in Your House": introduction

* The musical examples in this chapter are the author's transcriptions, reproduced by permission of Art Ensemble of Chicago Publishing (ASCAP). Each staff is labeled with the performer's initials. The examples represent pitches in the keys of the instruments being played, and may be read as scores for improvisers. The chapter text refers to pitches in concert key, and adopts the convention in which middle C is labeled C_4.

* In this example, diagonal arrows denote musical interactions between performers.

topic of Mitchell's composition, including performer-audience relationships and the reception of black music in France.

"A Jackson in Your House" begins with Bowie on trumpet, Mitchell on dinner chimes, Jarman on soprano saxophone, and Favors on double bass, playing an F-major fanfare in octaves. As Mitchell's final note rings out, he strikes a small cymbal; Favors and Jarman answer with a chorus of bicycle horns (see example 4.2). The meaning of Favors and Jarman's horn chorus is not clear, at least not right away. Bicycle horns and other "little instruments" routinely appear in Art Ensemble performances, and it is possible that in "A Jackson in Your House" the horns were chosen primarily for their acoustic properties. However, Favors and Jarman seem to be using the horns for another purpose: to say something about the fanfare. The musicologist Ekkehard Jost has written that the Art Ensemble's little instruments often "[stand] in a dialectical relationship to the music around [them]," and create a "confrontation of various levels of expression and style, in which the expressive power of one level is relativized by the other."[16] This is exactly what happens in the introduction of "A Jackson in Your House." From the perspective provided by the opening fanfare, the horn chorus is incongruous, even unmusical. Conversely, Favors and Jarman's horn response makes the

EXAMPLE 4.3 "A Jackson in Your House": percussion interlude
* In this example, the triangle is a symbol that means "improvise(d)."

fanfare melody sound quaint and out of place—"a pompous overture," in Jost's assessment, "whose Baroque grace is considerably impaired by percussive interjections."[17]

During the next section of the piece, Mitchell stays on dinner chimes and improvises a string of rubato phrases in the key of F. After each phrase, he plays an aphoristic response on some of his little instruments—bells, horns, and steel drum—complementing the metallic, vibraphone-like sound of his dinner chimes (see example 4.3). Mitchell's improvisation echoes the introductory fanfare and also foreshadows the upcoming main theme. Heard in relation to the entire performance, the fanfare and percussion interlude serve as an extended prelude. These passages also prepare the listener for the intermusical relationships that will emerge during the three statements of the main theme.

The full ensemble returns at 1:47 to present the main theme of "A Jackson in Your House." At first this section sounds like a reprise of the introductory fanfare, but in the fifth measure of the theme Mitchell switches from dinner chimes to wood blocks, cowbell, and drums, in order to play a linear accompaniment pattern that resembles the rickety percussion parts heard on early jazz recordings (see example 4.4). Mitchell's syncopated percussion work forms a quirky contrast to the foursquare, sequential melody performed by the rest of the group. If "music [has] . . . the functional equivalent of a past tense," as Ingrid Monson has asserted, then the members of the Art Ensemble are simultaneously portraying multiple styles and historical periods.[18] The main theme is a march melody, or perhaps a concert overture, but the percussion pattern belongs to turn-of-the-century New Orleans. Mitchell's accompaniment

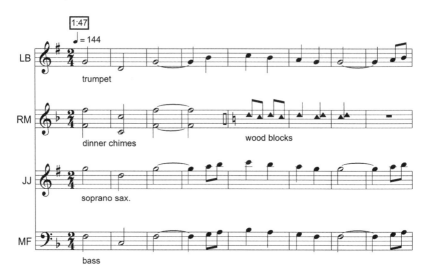

EXAMPLE 4.4 "A Jackson in Your House": theme statement 1, first two phrases

demonstrates both the similarities and the crucial differences between early jazz and its nineteenth-century antecedents, sounds formerly heard on Civil War battlefields, at Congo Square, and onstage at the French Opera House.

In the final phrase of the main theme, the members of the Art Ensemble perform a scale-wise melody borrowed from the introductory fanfare, then break into wild laughter (see example 4.5). Here, the ascending scale and ensuing laughter recall the bicycle-horn chorus from the beginning of the piece. The horn response played after the opening fanfare, however, was as spacious and restrained as the present outbreak of laughter is extroverted and surreal.

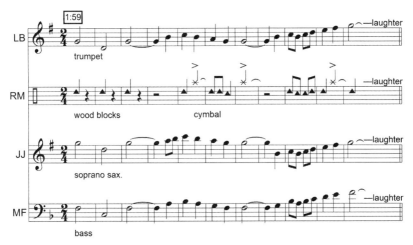

EXAMPLE 4.5 "A Jackson in Your House": theme statement 1, last phrase

Like many of the intermedia elements in "A Jackson in Your House," this vocal device conveys multiple levels of meaning. The musicians' laughter mocks the antiquated main theme, as in the introduction, and it calls attention to the stylistic divide between the theme and Mitchell's early jazz percussion playing. More audaciously, the Art Ensemble's uproar expresses the oppositional spirit of the performance itself. In the days leading up to the recording session for *A Jackson in Your House*, the band's concerts at the Théâtre du Lucernaire were acclaimed as the "sensational debut of the New Thing in Paris."[19] The Chicagoans contested this one-dimensional reception with a piece owing more to James Reese Europe and Sidney Bechet, who had charmed Parisians decades earlier, than to the free-jazz figures who served as inevitable points of reference in French critics' evaluations of the Art Ensemble.

The second version of the main theme is stated by Mitchell, who employs his best Bill Cosby voice to recite a rhyming poem over Favors's vigorous bass line. Mitchell has transformed the instrumental melody into a down-home toast to "Jackson," the cat he owned before the Art Ensemble traveled to Paris:[20]

> One two three
> There's a Jackson in your house
> All that he will do is chase your shoe and watch you in the tub
> Turn around and act the clown and scratch you on the rump
> One two three
> There's a Jackson in your house
> And he will never catch a mouse

EXAMPLE 4.6 "A Jackson in Your House": theme statement 2, Mitchell recitation

During the poem, Jarman and Bowie construct a madhouse accompaniment out of bicycle horns, stifled chuckles, and half-valve trumpet. When Mitchell reaches the end of his recitation, he turns the last note into a yodel, then a cascade of laughter, joining in the mirth created by the other musicians. Jarman gets the last word with a hip pun: "Jackson—that cat is something" (see example 4.6). The second theme is the funniest section of the performance, and the band's laughter can be perceived as a reaction to the witty poem, Mitchell's comical delivery, and the boisterous atmosphere around the recitation. This moment also illustrates the importance of humor to the musicians, a factor that distinguished their performances from much of the free jazz on the Paris scene in June 1969. "A Jackson in Your House" cheerfully refutes facile interpretations of their work: for instance, Philippe Adler's contention that the Art Ensemble's music was "violent and revolutionary."[21] If anything, "A Jackson in Your House" resembles the experimental theater productions and playful, semi-scripted happenings then taking place at the American Center.

In the next section of the performance, beginning at 3:04, the musicians play a collectively improvised rendition of the main theme in the New Orleans style. Bowie and Jarman collaborate on a contrapuntal melody, supported by Favors's two-beat slap-bass groove. This version of the theme would presumably provide a better fit for Mitchell's accompaniment. However, the rhythmic imprecision of Mitchell's percussion work makes the third theme statement sound slightly awkward, as if played by an amateur Dixieland band. The intermusical relationships heard earlier in the piece have given way to sharp parody.

This theme statement ends differently from its predecessors. Rather than pausing for laughter after they ascend the F-major scale, the members of the Art Ensemble detour into a tag ending that centers on the "shave and a haircut" rhythm played by Mitchell on wood block. All four musicians perform the "two bits" figure in rhythmic unison, but then Jarman plays an extra note on the very next beat. Mitchell exclaims "Oh, man . . . ," feigning disappointment with Jarman's calculated mistake, and the others loudly express their disapproval (see example 4.7). Jarman's wrong-note musical joke and the subsequent commotion represent a significant shift in the Art Ensemble's intermedia strategy. Previously in "A Jackson in Your House," the musicians' vocal interjections were humorous, and communicated critical messages in subtextual ways. Now the Art Ensemble's cultural critique is moving ever closer to the surface. "Let's get on down and play some more blues, man," Jarman urges. "We're gonna try to play some blues. Y'all are playing that ol' hacked-up [stuff]—ain't nobody want to hear none of that." Jarman's words convey the tight connections between the musical marketplace, the pressure it exerts upon performers to innovate yet remain within identifiable genre boundaries, and working musicians' utter dependence upon the favor of paying audiences, sympathetic critics, and industry gatekeepers. These constraints, George E. Lewis explained, were particularly apparent to the members of the Art Ensemble and their AACM colleagues, who understood that "black music had become the most commodified art in history, and the space of positions for alternative black musical expression was becoming vanishingly small."[22] In this respect, the Paris scene was no different from what the Art Ensemble had left behind in Chicago. As Jarman wrote in the liner notes to *A Jackson in Your House*, "humor as serious as life. . . . [i]t sounds like good old jazz, because it's just as good here as it was over there."[23]

Jarman's request to "play some more blues" signals a turning point in the Art Ensemble's cultural critique, and also marks the principal formal division of the piece. In response to Jarman, Favors initiates the long ending section of "A Jackson in Your House" at 3:36, playing a I–VI–II–V bass pattern in

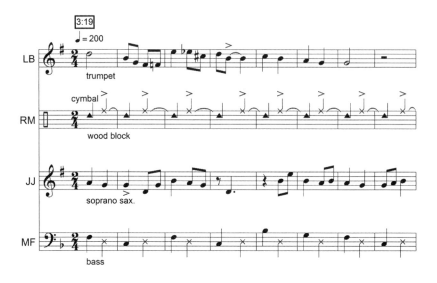

EXAMPLE 4.7 "A Jackson in Your House": theme statement 3, last phrase

the new key of B♭ major. The moderate tempo of Favors's bass vamp suggests the swing style of jazz, which Mitchell elaborates with a pentatonic clarinet melody. Though the contrast between the swing groove and the preceding theme statement is not immense, Jarman underscores the intermusical relationship with a monologue directed at the other performers: "Tryin' to play some blues!—You playin' some jazz there, huh?" (see example 4.8).

Jarman's spontaneous commentary recalls the writings of Anthony Braxton on the "reality of the sweating brow," a critical concept that explains West-

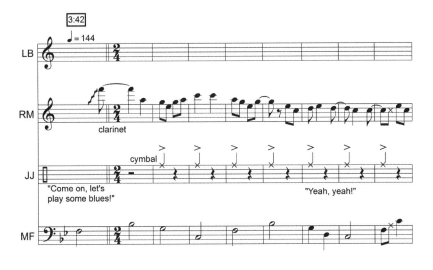

EXAMPLE 4.8 "A Jackson in Your House": swing vamp

ern perceptions of black performance. According to Braxton, the "'reality of the sweating brow' has to do with how white writers have come to interpret whether a given black musician is accurately 'doing the best' he or she can, or whether that musician is merely 'coasting'—or not 'really trying to be creative' . . . A black so-called jazz musician's activity . . . is viewed not so much with respect to his or her given music offering, but instead with respect to whether that person's emotional surface output is viewed as sufficient."[24] From this perspective, Jarman's energetic monologue could represent an audience talking back to the performers, as in a 1940s Jazz at the Philharmonic jam session, with enthusiastic fans crowded against the front of the stage, inciting their idols with shouts of "Go, man, go!" Alternatively, Jarman might be satirically enacting what certain listeners expected from the Art Ensemble: emotional displays, physical abandon, and sweating brows. This interpretation is consistent with some of the early reviews of the Chicagoans by French critics, such as Marc Bernard's characterization of their performances as "torrential and extremely violent," requiring from the musicians "total involvement— physical, psychological, and spiritual."[25]

Of course, these charged images were hardly unique to the Art Ensemble's reception in France, and are ultimately traceable to the black exotica phenomenon (discussed in chapter 3). This reality is central to the meaning of "A Jackson in Your House," as a compositional text and as a performed cultural critique. "A Jackson in Your House" sheds light on the band's experiences during the summer of 1969, and it also speaks to the history of jazz, from its New Orleans origins to latter-day jazz cultures in Paris and around the world. In the same way, Jarman's verbal commentary reaches beyond the Art Ensemble to embrace African American musicians past and present, and to resist commercialized or essentialist perceptions of black performance.

In the last section of "A Jackson in Your House," Bowie, Mitchell, and Favors play a sixteen-measure melody strain (at 4:34), then another new strain lasting twenty-eight bars (at 4:47). Jarman keeps time on a ride cymbal, sings along, and exhorts the others: "Yes it is—Uh huh—All right, man!" As the swing groove continues, it becomes clear that Mitchell could have composed any number of novel melodies over Favors's bass vamp, and it is increasingly difficult to predict when the musicians will end the performance. The members of the Art Ensemble exploit this sense of unpredictability by returning to the first swing strain, then linking this strain to a new tag ending. This gesture resembles the "shave and a haircut" figure from the third theme statement, but the musicians subvert expectations by prolonging the tag for an unusually long stretch of time. After a few false finishes, the performers finally reach the end: first Mitchell and Jarman, followed one beat later by Bowie and Favors. Curiously, they choose to downplay this clever conclusion—no bicycle horns, no laughing, no dialogue—so that listeners can reflect for a moment on what has transpired (see example 4.9).

"Get in Line"

The second track on *A Jackson in Your House* is "Get in Line," perhaps the most politically oriented composition in the Art Ensemble's repertoire circa

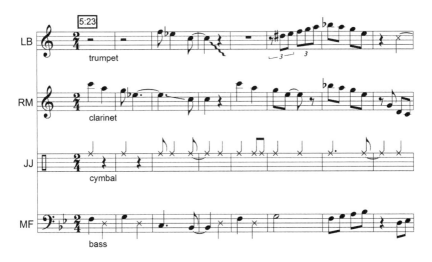

EXAMPLE 4.9 "A Jackson in Your House": first swing strain (return), tag ending

June 1969. "Get in Line" progresses through a series of musical styles and structures that seem to represent the experience of war (see example 4.10). To many Parisians, these sounds would evoke the Vietnam conflict, which had sparked the May 1968 protests and remained a divisive political topic in France one year after.[26] Furthermore, "Get in Line" also includes a theatrical script that depicts the U.S. Army as thoroughly afflicted by racism. This portrayal of the military would undoubtedly register as a political critique, especially for France's 1968 generation, which regarded American institutions like the army as imperialist enterprises.[27] Knowing this, one could be tempted

march music	0:00-0:35
intensity structure	0:35-4:19
percussion texture	4:19-5:47

EXAMPLE 4.10 "Get in Line": formal diagram

to hear "Get in Line" as an anti-war theater piece set to music.[28] Such an interpretation, though, would contradict numerous public pronouncements by the members of the Art Ensemble denying that their music had anything to do with politics. As Jarman explained:

> I used to be into the Student Peace Union, that kind of thing, during [college]. I've always been interested in politics, but now I'm more toward the left in a nationalistic way, black nationalism. But we, the Art Ensemble, we're not about politics.[29]

Bowie reaffirmed this distinction between individual political beliefs and the band's apolitical stance, while asserting that French critics writing about the Art Ensemble often had their own ideological agendas:

> The music is universal, our politics is the politics of the planet. . . . Our politics transcends religions, race and language, so we're dealing in another area. They all made it look like that, if you were black, you were political. That's all they would ask you about, you were put into it.[30]

The tension between "Get in Line" and Bowie's remarks about politics and the Art Ensemble points to another way to understand the piece. "Get in Line" is political, but unconventionally so. The musical and theatrical layers of the piece form a narrative that critiques racism and militarism, and also demonstrates how African Americans can respond to these issues without engaging in outright political activism, which was difficult in Chicago and impossible in Paris. The Art Ensemble's critique departs from the rhetoric often associated with Vietnam-era protest songs and free jazz, helping the Chicagoans contend with the new political environment they encountered in France. Additionally, "Get in Line" contains another narrative about social pluralism, which dramatizes the diverse aesthetic and political positions among the members of the Art Ensemble. This is consistent with the group's valuation of personal autonomy over orthodoxy, whether in politics or in music.

EXAMPLE 4.11 "Get in Line": opening bass ostinato

"Get in Line" opens with a two-note bass ostinato (see example 4.11). This bass line is almost identical to what Favors played during various portions of the previous track, and the immediate impression is that "A Jackson in Your House" has returned at a much faster tempo. Four measures later, the rest of the band enters. Mitchell, the composer of "Get in Line," plays a blistering chromatic melody on alto saxophone, which is doubled by Bowie on trumpet; Jarman, also playing alto saxophone, starts with a slower countermelody, and then joins Mitchell and Bowie for the final two bars of the phrase (see example 4.12). The upper-register melody, simultaneous countermelody, and oompah bass line imply that "Get in Line" is a march, reminiscent of the angular, stylized marches written by twentieth-century modernist composers— pieces like Charles Ives's "Country Band March" and Igor Stravinsky's "Marche du soldat." Mitchell was well versed in this repertoire, having performed much of it in the early 1960s, as a member of a South Side concert band sponsored by Local 208.[31] However, any attempt to hear "Get in Line" as a modernist concert march is confounded by what happens next. After tearing through the theme, the musicians fall silent for a few seconds. Then they reenter with a barrage of sound: whistles, bicycle horns, and a shocking exclamation from Jarman: "Get in line, n—, it's time to be a soldier! Get in line!" Jarman's outburst brings the first theme statement into sharper focus. "Get in Line" is a military march, not a concert march, and Jarman is an irate army officer addressing a black soldier. This theatrical scenario hit close to home for the four ex-servicemen in the Art Ensemble, especially Bowie and Jarman, who experienced racial discrimination while stationed at bases in the South.[32]

This interpretation of "Get in Line" as a theatrically inflected military march is confirmed in the next section of the piece. At 0:17, the group returns to the opening theme—and then, while Favors's bass vamp continues, his bandmates play interlocking melodies built from rhythmic patterns that are idiomatic to marches (triplets, dotted rhythms, etc.). Midway through the passage, Jarman breaks into a familiar army cadence call, chanting "Left! Right! Left! Right!" as if he is a drill instructor, commanding the other musicians to "get in line" and execute a quick-time march (see example 4.13).[33] The second theme statement ends abruptly, with all of the performers playing a three-note

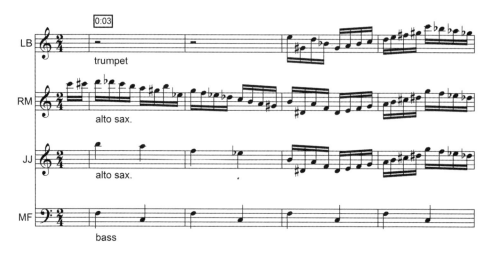

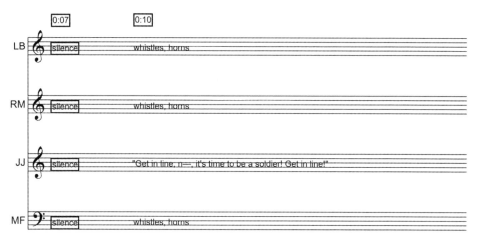

EXAMPLE 4.12 "Get in Line": march music, theme statement 1

figure in a crisp *one-and-two* rhythm. Like the stinger accents heard in many marches, this gesture provides musical closure as well as a vivid visual image of marching soldiers coming to a halt, *left-right-left*. This sense of resolution, however, proves to be fleeting.

After two seconds of silence, the musicians launch into an extraordinarily brief group improvisation, lasting only as long as it takes Bowie, Jarman, and Mitchell to release a single breath through their instruments. Another silent moment leads to more "short subjects"; then the process repeats again (see example 4.14).[34] Some of these improvised fragments resemble the idiomatic

EXAMPLE 4.13 "Get in Line": march music, theme statement 2

march rhythms from the previous section, but because Favors has abandoned his oompah ostinato, they never coalesce into a proper march. Instead, all four musicians play independent melodies, while staggering their breathing and phrasing to create the impression of a continuous texture. The members of the Art Ensemble are getting "out of line," theatrically speaking. In musical terms, they are gradually progressing toward an improvisation style that they would describe as an "intensity structure"—complex, dense, and highly energetic.[35] Or, to quote the poetic formulation offered by Jarman in the album

EXAMPLE 4.13 Continued

liner notes, the Chicagoans are "marching through the intense flood of the military world that surrounds us."[36]

The intensity structure that is materializing contrasts strikingly with the opening march music. Military marches, like the precision drills that they accompany, are defined by a few common characteristics. They possess rhythmic regularity: a steady, uninterrupted meter and a narrow range of tempos, suitable for walking or running. They are stratified, with instrumental groups performing specific functions, such as the bass and percussion instruments

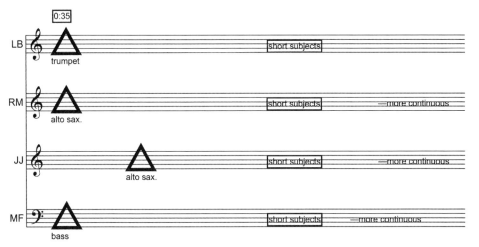

EXAMPLE 4.14 "Get in Line": short subjects, assembling the intensity structure

that imitate the footfalls of marching infantry. And finally, they are coordinated, with strict style norms that mirror the meticulous protocol governing all aspects of military routine, from training activities to actual combat. This careful scheme is overturned when the members of the Art Ensemble approach the intensity structure. Suddenly, there is no regular meter or tempo; each musician determines his own pacing independently of the others. They also shift from register to register, one timbre to another, with impressive speed, replacing stratification and coordination with a non-hierarchical structure that is "extremely dense, fast-moving, [and] ultimately static," as George E. Lewis put it.[37] If, during the two theme statements, the performers were marching or moving in formation, the music now conveys that their ranks have been broken, and that the Art Ensemble soldiers are operating in a chaotic, unpredictable environment—like the fields and forests of Vietnam. Jarman responds at 1:40, putting down his saxophone and shouting at the men under his command, in an attempt to gain control of a rapidly deteriorating situation (see example 4.15).

Jarman's verbal eruption seems to be triggered by developments in the music, specifically Mitchell's increasing prominence in the texture. For this reason, Mitchell's saxophone playing does not have to be heard as a solo (in the jazz sense) that contributes only to the musical layer of the performance. It would be more accurate to analyze this moment in theatrical terms. Here, Mitchell emerges as a distinct character who provides a dramatic foil to Jarman's officer persona. Furthermore, one can regard Favors and Bowie's instrumental sounds, siren noises, and police whistles as sonic backdrops

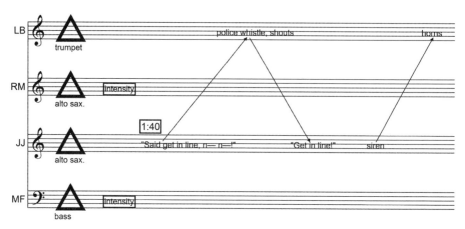

EXAMPLE 4.15 "Get in Line": intensity structure, Mitchell solo

that establish a theatrical change of scene, and set the stage for the mounting conflict between the characters played by Jarman and Mitchell.

In another effective dramatic touch, the performers let the exact nature of the dispute remain ambiguous. Mitchell could be protesting the officer's dehumanizing conduct or expressing solidarity with other black soldiers. Another interpretive possibility comes from Jarman's own combat experiences as a paratrooper in the U.S. Army, 11th Airborne Division. In the mid-1950s, Jarman and his fellow Pathfinders were deployed to Southeast Asia, where they conducted secret operations during the early stages of the Vietnam War. On one nightmarish occasion, Jarman's platoon was dropped near a Vietnamese village suspected of being a Communist hideout. Some of the paratroopers were killed in the landing, but Jarman and several others survived, and were ordered to proceed with their raid. They destroyed their target, only to discover that it held women and children, not Communist soldiers. The incident was incredibly traumatic for Jarman, both physically and psychologically. He sustained a severe leg wound while retreating, and was unable to continue in a combat role.[38] As he declared, "I had to get out of the line."[39] Jarman spent the rest of his enlistment playing saxophone in Augsburg, West Germany, an assignment much less arduous than dangerous paratrooper jumps.[40] With this story in mind, Mitchell's performance can be heard as a conscientious soldier rebelling against unlawful orders. Jarman himself might hear an echo of his own escape from Vietnam, saxophone in hand.

Thirty seconds into Mitchell's solo, Jarman calls out the soldier once more, and now Bowie reacts, playing a cadence gesture on trumpet at 2:13. His bandmates answer immediately, as they often do in response to his "brass

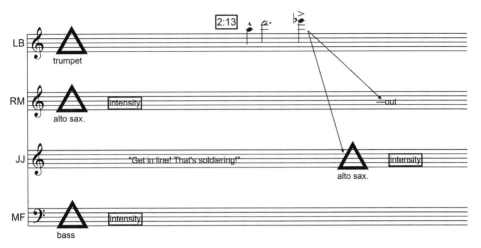

EXAMPLE 4.16 "Get in Line": intensity structure, transition

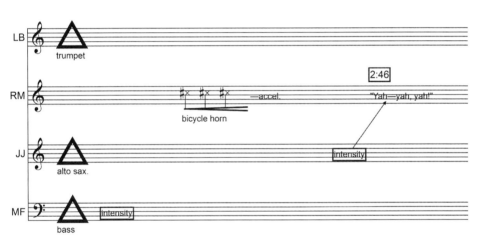

EXAMPLE 4.17 "Get in Line": intensity structure, Jarman solo

witnessing and signifying punditry."[41] Mitchell drops out, and Jarman reenters on alto saxophone, transforming his verbal assault into a spirited instrumental monologue (see example 4.16).

During the first few phrases of Jarman's saxophone performance, Mitchell rests. Then, as Jarman's line increases in volume, timbral complexity, and other markers of "intensity," Mitchell returns with a bicycle horn, playing a series of beeps and bleats that imitate Bowie's trumpet exclamations.[42] A few more soldiers, it seems, have joined the rebellion (see example 4.17). The dramatic conflict culminates about half a minute into the passage. Mitchell shapes his horn chatter into a steady pulse, which sounds like an emergency signal cutting through the dense texture generated by the other musicians. Shortly thereafter, Jarman reaches the peak of his saxophone improvisation, and Mitchell replies—not with a bicycle horn, but with his voice: "Yah—yah, yah!"

Mitchell's vocal cries can be interpreted in a number of ways. He could be encouraging his bandmates, catalyzing Bowie, Favors, and Jarman at an exciting musical moment. His cries might also hold some dramatic meaning, as rejoinders to the commanding officer or as representations of a soldier's distress during combat. Any dramatic interpretation, however persuasive, must nonetheless take into account the clearly comical tone that Mitchell adopts during this section of the piece. Here, Mitchell's performance registers not as genuine defiance or distress, but as a playful response that foregrounds the subjectivity of black soldiers. This is trickster logic, a kind of "meta-play" intended to be "disruptive of settled expectations," in the words of Brian Sutton-Smith.[43] Mitchell's cries are a critique of the power relationship between the officer and the soldier, and simultaneously a creative, improvisational move that establishes a "place where the 'writ does not run,'" where military protocol does not apply.[44] The soldier realizes that he cannot win at the officer's game, so he creates a new game, with himself at the center and the abusive officer at the periphery. This form of "subversive play"—according to bell hooks, whose theory of the ludic resonates with Sutton-Smith's—is often found in art forms informed by "radical black subjectivity."[45] "It seems to me a practical gesture," hooks observed, "to shift the scene of action if in fact the location of one's political practice does not enable change."[46]

Mitchell's playful response separates "Get in Line" from the rhetoric of many 1960s anti-war compositions, which often employed earnest pleading or world-weary cynicism.[47] In contrast, the members of the Art Ensemble are articulating what Aldon Nielsen called "the dada of the black experimentalist," a declaration that if the American "'power structure' . . . is reasonable, then we prefer not to be reasonable."[48] This conviction is at the core of Jarman's poem "AS BLACK/AND WILD AS IT CAN BE-":

> LEAVE
>   the war to those who NEED that . . .
>   WE MEAN TO DANCE AND SHOUT
>   TO HOLLER like damn mad fools
> (some will say) . . .[49]

In the wake of Mitchell's vocal cries, Jarman exits the stage, and by 3:07 only Bowie and Favors remain. The texture is much less dense than when the

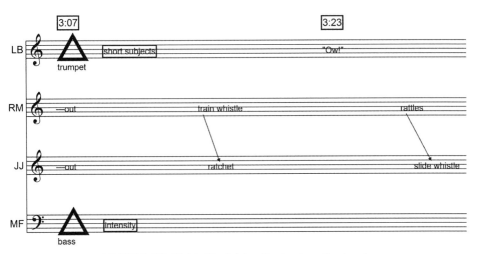

EXAMPLE 4.18 "Get in Line": intensity structure, Bowie solo

saxophonists were playing, despite Favors's forceful contributions on bass. After a short rest, Mitchell and Jarman return, playing some of the Art Ensemble's characteristic little instruments: a train whistle and a ratchet, then rattles and a slide whistle (see example 4.18). Earlier in the piece, one could easily analyze "Get in Line" as representational or mimetic. A military march was followed by a dispute between an officer and an African American enlisted man; the intensity structure seemed to represent soldiers breaking formation, and then contending with either the enraged officer or the sheer chaos of war. The little instruments played by Mitchell and Jarman, however, do not belong in a march, a theatrical battle scene, or even a standard Art Ensemble intensity structure. These are instruments heard in slapstick comedies and animated cartoons. Perhaps the whistles, rattles, and ratchet are functioning as another playful response, deconstructing the tense theatrical scenario as well as the intensity structure itself. Tellingly, the only vocal sound heard during this passage comes from Bowie, who pauses between trumpet phrases to holler at no one in particular, or at himself, confirming the subjective nature of the Art Ensemble's "subversive play." For a moment at least, the officer-soldier conflict has yielded to "the dada of the black experimentalist."

Mitchell returns on saxophone at 3:49, playing a fast-paced line that consumes the silences between Bowie's trumpet phrases. Jarman adds a few more ratchet scrapes, blurring the transition from the old texture to the new, and then enters on saxophone once again. The musicians have reconstituted the intensity structure that began three minutes earlier, creating a formal arch that spans the entire middle section of the piece (see example 4.19). This passage

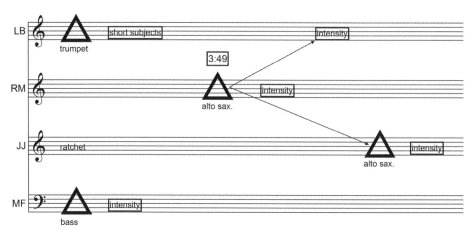

EXAMPLE 4.19 "Get in Line": reassembling the intensity structure

clearly recalls the early stages of the intensity structure, but the verbal texts and vocal sounds are missing. Jarman is not yelling invective, and there are no comical cries from Bowie, Favors, and Mitchell. Due to the absence of any theatrical elements, the Art Ensemble's music is no longer joined to a dramatic conflict, or to the wartime images of the opening march. Now the intensity structure can be reexamined for new meanings. One sonic connotation is readily apparent: the resemblance between this intensity structure and "energy-sound" playing, saxophonist Archie Shepp's term for a performance mode associated with second-wave free jazz.[50] As established in chapter 3, the reception of free jazz in France was shaped by the black exotica phenomenon, which by the late 1960s portrayed African American experimental music as both culturally and politically transgressive, the sonic manifestation of an essential black identity. This is the context for Bowie's claim: "They all made it look like that, if you were black, you were political."[51] Although such misperceptions gave the Art Ensemble a certain cachet on the Paris scene, the Chicagoans understood the real risks of appearing to be radical, given their precarious position as non-white immigrants to France, a nation still reeling from the May 1968 uprising. In one famous case, the African American trumpeter Clifford Thornton was denied entry to France in retaliation for the organizing he had done on behalf of the Black Panthers.[52] Viewed in this light, the "Get in Line" intensity structure can be comprehended not just as a protest against war and institutional racism, but also as a cultural critique of how African American music was received in late 1960s Paris. By denying that pieces like "Get in Line" were politically motivated, the members of the Art Ensemble could resist essentialist perceptions of their work and open up

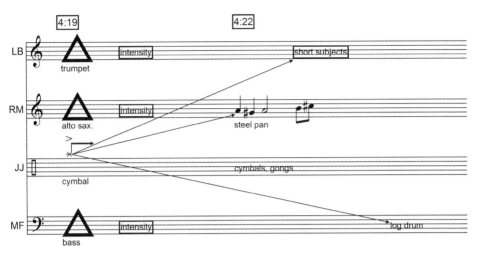

EXAMPLE 4.20 "Get in Line": percussion texture, metallic sounds

a space for expression that "continually opposes re-inscribing notions of 'authentic' black identity," as bell hooks wrote.[53] Instead of joining the contentious debate on black experimentalism, Bowie, Favors, Jarman, and Mitchell began to cultivate a discourse around their music that would become as "oppositional and liberatory" as the sounds they played.[54]

At the 4:19 mark of "Get in Line," Jarman suddenly pivots away from his microphone and starts crashing a cymbal with considerable force. Within seconds, the other musicians switch to various percussion instruments: gongs, steel pan, and a log drum. This swift transition ends the intensity structure, and introduces the final section of the piece (see example 4.20). As the percussion texture unfolds, Bowie continues to play trumpet, but the dominant instruments here are gongs, cymbals, and other large, metallic sound-makers. Unlike the dense and complex intensity structure, where a single second of musical time might contain dozens of notes, the new texture consists of massive, discrete events that sound like a series of deafening explosions: "total pandemonium," in Ekkehard Jost's description.[55]

A minute before the piece's end, the members of the Art Ensemble start shouting and "HOLLER[ing] like damn mad fools," to quote Jarman again.[56] This time, the performers' vocal sounds do not communicate disputation, distress, or any of the moods previously heard. Instead, they convey boundless joy—play and exultation. Mitchell reacts at 4:54 by moving from steel pan to bell lyre, playing simple melodies that diverge, both sonically and emotionally, from the rapturous contributions of his bandmates (see example 4.21). Mitchell's bell-lyre melodies form a deep contrast to the rest of the texture.

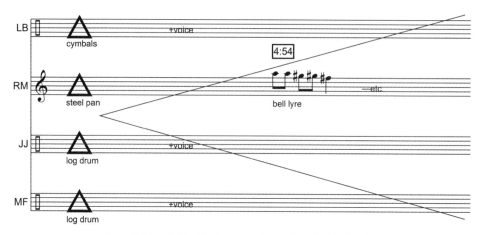

EXAMPLE 4.21 "Get in Line": percussion texture, Mitchell bell lyre

There is restraint against ecstasy, clarity in the midst of complexity. The other musicians are answering the intensity structure in a direct, unified way; even Jarman has discarded his dramatic persona to team up with Bowie and Favors. Still, Mitchell remains apart from his bandmates, and engages the intensity structure with an attitude of disregard. This response typifies Mitchell's oppositional approach to group improvisation.[57] It also shows the Art Ensemble's aesthetics in action, a pluralist model of music and social relations that counters essentialist views of African American performance, politics, and protest.

The musicians conclude "Get in Line" with another salvo of gongs, steel-pan strokes, and cymbal crashes. The thunderous resonance of all these metallic instruments creates the single loudest moment in the performance, overwhelming the recording-studio signal chain and prompting the audio engineer to adjust the mixing board on the fly. As this climactic passage proceeds, the members of the Art Ensemble keep shouting, demonstrating once more how play can transform one's situation—musically, theatrically, and politically. The last sounds heard are a cryptic trumpet line, followed by six pulsations from a small bell, quietly reverberating as the percussion texture fades away (see example 4.22).

"The Waltz"

A Jackson in Your House continues with another Mitchell composition, "The Waltz." This is the only purely instrumental track on the album; it has none of the intermedia elements heard in the other pieces, and "The Waltz" does

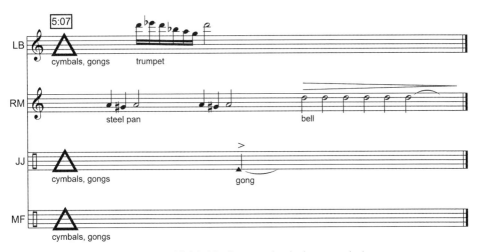

EXAMPLE 4.22 "Get in Line": percussion texture, conclusion

not carry as much emotional or critical weight as the tracks that precede it. Instead, its function is to provide musical contrast and a respite from the furor of "Get in Line." The composition's title indicates exactly how this is accomplished. "The Waltz" is in many ways a typical example of the genre. Played in triple meter, the piece is actually danceable, and its AABBA form is a familiar structure heard in numerous waltzes. The B sections, which are mostly diatonic and use only two chords, would fit perfectly into the repertoire of any Polish polka band in Chicago. In comparison, the A sections are more chromatic, even bordering on atonal, but do not otherwise breach the boundaries of the waltz genre (see example 4.23). With "The Waltz," the members of the Art Ensemble confirm Jarman's claim about the breadth of their performance practice: "We play. . . . [e]verything, really—because, ultimately, we play 'music.'"[58]

"The Waltz" is also distinguished by its extreme brevity. Including the eight-bar introduction, the piece is only forty-eight measures in length, and it lasts just over a minute. Heard in isolation, "The Waltz" could be the theme to a movie or television show. Its duration explains its placement in *A Jackson in Your House*, as the last track on the album's A-side. In many Art Ensemble concerts, short compositions such as "The Waltz" emerge at the end of extended improvisatory passages, creating a sense of arrival and enabling the musicians to move to something new and unrelated. This is precisely what happens on *A Jackson in Your House*. "The Waltz" closes off both "A Jackson in Your House" and "Get in Line," two pieces joined by similar bass lines

EXAMPLE 4.23 "The Waltz": full score

as well as by the critical texts and subtexts that they communicate. Having reached the end of the album's first side, we turn the record over and "wait passionately for an answer."[59]

"Erika"/"Song for Charles"

The second side of *A Jackson in Your House* is filled with a twenty-one-minute performance that begins with Jarman's "Erika," continues with Mitchell's "Song for Charles," and concludes with a long group improvisation (see example 4.24).[60] This performance, like the first two pieces on the album, contains several intermedia elements: poetry, text fragments, and vocal sounds.

EXAMPLE 4.23 Continued

Jarman recitation	0:00-3:39
"Erika" theme	3:39-5:25
transition	5:25-7:05
"Song for Charles" theme	7:05-7:39
open improvisation	7:39-20:59

EXAMPLE 4.24 "Erika"/"Song for Charles": formal diagram

However, the kinds of critical messages that characterize "A Jackson in Your House" and "Get in Line" do not appear in "Erika"/"Song for Charles." This has important consequences for the music on the album's B-side. The members of the Art Ensemble are not compelled to use intermusical relationships or evocative contrasts in style to advance cultural and political critiques; rather, they are free to explore alternative ways of linking music and intermedia.

One approach is heard in "Erika," which is based on Jarman's poem of the same name. Jarman recites the text, while the other musicians improvise an accompaniment based on the poem's imagery and form. Intermedia elements also make several appearances in the open improvisation that follows the "Song for Charles" theme, but they are not the sole factors determining how the music unfolds. Indeed, the Art Ensemble's performance makes it clear that verbal and vocal intermedia are just two components of a much larger toolkit for group improvisation. Sometimes musical sounds prompt other sounds, and texts inspire vocal or verbal replies. In other moments, the band members respond to a suggestive chord with spoken dialogue, or greet the reading of a poem with an eruption of instrumental music. There is, in "Erika"/"Song for Charles," a remarkable continuity of expression among verbal texts, vocal sounds, and music that parallels the Art Ensemble's innovative use of little instruments as equal partners to more conventional winds, strings, and percussion. Jarman, of course, would explain this concept with a poem:

> I seek new sounds
> because new sounds
> seek me
> Why, please tell me
> must i limit myself
> to a saxophone or clarinet![61]

"Erika" tells the story of a "little rebellious girl" and her parents, friends of Jarman's from Chicago.[62] Both the poem and its companion melody were at least two years old. Jarman recorded an instrumental version of "Erika" on 2 September 1967, and before that session both he and Mitchell played the piece with their own bands.[63] This was the same period when Jarman wrote "Non-Cognitive Aspects of the City," which like "Erika" draws on the "black urban surrealism" genre of poetry developed by Amiri Baraka.[64] Jarman had met Baraka some years earlier, back when the latter man was still known as LeRoi Jones. Like his Left Bank run-in with Allen Ginsberg, this encounter motivated Jarman to write poetry himself, and Baraka would become one of his main poetic influences.[65] In fact, there are specific references to Baraka's work in both "Non-Cognitive Aspects of the City" and "Erika"—Jarman's way of acknowledging the creative debt he owed Baraka. "Non-Cognitive Aspects of the City" is set in a forbidding landscape "where Roy J's prophecies become the causes of children."[66] A similar vision emerges in the very first stanza of "Erika," which introduces the girl named in the poem's title and describes her upbringing in 1960s Chicago:

> ERIKA
> child of our uncharted microtones
> thrown through the dawn the maze of
> longing
>   as she matures in Black America
> the Panther,paying homage to the people
> torn with gun,television hero
>   gone to madness-
> seeking the answer
>   can we.............endure[67]

Jarman bases his recitation on the phrase "our uncharted microtones," a poetic image with rich musical implications. Each line of the poem becomes a brief, atonal melody, placed with precision in a narrow vocal range rarely wider than a third. Jarman chants most of the text quietly, *sotto voce*, and emphasizes important words with careful note choices and by lengthening certain syllables. This approach is evident in the opening lines of Jarman's recitation. He intones "ERIKA" on the pitch C_3, holding the last syllable a bit longer than the others, then leaps up to a drawn-out $E\flat_3$ for "child," and returns to the lower register for the remainder of the line. The final word, "microtones," is recited just like "ERIKA," with all three syllables chanted on C_3 in a short-short-long

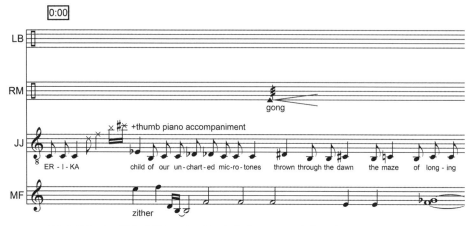

EXAMPLE 4.25 "Erika"/"Song for Charles": Jarman recitation, first part of stanza 1

pattern—an instance of melodic and rhythmic symmetry that ties together the first two lines of the poem (see example 4.25). In this moment and throughout his recitation, Jarman's attention to musical detail and transparent vocal timbre remind the listener of John Cage's idiosyncratic reciting style. One also hears a contrast between Jarman's measured, deliberate recitation and his more spirited vocals in "A Jackson in Your House" and "Get in Line," not to mention the other musicians' humorous, playful, and absurd contributions to the album.

During his recitation, Jarman accompanies himself with one of his handheld percussion instruments, a thumb piano. The practice of auto-accompaniment with little instruments had been a key feature of Jarman's solo poetry readings in Chicago, as well as the poetry pieces performed by the bands he led prior to joining the Art Ensemble.[68] In "Erika," Jarman uses the thumb piano to produce a musical layer that remains steady amid the changing textures created by the other members of the group. Bowie, Favors, and Mitchell take their cues from the poem itself, another aspect of the performance that is reminiscent of Jarman's earlier intermedia works such as "Non-Cognitive Aspects of the City." Here, the poem is divided into four stanzas, each of which begins with the name of the person portrayed therein: "ERIKA," "MOTHER," "FATHER," and "ERIKA" again. Accordingly, Jarman's bandmates shape their accompaniment into four distinct sections. During the first stanza, Favors plucks a zither while Mitchell tolls a gong and coaxes feedback sounds from an electric guitar. Bowie enters midway through the stanza, alternating between bass-drum strokes and delicate harmonica melodies (see example 4.26). Like Jarman's text, the Art Ensemble's accompaniment is shadowy and ominous.

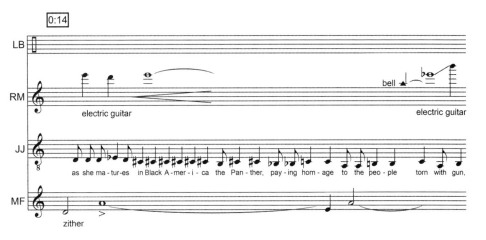

EXAMPLE 4.26 "Erika"/"Song for Charles": Jarman recitation, second part of stanza 1

Jarman moves into a slightly higher vocal register for the second stanza, which focuses on the psychological trauma borne by Erika's mother:

> MOTHER,once freaked with acid
> > product of the "NEW FRONTIER"
> becoming the maiden lonely,
> Heroshimas' crime,the horror,insane
> visions for her child/locked forever
> > in her womb.
> seeking the answer
> > > can we............endure[69]

To highlight this troubling imagery, Favors aggressively strums his zither, forgoing the light plucking technique he used in the first stanza. Mitchell switches to a new instrument, the C flute, improvising a chromatic melody that counterpoints Jarman's verbal recitation. Their attentiveness to the structure and content of the poem is matched by Bowie. As in the first stanza, he remains silent until Jarman has recited half of the text. Then Bowie returns on bass drum, playing a series of low, tenebrous tones that illustrate Jarman's bleak metaphor "locked forever in her womb." The second stanza concludes with the same two lines that ended the first stanza, "seeking the answer can we............endure." Mitchell and Favors frame these words with soft cymbal and zither sounds, echoing Jarman's poetic refrain by returning temporarily to the enigmatic texture of the first stanza (see example 4.27).

At 1:33, the musicians announce the third stanza with a major textural shift. Bowie performs a rapid flourish on harmonica and bass drum, Mitchell moves to alto saxophone, and for an instant both he and Favors play bells. Jarman, still accompanying himself on thumb piano, continues his recitation in an even higher vocal range (see example 4.28). He also accelerates the pace of his delivery, intoning each word like one of the brushstrokes urgently applied to canvas by Erika's father, who is painting a portrait of John Coltrane. Here, Jarman quotes Baraka's famous description of the late saxophonist, "the black saint whom Leroi calls 'the heaviest spirit'":[70]

> FATHER paints his nightmare,a black
>   sore of fear   in technicolor
> coated sorrow   coated "i" forgive
> a silver cup again - his youth,
> the bare facts of existence -
> image,the black saint whom
>   Leroi calls "the heaviest spirit".[71]

The saxophone line that Mitchell plays at the stanza's end is the opening phrase of the "Erika" theme. This theme comprises three sections: first, a series of eight short phrases; second, an oscillation around the pitch F_5, which can be repeated any number of times; and third, a pair of longer phrases that brings the entire theme to a close (see example 4.29). Thinking back to the previous stanza, it is possible to hear Mitchell's flute melody as the second and third sections of the theme, transposed into a different key—one sharp rather than two flats. This transposition fits better with the open tuning of Favors's zither, and can be accomplished easily with an expert musician's trick, by reading an E♭ alto saxophone part on the C flute.

EXAMPLE 4.27 "Erika"/"Song for Charles": Jarman recitation, stanza 2

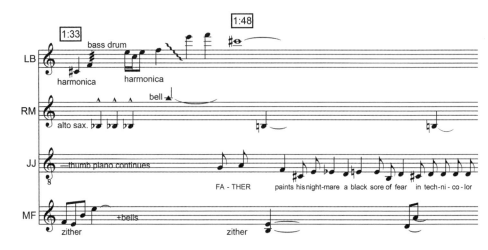

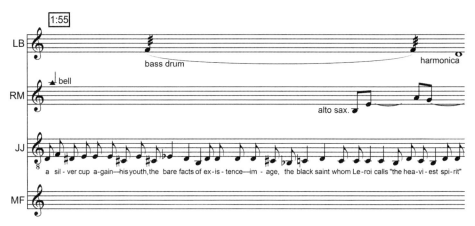

EXAMPLE 4.28 "Erika"/"Song for Charles": Jarman recitation, stanza 3

Jarman remains in a high, plaintive vocal range for the fourth stanza:

ERIKA
         after this America where humans
    wonder wandering -do peace movements
                        care
    her eyes,tender smile
              a flower garden,all gentle
    being must
              she
    endure   visionless   alone   _[72]

EXAMPLE 4.29 "Erika"/"Song for Charles": "Erika" score for alto saxophone

During Jarman's recitation, Mitchell plays the entire "Erika" theme on alto saxophone. She—Erika—has reappeared as the subject of the final stanza, and for the first time in the performance, Mitchell establishes a clear connection between the poetic and melodic representations of the "little rebellious girl" (see example 4.30).[73]

In the brief epilogue that follows the fourth stanza, Jarman alternates between reciting and singing, another demonstration of the continuity between intermedia and music in "Erika"/"Song for Charles," and on all of *A Jackson in Your House*. He addresses Erika and her parents, exhorting them to "rise up," and then sings "HARI OM," a Sanskrit mantra:

> "rise up"HARI OM "alone   "rise up"   hari   OM   alone   "rise up"
> hari OM
> "rise up"[74]

Jarman sings each syllable of "HARI OM" on C_4, one octave above the pitch he used during the first stanza for "ERIKA" and "microtones." He also returns to the short-short-long rhythm from the beginning of the piece, sustaining the final syllable "OM" in full voice as he transforms speech into song, poetry into prayer. This revelatory moment energizes Jarman's accompanists. Bowie, back on harmonica, plays a figure that starts and ends on C_4, the focal pitch sung by Jarman. Mitchell runs through the complete "Erika" theme once more, and Favors adds a colorful burst of percussion, accentuating the suddenly songful mood (see example 4.31).

Jarman recites the last line of the poem at 3:25, then moves to alto saxophone, setting aside his thumb piano. Fittingly, the first note he plays on

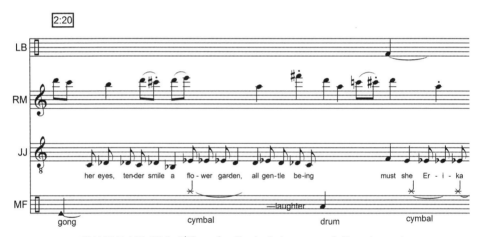

EXAMPLE 4.30 "Erika"/"Song for Charles": Jarman recitation, stanza 4

saxophone is the "HARI OM" pitch, C_4. With this gesture, "Erika" becomes an instrumental improvisation, no longer a poetry recitation with musical accompaniment. Seconds after Jarman picks up his alto saxophone, Bowie and Favors switch to trumpet and bass, respectively, and all four performers begin to converge toward the "Erika" theme (see example 4.32).

Bowie, Jarman, and Mitchell cycle through the theme's three sections, while Favors improvises a florid bass line in B♭ major, the key that "Erika" is in (see example 4.33). This musical consensus, though, lasts only until 5:25. It was Mitchell who first introduced the theme during the third stanza of Jarman's recitation, and now he is the first to diverge from "Erika." Even as Jarman plays another rendition of the "Erika" theme, Mitchell introduces a new melody—his composition "Song for Charles," which he wrote as a tribute

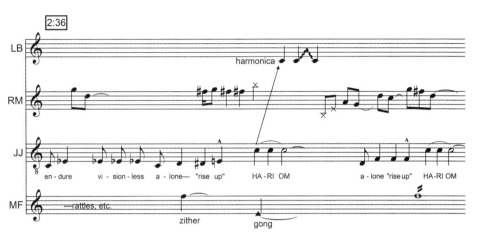

EXAMPLE 4.31 "Erika"/"Song for Charles": Jarman recitation, epilogue

to Charles Clark (see example 4.34). The members of the Art Ensemble follow the composer's lead here, just as they responded to Jarman throughout his poetic recitation. Within thirty seconds of Mitchell's entry, the other musicians take up the "Song for Charles" theme, one by one: Jarman, then Favors, and finally Bowie. The performers execute this transition in a smooth, almost imperceptible manner. The "Song for Charles" theme seems to emerge out of "Erika," and the modulation from B♭ to the new key of D♭ major happens with ease, facilitated by Favors's percussive bass line.

At 7:05, all four musicians arrive together at the "Song for Charles" theme. They play the first two phrases in unison, with bass commentary from Favors underneath the long tones that close each phrase. When Jarman and Mitchell

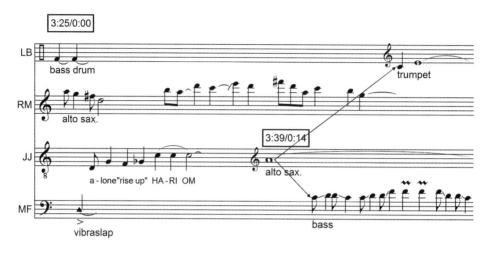

EXAMPLE 4.32 "Erika"/"Song for Charles": approaching the "Erika" theme

* In this example and the three that follow, the additional time points refer to durations on digital reissues of *A Jackson in Your House*, which divide "Erika"/"Song for Charles" into two tracks.

proceed into the third phrase of the theme, Favors continues his busy accompaniment, setting up a bass groove and forming a pathway out of "Song for Charles." Hearing what Favors is doing, Bowie also deviates from the theme, ornamenting the composed melody instead of interpreting it strictly. By the time Jarman and Mitchell play the theme's fourth and final phrase, the momentum generated by the other musicians is already pulling the saxophonists away from "Song for Charles." This impulse brings "Song for Charles" to

EXAMPLE 4.33 "Erika"/"Song for Charles": "Erika" theme, arrival

EXAMPLE 4.34 "Erika"/"Song for Charles": transition, approaching the "Song for Charles" theme

an abrupt end, and the members of the Art Ensemble immediately move into an open improvisation (see example 4.35). The decision-making and performance abilities on display here are a testament to the musical rapport that Bowie, Favors, and Mitchell had been cultivating since 1966, and to the strong connection they had developed with Jarman since he joined the Art Ensemble. According to Mitchell, their shared background in the AACM made it possible to integrate Jarman into the band so quickly: "Amongst the AACM members, we always played together. There were so many different combinations of concerts back then."[75]

The thirteen-minute passage that ends the performance is rather loosely related to "Erika" and "Song for Charles." During one moment, Jarman plays

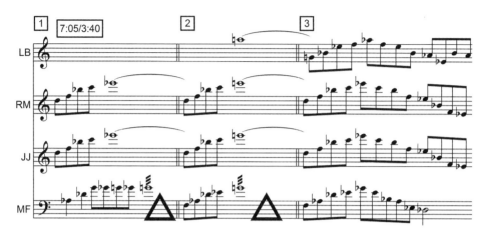

EXAMPLE 4.35 "Erika"/"Song for Charles": "Song for Charles" theme, arrival

on marimba some fragments of the "Song for Charles" theme, but in every other way this open improvisation is independent from the two compositions that spanned the first eight minutes of the performance. At times, the instrumental parts created by the musicians seem to be independent from one another as well, an approach to group improvisation that Mitchell described as involving an "almost infinite amount of choices."[76] The lone thread that unifies the open improvisation is not "Erika" or "Song for Charles," nor any other musical theme, but a multipart text recited by Mitchell. The various parts of the text include a poem in the style of an Afro-Caribbean folktale and a few cryptic lines—spoken in character and scattered throughout the performance—that sound like excerpts from an experimental theater piece.[77]

The first segment of this text emerges at 9:55, when Mitchell is on soprano saxophone and Favors is bowing his double bass. Mitchell plays a long tone, G_4, which Favors harmonizes with a bowed Ab_2, creating the astringent interval of a major fourteenth. After sustaining this skeletal chord for several seconds, they break away; then Mitchell grunts twice and says in a stern voice: "Give me a hand with these bodies up the basement. Give me a *hand* with these bodies—up the basement." Here, Mitchell appears to be playing the role of an investigator at a crime scene, as Aldon Nielsen has suggested.[78] In the context of an album dedicated to Charles Clark, who passed away less than three months before the recording session for *A Jackson in Your House*, Mitchell's evocation of a death by homicide is unnerving.

A minute later, Mitchell recites the second portion of his text, an absurdist take on West Indian storytelling:

> Little Sally.
> Little Sally wore a spally on the bottom of his back.
> Crick crack
> Crick crack
> Crick crack
> with his elbows far in front of him
> and a military pack.
>
> Crack crick
> Crack crick
> Crack crick
> Crack crick
> Crack crack!
> Crack crack!
> Crack crack!
> Crack crack!
> Slick, slick from one side to the other . . .

Mitchell's text is sound poetry, an exploration of the sonic qualities of spoken language. In traditional Afro-Caribbean folktale performance, phrases such as "crick crack" tell the audience that a story is about to begin, and encourage listeners to dialogue aloud with the storyteller.[79] Mitchell instead uses "crick" and "crack" for their sonic potential, and surrounds them with a strange tale governed not by narrative logic but by how it rhymes with the rest of the text. Bowie, Favors, and Jarman respond directly to Mitchell's recitation, imitating his colorful syllables with an outbreak of brilliant noises on trumpet, banjo, and piano. This is the first moment since the "Song for Charles" theme where all four musicians are playing simultaneously. Once again, music and intermedia have met, and merged, on common ground—the world of sound.

The members of the Art Ensemble extend the performance for nine more minutes, creating a handful of memorable exchanges while refusing to linger too long at any one improvisational destination. Mitchell ultimately ends "Erika"/"Song for Charles" at 20:54 with a final bit of text that can be heard as a return to the crime-scene scenario, or as his impression of a weary BYG producer closing down the recording session:

> Okay, boys, you can pack it up now—
>   [Jarman:] Ugh.
>   —and take it on home.

5 On the Road

We were a barnstorming band.[1]

Working Out

The Art Ensemble recorded at a prodigious pace during the summer of 1969. In a seven-week period from late June to mid-August, the band tracked six full-length LPs: three for BYG's Actuel series (*A Jackson in Your House, Message to Our Folks, Reese and the Smooth Ones*), two for Freedom Records (*The Spiritual, Tutankhamun*), and one for Pathé (*People in Sorrow*).[2] A seventh album, *Eda Wobu*, was recorded in October for the JMY label.[3] No other jazz players or experimentalists in Paris recorded as many albums as the Art Ensemble did that year. Archie Shepp made six LPs for Paris-based labels in 1969,[4] and Sunny Murray made four.[5] Anthony Braxton, Leroy Jenkins, and Leo Smith—the Art Ensemble's AACM colleagues—recorded just two albums in 1969, one as a trio and the other in a quartet with Steve McCall.[6] By this measure at least, the musicians were in greater demand than any of their peers on the Paris scene.

The Art Ensemble's popularity created a number of additional performance opportunities for the members of the group. In Paris, good bass players were hard to find, and Favors became the first-call sideman for a number of bandleaders, including Don Byas, Beaver Harris, and Cal Massey.[7] Bowie and Mitchell also worked regularly as freelance musicians, and along with Favors they participated in recording sessions led by Jimmy Lyons, Grachan Moncur III, Sunny Murray, Dewey Redman, Archie Shepp, and Alan Silva.[8] All four members of the Art Ensemble appeared on a Claude Delcloo album and an extraordinary seven-inch record by the Togolese actor Alfred Panou, in which Panou sang, shouted, and recited poetry over the Chicagoans' accompaniment.[9] Compared to his bandmates, Jarman was somewhat less busy as a freelancer, though he did play a series of duet concerts with Anthony Braxton.[10] In addition to music, Jarman devoted himself to theatrical pursuits: at the American Center in late 1969, he premiered his *Cable Piece*, a successor to the intermedia events he had presented in Chicago.[11] Jarman also joined a Paris theater company, where he and Leo Smith worked onstage—as actors, not musicians—in an experimental play.[12]

These recording sessions, concert dates, and acting jobs served several purposes. Supplemental income, even in modest amounts, was most welcome at a time when the Art Ensemble and the Bowies were still getting established in their new surroundings. Furthermore, becoming involved in multiple side projects helped the musicians simulate the activity level and creative ferment to which they had grown accustomed during the early years of the AACM. Some of these side projects would prove to be highly significant—for example, the Art Ensemble's extended collaboration with Brigitte Fontaine. A singer, actress, and poet, Fontaine was performing at many of the same Paris venues where the Art Ensemble worked, including the Théâtre du Lucernaire. She invited the members of the Art Ensemble and Leo Smith to take part in "Niok," her experimental production combining theater and song.[13] Like other French musicians of the 1968 generation, Fontaine was charting a path away from the traditional *chanson*, and she found the Art Ensemble's music to be perfectly suited for the song style she was developing with her creative partner Areski Belkacem, the French-Algerian percussionist.[14] Fontaine and Belkacem began composing pieces for the collaboration, and on 15 November 1969 the Chicagoans joined them in a Paris studio for the recording of *Comme à la radio*, Fontaine's third LP.[15] Prominently displayed on the album cover was "Art Ensemble of Chicago," immediately below Fontaine and Belkacem's names and well above the list of five highly regarded French musicians who also played on the recording, a clear indication of the Art Ensemble's position among Paris-based experimentalists at the end of 1969.

The collaboration between Fontaine and the Art Ensemble did not end with the recording of *Comme à la radio*. They continued to perform together for several months, mainly at venues on the Left Bank: Mondays at the Théâtre du Vieux-Colombier, 21 rue du Vieux-Colombier; Fridays and Saturdays at La Pagode, 57 rue de Babylone.[16] The Monday-night series at the Vieux-Colombier was launched shortly after the release of *Comme à la radio*, and attracted much notice in the press. *Le Nouvel Observateur*, in a preview of the first Vieux-Colombier concert, lauded the members of the Art Ensemble as "poly-musicians" who were "the musical revelation" of 1969.[17] This description must have intrigued the newsweekly's quarter-million readers, especially those who lived far away from metropolitan Paris and were unable to attend the Art Ensemble's earliest concerts during the summer of 1969. By 1970, the musicians would be touring throughout France, reaching new audiences who first encountered them not at the Lucernaire or the American Center, but in the pages of national publications or via broadcasts on France's public radio network, the ORTF—*comme à la radio*, as Fontaine would say. These mass-market outlets, predictably, were not free of the black exotica thinking often evident in French critics' reactions to the Art Ensemble. *Le Nouvel Observateur*'s review of the premiere performance at the Vieux-Colombier was entitled "Brigitte et quatre Noirs," quite in contrast to *Jazz Magazine*'s more neutral listing: "Brigitte et l'Art Ensemble."[18] Gabriel Dumetz, the *Jazz Magazine* reviewer, focused his comments on the quality of the musical interactions among Fontaine, Belkacem, and the Art Ensemble, while Philippe Koechlin of *Le Nouvel Observateur* emphasized Fontaine's crossing of the color line, which he portrayed as a colonialist foray into the Art Ensemble's "strange and beautiful jungle."[19] As Koechlin put it, "Brigitte Fontaine is crazy enough"—a play on words referring to her album *Brigitte Fontaine est . . . folle*—"to form a connection with the sorcerers from Chicago."[20] Such sensationalism aside, the Fontaine collaboration was a success. The Art Ensemble worked more frequently with Fontaine and Belkacem than anyone else (American or French, AACM or not), and in late 1970 the Académie Charles-Cros conferred upon *Comme à la radio* its Grand Prix du Disque, the French equivalent of a Grammy award.

In October 1969 the Art Ensemble traveled to Amougies, Belgium, to perform at the Actuel Festival. This was the group's first concert appearance outside France, after four months of performing almost exclusively in Paris.[21] The five-day festival was organized by BYG Records, and advertisements for the event described it as the "first continental festival" of counterculture music—in other words, continental Europe's answer to the massive concerts that had taken place in August 1969 at Woodstock, New York, and the Isle of Wight, just off England's southern coast.[22] However, unlike the Woodstock and Isle of Wight festivals, which were dominated by pop music, the roster for the

Actuel Festival was split evenly between rock bands and free-jazz groups. The appeal of this unique lineup was lost on the French authorities, who saw rock music, thousands of youths, and a few dozen African American experimentalists as a combustible mixture, if not the spark that could ignite another May 1968.[23] Several prospective sites in or near Paris were rejected, and BYG had to move the festival to Amougies, a small town located just across the Belgian border, some two hundred and fifty kilometers north of Paris.[24]

BYG was able to draw a sizeable crowd to the Actuel Festival, despite the distance between Paris and Amougies. According to press reports, the festival was attended by about twenty thousand people, a much larger audience than that of even the highest-profile free-jazz events in Paris.[25] This suggests that many of the festivalgoers were primarily interested in the rock acts on the program, not Don Cherry, Sunny Murray, or the Art Ensemble.[26] The possibility of a mismatch between the performers and the audience did not trouble BYG's Jean Georgakarakos, who—true to form—boldly proclaimed that the festival would "abolish the barriers" between pop music and free jazz.[27] What Georgakarakos left unstated were his ambitions for the BYG label. He and his artistic director, Claude Delcloo, had devoted the summer of 1969 to making recordings for the Actuel series, and the label had much product to sell. By presenting both pop and experimental musicians at the same festival, BYG could introduce rock fans to free jazz, creating a new audience for the music and thus a new market for BYG's recordings. Indeed, the free-jazz side of the festival lineup consisted entirely of artists who had recorded for BYG/Actuel. The festival's headlining pop acts, in contrast, were English progressive-rock bands with no prior relationship to BYG, including the Nice, Pink Floyd, Soft Machine, and Yes.

The Actuel Festival was held in an enormous tent, big enough to accommodate all of the attendees and an extra-large stage.[28] The stage was divided in half, with rock bands playing on one side and free-jazz groups on the other, perhaps for logistical reasons. Since rock bands had similar technical requirements, and likewise for free-jazz groups, the setup time between performances could be minimized when the two sides of the stage were used in alternation. Apart from its logistical efficiencies, this approach also meant that the festivalgoers were consistently confronted by conflicting sights and sounds, the visual and auditory elements that differentiated free jazz and rock music. Trumpets, double basses, and saxophones contrasted with psychedelic light shows and electric instruments played at full volume.[29] These contrasts were further amplified by the racial disparity between the performers of each genre.[30] Although Jean Georgakarakos hoped that the Actuel Festival would break down the metaphorical "barriers" separating rock and free jazz, it seems just as probable that any such barriers were reinforced.

The performers at Amougies were mindful of these barriers and rarely chose to challenge them. Several of the musicians sat in with other groups, but most of these collaborations did not involve crossing over to the other side of the festival stage.[31] The exception to this rule was guitarist Frank Zappa, the festival's emcee, who played with everyone from Pink Floyd to Philly Joe Jones.[32] Well versed in jazz, rock, and electronic music, Zappa was willing and able to surmount the genre barriers that the festival imposed. In contrast to Zappa, the members of the Art Ensemble happily entrenched themselves on the free-jazz side, emerging only to launch attacks on unfriendly territory.

The Chicagoans performed on the second night of the Actuel Festival—or rather, the third morning. Their set was scheduled for Saturday 25 October but did not begin until dawn on Sunday. By that time the festivalgoers were on edge: frustrated by the power failures that interrupted the performances, exhausted from staying awake all night, and chilled by the rainy, dismal weather. While waiting for the Art Ensemble to take the stage, they amused themselves by tossing lit firecrackers into one another's sleeping bags.[33] The members of the Art Ensemble, always aware of their surroundings, armed themselves and prepared to respond. Their weapon of choice was parody, which they had used to great effect on the BYG albums *A Jackson in Your House* and *Message to Our Folks*. At the festival, the first half of the musicians' set was relatively tame, at least by their standards. Then Jarman strode to the front of the stage, wearing a reddish-orange satin suit and scratching an electric guitar.[34] This was the opening of "Rock Out" (from *Message to Our Folks*), a Mitchell composition based on the famous drumbeat and rhythm-guitar pattern from James Brown's "Cold Sweat."[35] As the groove took shape, Favors and Jarman bent at the waist and contorted their faces in mock ecstasy, parodying the rock guitarists whom the audience had paid to see. The festivalgoers were extremely displeased by this provocation, and began to shout abuse at the Art Ensemble. Jarman reacted like a rock frontman and fed off the crowd's energy—at first absorbing the hostility, then elevating it to a level of participation "never seen on a Parisian stage."[36] As "Rock Out" reached a climax, he transformed the Art Ensemble's rock-band caricature into a startling striptease act, with the help of his tear-away suit:

> Joseph Jarman . . . grabbed the microphone like James Brown. In a raspy voice he shouted a parody, interchangeable lyrics from an imaginary pop song.

Have you seen my baby?
I love you.
Etc. . . .

In the manner of rock stars who throw objects touched by their divine hands to adoring fans, he ripped pieces of fabric from his suit, one after another, and cast them into the crowd—

Do you want it, do you really want it?

—until he was completely naked.[37]

The shock value of Jarman's striptease earned it significant attention in journalistic accounts of the Actuel Festival. However, mere transgression was not what motivated the musicians to take the stage at Amougies. Their performances could be provocative or critical, humorous or absurd, but at the core of the Art Ensemble's music was a central purpose, epitomized by the album title *Message to Our Folks*. For Favors, serving in the Art Ensemble as a "Music Messenger" was a higher calling:[38]

It seems that the people today are more interested in fairy tale music. . . . That's the great imbalance in our culture. You got to dig deeper into the spirit, soul, and the meaning of life to come up with something besides, "I love you baby." . . . I find that's what's wrong with society, too much make believe. Our ancestors sang about their surroundings and family.[39]

After the Actuel Festival, the members of the Art Ensemble found themselves working outside Paris more and more. Several factors contributed to this expansion in the group's performance opportunities. The Art Ensemble continued to receive favorable press coverage, from the usual concert write-ups to substantial feature stories.[40] By the end of 1969, the albums they had recorded that summer were beginning to be released, leading to further positive notice in jazz periodicals and other publications. *Le Monde*, France's national newspaper, announced the release of *People in Sorrow* by printing a poem authored by Jarman.[41] Additionally, the Chicagoans hired their first booking agent, Michel Salou, who helped them secure concert dates across France and elsewhere in Europe.[42]

Midway through December, Bowie, Jarman, and Mitchell participated in the 1969 Free Jazz Meeting in Baden-Baden, West Germany. Held from 12 to 14 December at the headquarters of the Südwestfunk radio network, the meeting was conceived as an international summit of Europe's top improvisers, with over twenty musicians receiving invitations.[43] The only non-Europeans to take part were the members of the Art Ensemble, Steve McCall, and three other North Americans residing in Europe: pianist Dave Burrell, bassist Barre Phillips, and trumpeter Kenny Wheeler.[44] At Baden-Baden, the musicians formed groups of various sizes and rehearsed one another's compositions. Jarman workshopped his piece "Holus Cliptic No. 3" and played in an octet led by Norwegian guitarist Terje Rypdal.[45] Bowie's contribution to the proceedings was "Gittin' to Know Y'All," a 32-minute composition for big band. In many ways, "Gittin' to Know Y'All" was the focal point of the Free Jazz Meeting. As composer and conductor, Bowie chose to include every instrumentalist present at Baden-Baden in the rehearsals and recording of his piece.[46] Bowie's score included solo, duo, and trio improvisations as well as ensemble passages, each musical configuration representing the kind of intercultural exchange that Joachim Ernst Berendt, the meeting's organizer, had hoped to facilitate. Despite Bowie and Berendt's intentions, the Free Jazz Meeting was not entirely successful in bridging the gaps between musicians of different racial backgrounds, national origins, and aesthetic orientations. The Europeans were at pains to distinguish their work from African American music—yet they remained more reliant on the idioms of mid-1960s free jazz than the Chicagoans, who had been developing alternative approaches to improvisation and composition since the days of the Experimental Band.[47] If this dissonance remained unresolved at Baden-Baden, the members of the Art Ensemble were nonetheless able to form some crucial connections.[48] Mitchell reunited with trombonist Albert Mangelsdorff, whom he first met a decade earlier at the Cave 54 jam sessions in Heidelberg, West Germany.[49] Jarman and Mitchell also had time to connect with percussionist Don Moye, who attended the Free Jazz Meeting as an uninvited observer.[50]

Don Moye

The Art Ensemble had been performing without a regular drummer since the summer of 1967, when Phillip Wilson left to join the Paul Butterfield Blues Band.[51] In the two years between Wilson's departure and their voyage to Paris, Bowie, Favors, and Mitchell occasionally employed guest drummers, including Thurman Barker and Robert Crowder. After establishing themselves in France, the members of the Art Ensemble felt the need to add a permanent drummer to the group, and in late 1969 they started reaching out to percussionists they knew.[52] At first, the musicians restricted their search to drummers with Chicago connections. They contacted both Barker and Crowder, but could not convince either drummer to give up his gigs in Chicago and relocate to

Paris.[53] The Art Ensemble also auditioned percussionists who were already living in Europe: Jerome Cooper, a Chicago native, traveled all the way from Copenhagen to sit in with the band at the Théàtre du Vieux-Colombier on a Monday night in March 1970.[54] Don Moye, who learned of the Art Ensemble's percussionist vacancy while at the Baden-Baden Free Jazz Meeting, "put [his] bid in like everybody else."[55]

Donald Franklin Moye Jr. was born on 23 May 1946 in Rochester, New York, a minor metropolis of about three hundred thousand inhabitants on the southern shore of Lake Ontario.[56] Like Lester Bowie, Moye came from a musical family. His cousin played vibraphone, saxophone, and drums; four uncles were amateur saxophonists; and his father, Donald Franklin Moye Sr., played drums in the marching band and jazz ensembles associated with the Elks lodge to which the family belonged.[57] Unfortunately, Moye's father died three days after the birth of his son.[58] Mr. Moye was killed in Bad Staffelstein, West Germany, during a protest on the army base where he was stationed.[59] Donald Jr. was raised by his mother, Ernestine Hicks Moye, who introduced him to the performing arts at an early age:

> I can remember going to see operas in the summer at open-air concerts in the park. We might see the opera one week and then the next week we'd go see the Mormon Tabernacle Choir. And then the next week Mahalia Jackson. There was always something. She took us out to a big variety of musical events, dance and theater.[60]

Growing up, Moye was particularly close to his grandmother Lelia Moye, a restaurant manager and caterer who provided the food service for the family's Elks lodge.[61] She lived next door to the lodge, in a second-floor apartment above the Pythodd Room, a Rochester nightclub that featured rhythm-and-blues acts, organ trios, and jazz bands. Moye's grandmother often hosted dinners for the entertainers working at the Pythodd, and young Moye was "fascinated and in awe of the musicians" he encountered: Kenny Burrell, Grant Green, Jack McDuff, and Jimmy McGriff.[62] Moye also gained an appreciation for gospel music while working at one of his first jobs: "I used to help out at the barbershop, and these cats were all Sanctified, Holy Rollers. They had all the Sanctified music, that's all they played. The singers would hang out there, so there was a whole scene."[63]

Moye was raised Baptist, but his elementary education took place at the parochial school operated by Holy Redeemer Catholic Church. Around the age of ten, Moye started singing in the youth choir at Holy Redeemer.[64] He also began taking drum lessons and performing with a local children's band. As a teenager, his interest in percussion grew, and he joined a Rochester drum and bugle corps, the Statesmen.[65] Playing with the Statesmen helped Moye explore the "technical part of drumming" while improving his music-reading skills.[66] By his senior year, Moye was proficient enough to join the Fabulous Crusaders, an award-winning drum and bugle corps. During Moye's tenure with the group, the Crusaders traveled to competitions in Canada, up and down the Atlantic coast, and throughout New York State.[67] Moye was also studying violin, playing bongos and congas with Puerto Rican friends from his Rochester neighborhood, and taking advanced classes in French, German, and Latin.[68]

A talented student and promising musician, Moye earned a scholarship to Central State University, where he matriculated in 1964 after graduating from Rochester's Benjamin Franklin High School.[69] Located in Wilberforce, Ohio, a tiny community about twenty miles east of Dayton, historically black Central State felt like a "little country school" to Moye: "I didn't have the distractions of a big city. I would get up and go to my classes and the rest of the time I would be playing and rehearsing."[70] Moye gradually outgrew Central State and its traditionalist faculty:

I got in trouble because I was hanging out with the blues cats in town. At school they took me on the rug about that—hanging out with blues dudes wasn't good for your [image]. The music school rehearsal facilities and auditorium were off-limits to people playing blues and [jazz] . . .[71]

Eventually I changed schools because there was not enough happening in Ohio. There were good teachers in the music department and they were very helpful but I felt I needed an urban environment.[72]

In 1966, after two years at Central State, Moye transferred to Wayne State University in Detroit, Michigan.[73] He enrolled in Wayne State's liberal-arts division, Monteith College, and played drums in the African Cultural Ensemble with students from Kenya and Ghana.[74] Outside the classroom, Moye spent much of his time at the Detroit Artists Workshop, a community organization cofounded by the political activist John Sinclair, then a Wayne State graduate student.[75] The Artists Workshop regularly presented art exhibitions, performances, and literary readings, all of which interested Moye. He was particularly passionate about contemporary literature, and at Artists Workshop events he met a number of prominent and emerging poets: Amiri

Baraka, Gregory Corso, Robert Creeley, Diane di Prima, Allen Ginsberg, and Chicago's own Joseph Jarman.[76] He also assisted the publishing efforts of the Artists Workshop Press, editing several volumes and serving as a circulation assistant for the press's arts journals, *CHANGE* and *whe're*.[77]

At the Artists Workshop, Moye got to know Charles Moore, a trumpeter and the operator of the Strata Concert Gallery in Detroit. Moore quickly became Moye's musical mentor.[78] He urged Moye to attend Roscoe Mitchell and Joseph Jarman's performances in Detroit (Mitchell with his Art Ensemble, and Jarman with his own quartet).[79] Moore introduced Moye to Detroit percussionists Doug Hammond, Ronnie Johnson, and Danny Spencer, who gave him lessons on the drum set, and with Moore's guidance, Moye began to seriously study jazz.[80] "I used to go over to his house every day and work with him," Moye remembered, "listening to records, analyzing charts, and stuff like that":

> I really started getting into the music more and actually getting gigs. I could always get by on my conga playing but in Detroit I started getting into situations where I could play drums, too. . . . I was playing a lot of different things: blues, pick-up gigs, a little rock here and there; but mostly, I was interested in so-called jazz. That's why I spent as much time as I did with Charles, because that is what he was into.[81]

Moye's studies of jazz and the drum set soon paid off. In the spring of 1968, he was playing congas in a jazz group led by saxophonist Arthur Fletcher. When the group's drummer left to join a rock band, Moye replaced him, and the musicians "came up with a scheme to go to Europe."[82] They named themselves Detroit Free Jazz, and in May, after a brief tour of several American cities, the group left the country. Although Moye was only a few credits short of his bachelor's degree, he quit Wayne State to go overseas with Detroit Free Jazz.[83] For Moye, traveling to Europe sounded better than staying in Detroit, especially following the assassination of Martin Luther King Jr. on 4 April 1968. As he would discover, though, Europe circa 1968 was just as tumultuous as America:

> I cut out for Europe from Detroit in '68 right after M. L. King's assassination and landed right in the middle of all the turmoil THERE: strikes, protests, and riots in Paris, Amsterdam, Prague, and numerous other centers of unrest where students, artists, intellectuals, and workers were united in violently challenging and confronting their institutions and govern-

ments. After the assassination of Robert Kennedy I was sitting in a cafe in Amsterdam, sipping on a Heineken with a *jonge genever* chaser, reading the *International Herald Tribune*, and, upon seeing the headlines, I pulled out my wallet, calmly extracted my draft card and Social Security card, tore them up, and threw the shreds into the nearest canal.[84]

With Detroit Free Jazz, Moye performed across Europe, from Munich to Milan, Switzerland to Sweden. He even traveled to Morocco, where he met pianist Randy Weston and played with the Gnawa musicians of Essaouira and Marrakesh.[85] Detroit Free Jazz managed to stay together until the early months of 1969. During a stop in Copenhagen, one of the musicians fell ill and had to return to the United States. The group disbanded, and Moye decided that he could make it on his own. As he explained, "drummers can work in Europe, at least at that time. I was always getting calls."[86] Before the breakup of Detroit Free Jazz, Moye had been earning extra money as a jazz sideman and as an accompanist for dance companies, "playing percussion for classes and performances."[87] Now a free agent, Moye relocated to Rome, where he found work as a staff percussionist for Radiotelevisione Italiana (RAI), the Italian public broadcaster. He also joined the jazz group led by soprano saxophonist Steve Lacy. When Lacy moved from Rome to Paris at the end of 1969, Moye followed. Once in Paris, Moye plunged into the city's music scene, working regularly with Lacy and the dance company of choreographer Elsa Wolliaston, while freelancing in ensembles led by experimentalists Ambrose Jackson, Noah Howard, Sonny Sharrock, Alan Shorter, and Alan Silva.[88]

After a brief stay at a hotel in the Saint-Germain-des-Prés district, Moye arranged to share drummer Oliver Johnson's basement apartment on rue Saint-Denis, one block east of the outdoor market at Les Halles.[89] He crossed the Seine daily to visit the American Center, where he kept his drums. For Moye, the Center was "the hangout at day and then there would be concerts at night. You could make contacts. It was kind of a networking area."[90] There he befriended the veteran bebop musician Arthur Taylor, one of his primary influences on drum set.[91] Since college, Moye had been learning various styles of African drumming, and he continued this pursuit at the American Center, studying with the Congolese percussionist Titos Sompa.[92] Moye's musical abilities also gained him entry into Paris's transnational community of African drummers—emigrants from former French colonies like Guinea, Ivory Coast, Mali, and Senegal. In these circles, Senegambian and Mande languages were spoken as much as or more than French. Moye, a budding polyglot, was able to absorb language and music side by side: "I got into the languages: Wolof and Bambara. I didn't learn a lot of grammar but I got familiar with their structures, sounds, slang, and colloquialisms. Music lives in the language, language lives in the music."[93]

For several years, Moye had aspired to join the Art Ensemble. He "got hooked on the dream of playing with them" back in Detroit, when he was in the audience for performances by Roscoe Mitchell and Joseph Jarman.[94] After Moye arrived in Paris, he became even more motivated to become a member of the Art Ensemble. The Chicagoans were thriving in France, living the good life at the farmhouse in Saint-Leu-la-Forêt and playing several concerts every week. "They was WERKIN all the time," Moye candidly observed. "Cats was WERKIN!"

> In the essence of the particularization of wanting to work with them, that was pretty much formed when I had seen them in Detroit. The open ended creative aspect of what they were trying to do is what hooked me. I knew they were looking for a drummer, and I knew that they was WERKIN all the time. They had trucks and a big crib out in the country. Everybody that was in Paris knew about that scene. Cats had motorcycles and all kinds of s—. That was a successful band doing their thing, you know.[95]

One night in late 1969, Moye was performing with Steve Lacy at a Paris venue. A representative from the Art Ensemble, either Jarman or Mitchell, heard Moye that night, and invited him to sit in with them during an up-coming gig.[96] A few days later, Favors and the saxophonists were scheduled to play a trio concert at the American Center. Moye showed up with his conga drums, as Favors recalled:

> When we were setting up for this gig—Roscoe, Joseph, and myself—here comes a conga drummer. He just came and set his drums up. I looked up—I didn't know him. So Roscoe and Joseph came to me and said, "Do you want him to play with you?" And being that I had experience with a conga player, after he played, I said, "Good congas, man." So Joseph, the kind of cat he is, said, "Yeah, he plays trap drums too." And he had just said to us he didn't know him. It was Moye. Joseph told me where he was play-ing in Paris. I went there that Tuesday night, and he was playing with [Mal Waldron]. So I spoke to him and said that we were looking for a drummer, and would he like to come out [to Saint-Leu-la-Forêt]. . . . Moye came out and Lester liked him and Joseph didn't have a voice in it because Joseph

was playing the "Parisian Kid." Roscoe had another drummer that he sorta liked, but me and Lester voted on Moye.[97]

Having reached an agreement, the members of the Art Ensemble accepted Moye into the group, concluding their months-long search for a drummer. Moye felt some apprehension about giving his notice to Steve Lacy, the bandleader who brought him to Paris. Much to Moye's relief, Lacy supported his decision, telling him: "Man, are you crazy? You better go and get on with your life. Go about your business."[98] Moye began taking part in the daily rehearsals at the Saint-Leu farmhouse in preparation for his first performances with the group, which took place in early 1970.[99]

It was not long before Moye realized how much the Art Ensemble expected from him. "Lester took me aside one day after rehearsal and said, very seriously, 'Don't even mess with us or get any more involved if you can't commit to playing Great Black Music at a very high level, becoming famous, and taking our place in the history of jazz.'"[100] Moye was up for the challenge, but "playing Great Black Music at a very high level" seemed rather difficult at first. In order to learn the Art Ensemble's "vast repertoire," he had to master several musical styles that he had not played before.[101] From Moye's perspective, the musical structures that presented the greatest challenges were "improvisational forms"—pieces like "Erika"/"Song for Charles," "Non-Cognitive Aspects of the City," and "People in Sorrow," in which the members of the band would create an extended performance from just a few bars of composed music.[102] This approach to group improvisation, a common practice in AACM circles, was new to Moye, whose formative musical experiences occurred far from the South Side of Chicago.

Although Moye faced a steep learning curve after joining the Art Ensemble, his new bandmates were "patient" and "helpful": "Apparently, they saw some potential in me that could be worked with."[103] Like the Chicagoans, he was a multi-instrumentalist, a skilled performer on drum set, congas, and other percussion instruments. He also brought to the group his expertise with music for percussion ensembles, in particular the traditional percussion musics of West and Central Africa. Over time, several Africa-inspired compositions would enter the Art Ensemble's repertoire, beginning with the title track of *Chi-Congo*, one of Moye's first recordings with the band.[104] This title seems to refer to Moye's studies with Titos Sompa, his Congolese percussion teacher, and the piece opens with a six-minute passage for percussion ensemble.[105] The first instrument to enter is an iron bell playing a timeline pattern, the rhythmic signature of countless percussion compositions from coastal West Africa. As the passage unfolds, the bell is surrounded by additional instruments: claves, Moye's conga drums, rattles, whistles, and balafon. Some of the musicians align their rhythms with the bell pattern, as in an African percussion ensemble, while the others play contrasting rhythms that work against the timeline, transforming the music and transporting the listener from the Congo's Brazzaville to Chicago's Bronzeville.

Moye's unique contributions to the group can also be heard on their soundtrack recording for *Les Stances à Sophie*, a film by director Moshé Mizrahi.[106] The album's first track is "Thème de Yoyo," a vocal feature for Fontella Bass, who frequently performed with the Art Ensemble in 1970. The drum-set part for "Thème de Yoyo" draws on James Brown's "Cold Sweat," much like the *Message to Our Folks* track "Rock Out." When the Chicagoans recorded "Rock Out" in August 1969, they had to make do with Bowie playing drums, but on "Thème de Yoyo," they take full advantage of Moye's precise and energetic drumming, which propels the group into a brilliant performance. The members of the Art Ensemble appear onscreen in *Les Stances à Sophie*, playing "Thème de Céline" at a Paris café. After their performance, the musicians sit down together to have a drink—all except Jarman, who joins the film's protagonist at her table. Céline, played by the lovely Bernadette Lafont, has written an anthropological study of the "moeurs sexuelles des indigènes d'Europe Occidentale." Jarman inspects the text and commends Céline for her work: "Something has to be done" about the sexual mores of Europeans, he affirms, "because it's a drag."[107]

The Great Escape

On 24 June 1970, the Art Ensemble performed at a benefit concert for the Black Panther Party. The benefit took place at the Maison de la Mutualité, on 24 rue Saint-Victor in the Saint-Germain-des-Prés district of Paris.[108] After May 1968, the political events held at the Mutualité, especially those involving the radical left, were closely monitored by French authorities.[109] Clifford Thornton's difficulties with the French immigration service began at another Black Panthers benefit, as Moye recalled:

[W]e were at Mutualité, that hall around the bottom end of Boulevard St. Germain. . . . That was where they had all the rallies for the Black Panthers. Clifford Thornton got up and gave a speech, jack. The s— he was saying, even the Black Panther cats were like . . . [laughs]. The people went wild, but when he was leaving the stage, the special inspector cats met him and escorted him on out. The next thing I knew, he was living in Switzerland.[110]

Like Thornton, the members of the Art Ensemble also drew unwanted attention from French officials because of their involvement in a Black Panthers benefit concert. Some weeks after the 24 June 1970 event, Radio Télévision Luxembourg (RTL), the French-language radio network, broadcast a program about the Art Ensemble. The program played up the musicians' connections, however distant, to the black nationalist movement. In Bowie's recollection, the RTL presenter "portrayed us as revolutionaries, damn near Black Panthers."[111] Furthermore, the program revealed that the Art Ensemble had a house in Saint-Leu-la-Forêt, a detail that alarmed local authorities. What happened next was, according to Bowie, "like a movie":

> The next day after the broadcast the police showed up at our door. Some inspector in a trench coat with a grimace on his face. He had two uniformed cats with him as back-ups. So our dogs had them stopped at the gate (that's from our military training). They told us if we didn't leave town they would escort us to the border.[112]

As luck would have it, the musicians were already preparing to depart for an out-of-town performance (possibly their 7 August 1970 concert in Berlin).[113] However, with the Saint-Leu police on alert, they could not return to the farmhouse anytime soon. So the Art Ensemble and the Bowie family went on an impromptu tour for several months, arranging performances wherever they could.[114] On the road, the musicians continued to practice cooperative economics, as they had done since arriving in Europe. No longer tied to a single place of residence, they lived in tents and their vehicles, drawing on the military experiences shared by every member of the group but Moye.[115] "All that bivouacking we did in the military helped us," Bowie stated—as did the Art Ensemble's unmatched *esprit de corps*:[116]

> We lived in a tent, but we lived hip. Hip sleeping bags, we had all the right stuff. We had a whole caravan of trucks, we had formations we got into with them. We were even *selling* trucks for a while. We went all over Europe like that, from way down in the south of France up to Scandinavia. I don't want people to think we've ever lived bad. We carried our own

environment, we were eating fried chicken and barbecue. People couldn't believe the food, they would come and eat with us and hang out.[117]

In this new lifestyle, Bowie explained, a "couple of grand from a gig would go a long way."[118] After leaving France, the musicians proceeded northeast, performing at festivals and art galleries, radio and television studios in Belgium, West Germany, and Denmark.[119] When the weather grew cooler and camping out became impractical, they moved on to Sweden, where they spent the winter living in hotels.[120]

By 1971, the Art Ensemble and the Bowies were ready to go back to the United States. Some of the band's peers—other black experimentalists who had traveled to Paris in 1969, such as Alan Silva and pianist Bobby Few— were deciding to settle in France for good, following the examples set by previous generations of American artists and musicians. Unlike these peers and predecessors, though, the members of the Art Ensemble never intended to become lifelong expatriates. "It was just employment opportunities," Moye asserted, "more chances to make a living playing the music of our choice."[121] Indeed, the group had worked steadily in Europe, playing concerts across the continent and recording no fewer than fifteen albums. Furthermore, the members of the Art Ensemble had reason to expect that new opportunities awaited them if they returned to America. Their AACM colleagues—Anthony Braxton, Leroy Jenkins, and Leo Smith—left France in 1970.[122] That May, the three musicians staged the first AACM concert in New York, performing in a sextet with Muhal Richard Abrams, Steve McCall, and bassist Richard Davis.[123] At the same time, the Art Ensemble's profile was growing in the United States, due to an impressive showing in *Down Beat* magazine's annual survey of jazz critics. In the 1970 Critics Poll, the Art Ensemble was recognized as "Talent Deserving of Wider Recognition" in the jazz combo category, placing second behind saxophonist Phil Woods's band. Additionally, all members of the group but Moye polled highly on their own instruments: Bowie finished third in the trumpet category, as did Favors on bass, while Mitchell and Jarman earned recognition on both alto saxophone and soprano saxophone.[124]

If America was calling the Art Ensemble, France was pushing the band away. A second run-in with overzealous French authorities may have been the greatest factor in the musicians' decision to come home. On 20 January 1971, they were en route to a performance in Caen, a city in Normandy about one hundred kilometers southwest of Le Havre. When they reached their destination, the local police detained and extorted them. A vigilant Art Ensemble fan reported on the incident in the pages of *Jazz Magazine*:

The musicians were detained by the French police for twenty-four hours and questioned in the presence of inspectors who were aware of all of their movements and activities. The pretext for this arbitrary detention was as follows: because their trucks were registered as *tourisme*, the musicians had not paid the required taxes on their instruments. They were fined twenty thousand francs. Part of this fine was due immediately, and a truckload of instruments was held as collateral. They were also subjected to blackmail: they could pay the fine and then leave French territory within eight days; they could pay the fine and numerous taxes during the rest of their stay; or, a third possibility, they could proceed with an extremely expensive trial that they would inevitably lose. These terms further demonstrate that the motive for their arrest was political and racist. The police officers openly reproached them for politicizing their music and . . . playing for the benefit of the Black Panther Party.[125]

According to Moye, the Caen police eventually determined that "all of our papers were in order," and the musicians were released from detention the next day.[126] However, in order to reclaim their property, the members of the Art Ensemble had to pay the confiscatory fine of twenty thousand francs, an amount that they had set aside for their transatlantic travel expenses.[127]

This financial setback delayed the group's return trip to the United States for several weeks. The musicians rebuilt their savings by going on a concert tour of France. In March and April 1970, the French culture ministry had organized Art Ensemble performances at dozens of regional Maisons de la Culture, a nationwide network of centers for the visual and performing arts.[128] After the incident in Caen, the musicians arranged to visit these Maisons de la Culture once again, earning enough from this series of concerts to pay for their passage back to America.[129] At the conclusion of the tour, they headed to the Mediterranean seaport of Genoa, Italy, just two hundred kilometers from France's southern coast. Then, on 11 April 1971, the Art Ensemble departed for the United States, sailing from Genoa to New York on the SS *Raffaello*.[130] Two years earlier, in the spring of 1969, Bowie had persuaded his bandmates and his family to leave Chicago for Paris. Looking back, Bowie considered the Art Ensemble's European adventure to be an unqualified success:

> Once we left Europe we knew we could always work there. That's the way we set it up. We wanted to go back to the States because we wanted to be home. If we couldn't get no work, that didn't matter because we would

be home. But we knew we could work in Czechoslovakia, or Warsaw or somewhere. We had set up a network. See, we approached this as world marketing for our music, not on just a local or national level, but world-wide. If you got your thing going internationally, you gonna work. You may have to go far, but you work.[131]

FIGURE 1 An early Art Ensemble performance at the University of Chicago, 1968.
Left to right: Malachi Favors, Roscoe Mitchell, Joseph Jarman.
Out of frame: Lester Bowie. Photo by Leonard E. Jones.

LA MUSIQUE A
BOUT DE BRAS

Ils sont noirs. Lorsqu'on s'a-
venture dans leur antre, au
Lucernaire, rue d'Odessa, on
croit assister à un rite magi-
que. Avec recueillement et
sérieux, quatre hommes explo-
rent une jungle d'instruments
baroques : des cuivres, cordes,
et percussions de toutes sortes.
Tour à tour austère, et violent,
religieux, et déchaîné, tel est
l'AACM de Chicago, lequel
depuis juillet présente un des
spectacles de free-jazz parmi les
plus fantastiques qu'on puisse
imaginer. Mais l'imagination
manque précisément aux pari-
siens, qui ont trop souvent
laissé bien des places vides dans
cette petite salle ultra-moderne,
où une bande d'amis organise
depuis quelques temps des
rencontres et des spectacles
d'avant-garde, au nez et à la
barbe des pouvoirs publics et
des CENSURES de toutes caté-
gories. Dans le bouillonnement
d'un très fantastique breuvage,
l'AACM récupère les formes

musicales les plus variées, en
exprime les essences vivantes et
rejette sans aucun ménagement les
carcasses exsangues dans les
vide-ordures où nous irons pui-
ser bientôt notre culture. Nos
petits esprits si bien condition-
nés réagissent sur commande :
«On dirait bien du Xénakis -
tiens, voilà Stockhausen, pulsation
en plus - ici un passage pop
- là on s'ennuie un peu - mélodie
de timbres - etc, etc». L'AACM
s'en fout. Laissant les traînards
et les cabots de toutes sortes
faire les poubelles et en tirer
quelques certitudes reluisantes
de graisse rance et universi-
taire, ils avancent sans se
retourner vers une exaltation
unique, celle de la création
permanente.
«Mais, dira-t-on, est-ce des
manières que de faucher à
d'honnêtes créateurs le fruit
de leur génie ? Quelle est cette
bande de truands qui opèrent
un racket permanent sur les
formes les plus sérieuses de
notre bonne culture ?» En entrant
au Lucernaire, attendez-vous
à ce que l'on vous fasse les
poches; vous y serez roué de
coups, détroussé, puis insulté, et
renvoyé tout nu et pleurnichant
à votre mère. Mais surtout ne
retournez pas chez vous. Si

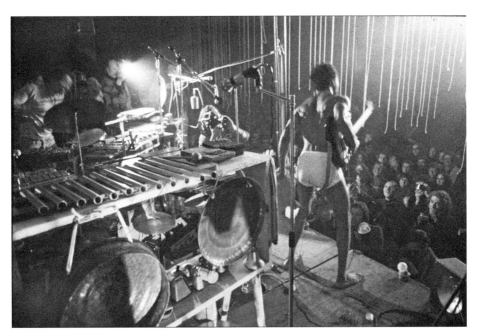

FIGURE 3 The Art Ensemble playing "Rock Out" at the Actuel Festival in Amougies, Belgium, 1969. Roscoe Mitchell (percussion), Joseph Jarman (electric guitar). Out of frame: Lester Bowie, Malachi Favors. Photo by Jacques Bisceglia.

FIGURE 2 Art Ensemble concert program for performances at the Théàtre du Lucernaire, Paris, 1969. Association for the Advancement of Creative Musicians Publicity Materials, Chicago History Museum, ICHi-74351.

FIGURE 4 Roscoe Mitchell in Paris, circa 1969. Photo by Jacques Bisceglia.

FIGURE 5 Recording session for the *Les Stances à Sophie* soundtrack, Boulogne-Billancourt, France, 1970. Left to right: Lester Bowie, Joseph Jarman. Out of frame: Malachi Favors, Roscoe Mitchell, Don Moye. Photo by Leonard E. Jones.

FIGURE 6 The Art Ensemble onstage at the Bergamo Jazz Festival, Italy, 1974. Left to right: Joseph Jarman, Don Moye, Lester Bowie, Malachi Favors, Roscoe Mitchell. Photo by Roberto Masotti.

FIGURE 7 AECO Records publicity photograph of Don Moye. Archives of the Art Ensemble of Chicago. Photo by Ted Gray.

FIGURE 8 Joseph Jarman backstage in Paris, 1978. Photo by Roberto Masotti.

FIGURE 9 Malachi Favors at the DuSable Museum of African American History, Chicago, 1979. Photo by Lauren Deutsch.

FIGURE 10 The Art Ensemble performing in Milan, circa 1980. Left to right: Roscoe Mitchell, Don Moye, Lester Bowie, Malachi Favors, Joseph Jarman. Photo by Roberto Masotti.

ART ENSEMBLE OF CHICAGO

Lester Bowie, Malachi Favors, Joseph Jarman, Roscoe Mitchell, Don Moye

P. O. BOX 53429
Chicago, Illinois 60653
Office: (312) 536-2200
Service: (312) 947-0664

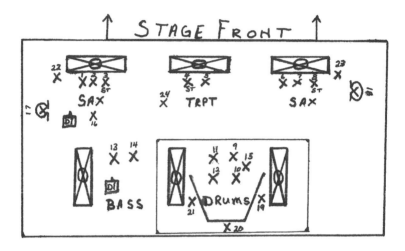

FIGURE 11 Art Ensemble stage plot on AECO stationery. Archives of the Art Ensemble of Chicago.

FIGURE 12 The musicians and their new color-coded flight cases, Europe, 1980.
Left to right: Joseph Jarman, Lester Bowie, Don Moye, Roscoe Mitchell, Malachi Favors.
Archives of the Art Ensemble of Chicago.

FIGURE 13 Lester Bowie at his home in Brooklyn, 1981. Photo by Lauren Deutsch.

FIGURE 14 Group portrait backstage at S.O.B.'s, New York, 1987. Left to right: Don Moye, Roscoe Mitchell, Lester Bowie, Joseph Jarman, Malachi Favors. Photo by Enid Farber.

FIGURE 15 The Art Ensemble performing at the AACM 25th Anniversary Festival, Chicago, 1990. Left to right: Roscoe Mitchell, Don Moye, Lester Bowie, Malachi Favors, Joseph Jarman. Photo by Lauren Deutsch.

FIGURE 16 The Art Ensemble's 25th-anniversary tour, Brussels, 1991.
Back row: the members of Amabutho and Brass Fantasy. Front row, left to right:
Malachi Favors, Joseph Jarman, Don Moye, Roscoe Mitchell, Lester Bowie.
Photo by Jacky Lepage, jackylepage.com.

FIGURE 17 Group portrait near the Art Ensemble's hotel, The Hague, circa 1993.
Left to right: Roscoe Mitchell, Lester Bowie, Malachi Favors, Don Moye, Joseph Jarman.
Archives of the Art Ensemble of Chicago. Photo by Hans Harzheim.

FIGURE 18 The Art Ensemble's percussion instruments on display at the Museum of Contemporary Art, Chicago, 2015. Photo by Lauren Deutsch.

6 Free Together

"We have five different people with five different lives and sets of experiences which are brought in to make up one music."[1]

Coming Home: Chicago and Beyond

The members of the Art Ensemble disembarked from the *SS Raffaello* onto a New York City pier, where they took turns loading their instruments into Malachi Favors's Volkswagen van and the two Ford trucks they brought from France.[2] After spending twenty-three months overseas, from June 1969 to April 1971, the musicians had finally returned to the United States. Much had changed in the past two years. Back in the spring of 1969, Joseph Jarman was mourning the death of Charles Clark and accepting an invitation to join Roscoe Mitchell's trio for a venture to Paris. Don Moye came aboard a year after Jarman, in early 1970, making the group a quintet, with a membership that would not change for a quarter-century. While in Europe, the Art Ensemble family also expanded in other ways. Lester Bowie and Fontella Bass welcomed two more children during their sojourn and were now the proud parents of four.[3]

When the musicians and the Bowies finished packing their possessions and preparing their vehicles for the road, they left

155

New York and drove to the Midwest. Their friends at home received them as "conquering heroes," and rightly so.[4] The members of the Art Ensemble had made their mark in Paris, a proving ground for generations of African American performers. They recorded fifteen albums, toured France twice, and played in a half-dozen other countries. Many of their European performances, according to Jarman, had taken place in "the best concert halls, with the best acoustics, with the best sound people, with the best wine in your dressing room, or the best beer, or the best chicken liver . . . and all you have to do is go on the stage and do your thing."[5] The Art Ensemble's achievements abroad, however, did not immediately translate into gigs back in America. So the musicians settled into new residences and reconnected with the communities they had left behind in 1969, determined to create their own opportunities at home.

The Art Ensemble stayed in the United States for the next few years, and the 1970s would become a pivotal period for the members of their group, like their time in Europe. During this momentous decade, they recorded for major labels, improved their business practices, and broadened their American audience. Just as significantly, the musicians reworked the cooperative social model that they had devised while living in France, allowing one another to launch independent careers as solo artists (although the Art Ensemble remained their highest priority). These crucial developments, all of which began to take shape in the summer of 1971, would define the band's second decade.

Favors and Jarman proceeded from the New York waterfront to Chicago, where they found lodging in the "musicians' building" at East 54th Street and South Drexel Avenue.[6] The building was owned and operated by the musicians' union, Local 10–208, as apartment housing for its members, and some of Favors and Jarman's associates were already living there.[7] The newly repatriated musicians fit right in. Jarman hit the ground running: he formed an ensemble called Return from Exile, its name an allusion to the Art Ensemble's European odyssey, and he looked for work as an educator specializing in music and theater.[8] He devoted much of the summer to teaching, first at the Circle Pines Center in rural Delton, Michigan. Three years earlier, Jarman had presented his intermedia *Gate Piece* at Circle Pines, and he returned there in the summer of 1971 as a lecturer and workshop director. After his Circle Pines residency, he traveled to Stockbridge, Massachusetts, to teach music and theater at the progressive Stockbridge School.[9] In comparison to Jarman, Favors stayed closer to home but was equally busy. His bass skills were in high demand, as during the Art Ensemble's time in Paris, and Favors quickly made his way into a variety of AACM groups. He and his AACM colleagues found themselves keeping the same morning-to-night routine of practicing, composing, and performing that they had first instituted in the early days of the Association.[10]

Like Favors and Jarman, Mitchell and Moye also drove from New York to Chicago, but they did not remain there for long. Instead, they soon headed south on Route 66 and caught up with Bowie, who had bypassed Chicago entirely in order to establish himself in St. Louis.[11] Shortly after arriving in his former hometown, Bowie purchased a house in University City, Missouri, an inner-ring suburb of St. Louis.[12] The house's previous owner was bassist Arzinia Richardson, a member of the Black Artists' Group (BAG).[13] Founded in St. Louis in 1968, BAG was a collective organization inspired by the AACM. Indeed, BAG was initially conceived as a St. Louis–based AACM chapter.[14] Bowie played a leading role in connecting the nascent community of experimental musicians in St. Louis with the Chicagoans whom they sought to emulate. He maintained a presence in St. Louis after his mid-1960s move to Chicago, returning frequently to bring AACM news to St. Louis musicians.[15] Prior to the formation of BAG, Bowie invited saxophonists Julius Hemphill and Oliver Lake to Chicago so they could hang out with Jarman and Mitchell. The four woodwind players spent several weeks practicing together at Promontory Point, a South Side lakefront park situated east of 55th Street and Lake Shore Drive.[16] Afterward, Hemphill and Lake returned to St. Louis and helped found BAG, serving as the organization's first chairman and treasurer, respectively.[17]

Mitchell and Moye's 1971 visit to St. Louis renewed the musician-exchange program pioneered by Bowie at a critical time in the history of BAG. During BAG's first two years of existence, the organization seemed to have considerable momentum. Its membership included musicians as well as artists from other disciplines, and both factions were represented in the organization's leadership: Hemphill and Lake worked alongside executive director Malinké Elliott, an actor, theater director, and poet.[18] When Hemphill assumed the directorship of an allied St. Louis program, Artists in Residence (AIR), BAG informally merged with AIR. This move gave BAG access to $100,000 in funding originally designated for AIR, half of a $200,000 grant that the Danforth and Rockefeller foundations awarded jointly to AIR and another local arts organization, the Performing Arts Training Center (PATC), founded by the renowned choreographer Katherine Dunham.[19] With these financial resources, BAG was able to acquire a building, produce concerts and intermedia events, and pay salaries to resident artists like the painter Emilio Cruz, who relocated from New York to St. Louis and set up his studio in the BAG building. (Cruz's art would subsequently appear on the covers of several Art Ensemble albums.[20]) By 1970, however, BAG's future was in doubt. Several members had departed, Hemphill was deposed as chairman, and the organization's funds were exhausted.[21] When Bowie, Mitchell, and Moye arrived in St. Louis, they tried to reinvigorate BAG by applying the lessons they had learned in Chicago and Paris.

Mitchell and Moye moved into the BAG building at 2665 Washington Boulevard, taking over the second-floor studio where Emilio Cruz and his wife, Patricia—a civil-rights activist and arts advocate—had lived and worked. This expansive studio had plenty of room for both musicians and their instruments, and they rehearsed with "all the cats from BAG" in an AACM-like environment.[22] Meanwhile, Bowie took full advantage of the performance space on the first floor of BAG headquarters. He launched a series of "all-night concerts that culminated at dawn with sunrise ceremonies on the sidewalks of Washington Boulevard," recalling the ninety-six-hour marathon concert he organized in 1968 after becoming the AACM's second president.[23] The musicians working on the "Sunrise Series," according to Moye, would "start one day at noon and play . . . until the sun came up the next day with continuous music featuring all the different groups."[24] In addition to participating in the Sunrise Series, Moye collaborated with a number of other artists linked with BAG. He performed with poet Shirley LeFlore and accompanied the Berea Messenger Singers, a women's choir at the church LeFlore attended, Berea Presbyterian.[25] Moye also resumed his studies of African drumming, learning djembe from the Senegalese percussionist Mor Thiam, who taught at Dunham's PATC.[26]

The Art Ensemble members' musical activities in St. Louis proved to be less consequential than the business tutorials they offered to BAG musicians. Many BAG members were disappointed by the reception of their music in St. Louis but were unconvinced that they could improve their lot by moving to Europe, as the Art Ensemble had done. Bowie, Mitchell, and Moye dismissed this skepticism and encouraged BAG musicians to "abandon their St. Louis efforts and relocate to Paris."[27] As Bowie said, "Just get there—you'll work."[28] The Art Ensemble's advice was not lost on Oliver Lake, who started making preparations for a European campaign modeled in every way on the Chicagoans' venture of 1969. Lake recorded a demo album, shipped copies to music-industry professionals in Europe, and formed a touring quintet with trumpeters Baikida Carroll and Floyd LeFlore, trombonist Joseph Bowie (Lester's youngest brother), and drummer Charles "Bobo" Shaw.[29] In the fall of 1972, Lake's ensemble set out for Paris. Their departure led to the dissolution of BAG, which was bereft of virtually all of the musicians and artists who had founded the organization in 1968 and sustained it into the early 1970s.[30] Across the Atlantic, Lake and his musicians followed the trail blazed by the Art Ensemble and replicated many of the group's successes. They rented a house in the Paris suburbs, bought two vans for transporting themselves to concerts outside the metropolitan area, worked the Chicagoans' connections, and found enough gigs to keep the quintet in Europe for more than a year, almost as long as the Art Ensemble's stay overseas.[31]

Social Practices

Throughout 1971, the members of the Art Ensemble reunited periodically for performances. During the summer, they played concerts in three separate locations. On 19 May, the group performed at the University of Chicago.[32] Their next concert took place several weeks later in Bloomington, Indiana, a college town equidistant from Chicago and St. Louis, the Art Ensemble's twin bases of operation that summer.[33] In August, the musicians played two nights at the Lenox Art Center in Lenox, Massachusetts, just across the state turnpike from the Stockbridge School, where Jarman was teaching.[34] The band convened again in December for a weekend stint at Alice's Revisited, a venue on Chicago's North Side known for booking blues artists like Muddy Waters and Howlin' Wolf.[35] This relatively sparse schedule of performances was reminiscent of the situation that confronted the Art Ensemble in the late 1960s, when the group was "working in the States maybe four times a year."[36] In 1969, the lack of gigs at home had driven the Chicagoans to France. Two years later, performance opportunities were still scarce, yet the members of the Art Ensemble no longer felt compelled to leave the Midwest. Instead, the musicians developed a new business strategy and adapted the cooperative social model that they had put into practice at the farmhouse in Saint-Leu-la-Forêt. (For more on the emergence of the Art Ensemble's social model, see chapter 3.)

Cooperative economics had helped the Art Ensemble prosper in Europe. The group minimized expenses and maximized earnings by living together and pooling all proceeds from Art Ensemble concerts and recording sessions. Through this strategy, the band achieved financial stability—and even generated a surplus that could be reinvested into important purchases, from vehicles to musical instruments. Of course, the principle of cooperation was not the only reason the group thrived overseas. The members of the Art Ensemble perfectly timed their journey to Europe. It coincided with the "high point of the new thing's popularity in France," and there was no shortage of work for experimental musicians, whether in Paris, elsewhere in France, or in other locations across Western Europe.[37] When the Art Ensemble returned to the United States, the members of the group continued to practice cooperative economics. After spending the summer of 1971 in St. Louis, Mitchell and Moye came back to Chicago and set up residence with Favors and Jarman in a nineteenth-century townhouse at East 60th Street and South Harper Avenue, near the University of Chicago.[38] Unfortunately, this effort at cooperation did not yield the surplus that the musicians had enjoyed in Europe, because the band's income had sharply declined. In contrast to Paris, steady work was unavailable to the Art Ensemble in the city of Chicago. Likewise, the European circuit of jazz festivals and theater gigs had no analogue in the United States circa 1971, making it difficult for the group to organize viable tours. A string of club dates would have been a poor substitute for a concert tour, and at any rate American jazz clubs were unlikely to hire a band whose music was as experimental as the Art Ensemble's. So the musicians devised an alternative strategy in which they balanced their commitment to financial and social cooperation by introducing a new, complementary ethic: autonomy.

The members of the group granted one another the freedom to pursue "side projects," additional musical endeavors that would be independent of the Art Ensemble.[39] To a limited degree, they had permitted this kind of autonomy before: in Paris, the musicians often played freelance gigs on the Art Ensemble's off nights. But after 1971, the band members' side projects took on special significance. Now they could dedicate themselves to side projects for weeks or months at a time during the intervals between Art Ensemble engagements. Through their side projects, the musicians could obtain individual incomes that were not subject to the cooperative. In turn, this enabled the members of the Art Ensemble to maintain the band's cooperative policy even when performances were few and far between, and to be considerably more selective when deciding which offers to take. No longer would the group agree to gigs that paid "less money than was acceptable."[40] Instead, they substantially increased the fee they charged for concert appearances.[41] In addition to improving the Art Ensemble's finances, the side projects benefited the band in many other ways. Working on side projects served to refresh the musicians and enhance their creativity, as Bowie explained:

> Each member of the Art Ensemble is free to do whatever he wants to do, not bound by anything. . . . that's why we work maybe a month and then we're off for maybe a month or two months. Each time we go off we go to our other bands. Then when I come back here I bring ideas, new songs,

new feelings and we all come together, rehearse and it keeps us alive. The individual freedom is emphasized, encouraged not stifled in any way.[42]

At the end of an Art Ensemble hiatus, the musicians put their side projects on hold and gathered at a house or apartment (often the home of one or more members of the group). Then they began their familiar routine of intensive daily rehearsals, starting each morning at ten o'clock and continuing until early evening.[43] These rehearsal periods lasted for at least one week, and could extend to several weeks, depending on the nature of the performances for which the musicians were preparing and the duration of the recently concluded hiatus.[44] After the Alice's Revisited engagement on the first weekend of December 1971, for instance, the band took a break for the rest of the month. During this hiatus, Jarman traveled to Paris, where he recorded a duet album with Anthony Braxton, *Together Alone*, and played a concert with a group that included Braxton as well as Alan Shorter on flugelhorn, Oliver Johnson on drums, and dancer Dawn Jones.[45] The Art Ensemble reconvened in early January 1972 at the South Side townhouse, where they rehearsed for two weeks leading up to their next concert dates, scheduled for 15 and 16 January at the University of Chicago.[46]

The Art Ensemble's efficient approach to rehearsal fulfilled several interrelated purposes. It revived a routine that had served the musicians well during their time in Europe, and it facilitated strong performances even after lengthy hiatuses. Furthermore, the Art Ensemble's devotion to rehearsing made it possible for the group members to elevate their performances from mere music-making into transcendent, spirit-filled rituals. According to Bowie, "it takes lots of rehearsal. You rehearse, practice just to enable you to be able to receive the spirit."[47]

Bowie's words reveal that even seemingly ordinary matters like rehearsal procedures could have profound implications for the Art Ensemble's musical and social practices. This was a reflection of the exceptionally close relationships that developed among the musicians during the 1970s, even as they gave one another greater autonomy. Indeed, the members of the Art Ensemble consistently characterized their post-1971 social model as the key to the band's musical accomplishments. Mitchell told an interviewer that "[i]f I view the Art Ensemble, I see it as five individuals. Each person all has their strong individual lifestyles and they were able to come together and blend these things into a cohesive ensemble."[48] Moye emphasized the mutual respect that helped the Art Ensemble strike a balance between collective goals and each group member's personal autonomy:

The essential element of that whole thing is respect. Everyone respects very much what everybody else is doing as an individual. . . . We realize that each person has to have a certain amount of leeway to realize his own ambitions, both within the Art Ensemble and on his own. So we purposely structured our whole thing in such a way as to allow the maximum realization of this. . . . That makes the group concept that much stronger.[49]

Jarman offered a different perspective in a conversation with Mitchell and two French critics, Laurent Goddet and Alex Dutilh. For him, the most remarkable aspect of the Art Ensemble's social model was not its allowance for autonomy. Instead, Jarman marveled at how the group's social practices gradually transformed the musicians' individual personalities and subjectivities:

The Art Ensemble is like a cake made from five ingredients: remove one of the ingredients and the cake no longer exists. When you look at the Art Ensemble from a certain distance, that's how it is, much more than any one individual whose personality you manage to isolate. . . . [W]e have developed an internal loyalty, an awareness of our interdependence. All of the experiences we went through together, our emotional experiences, positive or dramatic, all of the situations we found ourselves in collectively and individually—all of this has brought us closer together to the point that now we are of one mind.[50]

The members of the Art Ensemble based their social model on practices that emerged from the AACM. "When you look at what we're trying to do," Moye explained, "it's merely a reflection of a lot of principles . . . that we originally laid down in the bylaws of the AACM. So we reflect that whole spirit, only we try to carry it out in a smaller group context."[51] For example, in AACM business meetings, organizational decisions were made by consensus, and accordingly the Art Ensemble's decision-making process required that the group members reach unanimous consent on crucial matters.[52] However, the Art Ensemble's unwavering commitment to cooperation and autonomy ensured that its social model would evolve over the years into something distinctive and inimitable: a radical exemplification of the Association's principles, to paraphrase AACM historian George E. Lewis.[53] The AACM's activities were funded collectively by the members of the organization, but the Art Ensemble was the only AACM band that consistently practiced cooperative economics.[54] No other AACM group was able to foster the autonomous development and advancement of its members while also sustaining itself in the long term. In fact, during the 1970s the Art Ensemble became the longest-lived band in the history of the Association, a title it would never relinquish.

The Art Ensemble's longevity may have inspired Moye's notion of a "tree structure," his favorite metaphor for the group's social model. The tree envisioned by Moye was the African baobab, which has been known to live for more than a thousand years. During the dry season in its native habitat, the baobab loses its leaves and subsists on water stored in its enormous trunk. Its narrow, bare branches resemble tree roots, so much so that local folklore often describes the baobab as having been planted upside down. In Moye's metaphor, the trunk of the baobab represented the Art Ensemble. The branches extending directly from the baobab's trunk were the side projects, which functioned as creative outlets for the group members and also as conduits that brought new ideas back to the Art Ensemble. The smallest, leaf- and fruit-bearing branches, held a double meaning. They represented the other musicians participating in the side projects, and when reimagined as the baobab's "roots," they symbolized the musical forms engaged by the side projects and the Art Ensemble, the diverse sounds and traditions encompassed in the band's Great Black Music.[55]

Art Ensemble of Chicago Operations

After 1971, the Art Ensemble's prospects began to improve steadily, albeit at a slow pace that caused the musicians some frustration. "Fortunately or unfortunately," Jarman mused, "we're in it to such a degree that we cannot even begin to consider turning away from it."[56] The group worked only about a dozen times in 1972 and 1973, but each performance during that period was a major event that helped the Art Ensemble reach new audiences and achieve other vital goals. The band's 15 and 16 January 1972 concerts took place at the University of Chicago's Mandel Hall, an important concert venue with seating for almost one thousand. According to Moye, the musicians played to a full house, drawing several hundred listeners in the midst of a snowstorm: "10 degrees, 2 feet of snow, blizzard conditions, and the place was packed ... standing room only!"[57] The Art Ensemble hired an audio engineer to record the 15 January concert, a seventy-six-minute performance that Delmark would release as the double album *Live at Mandel Hall*.[58] (See chapter 7 for an analysis of *Live at Mandel Hall*.) In September 1972, the group's next two performances attracted even larger audiences: four thousand at the University of Wisconsin in Madison, and more than ten thousand at the Ann Arbor Blues & Jazz Festival, an attendance figure that rivaled the size of the crowd at the Actuel Festival.[59] The Ann Arbor concert yielded another live recording, *Bap-tizum*, a title chosen by Favors, who felt that "the spirit was there" during the Art Ensemble's set.[60]

The Art Ensemble's audience in Ann Arbor included Michael Cuscuna, a recently hired producer at Atlantic Records.[61] In the twenty-five years since its founding, Atlantic had grown from a small rhythm-and-blues imprint into a major label whose roster featured some of the biggest rock acts of the 1970s, from Led Zeppelin to Crosby, Stills, Nash & Young. Atlantic also maintained a jazz division that had been home to Charles Mingus, the Modern Jazz Quartet, Ornette Coleman, and John Coltrane. Cuscuna regarded the Art Ensemble as "the most significant and creative group in the new music since the original Ornette Coleman and John Coltrane quartets," and after the Ann Arbor Blues & Jazz Festival he offered the band a contract to make two albums for Atlantic.[62] *Bap-tizum*, the festival performance that impressed Cuscuna, would become the group's first release on Atlantic Records.[63]

Having a relationship with a major label paid off immediately. The albums that the Art Ensemble recorded in France were poorly distributed in the United States—if at all—but Atlantic discs were available everywhere.[64] This newfound visibility, coupled with the prestige of a contract with Atlantic Records, greatly enhanced the group's standing in the American music industry. Prior to 1973, the members of the Art Ensemble were virtually unknown among industry gatekeepers on the East Coast. This would change after the release of *Bap-tizum*. The promoter George Wein invited the Art Ensemble to perform at the 1973 edition of his Newport Jazz Festival, then held in New York City.[65] This performance, which took place on 5 July, was the musicians' first appearance at the premier jazz festival in the United States and also their New York debut.[66] Later that summer, the group experienced another breakthrough. The National Endowment for the Arts (NEA) awarded grants to all five band members to support the composition of new musical works. Bowie received $750, while the others received $1,000 each.[67] These modest amounts were typical for composition grants in NEA's jazz category, which was only in its fourth year of existence and much less well funded than the section dedicated to concert music.[68] The members of the Art Ensemble used their NEA grants to compose the music for their second Atlantic album, *Fanfare for the Warriors*, recorded in September 1973.[69] The compositions on *Fanfare for the Warriors* included the original version of Mitchell's "Nonaah," a landmark work that he would revisit again and again, composing variations for solo saxophone, chamber ensembles, and classical orchestra.[70] The album opens with Favors's "Illistrum," a percussion piece that supports a poetic recitation by Jarman. Here, Jarman recites his poem "ODAWALLA," an allegory about the divine forces who "guide the people of the Sun as they seek to leave . . . the grey haze."[71] The imagery in Jarman's text is often Afrocentric, particularly the recurring figure of "the people of the Sun," a poetic appellation for people of African descent. This phrase can also be understood as a reference to the members of the Art Ensemble, whom Jarman regarded as the inheritors of a divinely ordained musical tradition:

> ODAWALLA came through the people of the Sun
> to warn them of the vanished legions
> and to teach them how they may increase their bounty
> through the practice of the drum and silent gong
> (as taught by ODAWALLA) . . .[72]

By 1974, the musicians were poised to return to Europe. Their Atlantic albums had attracted attention from European critics, and concert promoters could expect favorable responses from continental audiences, who had been waiting three years for the chance to attend an Art Ensemble performance.[73] Accordingly, the band was able to orchestrate not one, but two European tours in 1974, each of which lasted two months. The Art Ensemble's first tour took place on familiar territory. From late January to mid-March, the musicians performed across France, following an itinerary that resembled their tours of 1970 and 1971. The Art Ensemble played a series of concerts at various regional Maisons de la Culture, as in 1970 and 1971, and every week or so the group visited Paris to perform at the headquarters of the ORTF radio network or at other high-profile sites like Le Gibus, a concert venue for jazz and pop music.[74] The tour concluded in Bergamo, Italy, where in late March the Art Ensemble appeared at the city's jazz festival.[75] After the Bergamo concert, the group traveled back to the United States, went on a three-month hiatus, and then returned to Europe for the summer. The Art Ensemble's second tour of 1974 capitalized on the release of *Fanfare for the Warriors*. Instead of retracing their steps in France, the musicians were able to perform at a number of new locations: urban jazz festivals in Finland, Italy, the Netherlands, Norway, and Switzerland.[76] For this tour, which stretched from late June to mid-August, the members of the Art Ensemble were joined by a special guest, Muhal Richard Abrams, who had appeared on *Fanfare for the Warriors*. At the time, Abrams was a rising star in the jazz world, and his presence alongside the Art Ensemble was a key selling point for promoters and concertgoers alike.[77] The tour's centerpiece was a 4 July concert at the Montreux Jazz Festival in

Montreux, Switzerland, Europe's answer to the Newport Jazz Festival. Instead of playing some or all of the seven pieces from *Fanfare for the Warriors*, the Art Ensemble and Abrams decided to play a set of entirely new music, including Jarman's composition "Theme for Sco" (his nickname for Mitchell) and several episodes of open improvisation. The ensuing performance was spacious and meditative, showcasing aspects of the Abrams collaboration that went unexplored on the more tightly formatted *Fanfare for the Warriors*. The members of the Art Ensemble arranged to have their Montreux concert recorded. They were pleased with how *Live at Mandel Hall* and *Bap-tizum* had turned out, and the venerable Montreux Jazz Festival seemed like an apt setting for the Art Ensemble's next recording. "In fact," Jarman stated, "we prefer recording a concert to making a record in the studio."[78] The Montreux concert, *Kabalaba*, would be the group's third live recording in as many years.[79]

In November 1974, the Art Ensemble went on yet another concert tour, a weeklong whirlwind visit to some of the biggest cities in Japan: Fukuoka, Kyoto, Osaka, and Tokyo. After this venture, the musicians remained at home in America for the better part of two years, traveling overseas only for the occasional one-off date in France or Switzerland.[80] The three tours undertaken by the group in 1974 were instrumental in securing the overseas market that proved crucial to the Art Ensemble's prosperity. As Bowie asserted, "we had to do our thing with a planetary approach. We had to hit the world market. We couldn't localize. It just could not be Chicago or New York. *The only way for us to survive was to develop a world audience.*"[81]

With their "world audience" in place, particularly in Europe, the members of the Art Ensemble could turn their attention to two additional objectives. First, they worked to improve all aspects of their business practices—bookkeeping, communications, contracts, and product sales—in order to meet the Art Ensemble's evolving needs as a group with an international profile and major-label affiliation. Second, the musicians "really got into developing our own audience in the States," as Moye recalled. "Any place where they were ready for the music, we took it directly to their door."[82] The Art Ensemble launched these two initiatives in the middle of the 1970s and reaped the rewards for the rest of the decade.

One business matter was especially urgent: gaining control of the group's compositions. The first recordings made by the Art Ensemble in Paris were for BYG Records, which possessed an in-house music-publishing company, BYG Music. The label and its publishing company claimed ownership of all Art Ensemble compositions that appeared on BYG albums, and the BYG principals never distributed royalties to the band.[83] After August 1969, when the group last recorded for BYG, the musicians quickly established their own publishing company through the Société des Auteurs, Compositeurs et Éditeurs de Musique (SACEM), the French performance-rights organization. This publishing company allowed the members of the Art Ensemble to earn royalties on their subsequent recordings. The Art Ensemble's SACEM publishing company remained active through 1973, the year when *Bap-tizum* was released. In 1974, prior to the release of *Fanfare for the Warriors* and *Live at Mandel Hall*, the members of the group joined the American Society of Composers, Authors, and Publishers (ASCAP) and established a new ASCAP-affiliated publishing company, Art Ensemble of Chicago Publishing.[84] By joining ASCAP, the performance rights organization with the greatest global reach, the musicians ensured that they would receive the maximum royalty payments for future broadcasts and performances of their music, whether in Chicago, Paris, or Tokyo.

The move to ASCAP inspired the musicians to exercise control over their work in other ways. In 1975, the Art Ensemble formed AECO Records, an independent label in which all five band members held an equal stake. Through AECO Records, the musicians could produce and release Art Ensemble albums as well as recordings of their various side projects.[85] Indeed, the initial three releases by AECO Records were side projects, solo albums by Moye, Jarman, and Favors.[86] These discs were followed by the first Art Ensemble recording on AECO, *Kabalaba*.[87] The members of the group sold AECO albums at their concerts and also via mail order, a typical sales strategy for smaller independent labels operating without extensive distribution networks. Furthermore, the Art Ensemble's product offerings were not limited to AECO discs. Fans of the band could purchase sheet music of the group's compositions, as well as Art Ensemble–branded bumper stickers, pins and buttons, photographs and postcards, T-shirts, wall posters, and window decals.[88] The Art Ensemble even sold books, beginning with Jarman's *Black Case*, a collection of his poetry and writings.[89]

The group members were equal financial partners in all of the Art Ensemble's enterprises, but each contributed to the cooperative in a unique way according to his personal interests and abilities. Much of the responsibility for the band's expanding business activities fell to the two-man team of Bowie and Moye. Bowie "negotiated deals and contracts" from his home base in St. Louis, while Moye remained in Chicago and focused on "administering the cooperative and generating work opportunities."[90] Moye needed an office to perform his administrative duties, and in 1975 he set up a modest workspace in the dining room of his apartment. At the time, Moye resided in the "musicians' building," the same South Side apartment house where Favors and Jarman had stayed during the summer of 1971. Evod Magek, a pianist and AACM member, lived near Moye in the "musicians' building," and he became the Art Ensemble's first employee, tasked with running the office when the band was on tour. In 1976, Moye moved to another residence and converted his former apartment into a dedicated office. The Art Ensemble now had the space and the financial means to bring on another staffer, and the group hired John Shenoy Jackson, an AACM member like Magek.[91] Jackson's AACM colleagues regarded him as an "administrative wizard," in recognition of the skill set he cultivated during a long public-sector career.[92] He started working for the Art Ensemble on a part-time basis, and when he retired from his government job at the end of the 1970s, he became the band's full-time executive secretary and bookkeeper.[93] Jackson's most significant administrative achievement came in 1979, when he helped the musicians incorporate their business as Art Ensemble of Chicago Operations (AECO). The members of the Art Ensemble used AECO to collect revenue, process business expenses, pay salaries, and manage their reinvestment efforts. AECO also served as the parent corporation of the band's record label and ASCAP music-publishing company, both of which were incorporated in conjunction with AECO in 1979. Each group member owned twenty percent of AECO and its subsidiaries, an arrangement that formalized the principles of financial and social cooperation upheld by the Art Ensemble since 1969.[94] The incorporation of AECO, like the other advances in the Art Ensemble's business practices, preserved the band's cooperative identity and helped the members succeed in a changing music industry. As Mitchell observed, "[t]he Art Ensemble was one of a very small number of groups that even survived the late '70s."[95] Clearly, it was imperative for the musicians to be about their business. However, the newly incorporated Art Ensemble was by no means a button-down, straitlaced organization. To celebrate the formation of Art Ensemble of Chicago Operations, the group members collaboratively composed a piece entitled "Funky AECO."[96]

In addition to updating their business practices, the musicians worked throughout the 1970s to expand their American audience. They were assisted in this effort by Kunle Mwanga, who became the band's booking agent in 1975. Mwanga was an established concert promoter with long-standing ties to the AACM.[97] During the 1960s, he attended many of Jarman and Mitchell's performances in Chicago, and in 1970 he produced the first AACM event in New York City, a sextet concert by Muhal Richard Abrams, Anthony Braxton, bassist Richard Davis, Leroy Jenkins, Steve McCall, and Leo Smith.[98] In April

1971, when the Art Ensemble returned to the United States on the SS *Raffaello*, Mwanga waited on the pier for the musicians to arrive and greeted them as they exited the ship. "I was on their case," he recalled, "because I wanted to immediately produce a concert with them."[99] Shortly thereafter, he organized the group's August 1971 performances at the Lenox Art Center.[100] At the end of the year, he moved to Paris, where he started working for Braxton as a booking agent and manager.[101] Mwanga reconnected with the members of the Art Ensemble in March 1974, during their tour of France: he was approaching the end of his tenure with Braxton, and the musicians suggested that he work with them in a similar capacity. He soon departed Paris and set up shop in Oakland, California. At the nearby Berkeley campus of the University of California, Mwanga instituted a monthly concert series and engaged the Art Ensemble for the January 1975 series premiere, the band's first gig in America after the November 1974 tour of Japan. The Berkeley concert met the musicians' expectations, and they decided to retain Mwanga as their booking agent, a position he would hold until 1977.[102]

Mwanga helped the Art Ensemble cultivate a larger domestic audience by staging concerts in a range of new venues and locales. The first performances he arranged after becoming the band's booking agent were in New York: two consecutive weeks at the Five Spot Café, a Manhattan jazz club known for presenting Thelonious Monk and Ornette Coleman, followed by a three-day stint at the East, a pan-African cultural center in Brooklyn.[103] The Five Spot gig in September 1975 was the group's debut appearance at a New York nightclub.[104] During the early years of the AACM, the members of the Association often refused to present their music in nightclub settings, if doing so would require them to conform to club owners' expectations.[105] A decade later, the Art Ensemble was finally welcome in a prominent jazz club, and the group members had no intention of changing their performance practice or masquerading as ordinary jazz musicians. Instead, they viewed the Five Spot engagement as an opportunity to challenge the cultural conventions surrounding jazz performance. *Down Beat* magazine reported on one of the Art Ensemble's sets at the Five Spot, which began with a trademark theatrical sketch:

> Bowie came out first, sporting a casino dealer's visor on his head and drinking from a pint of whiskey. Jarman and Moye staggered around the club like two winos, holding onto each other for balance, shooting off streamers and mumbling nonsensically. Bowie spotted them and yelled, "Over here! None of this music s—, we're gonna play some cards!" Somehow they found their way to a table set up in front of the stage, where a

deck of cards was produced. Bowie proceeded to deal furiously, cards flying everywhere, the three drinking, cursing and calling each other's bluff in a hilarious parody of a seedy card game. Even the Five Spot management got into the spirit, a waitress bringing a bottle of booze to their card table. However, Bowie, after sampling some of it, yelled out in feigned disapproval, "Man, what is this stuff? What kind of a jazz club is this?" Bowie then asked his buddies if they wanted to play some pool, waving a pool cue. One of them finally asked, "Where's Malachi?," and Favors made his entrance, while simultaneously Bowie extended the pool cue towards him, shouting, "Hey, Malachi, here's your cue!" And they got up on stage and commenced music-making.[106]

In the early months of 1976, the Art Ensemble returned to the road. The group performed at two different venues in Toronto, drove to San Francisco to play at the Great American Music Hall, and then returned to the East Coast for concerts at the Public Theater in New York and the Empty Fox-hole in Philadelphia.[107] Later that year, the musicians headed west again for a five-week concert tour of the California coast. The Art Ensemble's chief mode of transportation for these and other North American tours was a 1951 Greyhound bus.[108] The group's two German-built Ford trucks had fallen into disrepair not long after the musicians imported them from Europe, and replacement parts were difficult to find in the United States.[109] In 1972, when the Art Ensemble sold *Live at Mandel Hall* to Delmark Records, the musicians took the proceeds and traveled to Detroit, where they purchased the Greyhound bus directly from General Motors.[110] The bus, in Moye's description, was "black and silver with gold highlights, and an Egyptian pyramid painted on the rear panel."[111] The front panel was inscribed with the name Mitchell invented for the bus, "Ujibkum Chariot"—a moniker derived from the names of Bowie's dog, Kummi, and Mitchell's dog, Jibberimba.[112] "We named it after the dogs," according to Favors, "because they protected our instruments."[113] The members of the Art Ensemble also protected themselves by "carry[ing] heat on the road," as Moye recalled:

When we used to go out to the West Coast traveling cross country on our bus back in the 70s, you couldn't be too careful with them wild white people out there. We had shotguns and rifles. We've got film footage of rifle practice, and gun cleaning. We used to practice in the morning, then put the guns under the floorboards or up in the racks. We were never messin with nobody. But people would come up on us all the time (five Black men in their own bus full of instruments and two dogs). I remember one time . . . the bus broke down in the middle of the night in the corn fields. Some of them roving vigilante types came up on the bus in their pick-ups, unmarked squad cars with lights flashing and s—. They had their rifles and guns out. They said, "What you boys doin out here?" So we got back in the bus and came out with our guns and said, "What YOU BOYS doing?" They said "Uh uh we was just checking to see if y'all was alright cuz uh Billy Bob and err uhh Jeb here, theyz purty good mechanics. Well good night boss, y'all be careful now." And I said, "Right. Good night, Bubba."[114]

Mwanga organized two European tours for the Art Ensemble, one in 1976 and the other in 1977. The 1976 tour was an epic four-month trek across the continent: the musicians spent two months performing in France, Italy, and Switzerland, then a month in Scandinavia, and concluded the tour with concerts in Austria, Belgium, West Germany, and Yugoslavia. The 1977 tour lasted only one month but still covered a lot of ground: at one point, the group traveled some 1,400 kilometers from a gig in Zagreb, Yugoslavia, to Paris, the site of a weeklong residency.[115] The itineraries for both tours included occasional off days, which gave the musicians opportunities to showcase their side projects, often at the same venues and festivals where the Art Ensemble was playing. In August 1976, the jazz festival lineup in Willisau, Switzerland, included an Art Ensemble performance as well as a solo concert by Mitchell; a recording of this concert became the first side of his double LP *Nonaah*.[116] Nine months later, in May 1977, the Moers (West Germany) jazz festival featured sets by the Art Ensemble, the duo of Bowie and Moye, the duo of Favors and Muhal Richard Abrams, and the woodwind trio of Jarman, Mitchell, and Anthony Braxton.[117] In these and countless other instances, the Art Ensemble's growing popularity benefited not only the group as a whole but also the individual members in their careers as solo artists. This synergistic relationship could work in reverse as well. For example, Mitchell performed regularly in Toronto from 1973 to 1975, building a local audience that eagerly turned out for the concerts the Art Ensemble played there in 1976.[118] From the musicians' perspective, the Art Ensemble's longevity and the increasing viability of their side projects proved beyond a doubt that the group's post-1971 social model was triumphing: the tree structure was bearing fruit. As Jarman told jazz critic Nat Hentoff, "We already have been successful, because we have been able to stay together so long. And the longer our longevity is sustained, the more intimate we become with the music and the creative potential for it. That's the kind of success I'm talking about."[119]

Side Projects

The members of the Art Ensemble developed dozens of side projects after 1971. All of the musicians played solo concerts and recorded unaccompanied solo pieces, continuing the noted practice of solo performance that emerged in the AACM during the 1960s.[120] They also formed new ensembles of every conceivable size and instrumentation, ranging from duos, trios, and other small groups to Bowie's extraordinary fifty-nine-piece Sho' Nuff Orchestra.[121] The musicians often participated in one another's side projects, either as co-leaders or as sidemen. Furthermore, they sought out collaborations with fellow AACM members whose training in the Association ensured a degree of creative compatibility. Over the years, the community of performers involved in the Art Ensemble's side projects progressively expanded, as the musicians experimented with novel approaches to composition and improvisation and tested these discoveries with prospective collaborators whom they met in the course of their travels. For Bowie, the value that the Art Ensemble placed on the side projects reminded him of his experiences in the Armed Forces, another organization that cultivated strong, independent leaders:

> We used to call the Art Ensemble "OCS," which in the military means Officer Candidate School, where you train officers. We trained bandleaders, so that each one of us [was] able to know all the functions of carrying a group around, and to take that experience to other groups of musicians. . . . I mean, we take our experiences with the Art Ensemble to our individual groups; we in turn get this experience back, and we bring it back to the Art Ensemble, which enables us to keep growing in all ways.[122]

Many of Mitchell's side projects were based in the upper Midwest, the area where he put down roots in the 1970s. Even before the Art Ensemble ventured to Paris in 1969, he "was starting to want to get out of Chicago for a while, and get to a place by myself where I would have more time to work on things."[123] An opportunity to relocate presented itself soon after Mitchell and his bandmates returned to the United States. In 1972, Mitchell's friend David Wessel, a scholar and composer specializing in computer music, completed his doctorate at Stanford University and joined the faculty at Michigan State University in East Lansing.[124] Mitchell was intrigued by the lifestyle available in the rural areas outside East Lansing, and Wessel encouraged him to leave Chicago and settle in central Michigan. According to Mitchell, "I had a conversation with him, and he said, 'Come here and I'll help you find a place to live." That's when I decided to move into the country."[125] Mitchell's new residence was a farmhouse surrounded by some twenty acres of land, a secluded setting that suited him perfectly:

> I'm trying to slow myself down and do a lot of composing, do a lot of writing. That takes a lot of time. I like the freedom that the country gives me to be able to play at any time that I want to, no matter what hour, morning to night. I can get up at 3 o'clock in the morning and play if I want to. It's more of a free atmosphere and I just can't imagine how I could ever go back and live in an apartment building.[126]

In the fall of 1973, Mitchell and the other members of the Art Ensemble led a one-week workshop for Wessel's students at Michigan State. The musicians taught classes on composition, improvisation, and instrument design, among other subjects, and ended the workshop with a public concert.[127] For Mitchell, this was the first of many teaching engagements at the university level, experiences he would eventually parlay into a career as a professor of music. (The pinnacle of his academic career came in 2007, when he was appointed to the Darius Milhaud Chair of Composition at Mills College in Oakland, California.[128]) In 1974, Mitchell and approximately thirty young musicians from East Lansing established the Creative Arts Collective (CAC), a nonprofit organization "based on the fundamentals of the AACM."[129] The CAC staged concerts at local venues, following the model provided by the AACM, and also linked East Lansing musicians with veteran performers from other cities, primarily Chicago and Detroit.[130] Mitchell served as the CAC's president from its founding until 1977, when he moved to a 365-acre farm near Madison, Wisconsin.[131] The move to Wisconsin, however, did not keep him from collaborating with CAC members and other Michigan musicians. In 1980, he formed the Sound Ensemble, a quintet that included trumpeter Hugh Ragin and a rhythm section associated with the CAC: bassist Jaribu Shahid, drummer Tani Tabbal, and guitarist Spencer Barefield, who succeeded Mitchell as the CAC's president.[132] Also around this time, Mitchell introduced the Space Ensemble, a chamber trio with vocalist Thomas Buckner and multi-instrumentalist Gerald Oshita, two Bay Area musicians whom he met during the Art Ensemble's 1968 visit to California.[133] Like Mitchell, Buckner and Oshita were keenly interested in contemporary concert music as well as jazz, and the compositions that Mitchell wrote for the Space Ensemble drew equally from both of these styles. The Sound Ensemble and the Space Ensemble remained active until the end of the 1980s, when he formed two new side projects: the Note Factory, an expanded version of the Sound Ensemble with two bassists and two drummers; and the New Chamber Ensemble, which performed his concert-music compositions. By the 1990s, Mitchell was writing concert works for a variety of ensembles, including the classical orchestra. Many of these chamber and orchestral compositions were commissioned by Buckner or the New York conductor Petr Kotik, director of the S.E.M. Ensemble. Kotik, an accomplished composer in his own right, proved to be a vigorous advocate of Mitchell's music, and premiered more of his works than any other conductor in the United States or Europe.[134]

The side projects led by Bowie often drew inspiration from the music scene of his hometown. When he returned to St. Louis in 1971, he initiated collaborations with local performers, including members of BAG. By 1974, several BAG musicians had moved to New York, where they became vital participants in the loft-jazz scene, and Bowie started traveling to the city for performances with his St. Louis colleagues.[135] A few years later, in 1977, he too relocated to New York, joining in a "mass migration" of AACM members to the capital of the nation's music industry.[136] Bowie's move to New York coincided with an unfortunate event—legal separation from his wife—but after their marriage ended, Bowie and Fontella Bass were not completely estranged.[137] Instead, they continued to make music together, notably in his side project From the Root to the Source, which performed a blend of classic rhythm-and-blues songs and traditional gospel. Bowie needed three vocalists for this band, and he recruited some of the best he knew: Bass, her younger brother David Peaston, and their mother, Martha Bass. Peaston was a talented rhythm-and-blues performer, just like his sister, and both siblings were taught to sing by their mother, a former member of Clara Ward's acclaimed gospel group.[138] Bowie formed From the Root to the Source in 1979 and led the band for almost two decades.[139] During this period, the charismatic Bowie became one of the most beloved trumpeters in jazz and experimental music—"the major trumpet force on this planet," according to a *Coda* magazine critic.[140] He worked in a select few high-profile jazz groups, notably Jack DeJohnette's New Directions quartet and the Leaders, a post-bop sextet.[141] Bowie also successfully infiltrated the realm of pop culture, recording the theme song for the eighth season of *The Cosby Show* and appearing on his near-namesake David Bowie's album *Black Tie White Noise*.[142] Even as his fame grew, he remained committed to serving as an activist on behalf of the musicians' community, as he had done in Chicago and St. Louis. He became the second member of the Art Ensemble to form an AACM-style artists' collective when, in 1985, he cofounded the Musicians of Brooklyn Initiative (MOBI) with Oliver Lake and Cecil Taylor.[143]

Bowie's best-known side project was Brass Fantasy, an innovative nine-piece ensemble with eight brass players and one drummer. The concept of a brass-dominated nonet had interested Bowie for some time: "I first got the idea back in the early days of the AACM, when we used to do all sorts of different types of unorthodox groups."[144] He launched Brass Fantasy with a European tour in 1984 and kept the band going for fifteen years, long enough to make seven studio albums and two live recordings.[145] Brass Fantasy's repertoire included a handful of original pieces composed by Bowie and other members of the group, but much of the band's book consisted of hit songs from the 1950s to the 1980s and 1990s, recast in new arrangements that showcased the expressive possibilities of brass instruments. "I have a staff of writers," Bowie stated. "And when I feel a song—when I hear something on the radio that I like or it's just a song I like, I give it to one of the writers and ask them to give me an arrangement on it."[146] In 1997, he hired his youngest daughter, then in her teens, as his "repertoire consultant," and following her advice, he commissioned arrangements of songs by the Notorious B.I.G., the Spice Girls, and TLC.[147] For Bowie, Brass Fantasy was the last piece of the puzzle, the final link in the chain. With the Art Ensemble, From the Root to the Source, and Brass Fantasy, he had three groups that comprised his "total musical personality":

> The Art Ensemble is just an art group. It's experimental and searching and trying to extend the boundaries of the music, of the techniques, the compositions, the whole thing. . . . Brass Fantasy is what I call my avant-pop band. . . . Instead of my normal, white lab jacket, I wear a white, sequin lab jacket with Brass Fantasy, because it's a show band. What we try to do is to play popular music, but in a creative manner and in a way that people have never really heard of before. . . . It's about extending the language of the brass choir into the popular arena. The Root to the Source [is] a combination of gospel, jazz, and rhythm and blues. . . . [I]t takes those three to really express myself. I couldn't really express myself in any one way, or with any one group, or playing one particular sort of style.[148]

Jarman's post-1971 side projects closely resembled the creative pursuits he had engaged in before joining the Art Ensemble. He played solo concerts in which he sang, recited poetry, and played an array of musical instruments, as in his 1960s solo performances.[149] He also led Return from Exile, an all-AACM band, and in 1976 he began a long-term collaboration with his Art Ensemble bandmate Moye.[150] Jarman and Moye performed together in several different configurations. As a duo, they recorded the live album *Egwu-Anwu*—"Sun Song," in the Igbo language of southern Nigeria.[151] For tours and studio sessions, they often added a guest musician (pianist Don Pullen, bassist Essiet Essiet, multi-instrumentalist Johnny Dyani), expanding their group into a trio that they called the Magic Triangle. Moreover, Jarman's musical activities were not restricted to solo concerts and small-group performances. He continued to present large-scale intermedia events featuring musicians, poets, and other artists. One of his events, the 1975 production *Homage Song to the New Republic*, was funded by the NEA, which two years earlier had awarded composition grants to Jarman and the rest of the Art Ensemble.[152]

In 1982, Jarman moved from Chicago to New York, and announced his arrival with an intermedia performance at the downtown Public Theater.[153] This event, entitled *Liberation Suite*, featured his newly formed Sunbound Ensemble, an eight-piece band augmented by an actor, a dancer, and the poet Thulani Davis, Jarman's wife. The Public Theater sold out for Jarman's first concert appearance in his new city, and local critics received *Liberation Suite* as a successful New York debut.[154] Jarman and Davis settled in Fort Greene, the same Brooklyn neighborhood where Bowie lived.[155] During the 1980s, Jarman grew more involved with Buddhism and aikido, a Japanese martial art he had studied in Chicago.[156] He started teaching aikido professionally, and in 1990 he traveled to Kyoto, Japan, to be ordained as a Jodo Shinshu priest, thirty years after his introduction to Buddhism at a public library in Tucson, Arizona. He returned to the United States as Shaku Joseph Jarman, and he and Davis founded the Brooklyn Buddhist Association, which met in a storefront space that also served as his aikido dojo.[157] (*Shaku* is the title used by priests in the Shinshu school of Buddhism.) Many of Jarman's students at the Brooklyn Buddhist Association and Jikishinkan Dojo were musicians, and with them he formed LifeTime Visions, a musical ensemble with a spiritual mission. "I realized that I could express the Buddhist perspective through the music," Jarman affirmed, "and since then, that is what I have been doing."[158]

Moye saw Chicago for the first time in 1971, when he moved there with his bandmates. It was not long before he became a coveted sideman on the Chicago scene, known for his proficiency on hand drums and other percussion instruments as well as the drum set. Moye performed with local jazz combos, notably those of saxophonist Von Freeman and pianist Willie Pickens, two Windy City icons. He also played for the Darlene Blackburn Dance Troupe, Val Gray Ward's Kuumba Theatre, and the Pharaohs, a South Side funk band. Additionally, Moye joined a variety of experimental groups led by AACM veterans such as Muhal Richard Abrams, Fred Anderson, Amina Claudine

Myers, and Henry Threadgill.[159] Moye was one of several new members welcomed into the Association in the early 1970s, a cohort that also included
Chico Freeman (Von's son) and Ari Brown, both of whom would become
close collaborators. With Brown, he co-led a small group that performed
around Chicago and in Europe.[160] His partnership with Freeman gained momentum in the late 1970s, after the latter musician relocated to Manhattan.[161]
Moye's primary residence was in Chicago, but during this period he kept a
second apartment in New York, because he visited so frequently to work with
Freeman, Hamiet Bluiett, Julius Hemphill, and Don Pullen.[162] In 1983, Moye
and Freeman organized the first edition of the Leaders jazz sextet, with Don
Cherry in the trumpet chair; three years later, Moye invited Bowie to join the
group as Cherry's replacement.[163] Bowie returned the favor by hiring Moye
to play percussion for Brass Fantasy.[164] In the Leaders, Brass Fantasy, and the
Art Ensemble, Moye's responsibilities extended beyond the bandstand. He
served all three groups as road manager, in charge of logistics and handling
money.[165] In this position, Moye's language skills were just as useful as his administrative abilities: a fluent speaker of French, German, and Italian, he could
communicate about business matters nearly everywhere his groups toured.[166]

Moye's abiding interest in the percussion music of the African diaspora
would eventually take him all over the world, but it also helped him find
a like-minded musical community in his new hometown. After arriving in
Chicago, he joined the Sun Drummers, a percussion ensemble founded by
Atuque Harold Murray. With the Sun Drummers, Moye accompanied dance
troupes and directed workshops in the city's public schools.[167] Atu Murray's
knowledge of West African percussion traditions came from several years of
study in Ghana, and he taught Moye "the art of making drums, how to cure
skins and mount them on the drums, and functions of different instruments
in religious ceremonies and regular entertainment."[168] The Afrocentric philosophy of the Sun Drummers resonated with Moye: as he told *Black Music
and Jazz Review*, the group played "music from the sun," because "we are the
sun people."[169] He began using the phrase "sun percussion" to describe his
distinctive instrument collection as well as some of the side projects he led,
from solo performances like his 1975 album *Sun Percussion Volume One* to the
band Sun Percussion Summit, which he established in the mid-1990s.[170] For
Sun Percussion Volume One, he adopted the name Famoudou, after Famoudou
Konaté, a djembe drummer and arranger for Les Ballets Africains, Guinea's
national dance company—the very same ensemble that had inspired Favors
to start playing "little instruments."[171] In 1978, Moye added Dougoufana to
his name, in honor of a drummer from another African dance company, Le

Ballet National du Senegal.[172] However, this addition was only temporary, and Dougoufana Famoudou Moye soon became Famoudou Don Moye once again. At the end of the 1970s, Moye started traveling to Guadeloupe, Haiti, and Jamaica to learn about local styles of percussion music, "a drum tradition that comes pretty much in a pure form directly from West Africa."[173] He visited West Africa in 1985, on a concert tour with percussionist Hartmut Geerken and saxophonist John Tchicai. During this tour, the trio performed in Sierra Leone, Liberia, and Guinea, three neighboring countries on the Atlantic coast. At the Palais du Peuple in Conakry, Guinea, Moye enjoyed a "marvelous encounter," according to *Jazz Podium* magazine: "After the concert, a short man came up to the musicians and congratulated them on their music. It was the best West African drummer . . . Famoudou Konaté."[174]

Moye's investigations of African music did not stop at the Sahara, the geographical boundary separating North Africa from the rest of the continent. His 1968 visit to Morocco had exposed him to North African music, and he heard echoes of this tradition beyond Africa, in the "trans-Mediterranean culture" of southern Europe.[175] He learned much about Mediterranean music from the Sardinian bassist Marcello Melis, his rhythm-section partner in the old Steve Lacy group and a frequent collaborator from the 1970s to the 1990s.[176] Moye's personal connections with Melis and other European musicians helped him become a sought-after performer and clinician in Italy and elsewhere in Europe. By 2000, he was splitting his time between Chicago and Italy. Moye left Chicago for good in 2010, staying for a brief period in Morocco, and ultimately settling in Marseille, France, a cosmopolitan port city sited along the Mediterranean.[177]

Unlike the other members of the Art Ensemble, Favors never left the South Side of Chicago. Indeed, the group's European sojourn from 1969 to 1971 represented his only extended absence from the city of his birth. When Favors returned to the United States, he resumed faithful attendance at his family's church, Friendly Temple, where he served as a deacon and also as a musician, playing electric bass for Sunday worship services.[178] Beyond the church walls, he was something of a folk hero in Chicago's African American community, admired for his musical accomplishments and also for being a stalwart "race man."[179] As his friend Kahil El'Zabar said, Favors was "a major human being, but he still lived on the South Side where everyone knew him. That's supportive leadership."[180]

After 1971, Favors participated in a number of side projects, often with his Art Ensemble bandmates. He played in Jarman's Return from Exile as well as Bowie's 1970s groups, and in 1979 he joined From the Root to the Source.[181]

Additionally, Favors contributed to several projects led by Mitchell, including the recording of *The Maze*, Mitchell's inventive composition for percussion octet.[182] In 1975, he became Malachi Favors Maghostut, his new name a tribute to the Egyptian deity Hermes Trismegistus and the pharaoh Tutankhamun.[183] Favors described Maghostut as an ancient Egyptian word meaning "I am the host," an evocative phrase alluding to his intellectual interests in Egyptology, African history, and the connections between African spirituality and African American Christianity.[184] (The name was so evocative, in fact, that the writer Nathaniel Mackey adapted it for the title character of his novel *Djbot Baghostus's Run*.[185]) Favors's new name helped him establish an identity apart from the Art Ensemble, and he used it for all the side projects he led, from his solo concerts to his Maghostut small group, an ensemble he debuted in the early 1980s.[186] As a bandleader, Favors rarely performed outside Chicago, but he found ample opportunities to tour and record as a sideman with his AACM colleagues. Beginning in the 1970s, he worked in Europe with both Muhal Richard Abrams and Fred Anderson.[187] He joined Kahil El'Zabar's Ritual Trio at its founding in 1985 and traveled extensively with the group for nearly twenty years.[188] And in 2000, when he was well into his seventies, he became an original member of Wadada Leo Smith's Golden Quartet.[189] "So my thing is," Favors reasoned, "I'm just going to keep playing, as the old folks say, until the Lord says stop."[190]

7 *Live at Mandel Hall*

Everybody is the leader and the sideman simultaneously.[1]

Live at Mandel Hall was the first recording made by the "classic" five-person Art Ensemble after the band's return to the United States.[2] The album was also the first to reflect the post-1971 changes in the group's social model. Both of these factors recommend the 15 January 1972 concert at Mandel Hall as a worthy candidate for musical analysis.[3] However, the most compelling aspect of *Live at Mandel Hall* must be the superior quality of the performance. *Live at Mandel Hall* was an extraordinary event, perhaps the best Art Ensemble concert ever captured on audiotape. And yet, it was also a typical Art Ensemble performance, because its overall architecture and the improvisational techniques used by the musicians can be heard in every one of the group's concerts. Accordingly, the analysis that follows will address both sides of *Live at Mandel Hall*—its exceptional musical moments as well as the ways these moments relate to the core elements of the band's performance practice.

The members of the Art Ensemble prepared for the Mandel Hall concert in the usual fashion, with a series of daily rehearsals in which they practiced their repertoire of original compositions, from familiar material to newer pieces written in the previous few

intensity structure	0:00-4:38
"Duffvipels"	4:38-8:15
transition	8:15-19:18
"Checkmate"	19:18-29:11
transition	29:11-34:30
intensity structure	34:30-52:50
transition	52:50-75:05
"Mata Kimasu"	75:05-76:03

EXAMPLE 7.1 *Live at Mandel Hall:* formal diagram

months.[4] However, they waited until right before the concert to determine which compositions would make up the set list, as Favors explained: "About 10 or 20 minutes before we go on the stage, we say, 'What do you feel like playing?' and then we just play whatever we feel like playing at that particular time."[5] During the performance, the set list functioned as a provisional "sketch," in Bowie's description:

> [W]e put a basic sketch in our minds of what we may want to do, what tunes we may want to cover, but at the same time we don't limit ourselves. We will play a song that we haven't said that we were going to play, and we've conditioned ourselves, if something comes up, to go with it. . . . You don't say, "Hey, man, we're not supposed to play that this set." You just kind of go with the flow. So we kind of put a sketch, but we leave that sketch open to change. . . . I mean, sometimes we go on the stage with no idea. We have what we call "stoop and hit," which means just hit. We ask, "Hey, what do you feel like playing?" Nobody says anything. "Well, let's just stoop and hit." And we go on out there with no idea what we're going to play.[6]

The set list that the musicians chose on the evening of 15 January 1972 included just three compositions: "Duffvipels," "Checkmate," and "Mata Kimasu." They also decided to begin the performance with an "intensity structure," a characteristic style of group improvisation that often appeared in Art Ensemble performances (see example 7.1).[7] Some bands working in jazz and experimental music would consider such a set list far too short for a lengthy performance. But for the Art Ensemble and other AACM groups, three compositions and one stylistic framework could provide more than enough material. As Muhal Richard Abrams once observed, "I had to write quite a bit until I had musicians who could create a part, and then I wrote less and less. Now I can take eight measures and play a concert."[8]

Like most Art Ensemble concerts, the Mandel Hall performance was organized as a "suite," a nonstop performance lasting seventy-six minutes.[9] Instead of pausing after each piece, the group members connected it to the next entry on the set list with an "improvisational transition" (see example 7.1).[10] In certain instances, a transition might be scripted prior to the concert, but more often than not, transitions were spontaneously conceived and executed in real time. The musicians crafted each transition to fit the larger narrative arc of the performance, a procedure involving several different improvisational strategies. They could converge toward a particular composition or stylistic framework, or diverge away from it, two processes commonly employed in jazz performance and also in theatrical improvisation.[11] Alternatively, the members of the Art Ensemble could improvise in ways that were less about forging consensus and more about exercising autonomy—modes of performance where "[t]he instruments function completely independently," as Mitchell put it.[12] This conception of group improvisation was developed as early as the 1960s by various AACM members, including Anthony Braxton and Leo Smith.[13] Furthermore, such approaches to improvisation can be directly correlated with the Art Ensemble's post-1971 social model, in which individual autonomy was valued as highly as cooperation. The transitional passages of *Live at Mandel Hall*, and indeed the entire performance, can be understood as musical realizations of the Art Ensemble's social practices, a perspective that will be central to this analysis. The other key perspective behind the analysis is the contingent nature of improvisation. An audio recording or a musical transcription can provide a partial representation of a performance, but every sound wave or transcribed note reflects a multitude of decisions by the individual musicians, including choices not made and paths not taken. In improvisation, nothing is predetermined, and therefore this analysis focuses not only on the music as such but also on the decision-making processes from which the music emerged.[14]

Intensity/"Duffvipels"

The musicians open the performance with a spectacular, thunderous pulsation. Together they play a synchronized stream of low notes at the remarkably rapid rate of five attacks per second. Moye hammers away at his drum set,

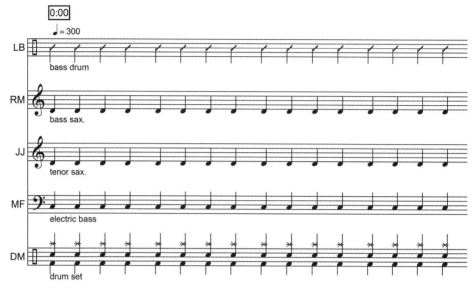

EXAMPLE 7.2 Intensity structure: opening pulse pattern

* The musical examples in this chapter are the author's transcriptions, reproduced by permission of Art Ensemble of Chicago Publishing (ASCAP). Each staff is labeled with the performer's initials. The examples represent pitches in the keys of the instruments being played, and may be read as scores for improvisers. The chapter text refers to pitches in concert key, and adopts the convention in which middle C is labeled C_4.

Bowie thumps a concert bass drum, and the others hit the lowest Cs that their instruments can produce (Jarman on tenor saxophone, Mitchell on bass saxophone, and Favors on electric bass). This sudden rush of sound is stunning to hear, not least because the musicians start out at what seems like full volume—and then get louder and louder (see example 7.2).

After forty-eight consecutive low Cs, Jarman begins an improvised solo by leaping up two octaves into the tenor saxophone's altissimo register. Mitchell promptly offers a counterpoint to this gesture, sliding downward to $A\flat_1$ at the very bottom of the bass saxophone's range. Then he lays out, leaving Jarman to contend with the thick texture created by his bandmates. Bowie is still striking the bass drum as fast as he can, falling only slightly behind the swift pace established at the outset. Favors and Moye, in contrast, have abandoned the pulse pattern to play irregular, fractal phrases that match the complexity of Jarman's saxophone line. In no time at all they have assembled an intensity structure, the first item on the set list. (For more on intensity structures, see the analysis of "Get in Line" in chapter 4.) The primary melodic voice in the intensity structure belongs to Jarman, but Favors soon introduces a short, repeating melody—two F_3s followed by three $B\flat_3$s—that becomes a

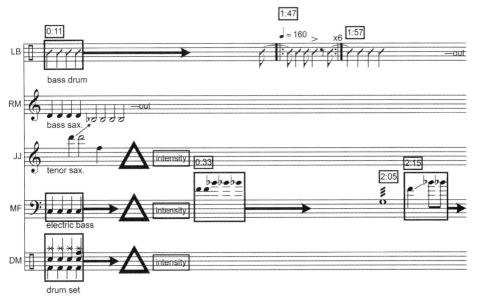

EXAMPLE 7.3 Intensity structure: building the intensity structure

* In this example, boxes indicate motives that repeat, diagonal arrows denote musical interactions between performers, and the triangles are symbols that mean "improvise(d)."

secondary focal point (see example 7.3). Here, Favors is responding to what both Jarman and Moye are playing. He echoes Jarman's altissimo line with an upper-register figure of his own, and he builds his melody from two pitches a perfect fourth apart, the same interval used to tune Moye's drum set. The saxophone and drum set can contribute more textural density than most other instruments in the Art Ensemble's arsenal, and for this reason Jarman and Moye are the performers best able to sustain this intensity structure.[15] However, when Favors deftly integrates his bass part with Jarman and Moye, he takes on much the same responsibility for the intensity structure as well as the power to help bring it to a close.

The first significant change in the texture comes not from Favors, but from Bowie. At 1:47, he moves away from the steady pulse to play a syncopated figure on the bass drum. Ten seconds later, Bowie reintroduces the familiar pulse pattern, restoring the intensity structure to its initial state. Favors elaborates on Bowie's idea, playing a drone on the bass's G string for ten seconds, then returning to his repeating F–B♭ melody (see example 7.3).

After the exchange between Bowie and Favors, the musicians prolong the intensity structure for two more minutes, urged on by Moye, who some-

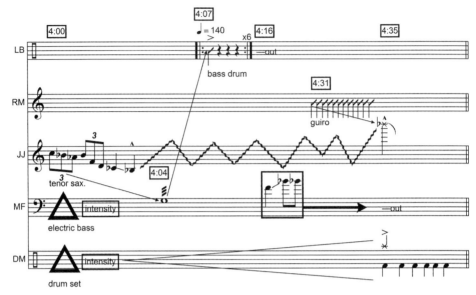

EXAMPLE 7.4 Intensity structure: ending the intensity structure

how finds a way to play even louder. Then, at 4:00, Jarman plunges into his
saxophone's low register, an area he had conspicuously avoided throughout
his solo. Favors quickly responds, revisiting the G-string drone he played
two minutes earlier, and Bowie follows his lead, playing six booming bass-
drum strokes. Any of these three gestures — Jarman's low-register line, Favors's
open-string drone, Bowie's drum accents — could be interpreted as a cue to
end the intensity structure. Yet, no one attempts to construct an ending, and
the intensity structure continues at full tilt: Jarman returns to the altissimo
register, Bowie drops out completely, and Favors goes back to his F–B♭ melody
once again (see example 7.4).

Seconds later, the volume level of Jarman's microphone begins to fluc-
tuate as he sways from side to side, drawing his bandmates' attention and
preparing them for a visual signal. Favors and Moye keep playing as they
await Jarman's next move. Then Mitchell, who has been silent for some three
minutes, reenters the fray, furiously scraping a guiro. The other musicians
react immediately. Jarman pivots away from the microphone, then reaches for
a high note, and at the same instant Moye plays a cymbal-and-drum accent,
decisively ending the intensity structure (see example 7.4). After this exciting
episode, the audience surely must ask if the Art Ensemble can maintain such
a high energy level for the entire performance. This question will arise anew

midway through the concert, when the musicians summon another intensity structure and develop it into a source of great drama.

As the sound of Moye's cymbal slowly decays, Mitchell shouts, "All aboard, all aboard—last train for Duffytown!" With this announcement, given in a comical voice reminiscent of a midcentury animated cartoon, Mitchell initiates his composition "Duffvipels," the next item on the set list. "Duffvipels" contains elements of intermedia, like many of the pieces he composed for the Art Ensemble. Some of these intermedia compositions involve theatrical scenarios that define a character or dramatic situation (for instance, "Get in Line" and "Song for Charles" from the album *A Jackson in Your House*, analyzed in chapter 4). Another compositional form used by Mitchell is the cinematic or television theme, a tuneful, through-composed piece usually deployed at a climactic moment in a performance ("The Waltz," also examined in chapter 4, is a prime example). "Duffvipels" is unique because it combines aspects of both formal types. As the musicians transition toward the piece, they improvise a theatrical sketch that depicts a train conductor and several passengers bound for "Duffytown." This intermedia vignette leads into the musical portion of the piece, which culminates with Mitchell's through-composed theme, creating the first major point of arrival in the concert.

Mitchell's bandmates respond to his verbal exclamation with various little instruments: bicycle horns, cymbals, and a ratchet. When he announces "all aboard" again, they answer by calling out the names of AACM members in attendance at Mandel Hall—Muhal Richard Abrams, Fred Anderson, Douglas Ewart, Kalaparusha Maurice McIntyre—beckoning them to board the imaginary train conjured up by the Art Ensemble. After this friendly salutation to their AACM colleagues, the musicians begin to lay the foundation for the "Duffvipels" theme. This process starts at 5:26, when Favors introduces the composition's bass line, an oompah pattern in the key of F that bears a strong resemblance to the bass vamps heard in two other Mitchell compositions, "A Jackson in Your House" and "Get in Line." Four measures later, Jarman briefly marks time by playing a few guiro scrapes and then yields to Moye, who joins in with an old-fashioned shuffle beat. The last performers to enter are Bowie and Mitchell. Bowie, on trumpet, offers a few playful phrases made up of mouthpiece noises and half-valve yelps, the sounds of a dawdling passenger trying to clamber onto the locomotive as it pulls away from the station. Mitchell grinds a ratchet, signifying on Bowie's trumpet line and mimicking the rotating gears of the train. Bowie brings the introductory passage to a close when he moves into the lower register of his horn and doubles Favors's bass

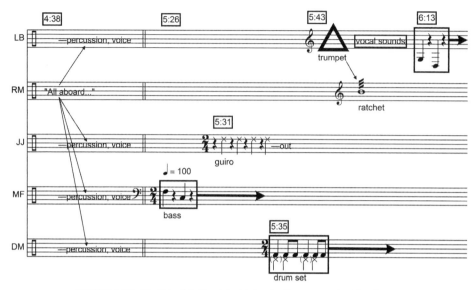

EXAMPLE 7.5 "Duffvipels": theatrical introduction, preparing the theme

line, alternating natural tones and raspberry-like pedal tones. This gesture, too, can be heard as representational. According to Mitchell, "'Duffvipels' was written at a time when I stopped smoking cigarettes and is a scramble of the words Devil Puffs."[16] It is easy to visualize a cartoon, perhaps drawn in the madcap style of classic American animation, in which a train's smokestack is rendered as a cigarette, with each of Bowie's trumpet tones matched to a puff of smoke. These sounds also serve an important musical purpose, telling Jarman and Mitchell to get ready for their upcoming entrance (see example 7.5).

Eight measures later, the musicians arrive at the "Duffvipels" theme, which is divided into four sections: an eight-bar A section written in the contrapuntal style of early jazz, a brassy seven-bar B section, a five-bar C section that ends with an upper-register squawk, and a five-bar D section that sounds like a beginning as well as an ending (see example 7.6). They repeat the melody once, then twice, and with each pass through the formally ambiguous D section, the theme seems more and more circular.[17] By the third statement of the theme, the unrelenting melodic loop has built up an overwhelming tension. During the fourth iteration of the theme, the members of the Art Ensemble finally break the loop: they play the A, B, and C sections as before, but instead of proceeding to the D section, they return to the C section and transform its melody into a rollicking vocal chorus: "Duffy deefy difey duffels" (see example 7.7). The vocal coda ties together all of the threads that make up "Duffvipels," from the cartoon voices of the train-station vignette to the

EXAMPLE 7.6 "Duffvipels": theme

melody composed by Mitchell. This moment of convergence has an immediate impact on the concertgoers, who applaud as soon as the vocal coda ends. George E. Lewis, who was in the audience at Mandel Hall along with many of his AACM colleagues, remembered that "'Duffvipels' hit me like a bomb."[18]

Transition/"Checkmate"

As the hall erupts in applause, Favors plucks the A string of his double bass, letting it resonate while he ventures onto the higher D and G strings, playing warm-toned glissandos and double stops. The other musicians gradually surround his solo line with quiet percussion sounds, and the next section of the performance begins. Moye described this passage as follows:

This is an improvisational transition, collective creativity, collective composition. A lot of stuff we play has all the elements and structure to qualify it

EXAMPLE 7.6 Continued

EXAMPLE 7.7 "Duffvipels": vocal coda

as being a composition. Usually we just named it for the practical purposes
of putting out a record. If we play concerts we don't name every section. . . .
We did a lot of sessions where we would say, "OK, open section number
one, open section number two, bass solo, bass section number one," and
later on if we want that to have a specific name, we give it a name.[19]

The Art Ensemble assigned titles and compositional credits to every piece of
music that appeared on commercial recordings, whether it was composed in

advance or in real time. This practice, according to Moye, helped the musicians challenge the misconceptions of record producers and other music-industry figures who assumed that the group's improvisations were unprepared or unrehearsed:

> You have to have a name for everything, a description, and a detailed analysis, otherwise they're going to label it as a random event, or "free jazz," or whatever. So we always make sure that if anybody asks us what we're doing, we always say the same thing generally. If they ask a general question, they get a general answer. If they ask a specific question, it's either "none of your business," or "why are you asking me when Moye is the one you should be asking?" They always try to make like it's some random event. But in the historical perspective, it's clear that the element of random stuff is minimal. They don't know about our rehearsal procedure.[20]

The members of the Art Ensemble did not always improvise in rehearsals.[21] Nevertheless, every aspect of their rehearsal method was designed to prepare the musicians to improvise together during concerts. In addition to practicing their book of compositions, they worked diligently to internalize a wide range of musical styles that would ultimately resurface in live performances. The group members called this approach "the hot 20," as Moye recalled:

> Our standard rehearsal format was to begin with what we called "the hot 20," because we made it a point to play 20 different kinds of music. Hit tunes, classical pieces, whatever was in the air; then we'd work on improvisation and original compositions. We believed that you had to be aware of all the forms in order to make your improvisations relevant.[22]

The musicians draw on a number of "hot 20" styles throughout *Live at Mandel Hall*, beginning with the eleven-minute transition that follows "Duffvipels." This transitional passage starts at 8:15, as a Favors bass solo loosely in the key of A minor. Moye joins in on bells and triangle, constructing a high-register, metallic accompaniment that complements the low, woody tones of Favors's unamplified double bass.[23] Jarman and Mitchell are the next to enter, playing marimba and bell lyre, respectively, and the texture reaches a point of temporary stability as a bass solo supported by atmospheric percussion. At 9:52, Bowie stealthily appears, using his trumpet to make soft, breathy mouthpiece noises (see example 7.8). Although these sounds fit with the accompaniment style adopted by the other musicians, Bowie's rather late arrival could be

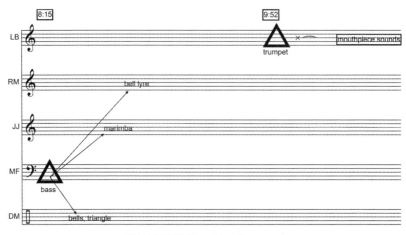

EXAMPLE 7.8 Transition: Favors solo

interpreted by his bandmates as an attempt to change the texture, not prolong it. However, if the others react to Bowie, it is hardly noticeable. The effect of his entrance may be felt most strongly by the listeners in the hall, who can observe Bowie, cheeks expanded, addressing the microphone with his horn.

After Bowie's understated entrance, Favors remains in control of the group improvisation. At 11:19, three minutes into the transition, he begins to play a slow, walking bass line in A minor, confirming the key suggested during his bass solo. Moye responds with a flourish of bells, then a light cymbal crash synchronized with one of Favors's quarter notes. On the very next beat, Favors moves into a scale-wise bass line that clearly outlines the A-minor triad before leading into an unambiguous cadence: B_2–E_3–A_2, a II–V–I progression in A minor. Bowie and Moye support Favors's attempt to articulate a cadence, playing simultaneous accents that make his quarter-note A_2 feel like a downbeat (see example 7.9). With this interaction, the texture shifts from an out-of-tempo bass solo to the related but distinct realm of the minor-key jazz ballad. In the new stylistic framework, Favors becomes a rhythm-section accompanist rather than a featured soloist, and Bowie is given an opportunity to take charge of the texture with a trumpet solo. However, Bowie refuses to play the soloist role, and instead contributes hand-muted tones that stay in the background, alongside Moye's delicate brushwork and Mitchell and Jarman's unobtrusive percussion sounds.

The musicians continue in the same vein for another four minutes, a long stretch of time for a stylistic framework as ambiguous as a jazz ballad lacking a clear-cut melodic lead. For Moye, this was one of the most precarious sections of the concert: "We have to be careful with this kind of playing—it has

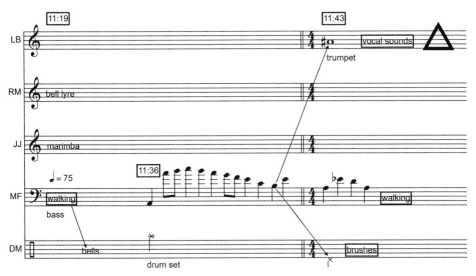

EXAMPLE 7.9 Transition: jazz ballad

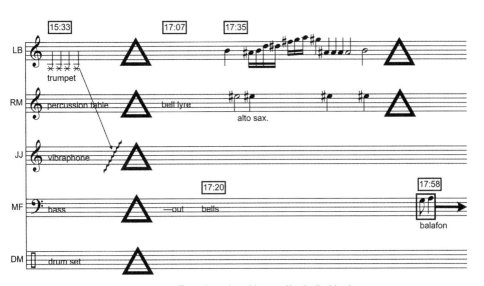

EXAMPLE 7.10 Transition: breaking up the ballad texture

to stay fresh. Sometimes a live performance starts meandering."[24] So Bowie decides to intervene at 15:33, offering a string of unpredictably timed G_3s that disrupts the rhythm section's groove. Jarman silences his vibraphone for an instant, then returns with a wash of rapid glissandos up and down the vibraphone's three-octave range (see example 7.10). The slow-tempo jazz ballad soon dissolves into a free-tempo exchange, a texture not unlike the

EXAMPLE 7.11 Transition: Bowie ballad phrases

bass solo from the very beginning of the transition. These two passages are similar in many ways, from the presence of multiple percussion instruments to the absence of a regular beat. However, in the broader arc of the performance, they fulfill completely different functions. During the bass solo, the members of the Art Ensemble diverged from "Duffvipels" and engaged in open improvisation, eventually settling on an identifiable stylistic framework, the minor-key jazz ballad. When this framework ran its course, the musicians brought back certain elements of the previous texture, but with a new possibility at hand: converging toward "Checkmate," the third item on the set list. Favors is the first group member to envision this outcome. At 17:20, he puts his bass down so he can play bells. A moment later, he switches instruments again, moving from bells to balafon, the West African xylophone he will play in "Checkmate" (see example 7.10). The sounds of Favors's balafon encourage the musicians to consider how they might arrive at "Checkmate," but the group does not immediately converge on the composition. Indeed, even after Favors has shifted to balafon, Bowie finally ventures into the jazz ballad style, playing several idiomatic phrases that would have fit perfectly over the slow groove that prevailed a few minutes earlier (see example 7.11). If Favors is moving the music forward, as Moye would say, Bowie is providing a backward glance at a stylistic framework that the band has left behind.[25]

The transition ends at 19:18, when the musicians abruptly transform the texture.[26] Jarman moves from vibraphone to balafon, Mitchell starts playing the small drums on his percussion table, and Moye stays on drum set but changes from brushes to mallets. Favors, who switched to balafon more than a minute earlier, introduces a two-note motive, B_4–$C\sharp_5$, played in a short-long rhythmic pattern. The balafon motive belongs to Mitchell's composition "Checkmate," and is one of the key components that define the piece (see example 7.12). "Checkmate" is a modular composition structured similarly to other modular works by Mitchell, Anthony Braxton, and minimalist composers like Philip Glass, Steve Reich, and Terry Riley. Such pieces are constructed from a handful of simple musical modules, some of which may be just one or two notes in length, and which can be rearranged into many different configurations.[27] "Checkmate" is based on four modules: Favors's balafon motive, single-note

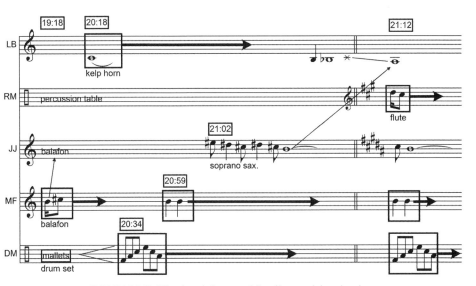

EXAMPLE 7.12 "Checkmate": assembling the modular structure

long tones (playable on any pitched instrument), a propulsive drumbeat, and a flute solo by Mitchell. In performance, the musicians deploy these modules in ways reminiscent of a chess game. Mitchell played chess daily in the late 1960s and early 1970s, and during the Art Ensemble's stay in Europe he had books of opening moves mailed to him from the United States.[28] These chess games motivated the composition of "Checkmate," as Mitchell recalled: "At that time a lot of people played a lot of chess. The result is 'Checkmate.'"[29] If "Checkmate" is like a chess game, the musical modules that make up the composition can be compared to chess pieces. A game of chess begins with the pieces arranged in a standard starting position. In the course of the game, they move independently along the board's eight-by-eight grid. At the endgame—namely, *checkmate*—some pieces have been captured and removed, and the others are dispersed across the board, far away from their initial locations. In Mitchell's "Checkmate," each of the musical modules (or chess pieces) is assigned to one or two members of the Art Ensemble. As the piece unfolds, the musicians interact with one another on a sonic chessboard, with rhythm and pitch as rank and file. By the end of "Checkmate," the modules will be thoroughly altered and realigned, and the music will barely resemble how it sounded at the outset. In this analogy, Mitchell's composition is like a scripted opening move, with the middlegame and endgame left to the devices of the performers.

The members of the Art Ensemble take their time assembling the composition's four musical modules. Favors plays the B_4–$C\sharp_5$ balafon motive for a full minute before Bowie enters on kelp horn (a horn made from lacquered seaweed), playing a sustained C_4.[30] Bowie's long tone is the second modular component of "Checkmate," and Moye soon supplies the third module when he reshapes his diffuse drum-set rhythm into a steady beat. Half a minute later, Jarman switches from balafon to soprano saxophone and plays a stepwise line that ends on a long-tone A_4, the pitch that is the tonal center of "Checkmate." In response, Bowie starts to gravitate toward A_3, one octave below Jarman's note. When Bowie lands on A_3, Jarman plays another long-tone A_4, and at the same time Mitchell begins his flute solo, the fourth and final musical module. At last, all of the musicians have converged on "Checkmate" (see example 7.12).

Mitchell bases his improvisation on just two notes, D_5–$C\sharp_5$, which he casts in the same short-long rhythm as Favors's module. In fact, Mitchell's figure is merely an inversion of the B_4–$C\sharp_5$ balafon motive. Mitchell builds phrase after phrase from this elemental figure, expanding and contracting it, then progressively introducing new melodic ideas that always find their way back to D_5–$C\sharp_5$ (see example 7.13). As Mitchell's solo evolves, his bandmates reinterpret their designated modules. Bowie and Jarman start playing shorter notes instead of long tones, and Favors distills his two-note balafon motive into a single pitch, B_4. A minute and a half into Mitchell's solo, at 22:38, Jarman selects a new long tone, $F\sharp_4$, a pitch that could be perceived as a new tonal center, shifting the texture from A major to its relative minor key. Moye hears Jarman's gesture as a turning point in "Checkmate," and answers with a series of cymbal crashes. The other musicians concur with Moye: Jarman drops out, Favors breaks up his pattern to play freely across the balafon, and Bowie sounds a fanfare of fourteen $F\sharp_4$s before falling silent. Mitchell responds in a complementary way, playing slower-paced melodies that match the increasingly sparse, spacious texture (see example 7.14).

Favors is the first to deliberately break with "Checkmate." At 25:39, five minutes into Mitchell's solo, Favors strikes a gong three times, then starts playing a ratchet, an instrument last heard during the theatrical prelude to "Duffvipels." Jarman, now on piccolo, offers a series of long-tone A_5s, returning to the tonal center of "Checkmate" as a concluding gesture. Then Bowie enters on flugelhorn, playing chord arpeggios in a dotted-rhythm pattern, figures that suggest a new stylistic framework—a march (see example 7.15). At this point in the performance, the musicians find themselves at an improvisational crossroads: many paths are open to them, but they can choose only one. Favors's gong crashes and ratchet sounds do not belong to "Checkmate," and

EXAMPLE 7.13 "Checkmate": Mitchell solo, opening phrases

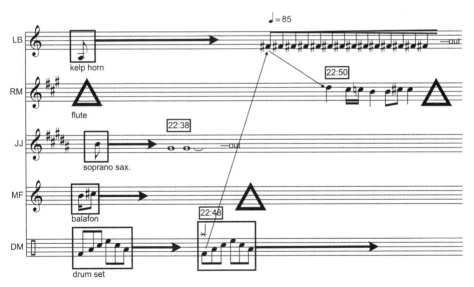

EXAMPLE 7.14 "Checkmate": reshaping the modular structure

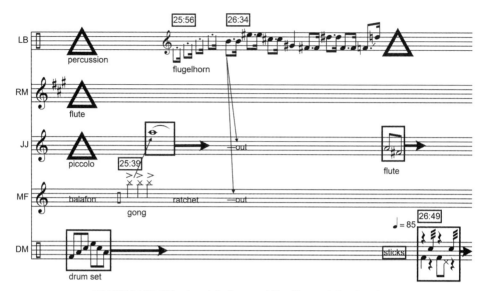

EXAMPLE 7.15 "Checkmate": disassembling the modular structure

might fit most comfortably in one of the Art Ensemble's transitional passages, which often feature percussion instruments. Bowie's march-like flugelhorn line, in comparison, provides not just a way out of "Checkmate" but also an alternative destination. Jarman is not as far along as Favors and Bowie. His long tones are not especially suitable for a transition, and he seems more focused on wrapping up "Checkmate" than on determining what will follow it. Mitchell and Moye, meanwhile, are still playing "Checkmate," but they too sense that the composition is near its conclusion.

The musicians' next collective decision will be crucial. After "Checkmate," there is only one more entry on the set list: "Mata Kimasu," a funk tune that will end the concert. They have been playing for just twenty-six minutes, and it is much too early to converge toward "Mata Kimasu." Instead, they must proceed from "Checkmate" into another open improvisation, as they did after "Duffvipels." This time, though, the group improvisation will have to last for approximately half an hour. Of course, the band members are up for the challenge, or for that matter any test of their music-making abilities. As Bowie declared, "[w]e . . . get into old country ass kicking with the Art Ensemble."[31]

Bowie steps into the breach with a crisp march melody that traces the contours of a B^7 chord. Favors and Jarman defer to Bowie and quickly exit the texture, while Mitchell makes a more subtle adjustment, synchronizing his flute line with Bowie's dotted rhythms. A few seconds later, at 26:49, Moye puts down his mallets, picks up two drumsticks, and starts playing a march

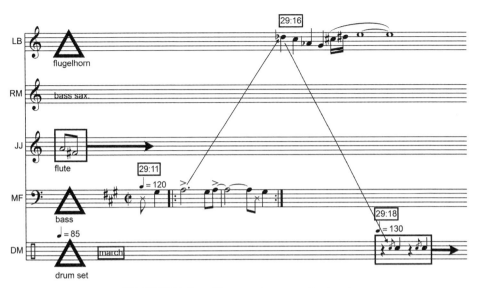

EXAMPLE 7.16 Transition: march groove, Bowie solo

beat at eighty-five beats per minute, confirming the tempo and musical style proposed by Bowie (see example 7.15). From Moye's perspective, this moment in the performance was all about the individual initiative taken by Bowie: "Lester just moved it forward."[32] Yet, it is also clear that Bowie could not have transformed "Checkmate" into a march without the cooperation of his bandmates. Just as in the group's business meetings, every major decision in an Art Ensemble performance was made by consensus.

Transition/Intensity ("Dautalty")

The musicians prolong the march for two and a half minutes, until nearly every trace of "Checkmate" has disappeared. All that remains is a tremolo figure, A_4–$F\sharp_4$, played by Jarman on flute. Then, at 29:11, Favors has an idea: a bass vamp in the key of A major that implies a tempo considerably faster than what prevailed during the march. The texture has become somewhat stagnant after the end of "Checkmate," and in this environment, Favors's irresistible bass line has an immediate, galvanizing effect. Bowie plays a soaring flugelhorn melody that evokes his hometown hero Miles Davis—"an angular approach to the *Sketches of Spain* thing," in Moye's description.[33] As Bowie guides his first phrase upward to D_5, Moye turns to his snare drum and starts playing flams on each upbeat, pushing Favors's tempo slightly and establishing a solid groove (see example 7.16). The speed and fluidity of this textural change are astonishing, even to the members of the Art Ensemble. "We don't practice stuff like that," Moye asserted. "That's a one-in-a-thousand shot there."[34] Although the musicians did not rehearse this transition before the concert, their myriad "hot 20" sessions over the years prepared them to improvise in any style, from minor-key jazz ballads to military marches and Spanish music. Furthermore, they could completely and convincingly shift from one musical style to another at a moment's notice, as demonstrated in this remarkable passage. This transition is one of the most thrilling episodes in the performance, as is the open improvisation that follows, and when the members of the Art Ensemble were preparing *Live at Mandel Hall* for commercial release, they chose to highlight these passages by giving them a shared title: "Dautalty."[35]

Two minutes into the "*Sketches of Spain* thing," Bowie plays three phrases in dialogue with Mitchell, now on soprano saxophone. Then Bowie yields to Mitchell, who at 31:39 takes over as the primary melodic voice and begins an improvised solo. The texture around Mitchell's improvisation recalls the opening of "Checkmate": Bowie and Jarman play long tones, and Favors anchors the texture with a repeating ostinato, while Moye drives the band with a compelling beat—here, a drum-and-bugle-corps cadence. And once again, Mitchell offers an improvisation distinguished by its deceptive simplicity, as he did during "Checkmate." In his "Checkmate" solo, he used a two-note motive as the foundation for an intricate melodic line. Similarly, in this improvisation, he selects two- and three-note fragments of the A-major pentatonic scale and plays them with alternate saxophone fingerings that change the intonation of almost every pitch (see example 7.17).[36] At other points in the performance, Bowie, Favors, and Jarman also explore microtonal playing, but during this passage Mitchell is the only member of the Art Ensemble to employ expressive intonation. His insistent microtones pull and tense against the rest of the texture, particularly the tempered intonation of Favors's bass line. Mitchell is carving out a unique space for himself in the group, setting the stage for an upcoming episode when he will pit his independence and autonomy against his bandmates' efforts to reach a musical consensus.

Jarman accompanies Mitchell with long tones on alto clarinet. He begins with A_2, the top note of Favors's line, and introduces a new, higher pitch in each phrase. In this manner he works his way up the A-minor scale, one long tone at a time, a gradual process that takes nearly three minutes. At 34:30, when Jarman finally arrives on A_3, Moye arrests his cadence-style beat to play a roll on his snare drum. Moye extends his drumroll for four seconds, letting the tension build, and then breaks into a ride-cymbal pattern played at an impossibly fast speed—essentially, what could be called a maximum

EXAMPLE 7.17 Transition: march groove, Mitchell solo

tempo. Mitchell seems to be undisturbed by Moye's rapid cymbal playing, and continues his solo as before. Jarman, though, elects to travel down the path cleared by Moye, switching to balafon and playing vigorous tremolos on $F\sharp_4$ and A_4. Together, Moye and Jarman have created another intensity structure (see example 7.18).

Favors is the next group member to join the intensity structure. After a brief, free-tempo interlude, he shifts to a walking bass line that comes close to the maximum tempo articulated by Moye. However, Mitchell maintains the deliberate pace he set at the beginning of his improvisation, instead of immediately adopting an intense mode of saxophone playing, such as the altissimo line crafted by Jarman during the intensity structure that opened the concert (see example 7.18).

Mitchell's resistance to the style chosen by his bandmates adds another layer of musical complexity to an already complex texture. Favors and Jarman are playing just a bit behind Moye's brisk tempo, but Mitchell's slow, austere saxophone melody occupies a different rhythmic realm altogether. The texture that the group members are developing could be characterized as multi-centered, an approach to group improvisation theorized by Mitchell:

> Let's say we were talking about an improvisational situation. What you would want is a music that offered completely free choices for everyone. That is, I wouldn't be doing anything that would inhibit your choices. Your

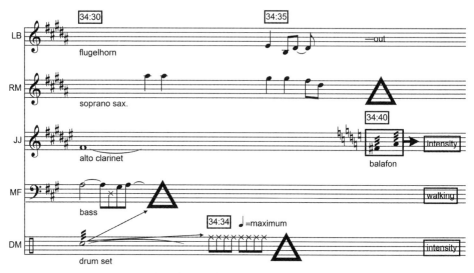

EXAMPLE 7.18 Intensity structure: assembling the intensity structure

choices would still be free and able to exist within the same space. . . . A
lot of the music we experience today is built around a particular center, or
drone, but in this situation we could have multi-centers. When we look at
the function of the rhythm section in so-called "jazz," a lot of the music
will have a particular beat and the bass can be walking a particular line and
the piano will be playing chords of some sort. Now to diffuse that whole
thinking, and create a pure music, would be more along the lines of what I
would be thinking about.[37]

In a multi-centered improvisation, the musicians attempt to remove all exter-
nal constraints on their decision-making. They need not adhere to the performance practices associated with a given musical style, or to their instruments'
standard playing techniques.[38] Indeed, they might not even audibly interact
with their bandmates, an activity often portrayed as fundamental to virtually
every mode of musical performance.[39] According to Mitchell, the musicians
must be as autonomous as possible in order for a multi-centered improvisation
to reach its potential:

The instruments function completely independently. You don't have to back
me up and I don't have to back you up either. And I really would prefer
your not following me. That cuts down on the full dimension of the music.
It makes the music one-dimensional.[40]

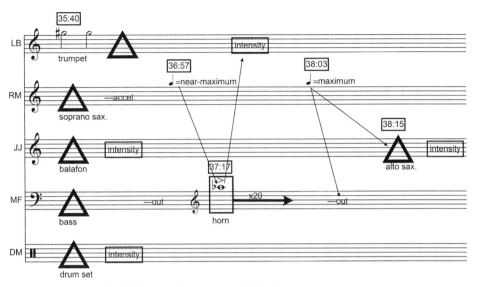

EXAMPLE 7.19 Intensity structure: Mitchell solo, increasing intensity

One minute into the intensity structure, at 35:40, Bowie enters on trumpet, playing smears and shouts in the upper register immediately above Mitchell's soprano saxophone. Bowie's bold "brass witnessing" adds another kind of intensity to the texture, and the other musicians react by playing faster and louder—except for Favors, who has been doing all he can on bass, and decides to take a brief rest.[41] Even Mitchell, the lone holdout from the intensity structure, starts to increase the speed of his saxophone line in response to Bowie. However, as Mitchell's tempo escalates, he manages to keep his volume stable, a challenging technique on any wind instrument. Mitchell's restraint keeps the texture from peaking too early, and demonstrates how a multi-centered approach can enliven an intensity structure through constant movement and development. Favors hears his bandmate slowly drawing nearer to the intensity style, and he encourages Mitchell with a handheld horn, playing exuberant blasts that Bowie parodies on trumpet. Mitchell finally reaches a maximum tempo at 38:03, some three and a half minutes into the intensity structure. Favors and Jarman drop out, temporarily creating more space in the texture for Mitchell. However, Jarman cannot stay away for long, and seconds later he picks up his alto saxophone and launches into a blistering solo, competing with Mitchell and Bowie to become the primary melodic voice (see example 7.19).

Jarman begins to dominate the texture with a series of rapid runs based on Db_3, the lowest pitch on his alto saxophone. Mitchell sees an opening to renew the intensity structure, and he shifts from soprano saxophone to

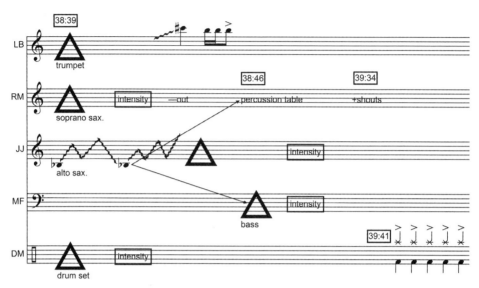

EXAMPLE 7.20 Intensity structure: Jarman solo

percussion table. By trading places with Jarman, who only recently switched from balafon to saxophone, Mitchell keeps the texture balanced between wind instruments and percussion. At the same time, he also transforms the group's timbral profile by substituting the rickety sounds of his percussion table for the clear tones of Jarman's balafon (see example 7.20). The musicians make moves like this throughout the concert, continually introducing new sounds into every composition or stylistic framework.[42] Intensity structures are not exempt from this rule: indeed, in *Live at Mandel Hall* and other performances, the members of the Art Ensemble employ an eclectic sonic palette that clearly differentiates their intense playing from that of non-AACM bands, particularly New York–based free-jazz groups. As Mitchell explained, "[w]e were unlike the music that was coming out of New York . . . because a lot of it was very intense, and that was it":[43]

> They never really played anything that was soft or anything like that. We were going around with these kelp horns and whistles. The Chicago people got intense, but they also got soft, and they also were incorporating other sounds into their music.[44]

The musicians' commitment to multi-instrumentalism enabled them to develop unique sounds in each performance. For the Art Ensemble, however, sonic novelty was not an end in itself, nor was multi-instrumentalism. Instead,

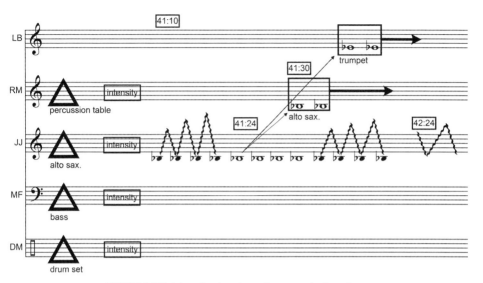

EXAMPLE 7.21 Intensity structure: Jarman solo, long tones

both practices were ultimately about musical expression. As Moye affirmed, "we've got all of these sounds there all of the time. We can move in and out of different situations and color them the way we want to."[45] During an Art Ensemble concert, one of the musicians can hear a sound played by his band-mate and replicate it, or respond with a contrasting tone color. Every sound, it seems, could be found in the group's vast instrument collection, including unexpected sounds that came to the musicians through inspiration, not their own intentions. The members of the Art Ensemble, according to Jarman, "were looking for specific sounds to express the music that was flowing through [our] consciousness. And that sound could be a bowl, a table, a piece of wood; whatever it took."[46]

At 41:10, almost seven minutes into the intensity structure, Jarman finds his way back to the lowest reaches of his alto saxophone, the register where his solo began. He plays a few phrases rooted on $D\flat_3$, then refines this idea into a string of long-tone $D\flat_3$s, calling out to Bowie and Mitchell with a simple, compelling line that begs to be doubled. Mitchell answers on alto saxophone, doubling Jarman's pitch, and then Bowie joins in on trumpet an octave higher. Their entrances free Jarman to explore another textural area, and he decides to float above their low-register long tones, darting up and down the har-monic series using the overblowing technique associated with intense styles of saxophone playing (see example 7.21).

Bowie and Mitchell play long-tone $D\flat$s for two minutes, then stop, re-

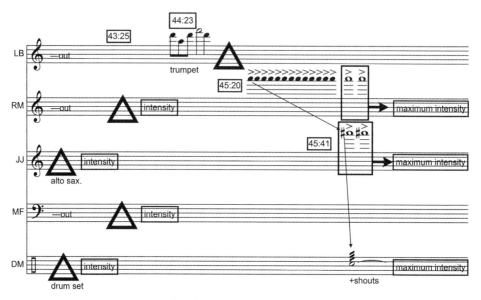

EXAMPLE 7.22 Intensity structure: reaching maximum intensity

freshing the texture once more. After a short rest, Mitchell returns with an energetic alto saxophone line that closely resembles Jarman's. This is the first time in the intensity structure when both saxophonists choose to play in a prototypically intense way, a development that could lead to a powerful musical climax. Mitchell slowly ascends to the altissimo register of his alto saxophone, three octaves above the low long tones he played a moment ago, and at 45:20 he starts blowing high, piercing C_6s as loud as he can. Jarman echoes Mitchell's upper-register long tones, but selects a different pitch, $C\#_6$, which he repeatedly bends toward D_6, accentuating the shattering dissonance he is forming with Mitchell. An instant later, Moye adds to the furor with a forceful roll on his snare drum, the same sound that triggered the intensity structure eleven minutes earlier. Over Moye's drumroll, the saxophonists continue their shrill, dissonant long tones, propelling the texture into an exhilarating state of maximum intensity (see example 7.22).

Moye prolongs his drumroll for almost a minute, an amazing span of time for a gesture that usually lasts no more than a few seconds. Then, at 46:38, he crashes a cymbal and reverts to the complex, dense style of drumming he has maintained for much of the intensity structure. The musicians built up an immense amount of energy during Moye's drumroll, and when it ends they keep playing at an even greater level of intensity than before. This choice is not without its risks. Extending the intensity structure will test the group members' physical stamina, already depleted after a marathon stretch

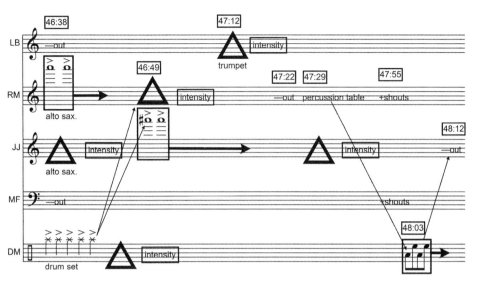

EXAMPLE 7.23 Intensity structure: reshaping the intensity structure

of strenuous playing. Furthermore, the drumroll could have served as a logical conclusion for the intensity structure, but now the musicians must devise another way to bring the texture to a close. Here, Mitchell seizes the initiative, moving from alto saxophone to percussion table and striking his wood blocks and cymbals. In register and timbre, these instruments overlap with Moye's snare drum and cymbals, and Moye yields this territory to Mitchell, focusing instead on his tom-toms and twin bass drums, the low-register instruments of his drum set. Jarman hears this significant textural change and puts down his alto saxophone (see example 7.23).

Art Ensemble intensity structures are often led by the saxophonists, but at this juncture neither Mitchell nor Jarman is playing saxophone.[47] Mitchell has already switched to percussion table, and with Jarman's exit the musicians have a second opportunity to end the intensity structure. However, Jarman refuses to let the intense feeling subside. Instead, he turns away from the audience at 48:18, addresses the drums at the center of the Mandel Hall stage, and nearly drowns out the rest of the band with a barrage of drum strokes. Jarman's move tilts the balance of the texture toward the group's battery of percussion instruments, transforming the intensity structure. Bowie reacts by funneling his trumpet line into low, blaring long tones. Favors sings along, matching Bowie's pitch with his voice and helping it be heard amid the clattering percussion. Bowie's long tones, like Moye's drumroll, could help end the intensity structure, but the musicians do not relent right away. So Bowie lays out for a moment, then returns at 50:14 with another series of long tones, each one

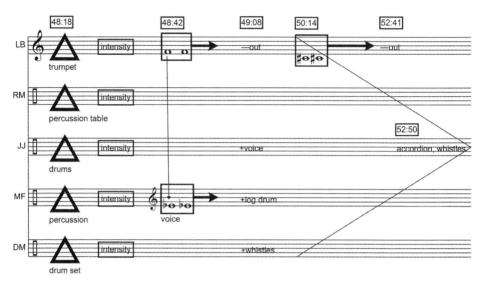

EXAMPLE 7.24 Intensity structure: disassembling the intensity structure

played quieter than the last. Bowie continues this decrescendo for two and a half minutes, until his persistence subdues the other group members, causing the intensity level to drop substantially. His goal accomplished, Bowie exits, further thinning the texture, and Jarman switches to accordion (see example 7.24). Finally, the musicians have allowed the intensity structure to disintegrate. After an epic eighteen-minute span, one of the lengthiest episodes in the entire concert, the members of the Art Ensemble have exhausted the possibilities of the intensity style. "[T]he color," as Moye would say, "has been worked."[48]

Transition/"Mata Kimasu"

As the intensity structure winds down, the musicians are confronted with the same choice they faced earlier in *Live at Mandel Hall*: how and when to arrive at "Mata Kimasu," the fourth and final item on the set list. At the end of "Checkmate," they decided against converging immediately on "Mata Kimasu," which would have brought the concert to a premature conclusion after a little more than twenty-six minutes. Now, nearly fifty-three minutes into the performance, the band members are less concerned about the precise amount of time that will elapse before they reach "Mata Kimasu." They must instead direct their attention to another matter—constructing a transition that will help "Mata Kimasu" deliver the desired emotional effect when it ultimately arrives.

The transition emerges seamlessly from the wake of the intensity structure. The musicians are already playing some of the percussion instruments that are frequently employed in transitional passages, and they are able to form a new texture from the materials at hand: bells, claves, and an assortment of drums. Favors plays log drum, an African instrument carved from a single piece of wood, and sings a traditional melody that he learned from Malian musicians during the Art Ensemble's years in France.[49] Over the next five minutes, his plaintive voice becomes the focus of the texture. When Favors's song ends, Moye takes over, playing a lively beat on conga drums. Moye's entrance sparks an impromptu percussion jam centered on his effusive hand drumming, with the other musicians contributing complementary rhythms on claves, cowbell, and tambourine.

At 63:27, eleven minutes into the transition, Moye closes off the percussion jam with a gong stroke. In Art Ensemble performances, single accents played on a resonant, metallic percussion instrument (such as a bell, gong, or triangle) typically represent a starting point, a new departure for the group improvisation. And indeed, this is the function of Moye's gong stroke, which divides the transition into two distinct passages. In the first passage, the musicians developed a percussion texture from the remnants of the preceding intensity structure. After the gong stroke, the group members move into the transition's second passage, where they introduce textural elements that prepare the arrival of "Mata Kimasu." The most crucial element of the emerging texture is Favors's double bass. Like "Duffvipels," "Mata Kimasu" will begin with a bass vamp that sets up the groove upon which the piece is based. When Favors enters on bass not long after Moye's pivotal gong stroke, his bandmates know that he could cue "Mata Kimasu" at any moment. So they settle into a texture resembling the concert's very first transition, a free-tempo bass solo with quiet percussive accompaniment that does not overshadow Favors's melodic line.

Favors's bass solo begins in C minor, then cycles through a number of keys. During the seventh minute of the solo, Favors finds his way to D minor, the key that "Mata Kimasu" is in. However, his high-register harmonics and open-string drones are worlds away from the funk style of "Mata Kimasu," and the other musicians decide to go on a brief excursion into a contrasting musical realm. Mitchell makes the first move at 72:35, offering slow-paced clarinet phrases drawn from the D-minor scale. Then Bowie and Jarman enter (on trumpet and flute, respectively), playing lyrical melodies that interweave with Mitchell's line. The texture begins to sound like "People in Sorrow," one of the best-known pieces in the Art Ensemble's repertoire. The core of "People in Sorrow" is its theme, a somber melody composed by Mitchell (see example 7.25). Although Mitchell's composition is just eleven measures long, it lends itself to expansive performances in which the musicians elaborate and

EXAMPLE 7.25 Transition: "People in Sorrow" score

EXAMPLE 7.26 "Mata Kimasu": opening groove

restate the theme over and over again—for instance, the forty-minute version of "People in Sorrow" on the 1969 Art Ensemble album of the same name.[50] At this point in the concert, the group members are not really considering a shift into "People in Sorrow"; even a few passes through the melody would seriously delay their arrival at "Mata Kimasu." Instead, the musicians have other aims in mind. This short, two-minute interlude allows the musicians to wrap up the protracted transition in a unified manner. More importantly, they will be able to form a stark musical contrast by moving from the reflective mood of the interlude to the raucous funk groove of "Mata Kimasu," subverting the audience's expectations and creating an effective finale for the performance.

Just after the seventy-five-minute mark of *Live at Mandel Hall*, Favors starts playing the "Mata Kimasu" bass vamp. Moye confirms Favors's tempo with a few finger snaps, then picks up a pair of drumsticks so he can contribute his part, a linear-style funk beat that links up with the repeating bass line. When Moye enters on drum set, he and Favors loop the one-bar groove several times as they await the arrival of Bowie, Jarman, and Mitchell, who will perform the "Mata Kimasu" theme (see example 7.26). Co-composed by Bowie and Moye, the theme is extraordinarily short, a mere six measures from start to finish.[51] It is intended to provide an emphatic conclusion to the performance, not a platform for further improvisation, and accordingly the musicians play the theme only once. The composition ends with a brash two-note tag that recalls

EXAMPLE 7.27 "Mata Kimasu": theme

the upper-register squawk from "Duffvipels." And just as in "Duffvipels," there is a massive sense of arrival when "Mata Kimasu" suddenly comes to a close—so much so that the concertgoers are too surprised to respond. After a few seconds, some audience members finally recognize that the performance is over, and their applause sets off an ovation that sweeps Mandel Hall (see example 7.27).

The impact of "Mata Kimasu" extended well beyond Mandel Hall, reaching listeners thousands of miles from Chicago and as far away as Japan. Delmark Records released *Live at Mandel Hall* in 1974, the year of the Art Ensemble's first Japanese tour. The record label had built a strong distribution network in Japan, and the musicians wanted to leave a positive impression on this new audience.[52] So they entitled the album's final track "Mata Kimasu," a Japanese phrase meaning "we'll come again." As promised, they would return to Japan several times in the 1980s and 1990s, a period when the Art Ensemble became one of the most widely traveled groups in jazz and experimental music (as will be discussed in chapter 8).[53] The band's globe-trekking was partly motivated by necessity. In an interview given before one of the group's Japanese tours, Bowie exaggerated only a little when he claimed that "[w]e can't buy a gig in Chicago, but we have to go to Tokyo."[54] The members of the Art Ensemble also learned something more significant from their extensive tours—their music, which so profoundly affected listeners at hometown venues like Chicago's Mandel Hall, could resonate just as deeply with audiences across the United States and around the world. This realization was a source of pride for the group, as Bowie explained:

> People will come from everywhere to see us play. Though our performances are rare in the States, there is a certain element of people who want to hear us, or who have been following us for years. The people at [a] Beverly Hills concert may have seen us the last time in Germany, France, or Japan. That's the benefit of world marketing. In fact every concert we play is sold out no matter where it is. It could be Istanbul or Los Angeles. . . . And that's what we went for from the beginning; to develop a real audience. That's who we play for now.[55]

8   Great Black Music

"In African music and Great Black Music all the arts were together."[1]

From Lagos to Ludwigsburg: The Art Ensemble on ECM

The Art Ensemble's 1977 European tour concluded in mid-June with two concerts in Rotterdam, the Netherlands.[2] Seven years earlier, in June 1970, the band made its Rotterdam debut at the Holland Pop Festival, during one of Don Moye's first tours with the group.[3] The musicians' return visit to Rotterdam in 1977 represented another turning point for the Art Ensemble. The group had toured Europe four times in the past four years, but there were no more international engagements on the horizon as the 1977 tour came to an end. Moreover, Kunle Mwanga had resigned from his position as the Art Ensemble's booking agent so that he could pursue his own performance career.[4] If the musicians wanted to go on another profitable tour in 1978, they would need to hire a manager who could negotiate with concert promoters and plan their tour itinerary. They also hoped to secure a recording contract that would surpass the terms of their two-album deal with Atlantic, which expired after the release of *Fanfare for the Warriors*.[5]

The members of the Art Ensemble chose to address these matters in the fall of 1977, after their customary post-tour hiatus.[6]

The business decisions they reached that fall would catapult the group into its period of greatest popularity, a fifteen-year span stretching from the late 1970s to the early 1990s. During this time, the band's audience significantly expanded, both at home and abroad, and the musicians enjoyed a newfound prosperity. The Art Ensemble also became an integral part of the American jazz scene, even as the group members asserted that their music encompassed far more than jazz. As they proudly proclaimed, the Art Ensemble played "Great Black Music, Ancient to the Future."

After the June 1977 concerts in Rotterdam, Malachi Favors, Joseph Jarman, Roscoe Mitchell, and Don Moye flew from Europe to the Midwest and revived their respective side projects. Lester Bowie, however, was not quite ready to return to the United States. Prior to the tour, he moved out of his house in suburban St. Louis, but he had not yet found a permanent residence in New York, where he would settle at the end of the year.[7] So he chose to delay his homecoming for a while. Bowie had always wanted to travel to Africa, and after watching the television miniseries *Roots*, which aired in January 1977, he resolved to make a pilgrimage to the continent at the first available opportunity. Although he "didn't know anyone in Africa," he had heard about Fela Kuti, the Nigerian musician and political activist.[8] By exchanging the return airfare that would have taken him back to America, Bowie could obtain a one-way ticket to Lagos, Nigeria, where Kuti lived. With $100 in his pocket, Bowie boarded a plane bound for Lagos, confident that his trumpet skills would find him a place in "the baddest band in Africa."[9] "Music life is a great time," Bowie declared, "if you just go on and trust it."[10]

This was not the first time that Bowie set off on "an expedition to somewhere," armed only with his trumpet.[11] He was the prime mover behind the Art Ensemble's 1969 journey to Paris, a move that transformed the group from a little-known Chicago band into an international phenomenon—one of the most successful and critically acclaimed ensembles in the history of jazz and experimental music. In 1975, Bowie's next adventure took him to Portland Parish, Jamaica, an agricultural area north of Kingston.[12] He quickly befriended the members of a Kingston reggae band, who granted him membership in the musicians' union and helped him find a house in Portland Parish.[13] Bowie subsisted in Portland Parish by teaching trumpet lessons to schoolchildren: "I had a workshop with all the local kids in the hills, this real small community. And they took care of me. If my food was running low, they would see to that: their parents would send crates of mangoes and pies up to me."[14] He remained in Jamaica for the better part of a year, leaving the island only for Art Ensemble performances.[15]

In contrast to his yearlong retreat in rural Jamaica, Bowie's 1977 visit to Nigeria was shorter but much more eventful. He arrived in Lagos a few months after the Nigerian military attacked Fela Kuti's compound, the Kalakuta Republic, brutalizing the residents (including Kuti's mother) and burning the entire property to the ground.[16] This assault, an act of retaliation against Kuti's political organizing, did not stop him from criticizing Nigeria's military government, nor did it diminish his visibility in Lagos. In the aftermath of the Kalakuta attack, Kuti was staying in a Lagos hotel, and Bowie was able to find his way there by hailing a taxicab and telling the driver, "Take me to Fela."[17] At the hotel, Bowie was greeted by one of Kuti's musicians, who escorted him to the bandleader's suite for an impromptu audition:

> It was funny. They had to wake Fela up. They woke him up, and Fela came in, and he said, "Oh, who is this guy?" He motioned for a guy to bring his record player, and he had some of those Jamey Aebersold type records. . . . So he put on this blues, a blues in B-flat, which is my specialty, right? So I played this blues, man! One-way ticket, you know I was blowin', baby. After I played a couple of choruses he said, "Stop. Somebody go get this guy's bags. He's moving in with me."[18]

For a period of two months, Bowie was Kuti's "guest of honor."[19] He lived at the hotel with Kuti and his band, the celebrated Afrika 70 ensemble, and appeared on five of Kuti's LPs, including *Stalemate*—where he was listed in the album credits as "Guest Artiste on Trumpet (A Good Afro-American)."[20] Bowie's tenure with Kuti lasted until August 1977, when tensions related to the Kalakuta attack made it "politically uncomfortable" for Afrika 70 to remain in Lagos.[21] Kuti and his band decamped to Ghana, and Bowie flew from Nigeria to Italy, where he awaited a money transfer from the Art Ensemble that would enable him to purchase return airfare to the United States.[22] While in Italy, Bowie fronted a small group called Laboratorio, a reference to the trademark white lab coat he had taken to wearing in performances with the Art Ensemble and his side projects.[23] Finally, in November 1977, five months after the end of the Art Ensemble's European tour, he flew to New York and began to make his home there.[24] Once Bowie had settled in, Favors, Jarman, Mitchell, and Moye traveled to New York, reuniting with their bandmate for a series of Art Ensemble business meetings that would lead the group to its next management team and a contract with a renowned record label.

The leading candidates for the managerial position were Marty Khan and Helene Cann, a husband-and-wife team who operated the management company Rasa Artists (later incorporated as Outward Visions). Khan entered the music industry as a performer. He studied saxophone with Sam Rivers, and during the early 1970s he played in Rivers's workshop band. In 1976, when Khan's performance career ended, he and Cann formed Rasa Artists, offering management services to Rivers and other musicians who worked in New York venues like Studio Rivbea, Rivers's downtown loft space.[25] AACM saxophonist Chico Freeman encountered Khan and Cann not long after his 1976 move to New York, and he recommended the couple to the Art Ensemble.[26] In late 1977, the group members met with Khan and Cann in New York to discuss a partnership arrangement, then convened a band-only meeting where they decided to go into business with Rasa Artists. Khan and Cann would work with the Art Ensemble for the next fourteen years.[27]

The first task Khan undertook as the Art Ensemble's representative was obtaining a new recording contract for the group. The band's most recent LPs, *Fanfare for the Warriors* and *Live at Mandel Hall*, had been released three years ago, in 1974.[28] Khan and the musicians believed that a new album would make the group more competitive for domestic and international bookings. The Art Ensemble decided to target ECM Records, a West German label specializing in jazz and experimental music.[29] ECM had been interested in the band for some time. The ECM producer Thomas Stöwsand became an avid fan of the Art Ensemble when he witnessed their performance at the 1970 German Jazz Festival in Frankfurt: "I had never seen anything like this before, with all the costumes and makeup."[30] Stöwsand's enthusiasm for the group was infectious. He encouraged Manfred Eicher, the founder of ECM, to check out the Art Ensemble, and Eicher began listening closely to the band's recordings.[31] A particular favorite was *People in Sorrow*, which Eicher often played while working at the label's office in Munich.[32] At the end of 1977, when the group contacted ECM to propose a recording contract, Stöwsand happened to be in New York on a business trip. Khan set up an in-person meeting with Stöwsand, and days later they reached a "handshake agreement" on a contract between the ECM and the Art Ensemble.[33] In May 1978, during the band's five-week European tour, the musicians visited Ludwigsburg, West Germany, to record their first album for ECM, *Nice Guys*.[34]

The Art Ensemble's signing with ECM Records was perceived as a "major event in the world of jazz."[35] At the end of the 1970s, the jazz recording industry was in flux, especially in the United States. Prominent jazz labels such as Blue Note had stopped releasing new recordings, while many of the labels that remained active focused on bands that fused jazz with rock, funk, and soul.[36] In contrast to its competitors, ECM had grown steadily since its 1969 founding, and its catalog included hundreds of acoustic jazz albums as well as fusion offerings by artists like Pat Metheny.[37] With each recording it issued, regardless of genre, ECM reinforced its position as an industry innovator, an image that would be further enhanced by its association with the Art Ensemble.

One reason for the label's cutting-edge reputation was the famous "ECM sound," a distinctive approach to record production that gave its albums "superior clarity and a deep sense of space."[38] The Art Ensemble's ECM recordings were engineered by Martin Wieland, a veteran *Tonmeister* who had worked with the label for nearly a decade prior to the *Nice Guys* sessions.[39] He soon discovered that his years of experience as an audio engineer had not entirely prepared him to record the group's unpredictable music: "[R]ecording the Art Ensemble is always a challenge, because nobody knows what is going to happen in the next second. I believe not even the musicians. It just develops."[40] Fortunately, Wieland was able to accurately capture the Art Ensemble's unique sound spectrum while bringing out nuances in the high-frequency range that had been neglected on the band's earlier recordings.[41] The musicians were generally satisfied with Wieland's work. "I heard the test pressings," Moye remarked after listening to *Nice Guys*, "and it sounds like us."[42]

If the members of the Art Ensemble appreciated the production values of their ECM recordings, they were equally attuned to other aspects of the label's business model. According to Favors, ECM consistently upheld its profit-sharing arrangement with the band, paying the musicians a percentage of the revenue from their album sales.[43] No other record label had dealt so forthrightly with the Art Ensemble. In Moye's estimation, "[ECM] is an honest company, unlike BYG and Atlantic. We trust Manfred Eicher and Thomas Stöwsand."[44] The Art Ensemble's sales figures were boosted by ECM's international distribution network, which in North America was operated by Warner Brothers, a major label.[45] The group members knew that their ECM albums would receive wide exposure, even more so than their Atlantic discs, and they endeavored to make their recordings accessible to the broadest possible audience.[46] This strategy paid off. Both *Nice Guys* and *Full Force* (the band's second ECM recording) sold over forty thousand copies in the United States and thousands more overseas—impressive numbers for a group whose Atlantic LPs had sold only a tenth as many units.[47] The Art Ensemble's popular appeal was also reflected in the annual polls sponsored by *Down Beat* magazine. The *Down Beat* Critics Poll selected the Art Ensemble as "Acoustic

Jazz Group of the Year" for three consecutive years after the 1979 release of *Nice Guys*.[48] *Nice Guys* and *Full Force* placed highly in the magazine's Readers Poll, a first for the Art Ensemble.[49] And in 1981, the Critics Poll chose *Full Force* as "Jazz Album of the Year."[50]

ECM organized European tours for the Art Ensemble and its other recording artists. The label viewed these tours as promotional ventures that would stimulate album sales, ECM's core business, and the company fully funded the tours at no cost to the Art Ensemble.[51] In addition to covering the musicians' lodging and travel expenses, ECM also paid for their American road crew to accompany them to Europe.[52] The Art Ensemble had never toured Europe with a "paid crew," and Moye welcomed the change:

> We basically had been moving all of our equipment around ourselves; driving, setting up, playing the gig, breaking down, and driving on to the next hit. We had been doing that since I joined the band in '70. So that s— was starting to get old; we had too much equipment to move by ourselves *and* do the gig too.[53]

ECM artists kept all of the profits from the European tours sponsored by the label.[54] The members of the Art Ensemble treated this income as an opportunity for reinvestment, in keeping with the cooperative principles they had followed since 1969. After the group's second ECM tour, a five-week outing in the spring of 1979, the musicians reinvested the proceeds into a major equipment purchase: thirty-six flight cases, each custom-manufactured to the band's specifications. Some of the cases were used to transport Art Ensemble merchandise and the musicians' concert wardrobes, but most were designed to carry their massive inventory of instruments.[55] With these flight cases, the members of the Art Ensemble could present their entire instrument collection in concerts for the first time since 1971, when they were crisscrossing Europe in a fleet of trucks.[56] Each musician's cases were painted a different color— black for Bowie, blue for Jarman, green for Mitchell, "sun percussion" yellow for Moye, and red for Favors. This color-coding system, according to Moye, allowed the Art Ensemble's road crew to "easily coordinate performance setups and placement of equipment in designated areas . . . which corresponded to the details of the stage plan for every show."[57] The case coloring also contributed to the remarkable visual spectacle that began to take shape hours before each Art Ensemble concert. Jarman depicted this kaleidoscopic scene in his liner notes for the group's third ECM album, *Urban Bushmen*, recorded live at the Amerika Haus in Munich:

They arrive, we are amazed and holding our breath as the large travel cases open to reveal smaller cases and yet smaller cases until the whole space is filled with cases. We see FIVE different colors of cases with various markings, numbers, names, stickers from other concert sites, airline cargo markings, train stickers, and other non-descript sign-symbols. Some of the cases are colored red, some blue, green, black, and many are painted a sunbright yellow. Soon the cases are pushed, pulled, and hauled into five different shapes of color; we begin to feel a sense of order growing out of the mass of metal, wood, skin, and fiber. Area by area the machine unfolds.

A special made gong stand holds gongs of various sizes from ten to forty inches in diameter, bells are hung from inverted racks that look like sculptured icons in motion, unusual stands hold drums, wood blocks, cymbals, and sound makers we never dreamed of. The space is TRANSFORMED into a semi-circle of gold, bronze, brass, silver, and copper, a beautiful shining sound object waiting to tone the infinite sound of the ART ENSEMBLE OF CHICAGO. Finally a huge bass drum is placed in the center of the semi-circle, the machine is ready.[58]

A Fascinating Commodity

From the late 1970s to the early 1990s, the Art Ensemble's popularity was at a peak. The group's recordings for ECM increased the demand for Art Ensemble performances all around the world. The 1980 tour in support of *Full Force* took the musicians to a number of new destinations, including Mexico, Brazil, Russia, and Australia.[59] In Europe, the band became a major concert draw, appearing at jazz festivals, concert halls, and theaters across the continent. No longer could the Art Ensemble be considered a "local act in Paris," as Favors put it, although French audiences would never forget the Chicagoans' astonishing debut in the summer of 1969.[60] The Art Ensemble was able to tour Europe every year from 1976 to 1984, traveling from Great Britain to Greece, Poland to Portugal.[61] Also in 1984, they made a triumphant return to Japan, ten years after their first concert tour of the country.[62] The Art Ensemble would visit Japan again in 1986, 1988, and 1990.[63] Back in May 1969, days before the group left Chicago for Paris, Bowie predicted that he and his bandmates would "carry their music everywhere."[64] Two decades and five continents later, the Art Ensemble proved Bowie right.

The band's American audience grew in parallel with its international fan base. The musicians benefited enormously from the promotional efforts of Warner Brothers, ECM's North American distribution partner—at one point, they shared a publicist with Prince, Warner's biggest star.[65] However, Warner Brothers and ECM could not claim all of the credit for the band's popularity with American concertgoers. Indeed, the Art Ensemble continued to organize lucrative domestic tours for several years after the 1985 release of *The Third Decade*, the last of the group's four albums on ECM. In order for the band to remain a successful touring act, the musicians had to cultivate new communities of listeners in the United States that they did not reach during the group's first and second decades.

During the late 1960s and early 1970s, much of the Art Ensemble's domestic audience was concentrated in Chicago.[66] The musicians also had small but dedicated followings in a few scattered locations—mostly college towns—where they had spent a month or so rehearsing in a rented house.[67] "We traveled all over the States in our bus," Moye recalled. "[W]e'd put some cash together, hit the road, and rent a house-rehearsal space and play every day for 8 to 10 hours consistently. We did that in Ann Arbor; San Jose, California; Eugene, Oregon."[68] Later in the 1970s, the group began to tour more extensively, broadening its geographic base and building audiences on the East and West Coasts. The Art Ensemble also started to attract notice from the jazz community, a process that accelerated after the band signed with ECM. When the musicians performed at a New York jazz club, they could play to nearly a thousand listeners in the course of a weeklong engagement. For concert appearances at larger New York venues like the downtown Entermedia Theater, however, the attendance figures could be somewhat different, as Marty Khan learned during the Art Ensemble's 1978 tour:

> People would follow them around. If they were playing three or four dates on the East Coast, people would travel to all three or four cities. If they were doing four performances, people would show up for all four shows. It was that type of a community. . . . On that first tour, we did a concert and we only drew about 375 people, anticipating 600–700 people because the clubs would draw 800–1000. What it really was, is that 800–1000 was comprised of around 350 fans who were coming two and three times.[69]

This setback did not deter the musicians from working in theaters and concert halls, the performance settings they preferred. Instead, they chose venues of a size that would maximize the leverage provided by their loyal fan base. When Khan was booking the New York leg of the 1979 American tour, he arranged for the group to play two consecutive nights at the Public Theater, an intimate downtown space:

[W]e put them into the Public Theater for four performances on a weekend in a 300-seater, knowing that we were going to sell out 200–250 of those tickets across the board, and there would be only about 50 tickets available, so they would always sell out. And as a result of selling out two or three times in a row, we developed a demand for them. . . . [P]eople never want anything more than what they can't have.[70]

One year later, the Art Ensemble returned to New York to open the 1980 Newport Jazz Festival. Thirteen hundred concertgoers attended the band's midnight performance at Town Hall, by far the largest audience the musicians had ever drawn in New York.[71] The Art Ensemble's fan base had exploded.

The musicians' growing popularity significantly increased their earning potential. The Art Ensemble worked with Khan to establish a "touring circuit" of cities where the group could play year after year.[72] This circuit included major markets like New York, Chicago, and the Bay Area, as well as dozens of smaller metropolises in between.[73] Performing in minor markets could be risky: ECM did not sponsor the band's American tours, and the musicians incurred substantial expenses when transporting their instruments from gig to gig.[74] Over the years, though, they steadily enlarged their profit margins by forming partnerships with promoters who could help the group build devoted local followings. In 1978, for instance, the promoter Bill Warrell brought the musicians to Washington, D.C., for a series of concerts at the Corcoran Gallery of Art.[75] This was Warrell's first production at the Corcoran Gallery, and he could only afford to pay the band $2,000.[76] In subsequent years, Warrell was able to offer the Art Ensemble more money for each performance, and by 1988, the group earned $10,000 for an outdoor concert that Warrell staged at Freedom Plaza, two blocks from the White House.[77] The band experienced similar rates of growth in markets across the country. On the 1980 *Full Force* tour, the Art Ensemble made $100,000 over an eight-week period, earning an average of $2,500 for each concert date.[78] In 1991, the musicians received the same amount, $100,000, for only eight performances, a fivefold increase in the amount earned per show.[79]

To Khan, the Art Ensemble was a "fascinating commodity," an experimental performance group that was nonetheless highly marketable.[80] American newspapers and music magazines printed countless stories about the band, many illustrated with images of the musicians wearing their stage attire and face paint. "We were able to get a lot of attention from newspaper editors and magazine editors who didn't care one way or another what the music contained," Khan observed. "[They] were just looking for a compelling photograph."[81] Jazz listeners, in contrast, cared deeply about the music, and the Art Ensemble obliged them with ready virtuosity, unparalleled group improvisations, and a repertoire that featured numerous original jazz compositions, including the band's theme, "Odwalla."[82] However, Khan and his partner Helene Cann, a publicity specialist, did not market the Art Ensemble as an ordinary jazz group. Instead, they focused on positioning the musicians in the performing-arts world, "reaching out to the same kind of audience that would come and see the Kronos Quartet or the Alvin Ailey dance company."[83] This was an unprecedented move: never before had a band crossed over from jazz to performing arts. The template established by the Art Ensemble became a model for other jazz and experimental music groups with crossover potential, such as the World Saxophone Quartet. But the members of the Art Ensemble were the first—they were the "battering ram," Khan stated, that allowed jazz musicians to enter the performing-arts world.[84]

Performing-arts audiences were intrigued by the Art Ensemble's music and absolutely enthralled by the band's innovative use of intermedia. Indeed, the musicians' costumes, bodily movements, instrument arrays, and stage designs worked together to create visual displays that rivaled any dance performance or concert-music production. To raise the Art Ensemble's profile in the performing-arts field, Khan and Cann employed a dual strategy. They produced tours that paired the band with the Alwin Nikolais Dance Theater and the Women of the Calabash, groups whose performances combined music, costuming, and movement in ways comparable to the Art Ensemble's.[85] Additionally, Khan and Cann centered their publicity campaigns on the band's longtime slogan, "Great Black Music, Ancient to the Future," a concept that appealed to the performing-arts world as well as certain segments of the jazz community. In this way, the musicians developed two distinct, complementary audiences, a rare achievement for performers in any field. According to Khan:

> The Art Ensemble became the leading commodity for those presenters who were embracing the whole avant-garde reality. . . . It was really our world, because the performing-arts world is supposed to be the cutting edge, and [the Art Ensemble] is the cutting edge.[86]

More Than a Marketing Scheme: The Meaning of Great Black Music

For Khan and Cann, "Great Black Music, Ancient to the Future" was an important component of their strategy to market the Art Ensemble to performing-arts audiences. From the musicians' perspective, however, Great Black Music was much more meaningful. The group members emblazoned their slogan on album covers, stage backdrops, and even Bowie's bass drum, ensuring that anyone who heard their recordings or attended their concerts would associate Great Black Music with the Art Ensemble. They also offered elaborate interpretations of the slogan in a variety of forums, including interviews with critics, who invariably asked the band to reveal the precise meaning of Great Black Music. In these discussions and other public pronouncements, the group portrayed the Great Black Music concept as the key to understanding the Art Ensemble's multifaceted performances, which seemed to "def[y] categorization," as Bruce Tucker wrote after viewing the concert video *Live from the Jazz Showcase*.[87] (See chapter 9 for more on *Live from the Jazz Showcase*.) The Great Black Music concept, according to the members of the Art Ensemble, could explain every aspect of their performance practice, from the diversity of their repertoire to their involvement with multiple forms of intermedia. The musicians also used their slogan to intervene in cultural and political debates, staking out the Art Ensemble's positions on a number of important issues, including the ascent of a powerful traditionalist faction on the American jazz scene during the 1980s and 1990s.

Great Black Music was initially conceived not for the Art Ensemble but for the AACM. In 1968, when Bowie became the AACM's second president, the organization was in need of a better slogan. "We had these bumper stickers saying 'Jazz is Alive,'" Bowie remembered, "and the membership didn't go for jazz."[88] So he asked Favors to help him devise a new slogan that would more accurately describe the Association's musical ambitions. In Favors's recollection, the two bandmates "had a big debate over the labeling of our music which lasted for hours. We finally came to the conclusion of 'Great Black Music.'"[89] The term caught on within the AACM, Bowie claimed, because it represented something "broader" than jazz.[90] More importantly, just like the earlier term "creative music," it enabled AACM members to take the lead in defining their own work, an opportunity seldom granted to African American artists.[91] The members of the Art Ensemble took up this project in earnest after moving to France in 1969, when they adopted Great Black Music as the band's slogan (later adding Ancient to the Future, a phrase invented by Favors).[92]

The Great Black Music concept had deep ethical implications. Bowie thought that it helped the Art Ensemble avoid the loss of "dignity" experienced by musicians who were prevented from naming what they had created.[93] As he proudly asserted, "we are one of the only groups of musicians that have labeled our own music, given it our own name.... [N]ever before were we even allowed the dignity of even selecting a name for our own music."[94] In Moye's view, such denials of dignity and agency were often linked to economic injustice. "[T]hose terms," Moye observed, "were always coined by people that actually ended up being in a position of exploiting the music."[95] Proclaiming Great Black Music, therefore, enabled the group members to empower themselves and demand ethical treatment from the music industry. Furthermore, the ethical compass provided by Great Black Music extended well beyond the band's own business dealings. The musicians did not portray themselves or their AACM colleagues as the only exponents of Great Black Music.[96] Instead, they used the slogan to honor their musical forebears—individuals and entire societies whose contributions to global culture went unacknowledged for far too long. Favors and Bowie discussed this aspect of Great Black Music in an interview with Rafi Zabor:

> Favors: A lot of people criticize us for using the term, but as I know history, no one ever gives black people credit for doing anything. No one else is going to say that this is Black or African. Even in so-called jazz, people have tried to take that away from us, or say that so-and-so did this, when actually our ancestors did it. That's why we have to stress these terms.
>
> Bowie: I went and saw this cat with the Senegalese Ballet, he played a song that was 2500 years old and it had the whole of the sonata form in it. Now what were they doing in Italy 2500 years ago? We were always led to believe that all they did in Africa was drums and dance. We never knew about all these cats with circular breathing, reeds, oboes, choirs, everything. . . . *Man* came from Africa, even the scientists admit to that! So does the music, that's why it's so strong.[97]

The members of the Art Ensemble studied a number of traditional and contemporary musical styles from North, South, Central, and West Africa, and the group's slogan expressed their belief that all African musics, despite their differences, were ultimately related.[98] Great Black Music, in other words, was a pan-African concept. It was not constrained by ethnic divisions or national boundaries within Africa—nor was it strictly confined to the African continent. According to the Art Ensemble, Great Black Music could be found throughout the African diaspora. "[W]hen we say 'Great Black Music,'" Favors explained, "we mean all of this great black music that has influenced American music, that has influenced South American music, and the world."[99] Crucially, styles of Great Black Music that emerged in the global diaspora were on equal footing with forms that originated in Africa. This expansive conception of Great Black Music was endlessly inspiring to the Art Ensemble. As Jarman affirmed, "Rhythm and blues; rock and roll; spirituals; swing; Dixie; reggae; bebop; funk—all these things are available to us as practitioners of Great Black Music."[100] Some of the most significant styles of twentieth-century music were represented on Jarman's list, and the members of the Art Ensemble were confident that Great Black Music would continue to be a vital element of global culture in the twenty-first century and beyond. This implied that Great Black Music, in its many manifestations from the Ancient to the Future, was without limit. "We can be free," Bowie reasoned, "to interpret everything that's ever been played, [and] things that have never been played." He continued, "I feel we have created a truly WORLD music, comprised of music from everywhere, for people everywhere."[101]

The Art Ensemble's slogan appeared at a moment in history when race and ethnicity were intensely politicized, and certain critics dismissed Great Black Music as a reductive notion that was better suited for a protest march than a concert stage.[102] However, the musicians' interpretations of the slogan were far from one-dimensional. Great Black Music was at once a pan-African theory of culture, an expression of diasporic consciousness, and a radical declaration that black music could be whatever the Art Ensemble wanted it to be. The last of these three perspectives was particularly meaningful to Mitchell, who reflected on the relationship between Great Black Music and his own sense of personal identity:

> Music doesn't have color, music is infinite. . . . But I equally reflect my existence as a black man and the world in which I live, a world in which it is ever easier to communicate with all kinds of individuals and cultures. In a few hours, you can be physically on the other side of the globe. In a few seconds, you can exchange your ideas, your sentiments, or your impressions with anybody, anywhere. The basic experience, however, is always the same: you express that which influences you, that which permits you to progress in your knowledge of beings and things, and to forge a vocabulary and a language that permits you speak freely, and to be yourself when in contact with others.[103]

For Mitchell, the significance of Great Black Music was the central role it played in his development into a great black musician—or, as he phrased it, a "super musician."[104] Mitchell aspired to be "someone that moves freely in music," able to compose in any style and improvise fluently with any musician, anywhere.[105] He believed that Great Black Music was one of the major traditions worldwide that could provide a super musician with a "well established background," a necessary condition for mastering composition and improvisation.[106] In the late 1960s, though, critics and audiences did not always recognize that the music of Africa and its diaspora could provide a solid foundation for a group of would-be super musicians who wanted to achieve total musical mobility. And this, according to Mitchell, is why the Art Ensemble had to invent the concept of Great Black Music: "Well, nobody was calling the music great."[107]

The Great Black Music slogan also helped the members of the Art Ensemble contextualize the intermedia elements of their performances. Sometimes they drew connections between their intermedia practices and African modes of performance, while at other times they compared their work to influential performance traditions from black America, elsewhere in the African diaspora, and even Europe or Asia. In Jarman's view, the band's use of theater and poetry could be linked to a number of antecedents. He and his bandmates came of age during the 1940s and 1950s, an era when African American popular music often involved theatrical gestures and broad humor. Jarman's upbringing near the entertainment district on the South Side of Chicago gave him a front-row seat to these developments: "I remember being very young and going to hear the [Eddie] 'Cleanhead' Vinson Band. And this man comes out with a bald head and a big super comb and combs his 'hair.' It was theater."[108] Decades later, Jarman discovered another approach to intermedia performance at an arts festival in Morocco:

> [T]hat experience was the confirmation for these ideas I had. Because all of the performers were actors, and dancers, and singers, and poets, and everything. It was just one entity. . . . For me now, [making] music with my voice and body is the same as [making] music with a traditional musical instrument. Also for me now the body has become a musical instrument as well as a movement instrument.[109]

Jarman felt that his band had the potential to accomplish what he had witnessed in Morocco, the complete integration of music and other performing arts. After all, the members of the Art Ensemble, like their Moroccan counterparts, were practitioners of Great Black Music. "In African music and Great Black Music," Jarman claimed, "all the arts were together." He further said, "We are trying with the Art Ensemble to revive this tradition, to make people understand that they are free, that there's no separation between these forms."[110]

The musicians offered a similar range of explanations for the face paint and costumes they wore onstage. Favors, who introduced face painting to the Art Ensemble, considered it to be a pan-African practice associated with worship ceremonies and other important rituals. "It's a tradition in my ancestry," Favors stated. "[W]henever an event took place in Africa they masked up, and in sort of a spiritual vein."[111] In contrast, Jarman contended that face paint and masking were "not unique to black culture":

> We use face paint, for example, not as war paint but in place of masks, which are used in cultures of every ethnicity to subjugate the personality of the performer so he can more easily become a representative to the community. Masks and costumes make universal statements, and are archetypal symbols.[112]

Not all of the band members painted their faces. Favors, Jarman, and Moye regularly wore face paint and occasionally donned masks, while Bowie and Mitchell never painted for performances.[113] As with the Art Ensemble's social and business practices, personal autonomy was essential to all aspects of the group's performance practice. "In our music," Bowie noted, "each member is free to express himself individually, in any way he feels he wants to. . . . Everything is based on individual creativity, free expression."[114] This principle was also evident in the stage costumes worn by the Art Ensemble. Instead of adopting a standard uniform, each musician chose his own concert apparel. During the late 1960s and early 1970s, their attire could be rather eclectic. Bowie might appear onstage wearing a bow tie, a train conductor's cap, or a chef's outfit.[115] By the Art Ensemble's second decade, though, the group members' wardrobe choices began to align into a perceptible pattern. Jarman described this costuming scheme as a historical "spectrum," a visual depiction of Great Black Music:

> [I]f you look at the spectrum, we were representing history, from the "Ancient to the Future." And that slogan came from that realization. Malachi always represents the oldest entity because he would always wear these long full flowing robes. And he would look like an African/Egyptian Shaman. His persona would emulate that, and his music and his style. He is very ancient. Then Moye was really in the midst of the African tradition. His drumming, his style, his approach, his feeling and his interests, were not a single African tradition, but a total African tradition. . . . My position was more moving toward the contemporary. I was Eastern oriented. These three

were the pantheistic element of Africa and Asia. Roscoe represented the mainstream sort of Shaman, the Urban Delivery Man, delivering healing qualities. . . . Lester was always the investigator, wearing cook clothes, which is healing, creating energy and food. Then he advanced his awareness and went to the doctor's experimental laboratory. All of this Black imagery going from the "Ancient to the Future" is represented in this stage attire.[116]

Jazz Wars

The relationship between the Great Black Music concept and jazz was rather complex. The members of the Art Ensemble regarded their slogan as a way to transcend the limitations of jazz, especially its position in the music industry. "We want to avoid the stigma of jazz," Bowie explained. "When you say 'jazz,' it means, 'uh-oh': You're the lowest paid guys on the concert, you have the worst hotel, you're the least respected. The name 'Great Black Music' generates more respect."[117] Despite these concerns, the group members were not interested in abandoning jazz entirely. Jazz was a major influence on their performance practice—indeed, it was one of the vital "roots" of Great Black Music, according to Bowie.[118] Moreover, jazz listeners and jazz critics were some of the musicians' biggest supporters, as evidenced by their album sales and their impressive run atop the *Down Beat* polls in the 1980s. The members of the Art Ensemble were fully aware that they occupied an important place on the American jazz scene, even as they found new audiences in the performing-arts world. Accordingly, when the jazz community erupted in controversy over the rapid rise of a traditionalist movement headed by Wynton Marsalis, the musicians were compelled to respond.

Marsalis and the Art Ensemble did not start out as antagonists. In fact, for an all-too-brief period in 1982, the twenty-year-old Marsalis was a bandmate of Bowie's.[119] In the years since his 1977 move to New York, Bowie had established himself as an elder statesman on the city's jazz scene and a mentor to many younger musicians.[120] One of the musicians in Bowie's orbit was Malachi Thompson, a fellow AACM trumpeter who relocated to New York around the same time as Bowie.[121] In the spring of 1982, Bowie and Thompson formed the New York Hot Trumpet Repertory Company, a precursor to Bowie's Brass Fantasy with an even more unusual lineup: five trumpets, no low brass instruments, and no rhythm section.[122] To fill the three open trumpet chairs, Bowie and Thompson hired Olu Dara, Stanton Davis, and Marsalis, who had just left Art Blakey's Jazz Messengers and was primed to launch his solo career.[123] Marsalis played with the New York Hot Trumpet Repertory

Company for just a few months. He had ample performance opportunities with his own quintet, and his debut album on Columbia Records, released earlier in 1982, was becoming a critical success.[124] When Marsalis quit the New York Hot Trumpet Repertory Company, Bowie did not miss a beat. He brought in Bruce Purse to replace Marsalis, and the band kept working.[125] However, the circumstances surrounding Marsalis's sudden departure made Bowie suspicious of his ex-bandmate. "Wynton was with us until the label executives from Columbia advised him to get away from that maniac assed Lester Bowie before he f— up his whole career," Bowie recalled. "There was never an argument. I felt Wynton was being used and was an enemy of the music."[126]

The rift between Bowie and his former collaborator deepened during the 1980s and 1990s. Marsalis's ties to leading cultural institutions, including Columbia Records, Jazz at Lincoln Center, the *New York Times*, and the Public Broadcasting Service (PBS), gave him a prominent public platform, and he became a self-assured spokesman for his vision of jazz. For Marsalis, jazz was the grandest musical achievement of African American culture (and American culture in general). He took a dim view of musicians whose work deviated from what he considered to be the fundamentals of jazz—swinging, blues-based approaches to improvisation and composition advanced by iconic figures such as Louis Armstrong and Duke Ellington. Marsalis prosecuted his case vigorously, often disparaging jazz-fusion players and others whom he judged to be outside the jazz tradition, including the Art Ensemble.[127] These attacks did not sit well with Bowie, who gradually emerged as one of Marsalis's fiercest critics. At first, Bowie's critiques were relatively gentle, and directed at Marsalis's trumpet playing rather than his intemperate public persona. In a 1984 *Down Beat* interview, given while Bowie was an artist in residence at Harvard University, he sounded like a teacher admonishing a wayward student:

> The hardest thing to do is develop identity. You have to go through everybody before you. I hope Wynton will continue to develop and not be scared of those boys at [Columbia Records] making all those big claims. . . . Wynton, to me, is a genius, but he has a long way to go, and he's the first to tell you. With Wynton's chops and my brains, I could've been one of the greatest.[128]

Nine years later, in another *Down Beat* article, Bowie once again expressed doubts about Marsalis's improvisational abilities: "How long did it take Lee

Morgan to play something of his own, or Clifford [Brown], or Booker Little? Wynton's a good musician, but he's been totally miscast. No way in the world is he the King of Jazz, the King of Trumpet."[129] But this time, the core of Bowie's critique was aimed at the power that Marsalis wielded as the newly installed artistic director of Jazz at Lincoln Center:

> Why is it that these sorts of responsibilities are pressed on a negative person? He even accused Miles [Davis] of treason. Because Miles played a Cyndi Lauper tune ["Time After Time"]? In the '50s, "Surrey with the Fringe on Top" was on the Hit Parade. That's part of the thing to be contemporary, to express yourself. Wynton's trying to tamper with the music's development, and I see some kind of evil overlay on that.[130]

Bowie's challenges to Marsalis did not go unanswered. In May 1994, Marsalis brought his trumpet to a New York jazz club where Bowie was performing with his band Brass Fantasy. Marsalis's plan was to interrupt Brass Fantasy's set and provoke Bowie into an old-fashioned trumpet duel that would somehow settle the score with his adversary. This stunt did not amuse Bowie, according to a *New York Times* account: "After addressing Mr. Marsalis as 'boy,' Mr. Bowie, who is . . . 20 years older than Mr. Marsalis, wouldn't invite him to play."[131] Marsalis, never one to forgive and forget, got retribution in the PBS documentary series *Jazz*, directed by Ken Burns.[132] (Marsalis served as the film's senior creative consultant.[133]) In the final episode of the series, Bowie briefly appeared on camera, telling the story of why the Art Ensemble adopted the Great Black Music slogan. Then the narrator took over, charging the Art Ensemble with a grave offense against jazz: not having a "black audience."[134] To support this allegation, the narrator cited two pieces of evidence, both of which were demonstrably false. The first claim, that the group "once found itself playing to just three people in its own hometown," was in fact a self-effacing anecdote told by Anthony Braxton about one of his 1960s performances.[135] The second bit of evidence was just as misleading. The Art Ensemble supposedly "attracted its largest following among white college students — in France," the narrator intoned, all but accusing the group members of being inauthentically black.[136] This assessment of the Art Ensemble's fan base might have been accurate (if trivially so) when the musicians were actually living in France, but in the decades thereafter, the group developed a diverse audience in locations around the world.

In Bowie's view, the Art Ensemble's audience was precisely as diverse as the communities where the band performed: "[I]f we play in America and you get ten blacks out of a hundred, that's about the proportion that you would expect in this country. If we play in France, we get 95% Frenchmen."[137] Marty Khan claimed, contrary to Bowie, that the group's fan base in the United States was nearly fifty percent black.[138] Indeed, in 1982 the Art Ensemble won an NAACP Image Award, an indication that the band had a substantial following in the African American community.[139] However, even Bowie's modest estimate of the Art Ensemble's African American fan base would compare favorably to the diversity of the general jazz audience—or, for that matter, the audience demographics for Marsalis's own Jazz at Lincoln Center Orchestra.[140] In 1998, when the Art Ensemble earned its fifth "Acoustic Jazz Group of the Year" award from *Down Beat* magazine, Mitchell remarked that "we did a sold-out concert in New York at Alice Tully Hall," then the home of Jazz at Lincoln Center: "Marsalis doesn't even fill a hall like that."[141]

The public debate between Bowie and Marsalis was intensified by the personal rivalry between the two trumpeters. Every year from 1982 to 1995, either Bowie or Marsalis was named the best trumpet player in *Down Beat's* Critics Poll. Like two evenly matched prizefighters in their prime, neither Bowie nor Marsalis held on to first place for more than three consecutive years, and once (in 1993) they battled to a draw.[142] In the same poll, the Art Ensemble and Marsalis's band contended annually for the title of "Acoustic Jazz Group of the Year." Despite the huge publicity advantage enjoyed by Marsalis, the Art Ensemble managed to win twice as many group awards, prevailing in 1980, 1981, 1982, 1985, 1998, and 1999.[143]

Competitions for concert ticket sales and *Down Beat* awards could add fuel to the fire, but ultimately the Bowie-Marsalis dispute was not about music-industry politics. Bowie and Marsalis were instead engaged in a philosophical debate about the nature and practice of Great Black Music. And as in all debates, the personal differences between the two parties, no matter how small, further dramatized their philosophical disagreements. In some ways, Bowie and Marsalis were more alike than they cared to admit. Both Bowie and Marsalis were engaged in the same cultural project of elevating black music. The two men both understood how to convey cultural messages through their stage attire—witness Bowie's experimentalist lab coat and Marsalis's closetful of tailored suits, courtesy of Brooks Brothers, the "official clothier" of the Jazz at Lincoln Center Orchestra.[144] As young musicians, they emulated the same trumpeters, Louis Armstrong and Miles Davis, and both emphasized the importance of studying the jazz tradition. But it was at this point that they parted ways.

Unlike Marsalis, Bowie viewed jazz history through a progressive lens. The members of the Art Ensemble were "traditionalists in [a] sense," according to Bowie, because "rebellion is the actual tradition of jazz."[145] From this perspective, Marsalis's devotion to the performance practices of previous generations seemed paradoxical. As Bowie pointed out, "revolution is for young people: that should be Wynton's job."[146] In Bowie's diagnosis, Marsalis failed to strike the proper balance between the Ancient and the Future, between his interests as a historian of jazz and his responsibilities as a creative artist. "You do have to go through the music of the past, to learn how to play," Bowie argued, "but once you do that, that's it. Because jazz is not some academic exercise."[147] Bowie and his bandmates, of course, were not categorically opposed to the kinds of research and educational efforts sponsored by Jazz at Lincoln Center.[148] Mitchell had taught at universities across the country, Bowie served as a resident artist at Harvard and two other Ivy League schools (Dartmouth College, Yale University), and the others routinely led master classes in conjunction with their performances.[149] However, the group members were deeply concerned about how jazz was being taught by Marsalis and his allies. Marsalis, echoing his intellectual mentor Albert Murray, insisted that improvisers should "elaborate, extend, and refine" the musical materials inherited from the early masters of blues and jazz.[150] This strict, purist prescription left little room for innovation.

The members of the Art Ensemble had resisted traditionalist thinking since the 1960s, when they first introduced the Great Black Music concept. To Mitchell, Marsalis was only the latest entrant in a parade of musicians and critics who "turn[ed] away [from] new ideas and sounds" and tried to limit, not expand, the horizons of jazz.[151] In contrast, Mitchell and his bandmates envisioned an unbounded, Ancient to the Future tradition in which "the creative process is . . . still going on."[152] For the Art Ensemble, Great Black Music could encompass the living traditions of Africa and its diaspora, as well as sounds from all periods and all places, every mode of performance, and anything that the group members imagined. As Mitchell declared, "[m]usic is exploration and the Art Ensemble has such a wide variety of musics to choose from."[153]

9 Live from the Jazz Showcase

Music is seen as well as heard.[1]

All of the sonic and visual elements of Great Black Music are on display in *Live from the Showcase*, an Art Ensemble concert video recorded on 1 November 1981 in Chicago.[2] The musicians were in town for a three-day engagement at the famous Jazz Showcase nightclub, a Chicago institution since 1947. The Jazz Showcase was an ideal place to film a concert video. At the time, the nightclub was located in the Crystal Ballroom of the historic Blackstone Hotel, at South Michigan Avenue and East Balbo Drive in Chicago's Loop district.[3] The band's enthusiastic hometown following ensured a capacity crowd, while the ballroom's open layout allowed the videographers to move freely around the perimeter of the low-slung stage, capturing three hundred and sixty degrees of the Art Ensemble.[4]

Live from the Jazz Showcase reveals what audiences experienced at Art Ensemble performances in the 1980s, the decade when the group toured most extensively. Many of the compositions on the Jazz Showcase set list were fixtures of the band's concert repertoire. The musicians played "Promenade: Coté Bamako," "New York Is Full of Lonely People," and "A Jackson in Your House" during the 1980 tour in support of the ECM album *Full Force*, and nearly

silence	0:00-0:57
"We Bop"	0:57-7:52
transition	7:52-11:04
"Promenade: Côte Bamako"	11:04-21:14
"New York is Full of Lonely People"	21:14-25:46
transition	25:46-37:52
"A Jackson in Your House"	37:52-40:56
Encore: "Funky AECO"	40:56-47:14
Encore: "Odwalla"	47:14-52:15

EXAMPLE 9.1 *Live from the Jazz Showcase*: formal diagram

every Art Ensemble concert since the fall of 1972 had ended with "Odwalla."[5] The other compositions performed by the group at the Jazz Showcase, "We Bop" and "Funky AECO," appeared on live recordings and studio albums later in the 1980s (see example 9.1).[6] *Live from the Jazz Showcase* also makes visible the full range of visual intermedia employed in Art Ensemble concerts, a crucial aspect of the band's performance practice. We see a "Great Black Music, Ancient to the Future" banner suspended above the stage, and below it, the group's immense collection of musical instruments: "a beautiful shining sound object," as Jarman phrased it, "waiting to tone the infinite sound of the ART ENSEMBLE OF CHICAGO."[7] We also see Moye's face paint, the masks worn by Favors and Jarman, and the musicians' stage attire, as well as the gestures and movements they make while performing. In sum, we see each and every visual "enhancement of the music"—the intermedia elements that, according to Moye, elevate an Art Ensemble concert from a music-only event into a form of "total creative expression."[8]

Live from the Jazz Showcase shares several key features with the albums analyzed in chapters 4 and 7. As in *Live at Mandel Hall*, another concert recording, group improvisation is at the core of the performance.[9] The musicians work together in real time to execute the set list, interpreting each composition and then seamlessly connecting it to the next piece with an "improvisational transition."[10] And as in the studio album *A Jackson in Your House*, the members of the Art Ensemble combine music and intermedia throughout the Jazz Showcase concert, creating a series of compelling narratives.[11] In *A Jackson in Your House*, these intermedia narratives are shaped by theatrical scenarios and poetic texts, but in *Live from the Jazz Showcase*, the Art Ensemble's narratives emerge from the interactions between sound and image. The group members accompany the music with a rich visual counterpoint, in which five costumed performers play myriad instruments, move about the stage, and engage in spontaneous choreography.[12] The intermedia narratives presented by the band at the Jazz Showcase take on many different forms. The musicians might call attention to the ritualistic dimensions of the concert, use gestures to dramatize a transitional passage, or move their bodies in ways that evoke the history of a musical style. As the performance unfolds, these diverse narratives gradually coalesce into one resonant theme: the limitless possibilities of Great Black Music.

Silence/"We Bop"

The Jazz Showcase concert begins not with sound, but with silence. The members of the Art Ensemble take the stage and move to their usual stations.[13] Moye is up center, at the back of the stage, and Favors stands to his left. The others position themselves along the front of the stage. Jarman is down left, ahead of Favors, with Bowie and Mitchell to his right. Once the musicians reach their places, they turn to the left, soundlessly, and almost a minute passes before the first note is heard.

For the Art Ensemble, opening a concert with a moment of silence was not out of the ordinary. In fact, it was just as integral to the band's performance practice as "Odwalla," the theme played at the close of most concerts. The moment of silence, according to Moye, helped "focus the energy in the room onto what is happening on stage," capturing the audience's attention even before the music began.[14] Meanwhile, the group members used the moment of silence as a time for spiritual preparation. Together they offered a wordless invocation—a "prayer for unity and peace throughout the universe," in Jarman's description.[15] The musicians inherited this practice from the AACM. From the earliest days of the Association, business meetings began with the attendees facing east for a silent prayer, and the members of the Art Ensemble brought this ritual into their concerts, with one slight modification.[16] In their hometown of Chicago, it was easy to determine which way was east, but when the musicians started traveling the world and performing in unfamiliar settings, getting oriented became more difficult. "It used to be east," Bowie recalled. "Now we face Jarman. The decision just came to us. And it's more effective. Besides, we couldn't keep track of where east was."[17]

The Art Ensemble's silent invocation also served a specific musical purpose. Silence was central to the group's conception of music.[18] In the 1960s, Mitchell told a bandmate that "the first music was silence—just total silence," and one can imagine the moment of silence at the beginning of the Jazz Showcase performance as a representation of this primeval period in music history.[19] However, Art Ensemble concerts did not involve orderly progressions from Ancient sounds to Future sounds, or any other teleological interpretations of Great Black Music. "[I]t doesn't have to be a chronological thing," Bowie explained. "It doesn't have to be, 'Here comes the blues and here comes the gospel.' It can start with the avant-garde and end with the blues. I mean, I know the audience, they aren't dumb!"[20] The invocation instead functioned as a silent prelude, an imperceptible background that brought the Art Ensemble's music into greater relief. As Mitchell observed, "[i]f you're just sitting somewhere and it's totally silent, a lot of people don't even have that luxury anymore, living in a city. In a concert hall, you can have that. When you interrupt that with a sound, then you have music."[21]

In other performances, the members of the Art Ensemble conclude the invocation by striking a gong, but at the Jazz Showcase, Jarman interrupts the long silence with a blast on a whistle.[22] Then the musicians pivot rightward, turning away from Jarman's side of the stage to face the audience. The first piece on the set list is Bowie's "We Bop," a jazz composition that typically begins with a fast-paced statement of the theme.[23] Instead of attempting to smooth the transition from the serene invocation to the lively feel of "We Bop," the group members simply leap right in. Bowie counts off two beats, then taps his foot three times to lock in the quarter-note pulse that underlies the melody. On the next beat, he enters along with Jarman and Mitchell, and together they play the "We Bop" theme (see example 9.2). Bowie and Mitchell, on trumpet and alto saxophone, respectively, are in unison, while Jarman, on tenor saxophone, doubles the melody one octave lower. Favors (on double bass) and Moye (on drum set) support their bandmates with a swinging, up-tempo groove, and for about forty seconds, the Art Ensemble sounds like a conventional bebop quintet. This impression is enhanced by the structure of Bowie's theme. The theme is in ABCB form, a variant of the 32-bar song form that is so common in jazz, and the chord progression is borrowed from the jazz standard "I Got Rhythm." ("We Bop" is in B♭ major, the usual key for a theme that uses the "Rhythm changes" progression.) In another nod to the jazz tradition, Bowie bases the C-section melody on the opening motive of Sonny Rollins's "Pent-Up House," a classic hard-bop tune from the mid-1950s.[24]

EXAMPLE 9.2 "We Bop": "We Bop" score for trumpet

* The musical examples in this chapter are the author's transcriptions, reproduced by permission of Art Ensemble of Chicago Publishing (ASCAP). Each staff is labeled with the performer's initials. The examples represent pitches in the keys of the instruments being played, and may be read as scores for improvisers. The chapter text refers to pitches in concert key, and adopts the convention in which middle C is labeled C_4.

During the opening phrases of "We Bop," the concertgoers get their first look at the group's stage costumes. Bowie wears his white lab coat over casual clothing: a red oxford shirt and crisply cuffed jeans. Mitchell is even more relaxed in tan corduroys, a burgundy turtleneck, and a yellow knit cap, looking "as if he had paused in the course of his ordinary day to play some . . . extraordinary music."[25] As usual, neither Bowie nor Mitchell wears face paint or anything else that would turn heads on the streets outside the Jazz Showcase (except perhaps the expensive gold watch perched on Bowie's wrist). Moye, Jarman, and Favors are also dressed in their typical concert attire, but unlike Bowie and Mitchell, their clothing appears more ceremonial than casual, more African and Asian than American.[26] Moye is clad in a four-piece ensemble—pants, shirt, vest, and kufi cap—made of richly textured, earth-toned fabrics. His face paint design is also multicolored, with a sun-like yellow circle drawn on his forehead. Jarman's outfit is similar to Moye's, though the color scheme is cooler, and his face is covered not with paint but with a turquoise-and-silver mask that gleams when hit by the lights. The boldest colors on stage, however, belong to Favors. He wears a bright red tunic and pants, a wide black belt decorated with cowrie shells, and a black mask. Instead of a cap, Favors sports a gold headcloth like that of an "African/Egyptian Shaman," a costuming detail that provides an Ancient bookend to Bowie's Future-oriented laboratory coat.[27] "We are trying to represent the complete history of Great Black Music," Jarman explained. "Lester always looks like a doctor, a scientist—something very contemporary. . . . And then there is Malachi who is always ancient."[28]

After the musicians state the "We Bop" theme, they set out on two very different paths. Bowie keeps playing in the bebop style, offering an improvised melody line that elaborates on the 32-bar form and chord progression set out in the theme. Favors and Moye follow Bowie's lead, maintaining the walking bass line and dancing ride-cymbal rhythm that they introduced at the beginning of "We Bop." In contrast to their bandmates, Jarman and Mitchell studiously avoid doing what might be expected of two saxophonists in a typical bebop performance. During Bowie's trumpet solo, they could wait patiently for their own solo turns, or even accompany Bowie with an impromptu background riff. Instead, Jarman and Mitchell put down their saxophones and start playing percussion. Mitchell alternates between bell lyre and a set of tiny cymbals, while Jarman focuses on his own array of metallic percussion. At first, they use their percussion instruments to comment on important events in the 32-bar form. Partway through the first chorus of Bowie's solo, Mitchell moves from cymbals to bell lyre and plays a shimmering B_4, marking the arrival of the G^7 chord in the third measure of the C section by sounding that chord's most chromatic pitch. Fourteen measures later, Moye leaves some space at the end of a drum fill, and Jarman steps in, striking a pair of bells at 2:14 to announce the beginning of Bowie's second chorus.

As the trumpet solo continues, Mitchell and Jarman's percussion sounds gradually develop into an independent texture that is untethered to the repeating 32-bar form and bebop style articulated by their bandmates. Jarman is surrounded by an extensive arsenal of percussion instruments, including more than thirty bells and gongs, and he takes the lead in shaping the nascent percussion texture. One minute into Bowie's improvisation, Jarman plays a series of disconnected bell and gong strokes, working against the groove created by the rhythm section and blurring the boundary between the second and third solo choruses. Jarman's percussive attacks grow denser and denser during each ensuing chorus. By 5:14, the top of Bowie's seventh chorus, Jarman is stomping on a bulb horn, producing an insistent chatter that nearly overshadows the trumpet solo. Bowie answers with a string of middle-register long tones that break away from the 32-bar form, just like Jarman and Mitchell's percussion contributions. After playing several long tones, Bowie abruptly moves into the upper register at 5:28, then twists to his left, aiming his trumpet squarely at Jarman. Bowie's upper-register fanfare earns an immediate response from Jarman, who starts crashing a pair of handheld cymbals. Jarman and Bowie trade salvos for fifteen seconds, bringing the trumpet solo to a climax. Then Bowie relents, sitting down on his chair at the center of the stage and playing one last middle-register smear, which Jarman punctuates with another cymbal crash. Bowie's four-minute, seven-chorus improvisation has come to a close (see example 9.3).

When Bowie exits, the musicians must decide whether to end "We Bop" and transition to the next entry on the set list. Favors and Moye temporarily suspend the groove, each waiting to see what the other will do. Then Favors returns to the walking bass line he played during the theme and trumpet solo, and Moye concurs, synchronizing his cymbal pattern with Favors's steady pulse. Favors is once again outlining the "We Bop" chord progression, and Mitchell or Jarman could easily prolong the piece by taking a saxophone solo. Both, however, choose to stay on percussion. Mitchell coaxes fragmentary melodies from his bell lyre, and Jarman remains engrossed in his assortment of bells and gongs. Mitchell and Jarman's decision keeps the group improvisation balanced between two opposing possibilities. They are still exploring the percussion texture that emerged early in Bowie's trumpet solo, while Favors and Moye show no signs of abandoning "We Bop." The tension between the percussion texture and "We Bop" persists for a full minute, until 6:42, when

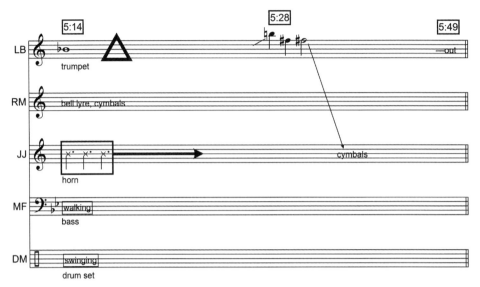

EXAMPLE 9.3 "We Bop": Bowie solo, chorus 7

* In this example, the box indicates a motive that repeats, the diagonal arrow denotes a musical interaction between performers, and the triangle is a symbol that means "improvise(d)."

Bowie reenters on trumpet. Favors and Moye have just arrived at the midpoint of the 32-bar chorus—a perfect place for Bowie to begin another bebop-style solo or prepare to restate the "We Bop" theme. Instead, Bowie integrates his trumpet line into Jarman and Mitchell's percussion texture. He soon finds his way to the upper register, the range he ventured into at the climax of his trumpet solo a moment earlier. Mitchell and Jarman react by moving from metallic percussion to drums, echoing Bowie's upper-register bursts and inviting sympathetic responses from Moye and Favors (see example 9.4). When this exchange concludes, Bowie lays out, and "We Bop" instantly breaks down. Favors arrests his walking bass line, and Moye uses his snare drum and tom-toms to dialogue with the drums played by Jarman and Mitchell. The percussion texture has finally prevailed.

Transition/"Promenade: Coté Bamako"

The members of the Art Ensemble proceed from "We Bop" into the first transitional passage of the performance. Unlike some transitions, this episode will not have to be assembled from scratch. The rich percussion texture that overtook "We Bop" is an optimal point of departure for a group improvisation—indeed, in countless Art Ensemble concerts, percussion sounds serve as the

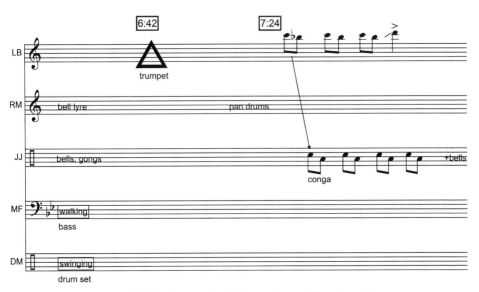

EXAMPLE 9.4 "We Bop": percussion texture, disassembling the swing groove

building blocks for improvised transitions. Moreover, this passage's ultimate destination will also center on percussion. The next item on the set list is "Promenade: Coté Bamako," a drum composition by Moye. In performances of "Promenade," Moye acts as the lead drummer, responsible for initiating the piece and directing his bandmates as they play their parts.[29] Accordingly, until Moye gives the cue for "Promenade," the musicians can improvise in an open-ended fashion, drawing on elements of the percussion texture or offering musical ideas that are entirely new.

At the beginning of the transition, the texture is dominated by the drumming of Jarman, Mitchell, and Moye. Jarman also works to reintroduce the bells and gongs that he played during "We Bop." He holds mallets in both hands, and at one point he extends his left arm outward to strike a bell and a conga drum in alternation while simultaneously tolling a gong to his right. Then he shifts positions so he can grab a handful of confetti from a bag resting on the table near his gong collection. With a skyward leap, Jarman tosses the confetti into the air at 8:48. Before it can fall to the ground, he rushes to his rack of bells, ringing as many as six bells per second and creating a splendid clangor. Jarman's high-register bell chorus transforms the texture. Moye responds by moving from drum set to triangles, and Mitchell returns to his bell lyre. In just a few seconds' time, all of the drums heard prior to the confetti toss have been replaced by metallic percussion. Even Bowie, who has rested since the end of "We Bop," rejoins the texture playing trumpet, the

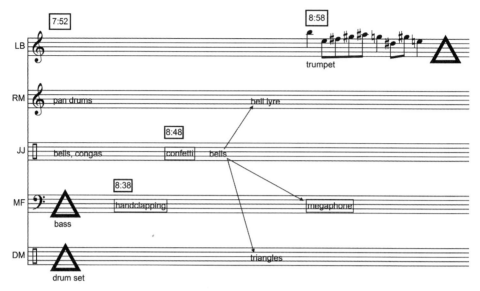

EXAMPLE 9.5 Transition: Jarman confetti toss, metallic sounds

instrument of his that most closely matches the range and timbral profile of Jarman's bell rack (see example 9.5).

As the transitional music unfolds, Favors acts out his own wordless drama. For more than three minutes, the entire length of the transition, he barely makes a sound. Instead of playing an instrument, he communicates with his bandmates and the audience through a series of enigmatic physical gestures. Early in the transition, Favors lays his bass aside and stands silently in the middle of his station. Suddenly he gazes upward, reaches above his head, and claps his hands together, as if catching a fly. His next gesture is even more mysterious. After Jarman's confetti toss, Favors grabs a blue-and-gray megaphone and holds it near his mouth—but no sound escapes. On other occasions, Favors was known to advise listeners that "there may be a message in the music for you."[30] At the Jazz Showcase, though, he remains mute, letting the concertgoers develop their own interpretations of the sounds and sights presented by the Art Ensemble (see example 9.5). The mystique conveyed by Favors is heightened by the mask he wears. Fashioned by his AACM colleague Douglas Ewart, who also made the mask worn by Jarman, Favors's mask completely covers his face, with small openings for his eyes and mouth.[31] An Egyptian all-seeing eye is embossed on the forehead, and during the transition it seems to shine brighter than Favors's own eyes, which are painted the same shade of onyx as his mask. Because of the mask, Favors's facial expressions are hard to read, but this only makes his performance more captivating. With

EXAMPLE 9.6 "Promenade": Moye composite rhythm

his face obscured, the audience must focus intently on Favors's gestures and bodily movements, which carry much of the message he delivers during the Jazz Showcase concert.

At 11:04, three minutes into the transition, Moye approaches a pair of drums placed stage right, just past Mitchell's station. He then starts playing an intricate rhythmic pattern in 8/8 time, a signal for the group to begin his composition "Promenade" (see example 9.6). The instruments employed by Moye are "pan drums," which were specially made for the Art Ensemble in advance of the 1980 *Full Force* tour.[32] The craftsman, Chicago percussionist Musa Mosley, hand-built the drums from local materials: "100% pure American beef hides and hardwood from the South Side."[33] Mosley's instrument designs were indebted to the single-headed, rope-strung drums widely used across Africa, and he called his creations pan drums because he considered them to be pan-African in origin.[34] Mosley made several pan drums for the Art Ensemble, and with these instruments the band could perform Moye's compositions for drum choir, including "Promenade." Pan drums (and Favors's African log drum) are the only instruments played during "Promenade," which is written in the style of a Mandinka percussion piece, as suggested by the composition's subtitle, "Coté Bamako."[35]

The pan drums used by Bowie, Jarman, and Mitchell are all positioned within a few feet of Moye's drums on the right side of the stage. Jarman's drum is immediately to the right of Moye, and Mitchell's drum is on Moye's left. Bowie's pan drum is equipped with a shoulder strap, allowing him to play while marching along the front of the stage, not far from Moye. According to Moye, the other musicians "kept losing the damn beat" during performances of percussion pieces like "Promenade."[36] For this reason, Moye's bandmates placed their pan drums in close proximity to him, so that they could quickly establish eye contact with him if they faltered while playing. Even Favors, who remains in his stage-left station for "Promenade," can turn to his right and look directly at Moye. By virtue of this stage setup, the members of the Art Ensemble face one another during "Promenade," instead of addressing the Jazz Showcase audience. As "Promenade" takes shape, the concertgoers may

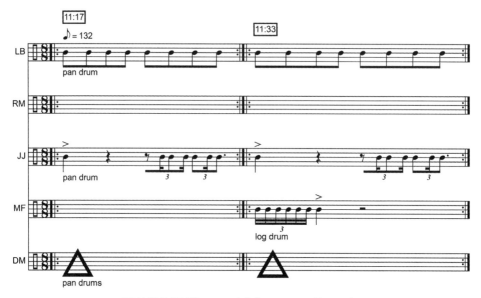

EXAMPLE 9.7 "Promenade": three supporting parts

feel less like listeners at a jazz club and more like observers of a performance-art event or music-centered ritual. This shift in perspective also affords the audience a closer look at a key component of the concert experience: the group members' performance personalities, from Bowie and Jarman's extro-version and Moye's confident stage presence to the more reserved demeanors of Mitchell and Favors.

"Promenade" is a solo feature for Moye, whose pan-drum improvisation is supported by four interlocking parts played by the other musicians. But before he can start his solo, he must first invite the rest of the group into the new texture. The 8/8 drum pattern that Moye uses to cue "Promenade" is a composite rhythm. It includes the essential elements of three parts assigned to his bandmates: Bowie's eighth-note pulse, Jarman's short-long rhythmic figure, and Favors's sixteenth-note triplets. When these parts are played together, they produce a resultant rhythm that is almost identical to Moye's pattern.[37] By beginning "Promenade" with a composite rhythm, Moye gives the other group members a chance to hear their parts before they enter. After Moye plays his pattern four times, Bowie and Jarman join in, and Favors enters five measures later at 11:33 (see example 9.7). Once Mitchell brings in the fourth and final supporting part, the rhythmic framework of "Promenade" will be complete, and Moye's pan-drum solo can commence. However, when Mitchell starts playing, Favors drops out, just two bars after he entered (see example 9.8).

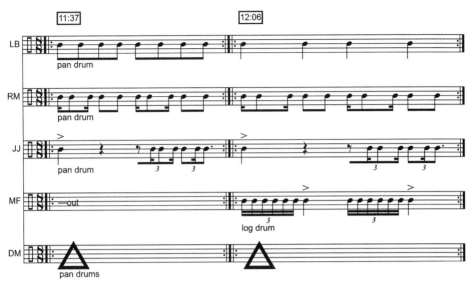

EXAMPLE 9.8 "Promenade": four supporting parts

EXAMPLE 9.9 "Promenade": Moye composite rhythm, cueing Favors

Although Favors knows he has to return as soon as possible, he seems hesitant, perhaps because his part is difficult to reconcile with Mitchell's. Both parts involve subdividing the eighth-note pulse, but Favors splits each eighth note into sixteenth-note triplets, while Mitchell plays an uneven short-long-short rhythm built from duple subdivisions. When Favors finally reenters, some fifteen seconds later, he is one beat ahead of the other group members. Moye instantly senses that his bandmate is lost, and he turns toward Favors so that both musicians can see each other. Then Moye raises his arms dramatically, beckoning Favors to pay close attention to what will happen next. Once he is certain that Favors is tuned in, Moye hammers out a new composite rhythm that blends Mitchell's duple rhythm with the triplet-based patterns assigned to Jarman and Favors. In the following bar, Moye performs Favors's own part, and this prompt is all that Favors needs (see example 9.9). Midway through the measure, at 12:06, Favors rejoins the texture playing his sixteenth-note triplets. At last, one minute after Moye introduced "Promenade," all four supporting parts are in place (see example 9.8).

pan drums

EXAMPLE 9.10 "Promenade": Moye transitional rhythm, metric shift

Now that Favors is properly aligned with the other musicians, Moye can proceed into his solo. He improvises on pan drums for two minutes, developing each of the four supporting rhythms that define "Promenade." At times he uses his drumsticks to play on the wooden shells of his pan drums, creating a distinctive timbre that further differentiates his lead drumming from the accompanying roles played by Bowie, Favors, Jarman, and Mitchell. During Moye's solo, his bandmates make only minor adjustments to their assigned parts. Bowie occasionally lapses into half time to rest his arm, and a minute into Moye's improvisation, Jarman deviates from his part and plays a continuous stream of rapid triplets. Moye reacts with a complex triplet line of his own, triggering a wave of applause from the concertgoers.

The audience's response to this improvised exchange tells the Art Ensemble that the time is right to change the texture. The group members have been elaborating the same rhythmic framework for the better part of three minutes, and if they want to prevent the music from growing too repetitive, they must assemble a contrasting texture using the musical materials of "Promenade." The task of guiding the band into another area of "Promenade" will fall to Moye, who is still serving as the lead drummer. When Moye is ready to end his improvisation, he looks up from his pan drums and glances toward Favors and Mitchell. Then, at 13:51, he doubles Mitchell's part, playing the 8/8 pattern three times. He starts to play Mitchell's rhythm again, but after four beats he stops, stays silent for two beats, and launches into a brand-new figure. Moye's new pattern is unambiguously in 8/8 time, which makes the preceding material (four beats drawn from Mitchell's part, followed by a two-beat rest) sound like a 6/8 measure (see example 9.10). This metric shift has a major impact on the supporting parts. Now all of the other musicians are two beats behind Moye. Before Moye can repeat the new 8/8 pattern, Bowie, Favors, and Jarman pare down their parts to single drum strokes, avoiding any potential rhythmic conflicts with the lead drummer. Mitchell, however, keeps playing his supporting part, because it fits perfectly into the new metric context. Indeed, the metric shift gives new life to Mitchell's pattern. The displacement of his short-long-short rhythm to the weaker beats of each measure makes the ensuing downbeats much stronger, and the musicians see

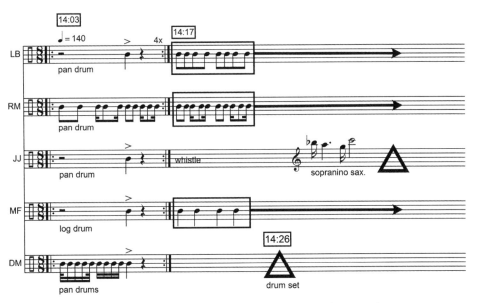

EXAMPLE 9.11 "Promenade": building a new groove, Jarman solo

an opportunity to build a powerful groove on top of the rhythmic foundation provided by Mitchell. Bowie resumes his eighth-note pulse, while Favors adds a reinforcing pulse pattern that is half as fast. Favors's slower rhythm unites the parts played by Mitchell and Bowie, and the groove immediately takes off (see example 9.11).

Moye and Jarman do not want to complicate the emerging groove with additional layers of pan-drum rhythms. So at 14:17, they leave the right side of the stage and return to their stations. Moye moves to his drum set and keeps time on cymbals and cowbell, relinquishing his lead-drummer role. The new texture that is forming demands a soloist, and Jarman is poised to fill this void. Seconds after Moye switches to drum set, Jarman picks up his sopranino saxophone and starts improvising, playing a free-tempo line in the key of B♭ minor (see example 9.11). The sound of Jarman's saxophone line reminded Moye of music he heard during a 1968 visit to Guelmim, Morocco, and after the Jazz Showcase concert, he and his bandmates titled this passage "Bedouin Village."[38]

The textural shift from Moye's pan-drum improvisation to Jarman's saxophone solo reveals much about the Art Ensemble's conception of Great Black Music. Fourteen minutes earlier, the group opened the concert with "We Bop," Bowie's tribute to a canonic style of African American music. Then, after a transition featuring percussion instruments from across the globe, the musicians found themselves in Bamako, along the banks of the Niger River in Mali, West Africa. When Jarman took over the soloist role from Moye, the Art Ensemble set off on another musical journey, traveling a thousand miles northward from Bamako to Guelmim, at the far western edge of the Sahara. In history, culture, and geography, Bamako and Guelmim are worlds apart from each other, but the musicians are able to link Mali to Morocco with a simple, elegant gesture—changing the metric context around Mitchell's pan-drum part.

The rhythmic techniques employed in this passage came to the group members from their studies of Great Black Music.[39] According to Jarman, the Art Ensemble's commitment to practicing and performing the full spectrum of Great Black Music "required the group to investigate an infinite number of forms."[40] Through these investigations, the band discovered that certain sounds and structures, like Mitchell's versatile pan-drum rhythm, transcended all musical and cultural boundaries. By playing Great Black Music, the members of the Art Ensemble could bring to their audience a universal musical experience, because the spiritual connections that arise between performers and listeners are based not on shared ethnicity, but rather on their common humanity. As Jarman recalled:

> Moye would teach us African rhythms with specific forms. . . . When we worked on it and did it right, you could feel the spirit click in, you could feel the spiritual uplift of the universality of the music. Even if it was a Southeast Asian form, when we got to the right level of that, you could feel the spirit click in.[41]

During this part of the performance, no one feels the spirit more than Favors. *Live from the Jazz Showcase* was filmed on a Sunday, only a few hours after the morning worship service at Favors's South Side church, Friendly Temple. Like other congregations affiliated with the Church of God in Christ (COGIC), Friendly Temple encouraged believers to receive the spirit while worshipping.[42] According to Favors, church members who felt the spirit's presence might respond by "testifying, singing, dancing, shouting, clapping of hands, speaking in tongues, and great congregational praise."[43] For Favors, an Art Ensemble concert could be just as spiritually charged as a COGIC worship service, and at the Jazz Showcase, the "spirit of music" leads him to perform a spontaneous dance.[44] Four minutes into Jarman's saxophone solo, at 18:42, Favors switches from log drum to maracas, an instrument that allows him to move his body more freely. At first he dances only from the waist up, rocking his shoulders forward on every beat. Then he closes his eyes, tilts his head backward, and lets the spirit take control of his dance. After a while, his eyes open, and he looks from his left to his right in an effort to regain his bearings. Next, Favors starts dancing with his entire body, swaying from side to side and gradually working himself into a crouching position. Through all of this, he never interrupts the sixteenth-note pulse he is playing on maracas, which becomes just as vital to the texture as Jarman's sopranino saxophone. Eventually Favors decides to put down his maracas, taking away the beat that has sustained the texture since the beginning of "Promenade." Jarman reacts by slowing the pace of his saxophone line, and the momentum behind his improvisation soon dissipates. One minute later, Jarman exits, and the second major episode of the performance comes to an end.

"New York Is Full of Lonely People"/Transition/"A Jackson in Your House"

At the conclusion of Jarman's saxophone solo, the video fades out. When it fades in again at 21:14, the musicians are playing another piece—Bowie's composition "New York Is Full of Lonely People," a jazz ballad in B♭ major.[45] This transition seems to take only a second, but in fact more time has elapsed: the video returns at the top of Favors's double-bass solo, omitting the band's statement of the opening theme.[46] Favors improvises for a little over two minutes, playing two choruses of the 16-bar AABA form. He is backed by Moye (on drum set) and Mitchell (on pan drum and bell lyre), whose accompaniment starts out sparse, then grows denser as the bass solo continues. The texture becomes even more active when Favors yields to Bowie, the next soloist. Favors's solo was understated, more of an ornamented bass part than an independent melodic line, but Bowie takes a different approach for his trumpet solo. He enters playing much louder than his bandmates, who quickly raise their dynamic level to match his volume. When he reaches the end of his solo chorus, he holds out his last note, a middle-register G♭$_4$, telling the group to prepare for the closing theme.

Instead of stating the theme in its entirety, the musicians conclude "New York Is Full of Lonely People" with just the second half of the theme, a standard performance strategy for a piece in the jazz-ballad style. Unlike most jazz ballads, however, the penultimate B section is played out of tempo rather than in strict time. As Bowie prolongs the final note of his solo, Moye breaks into a busy drum fill, disrupting the steady beat. Then, at 24:38, Bowie cues the B section with a downward swoop of his trumpet. Mitchell and Jarman

EXAMPLE 9.12 "New York Is Full of Lonely People": closing theme, "B" section

have switched to saxophones, alto and tenor, respectively, and they play the B-section melody with Bowie. Favors and Moye support the horn players with an intricate, free-tempo background texture (see example 9.12). The B section leads directly into the ending A section, played at a tempo much slower than that of the preceding solo choruses. In the third measure of the A section, Bowie leads his trumpet line to $G\flat_4$, the same pitch he used to end the trumpet solo. And once again, the group members interpret this pitch as a signal to suspend the groove. Moye switches from drum set to triangles, and the others start playing out-of-tempo long tones. Bowie leaps down from $G\flat_4$ to A_3, then resolves his line to $B\flat_3$, closing off "New York Is Full of Lonely People" (see example 9.13).

The next item on the set list is the Mitchell composition "A Jackson in Your House." Favors moves toward the piece right away. As the horn players continue sounding the long tones that ended "New York Is Full of Lonely People," Favors introduces an oompah bass vamp in the key of F. This is the bass line for "A Jackson in Your House," but the other musicians do not immediately react, perhaps because of the tempo adopted by Favors. He starts the vamp at ninety-six beats per minute, a relatively slow tempo that could also suggest another composition with a similar bass pattern, Mitchell's "Duffvipels" (from *Live at Mandel Hall*, analyzed in chapter 7).[47] From 26:11 to 26:43, Favors gradually speeds up, shifting the bass vamp into a faster tempo range that could only represent "A Jackson in Your House." When Favors stabilizes his

EXAMPLE 9.13 "New York Is Full of Lonely People": closing theme, "A" section

tempo at one hundred and forty-four beats per minute, Moye finally responds, using handheld birdcalls to produce a chorus of laughter-like sounds.[48] Moye's birdcalls evoke the bicycle horns and riotous laughter heard on the original recording of "A Jackson in Your House" (from the 1969 album of the same name, analyzed in chapter 4).[49] This intermusical relationship does not escape the horn players' attention.[50] As soon as Bowie hears Moye's birdcalls, he stops playing long tones, and shortly thereafter the saxophonists exit. When Jarman and Mitchell return a few seconds later, though, they do not play the theme of "A Jackson in Your House," or any other musical motives from the composition. Instead, they build a vivid, fragmented texture centered on the raucous sounds of Moye's birdcalls. Mitchell switches rapidly from one wind instrument to another, while Jarman mimics Moye—laughing and chattering into his microphone, then playing whistles and other small noisemakers. Not to be outdone, Moye adds to the commotion by stepping rhythmically on two bulb horns placed at his feet (see example 9.14).

As the texture unfolds, Bowie sits quietly in his chair, taking in his surroundings. Suddenly he stands up, brandishes a pistol, and fires several rounds into the air, "blanks of course" (see example 9.14).[51] Bowie's penchant for theatrical gunplay was well known. *The Bear Comes Home*, a novel by the jazz critic Rafi Zabor, includes a fictionalized account of an early 1980s Art Ensemble appearance at the Bottom Line nightclub in New York: "[S]omeone called

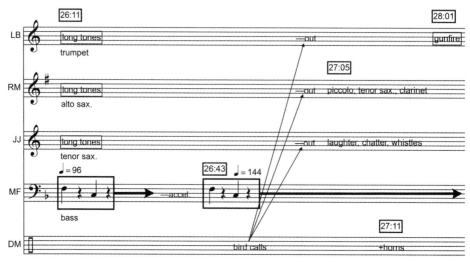

EXAMPLE 9.14 Transition: Favors bass vamp, Bowie gunfire

Jarman's impossibly uptempo Coltrane tribute, 'Ohnedaruth,' and all the horn players blew their brains out in succession. Bowie played last, pulled out his pistol at the end of his outing and emptied his clip of blanks into the lights."[52] For legal and other reasons, most concert venues tried to discourage Bowie and his bandmates from discharging firearms onstage, and the Jazz Showcase was no exception.[53] The club's proprietor, Joe Segal, discovered Bowie's pistol before the performance and confronted the group, as Moye recalled:

Joe Segal said, "I heard you carried that. You can't use that in here." "OK, Joe, no problem." We used that s— anyway.[54]

The musicians often incorporated elements of theater into their performances, and on a few occasions they employed guns as stage props in theatrical scenarios that offered cultural and political critiques. During a 1967 concert, one member of the group danced with a life-sized Raggedy Ann doll while another musician "trail[ed] after them with a shotgun," parodying American anxieties about integration in the wake of *Loving v. Virginia*, the Supreme Court decision that legalized interracial marriage.[55] And for a performance in 1979, the year of the Iranian Revolution, the Art Ensemble attempted to hire an actor who would "run across the stage dressed [like] the Ayatollah" as the musicians fired shotguns, set off firecrackers, and dropped confetti on the audience.[56] At the Jazz Showcase, the audience may perceive Bowie's gunplay as a purely theatrical gesture, but the members of the Art Ensemble hear the pistol volley as a turning point in the group improvisation. Favors ends the oompah bass vamp he has played for the past two minutes, and the others abandon the laughing sounds that alluded to "A Jackson in Your House." The musicians have put aside Mitchell's composition, at least temporarily. Instead of proceeding directly into "A Jackson in Your House," they will transition to the piece via an open improvisation.

Bowie's gunfire leads to a significant textural change, one of many in this lengthy transition. As if on cue, the group members develop each texture for about two minutes before creating a new one. This improvisational strategy is highly effective: the transition never loses momentum, and with the advent of each contrasting texture, the transition's ultimate destination becomes harder to predict. When the first section of the transition ends, punctuated by Bowie's gunshots at 28:01, the musicians build a new texture from their colorful sonic palette. Bowie summons a deep rumble from his concert bass drum, and Moye blows into an emergency horn, which Jarman and Mitchell echo on whistles and reeds. Favors, too, decides to rejoin the texture—but the instrument he selects, a plastic whirly tube, is too faint to be heard over the mounting ruckus. In an earlier transitional passage, Favors spoke inaudibly into a megaphone, and once again he chooses to contribute to the group improvisation with a physical gesture that is soundless yet expressive. As he stands in his station upstage, he raises the red whirly tube above his head and rotates it at a constant speed, adding a discernible visual rhythm to an otherwise free-tempo texture.

Bowie picks up on Favors's silent rhythm, and he starts playing an emphatic pulse on his bass drum at 29:57. Moye and Jarman quickly align their patterns with Bowie's beat, and together they form a new pulse-driven texture, the third section of the transition. Eventually Bowie strays from his pulse to play a string of subdivided rhythms. In response, Moye moves from pan drums to an alarm bell and introduces an alternative pulse pattern at a pace several times faster than Bowie's tempo. The group members react to this striking sound in different ways. Mitchell, who has switched from tenor to soprano saxophone, hears Moye's bell as analogous to a brisk ride-cymbal rhythm, and he shifts into an intense style of saxophone playing, sounding much like he did on the long "intensity structure" from *Live at Mandel Hall*.[57] Contrary to Mitchell, Jarman and Favors are drawn to the alarm bell's high-register resonance, not its resemblance to a ride-cymbal beat, and they move to instruments with brighter timbres: bells and balafon, respectively (see example 9.15). This interpretation of Moye's alarm bell proves the most persuasive, perhaps because it offers the musicians a pathway into the transition's fourth section—a percussion texture centered on luminous bell sounds. Mitchell exchanges his soprano saxophone

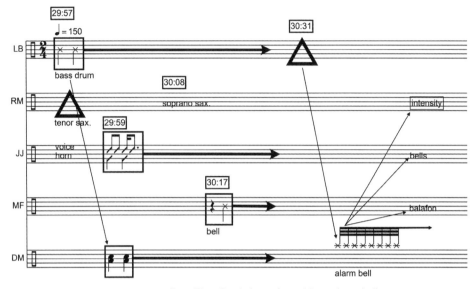

EXAMPLE 9.15 Transition: Bowie bass drum, Moye alarm bell

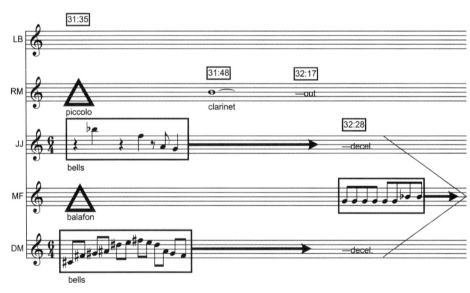

EXAMPLE 9.16 Transition: "Morning Bells," Favors balafon

for a piccolo flute, and Bowie drops out. Meanwhile, Moye approaches his rack of pitched bells, and at 31:35 he begins a repeating pattern that moves up and down a seven-note scale. Jarman streamlines his own bell part into a four-note ostinato, deftly interweaving it into the scale-based pattern played by Moye (see example 9.16). This is Moye's "Morning Bells," a compositional sketch inspired by music from Calabar, a port city in southeastern Nigeria.[58] "Morning Bells" has a simple, flexible structure. Moye and Jarman can invoke the piece by playing ascending or descending lines on pitched bells, and here they use the piece to create a temporary focal point in the group improvisation.

After a minute and a half, "Morning Bells" runs its course. Moye and Jarman play slower and softer, letting Favors's quiet balafon part emerge (see example 9.16). Favors has been improvising on balafon since the third section of the transition, and he keeps playing even when Bowie returns on flugelhorn, cueing the transition's fifth and final section. Bowie's flugelhorn line is firmly in F major, and it forms a curious counterpoint against the non-tempered heptatonic tuning of Favors's balafon. Instead of immediately resolving this tension, the group keeps the texture balanced between the two opposing musical layers. Mitchell enters on tenor saxophone, offering a series of F-major phrases that complement Bowie's melody. Favors receives support from his rhythm-section partner Moye, who plays sympathetic rhythms on talking drum, while Jarman gently crashes a suspended cymbal, blending the contrasting musical layers into a single texture.

Bowie and Mitchell gradually find their way to a familiar melody: Albert Ayler's "Bells," one of the few pieces in the Art Ensemble's repertoire not composed by the band members.[59] They play the theme out of tempo, and conclude "Bells" at 37:43 with a string of long tones, not unlike how the group ended "New York Is Full of Lonely People." In an extraordinary display of musical memory, Favors reintroduces the oompah bass vamp he played at the beginning of the transition, some twelve minutes earlier. Moye sees that Favors is trying to revive "A Jackson in Your House," and he answers by grinding a ratchet. Then he plays his handheld birdcalls, the same response he gave during the first appearance of the bass vamp. This time, Favors's bass line and Moye's birdcalls do the trick. Bowie switches from flugelhorn to trumpet, Mitchell picks up his clarinet, and the musicians get ready to play "A Jackson in Your House" (see example 9.17).

After a twelve-minute detour through five distinct textures, the members of the Art Ensemble finally converge on the main theme of "A Jackson in Your House" at 38:39. The arrangement they use is adapted from the 1969 studio recording, which included an extended introduction, multiple statements of the theme, a humorous poetic recitation, and a concluding section in the swing style. In concert settings, the band tended to omit certain portions of Mitchell's composition, as Jarman recalled: "Each [performance] was different, and in order to keep it more open we usually played parts of 'A Jackson in Your House' rather than the whole structure."[60] This strategy ensured that

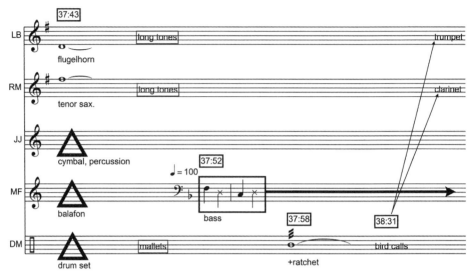

EXAMPLE 9.17 "A Jackson in Your House": Favors bass vamp, Moye birdcalls

"A Jackson in Your House" would fit into the overall narrative arc of the performance. A 1979 Art Ensemble concert in Athens, Georgia, began with the piece's swing section, which served as a point of departure for a lengthy open improvisation.[61] One year later, in Milan, Italy, "A Jackson in Your House" was the final item on the concert set list. The Art Ensemble preceded it with a wide-ranging transition, announced the piece with a chorus of birdcalls, and played the theme twice to close the performance.[62] At the Jazz Showcase, the composition is at the end of the set list, as in Milan, and the musicians choose a similar arrangement that helps the piece function as a point of arrival.

Despite its abbreviated form, the arrangement employed by the Art Ensemble preserves one of the piece's core features: intermusical relationships between various styles of jazz. During the first theme statement, Mitchell wields two woodwinds at once, playing a countermelody on tenor saxophone while repeating an F_4 on clarinet. His unconventional two-instrument technique catches the audience's eye, and his purposely awkward rhythms threaten to disrupt the other horn players, who are presenting a straightforward interpretation of the theme over Favors and Moye's slow groove (see example 9.18). The theme is followed by a brief rhythm-section interlude, which gives Mitchell a chance to put down both horns and pick up his soprano saxophone, an instrument with a range in between Bowie's trumpet and Jarman's sopranino saxophone. After the interlude, the re-voiced horn section plays the theme a second time, using a contrapuntal approach reminiscent of early jazz. When

EXAMPLE 9.18 "A Jackson in Your House": theme statement 1, first phrase

EXAMPLE 9.19 "A Jackson in Your House": Bowie riff, preparing theme statement 3

the musicians arrive at the last phrase of the theme, they play it in unison and hold the final note for an extra beat. If they wished, they could end the piece right there. But a pair of theme statements in roughly the same style might not provide a payoff proportionate to the epic transitional episode that brought the Art Ensemble to "A Jackson in Your House." So Moye plays a brief roll on his snare drum, extending the theme's final note a little longer and building anticipation for what comes next.

When Moye breaks off his drumroll, the group falls silent for an instant. Then, at 39:59, Bowie returns with an eight-bar trumpet riff at a much faster tempo (see example 9.19). Bowie's exuberant phrase sets the tone for the closing statement of the theme. Jarman takes the composed melody, with improvised elaborations from Mitchell and Bowie, while Favors and Moye play a rousing two-beat groove. Indeed, the rhythm section's groove is so irresistible that Bowie, Jarman, and Mitchell are compelled to dance as they play the theme. They strut and dip in time with the bracing backbeat of Moye's

EXAMPLE 9.20 "A Jackson in Your House": theme statement 3, tag ending

snare drum, conjuring up not just the original recording of "A Jackson in Your House" but also the turn-of-the-century African American dance culture from which jazz emerged.

The theme concludes with a clever tag ending based on the 1969 recording. The members of the Art Ensemble play an ascending line three times, then a "shave and a haircut" figure—a clichéd phrase that in 1969 served as the setup for a musical joke. Here, however, the outcome is completely different. The lively closing theme and its crisp tag ending create a striking intermusical contrast with the first two theme statements, an effect that is heightened by the band's dancing and audacious showmanship. Ordinarily the audience at an Art Ensemble concert can only expect the unexpected, but once the musicians reach the "shave and a haircut" phrase, everyone in the Jazz Showcase knows what must follow. The group members play the "two bits" figure together, triumphantly, and the concertgoers respond immediately with an appreciative round of applause (see example 9.20).

"Funky AECO"/"Odwalla"

Jarman leans toward his microphone, acknowledges the audience, and introduces the group: "Roscoe Mitchell, Lester Bowie, Famoudou Don Moye, Malachi Favors Maghostut, Joseph Jarman." The audience's ovation continues for several seconds after Jarman finishes speaking, and he and his bandmates decide to repay their fans with two encore selections, "Funky AECO" and "Odwalla." Earlier in the performance, the group members engaged in open improvisation and played music from Mali, Morocco, and Nigeria. Now, at the concert's end, they offer two more compositions—one in the funk style and the other a modal jazz tune—that provide further proof of how diverse Great Black Music can be.

But "Funky AECO" and "Odwalla" illustrate more than the breadth of the band's repertoire. They also represent some of the essential qualities that set the Art Ensemble apart from every other band in jazz and experimental music. "Funky AECO," composed by the entire group, commemorates Art Ensemble of Chicago Operations (AECO), the corporation that the band members established in order to advance their practice of cooperative economics. The musicians' business practices, of course, went hand in hand with their social principles of cooperation and autonomy, the values that sustained the group for decades. Indeed, without their steadfast commitment to cooperation and autonomy, the Art Ensemble would not have survived the fifteen years between the group's 1966 founding and the 1981 Jazz Showcase concert, let alone the twenty-nine years from the Showcase concert to the band's final performance in 2010.[63]

"Odwalla" captures yet another side of the musicians: their use of intermedia to convey messages (to their folks) about black culture and identity. Mitchell's instrumental composition inspired Jarman to write the poem "ODAWALLA," an origin myth for Great Black Music. The poem describes a pantheon of gods, among them ODAWALLA, and "the people of the Sun," who inhabit a "ghost world" afflicted by a "grey haze." From the people of the Sun several heroes arise, and with the guidance of ODAWALLA they learn of "the practice of the drum and silent gong," sacred musical instruments that possess the power to unify the Sun people and restore their divine nature. The heroes join forces, and at just the right moment ODAWALLA sends a vibration into the ghost world, "causing the silent gong to sound silent." With this, the people of the Sun become a "body whole"—the godlike figure KAW ZU PAM—and at last they can leave the ghost world behind.[64] In the poem's final stanza, Jarman addresses his audience directly, intimating that the story about the people of the Sun is more than a myth. It is a prophetic vision about the possibility of redemption in a fallen world. The "grey haze" is "here now," Jarman says, but so are the liberating drum and silent gong:

> the grey haze Sun People drum
> Silent gong---here now
> here now-between us
> grey haze Sun
> People[65]

The performance at the Jazz Showcase began with a moment of silence, and it concludes with Moye's "sun percussion." With a drum flourish and cymbal crash, Moye closes off "Odwalla" at 50:40, bringing the concert to its end. Bowie, Jarman, and Mitchell take a bow and exit, while Favors and

Moye stand, arms raised, at the back of the stage. With outstretched hands, they take in the applause, then bend forward and return it to the audience. After this gesture, Favors follows his bandmates offstage, but Moye has one more rite to perform before he departs. He emerges from behind his drum set holding a ceremonial staff, and he hoists it into the air while marching along the front of the stage, "ritualizing and symbolizing and raising the music up to a higher level."[66]

Conclusion

We SURVIVE for the spirit of GREAT BLACK MUSIC and for the
spirit of GREAT BLACK MUSIC alone.[1]

Sirius Calling

The Art Ensemble's tenure on ECM Records ended in 1985, after
the release of *The Third Decade*.[2] The members of the Art Ensemble had always given their album titles careful consideration,
ever since the mid-1960s, when Malachi Favors and Lester Bowie
joined Roscoe Mitchell to form the core of the band that recorded
the LP *Sound*.[3] Some twenty years later, the musicians used the
title *The Third Decade* to celebrate their incredible longevity—and
to suggest that their best years were yet to come. They would
continue working together (in one configuration or another) until
2010, bringing the Art Ensemble into its fifth decade and making
it one of the most enduring groups in music history.[4] Some of
the musicians, sadly, would not make it to the finish line with
their bandmates. Yet, their revolutionary performances and social
practices ensured that the Art Ensemble would live on even after
they were gone.

The musicians parted ways with ECM and immediately signed
a new recording contract with DIW, a Tokyo-based independent
label.[5] Unlike ECM, the DIW label was not internationally re-

261

garded as a leader in jazz and experimental music, nor did it have an extensive distribution network outside its home country. However, recording for DIW had many other advantages. The Art Ensemble was touring Japan every other year in the mid-1980s, developing a sizeable local audience that would eagerly purchase the band's DIW releases.[6] In fact, the group's first DIW album, *Live in Japan*, was taped in Tokyo, one of the stops on their 1984 Japanese tour.[7] DIW also offered the musicians something they had never experienced before: complete control of their recording projects. The group members produced all of their DIW albums themselves, supervising the recording sessions as well as the mixing and mastering processes. Crucially, the musicians were able to choose what they wanted to record, not just how it would be recorded, and they used this creative freedom to produce a unique set of ten albums, the band's most varied discs since the Paris years.[8] For the three albums in the *Dreaming of the Masters* series, the Art Ensemble broke precedent and recorded music by other composers, from John Coltrane and Duke Ellington to Jimi Hendrix, Fela Kuti, Bob Marley, and Otis Redding.[9] The second *Dreaming of the Masters* album was dedicated to the bebop pioneer Thelonious Monk, and for this project the group hired another legendary pianist, Cecil Taylor, who was living in Brooklyn not far from Bowie and Joseph Jarman.[10]

The recording with Cecil Taylor was one of several collaborative projects that the Art Ensemble brought to DIW. And as with Taylor, whose relationship with the band began with a performance at the 1984 Paris Jazz Festival, the members of the Art Ensemble auditioned each potential collaborator in a concert setting before producing a recording.[11] In 1990, they made a live album with Bowie's side project Brass Fantasy, which had been touring with the Art Ensemble for years.[12] The group also recorded two discs with Amabutho, a five-man Zulu chorus that had performed with Bowie and Don Moye at a festival in London.[13] On the covers of both Amabutho discs, the musicians billed themselves as the "Art Ensemble of Soweto" in order to express their solidarity with the Amabutho singers, who were living as exiles in Great Britain in protest of the apartheid regime then ruling their native South Africa.

The members of the Art Ensemble were never afraid to address urgent political issues, and in 1989 and 1990, when the Amabutho albums were recorded, the international outcry against South African apartheid was at its peak. However, from the Art Ensemble's perspective, the Cecil Taylor and Brass Fantasy collaborations were just as meaningful as the Amabutho project. The musicians considered their social practices to be a powerful political statement, a testimony to the great things African American artists could accomplish through cooperation—"how to band together and make a way when there is no way," as Mitchell put it.[14] Indeed, those who got to know the Art Ensemble on a personal level, from collaborators to the group's managers, were able to see firsthand how the musicians had transformed their lives through social and economic cooperation.[15] By the 1990s, all five band members owned their homes, a significant achievement for anyone working in jazz and experimental music. Before long, Cecil Taylor, the Brass Fantasy players, and a number of other musicians were going to Bowie for financial advice. Moye called this the "Lester Bowie forum":

That's how I got two homes, and everybody in the band has homes too. Lester turned a lot of people on to the whole schematics of that—Craig Harris, Oliver Lake, Steve Turre, Cecil Taylor, Betty Carter—turned 'em on to quality of life for your ass. Cats used to come around and talk to Lester about getting a home, and he'd customize a program for 'em. He was like, "Do you want a house, or are you just a renegade m—f—?"[16]

In 1991, the group celebrated a major anniversary. It had been twenty-five years since Roscoe Mitchell introduced his Art Ensemble in a concert at the Harper Theater in Chicago.[17] Back in 1966, only a few hundred people, most of them on Chicago's South Side, had heard of Mitchell and his bandmates. Now the Art Ensemble of Chicago was known to audiences around the globe, from Tokyo to Istanbul, Los Angeles to London. To commemorate their twenty-fifth anniversary, the musicians embarked on a long European tour, bringing with them Brass Fantasy and Amabutho, their most frequent collaborators.[18] For the members of the band, these collaborations were a creative boon, a composer's dream. When they joined forces with Brass Fantasy or Amabutho, the musicians could compose and arrange music for a larger, hybrid ensemble with expanded instrumental or vocal resources. In both of these blended groups, though, the Art Ensemble remained at the very center, preserving the musical and social intimacy that helped the band members improvise together at the highest level. After the twenty-fifth-anniversary tour, the Art Ensemble sought out even more collaborators, performing and recording with pianist Don Pullen, blues musicians from New York and Chicago, and the Deutsche Kammerphilharmonie.[19] The collaboration with the Deutsche Kammerphilharmonie culminated in the fall of 1993 with a spectacular performance in Bremen, Germany. Three German composers—Wilfried Maria Danner, Klaus Obermaier, and Robert Spour—created concertos for the Art Ensemble, surrounding the musicians with stunning orchestral textures reminiscent of their own improvisations. At the concert's end, the audience saluted the members of the group with one of the longest ovations they had ever received.

The concert with the Deutsche Kammerphilharmonie was a resounding success, but for Jarman, it must have been bittersweet. This would be his last performance with the Art Ensemble for a long while. He was stepping away from the band (and all his other musical endeavors) to focus on what had become his most important side projects: the Brooklyn Buddhist Association and Jikishinkan Dojo.[20] Jarman had been serving as a Buddhist priest for three years, since 1990.[21] Music was no longer giving him the same sense of fulfillment he got from teaching Buddhism and aikido, and his tours with the Art Ensemble were taking him away from his students for months at a time. According to Jarman, "I had to choose between the constant traveling with the Ensemble because it constantly traveled. That was its thing. Or [I could] devote more time to these other studies and practices."[22] So he decided to take an indefinite leave of absence from the group. Jarman's bandmates were sad to see him go, of course, but they had always given one another the personal autonomy to pursue side projects and go on sabbaticals. As Moye stated: "Our agreement in the group was anybody that had critical issues in their life, they have to be addressed and we respect and support their ability to do that. He had to take care of some things that were critical in his life, which would make him be able to come back and play."[23]

The musicians' resilience was tested in 1998, when Bowie was diagnosed with liver cancer.[24] Although his illness was terminal, he kept performing as long as he was able. After a lifetime on the road, Bowie did not want to spend his final months at home waiting to die, nor did he want the Art Ensemble or his side projects to stop working because of his declining health.[25] In the fall of 1999, he brought Brass Fantasy to Europe, but after a few performances, he was too sick to continue the tour. His second wife, photographer Deborah Bowie, brought him back to Brooklyn, where he died on 8 November 1999 at the age of fifty-eight.[26] Bowie's memorial service was held in midtown Manhattan at St. Peter's Church, a Lutheran congregation with a tradition of ministering to the jazz community.[27] Hundreds of friends, family members, and musicians were in attendance, including just about every trumpet player in New York.[28] The memorial featured a heartfelt musical tribute to Bowie by the Art Ensemble: Mitchell, Favors, Moye—and Jarman, in his first appearance with the group since 1993.[29]

After Bowie's death, Jarman began to think about rejoining the Art Ensemble.[30] However, he had not practiced during much of his sabbatical, and in late 1999, he was still working to regain his technique.[31] So the three remaining members kept the band going without Jarman, maintaining their rigorous tour schedule and returning to ECM Records to make a trio album entitled *Tribute to Lester*.[32] "The Art Ensemble is an institution," Mitchell affirmed. "The way it was always run was that we dealt with whatever was there. You will notice that [practice] throughout our history, way back from when we had Phillip Wilson and he left to go with Paul Butterfield."[33] In the late 1960s, Bowie, Favors, and Mitchell invited Jarman to play with them after Phillip Wilson's exit, not to replace the departed drummer but rather to enhance the group's music. History repeated itself in January 2003, when Jarman finally came back to the band after a ten-year absence.[34] And just as in the 1960s, when the Art Ensemble helped Jarman cope with the loss of Christopher Gaddy and Charles Clark, reuniting with the group in 2003 made him feel whole again. As Jarman recalled, "Roscoe actually gave me a call and convinced me it was time to get back to work":

> When I first left, for three years I didn't play any music at all, and I found I
> was depressed because I wasn't playing. . . . I shouldn't have been surprised:
> I'd been playing music for 50 years. . . . During those years, Lester was a
> neighbor of mine, and he was constantly urging me to get back to the Art
> Ensemble. After Lester's transition, when Roscoe hooked up with me, I
> wasn't reluctant at all.[35]

With Jarman on board, the musicians immediately hit the road. In early 2003, they flew to Europe for a series of performances, then returned to the United States, where they made two albums for the independent label Pi Recordings.[36] Jarman's return to the band had long been anticipated, and interest in the newly reconstituted Art Ensemble was high. Newspapers and jazz magazines rushed to print profiles of the group, creating a wave of positive publicity. Concert promoters took notice, and soon the Art Ensemble's tour schedule was full through 2004.[37]

This sudden upsurge in work opportunities energized the musicians, who might have gone on performing together for years. But then tragedy struck. In January 2004, Favors went to a Chicago hospital complaining of stomach trouble. The diagnosis was late-stage pancreatic cancer, and he had only days to live.[38] On 30 January 2004, Favors passed away at the age of seventy-six.[39] Love ran deep for Favors in his hometown of Chicago, and his family knew that his funeral would draw a crowd. Instead of holding his service at the family church, Friendly Temple, they moved the funeral to Love Community Church, a suburban COGIC congregation that was large enough to accommodate more than five hundred mourners.[40] Favors was eulogized by his nephew Rev. Edwin Walker (the pastor of Friendly Temple) and by a number of his dearest friends, including Moye. AACM member Douglas Ewart gave a speech that hailed Favors as "one of our most profound messengers," a worthy successor to his namesake, the prophet Malachi.[41]

Favors's transition came just weeks before the group's spring 2004 tour. Jarman, Mitchell, and Moye wanted to honor Favors and Bowie by playing some of their old repertoire, quintet compositions that they wrote for the classic Art Ensemble. In order to do so, they would have to fill out the group with two guest musicians. Mitchell reached out to trumpeter Corey Wilkes and bassist Jaribu Shahid, both of whom played in his band Note Factory.[42] Wilkes was a young man, still in his mid-twenties, while Shahid had been working with Mitchell since the late 1970s.[43] The Art Ensemble's two guests performed brilliantly on the spring 2004 tour, particularly during a weeklong residency at the New York jazz club Iridium. The group recorded the Iridium dates, gathering enough material to fill a double album, *Non-Cognitive Aspects of the City*, which was released on the Pi label in 2006.[44]

For many listeners, this would be the last time they heard the Art Ensemble make new music. The musicians toured infrequently after 2004, visiting Europe in 2006 and the East Coast in 2010.[45] And then the band fell silent. Moye moved out of the country, Jarman's health prevented him from playing regularly, and Mitchell busied himself with his many side projects.[46] The members of the Art Ensemble had performed together for more than forty years, traveling all over the world and making no fewer than fifty albums. Now their music is a memory, dwelling in the hearts of the group and their audience—and resounding softly in the pages of this book.

There's a Message for You

The members of the Art Ensemble left a remarkable legacy that was as multi-faceted and inspiring as their performances. All five were extraordinary instrumentalists, ranking among the most virtuosic and creative players in jazz and experimental music. They were also responsible for a number of crucial innovations that were adopted by their AACM colleagues and musicians across the globe. Anyone who improvises with "little instruments" is indebted to Favors, and any aspiring multi-instrumentalist is following in the footsteps of Mitchell, Jarman, and Moye, who mastered a veritable orchestra of woodwinds and percussion. Likewise, the Art Ensemble's brilliant intermedia performances provided a valuable model for groups that sought new ways of combining sound, poetry, theater, costume, and movement into an integrated whole. All of these advances were widely influential in the AACM and beyond, and after the Art Ensemble, jazz and experimental music would never be the same.

Some of the band's contributions, however, were so unique to the Art Ensemble that they simply could not be imitated. No composer but Mitchell could have written "Care Free," the forty-five-second gem that closes the A-side of *Full Force*, and no other horn section could make that final E-major chord sound so glorious, with the highest and lowest pitches played perfectly out of tune, just enough to make the triad truly sing.[47] Each Art Ensemble performance was different, of course, but they all had a few transcendent moments like the end of "Care Free"—revelatory passages of music that could only have come from Bowie, Favors, Jarman, Mitchell, and Moye. Audiences could never predict when the next "one-in-a-thousand" passage would occur, but from the group's perspective, these episodes did not happen by chance.[48] Every concert and recording session was shaped by careful compositional designs, years of intensive rehearsals, and the musicians' unparalleled improvisational skills. Indeed, recordings like *A Jackson in Your House*, *Live at Mandel Hall*, and *Live from the Jazz Showcase* featured some of the best compositions and improvisations of the 1960s, 1970s, and 1980s, or any era.[49] In the past fifty years, only a handful of improvising groups could approach the heights that the members of the Art Ensemble reached whenever they took the stage. It was for this reason that many listeners and critics considered the Art Ensemble to be one of the most important bands in the history of jazz and experimental music.[50]

From 1966 into the twenty-first century, the Art Ensemble had few rivals, and in one key respect—longevity—the group was without peer. The musicians' early performances were so groundbreaking that their musical legacy would have been secure even if they had parted ways sometime in the 1970s. But they defied the odds and stayed together for decades. And the Art Ensemble's longevity, like the consistently high quality of the band's performances, was the result of years of deliberate effort. As Bowie explained: "What people have to understand is that in this business a lot has to do with luck. A lot has to do with direction and vision. You don't get the luck until you are headed the right way. You don't get blessed if you are doing the wrong s—."[51] The musicians began practicing cooperation and autonomy during their first few years together, and these social practices became the foundation of all their accomplishments. When they were making very little money, cooperative economics helped them survive. And once their income started to increase, cooperation allowed them to fund new business operations and turn the Art Ensemble into a decades-long investment. Similarly, the group's commitment to autonomy gave the members the freedom to launch independent side projects, which in turn enabled them to invest even more into the business of the Art Ensemble. Some of these side projects became major successes, notably Bowie's Brass Fantasy. But the Art Ensemble always remained the musicians' top priority. At least once a year, the group members set aside all other obligations so they could get together and rehearse for several days, even several weeks. Then they went on tour, using the proceeds to finance business ventures or their next group retreat. With this level of devotion—to the band and to one another—the musicians believed that they could not fail. "This thing," Moye declared, "is about 35 years of cooperative economics. More than music it's about sustaining our lives."[52]

The members of the Art Ensemble were ideal partners for one another, onstage and off. Bowie, Jarman, and Mitchell complemented one another marvelously, while Favors and Moye had a rhythmic rapport that would be the envy of any bass-and-drums team. But it was their fierce loyalty and shared values that made the Art Ensemble much more than the sum of five very different personalities. Mitchell was the driving force, so unshakeable that his bandmates called him "Rock," though it was often Favors who kept the others grounded through his wisdom and spirituality. Bowie's irresistible charisma made him the face of the Art Ensemble, whether he was playing trumpet at center stage or negotiating a record contract. Jarman was "The Voice," the eloquent seeker who lent the band much of its mystique. And Moye's boundless energy kept the group moving ahead to the next gig, the next tour, the next collaboration. Musicians like this have always been as rare as diamonds, and groups as creative and long-lived as the Art Ensemble are even rarer. For Favors, this was a sure sign that he and his bandmates had a higher calling:

> I feel blessed that I got with the Art Ensemble, because I know I'm playing with some chosen brothers; otherwise how would we be together [so many] years. . . . There are few of us musicians left who play what I call "truths in music." You can't be an exact vehicle for the Word through your horn because you're still human. But it's very few of us left [who] even to a degree, let that happen. As they say in the church, "Let the Word come on out."[53]

Notes

Introduction

1. Epigraph: Jarman, *Black Case*, 99.
2. Calloway, "Yusef Lateef Set," 19.
3. Moye, e-mail message to author, 22 October 2005.
4. Art Ensemble of Chicago, *Bap-tizum*.
5. Favors, quoted in Beauchamp, *Art Ensemble of Chicago*, 30.
6. Favors, quoted in Beauchamp, *Art Ensemble of Chicago*, 30.
7. Beauchamp, *Art Ensemble of Chicago*, 30.
8. Bowie, *Serious Fun*.
9. Bowie, quoted in Beauchamp, *Art Ensemble of Chicago*, 47.
10. Radano, *New Musical Figurations*, 87.
11. Lewis, *A Power Stronger Than Itself*, 227.
12. Lewis, *A Power Stronger Than Itself*, 103.
13. Higgins, "Intermedia," 3.
14. Lewis, *A Power Stronger Than Itself*, xxvii.
15. Beauchamp, *Art Ensemble of Chicago*; Looker, *"Point from Which Creation Begins"*; Radano, *New Musical Figurations*.
16. In the field of jazz studies, recent exceptions to this rule include Elsdon, *Keith Jarrett's* The Köln Concert; Magee, *The Uncrowned King of Swing*; and Solis, *Thelonious Monk Quartet with John Coltrane at Carnegie Hall*.
17. Art Ensemble of Chicago, *A Jackson in Your House*.
18. Art Ensemble of Chicago, *Live at Mandel Hall*.
19. Art Ensemble of Chicago, *Live from the Jazz Showcase*.

Chapter 1

1. Epigraph: Jarman, quoted in Figi, "Art Ensemble of Chicago," 47.
2. Lemann, *The Promised Land*, 64.
3. Lemann, *The Promised Land*, 64; Duncan and Duncan, *The Negro Population of Chicago*, 23.
4. Boyer, *How Sweet the Sound*, 57–102.
5. Gregory, *The Southern Diaspora*, 137–138.
6. Iain Anderson, *This Is Our Music*, 129; Bone and Courage, *The Muse in Bronzeville*, 64–69; Kenney, *Chicago Jazz*, 17–23, 163–164.
7. Crawford, "Black Light on the *Wall of Respect*," 23–42; Lewis, *A Power Stronger Than Itself*, 166–169.
8. Gregory, *The Southern Diaspora*, 23–24; Wilkerson, *The Warmth of Other Suns*, 9.
9. Duncan and Duncan, *The Negro Population of Chicago*, 21.
10. Duncan and Duncan, *The Negro Population of Chicago*, 302.
11. Gregory, *The Southern Diaspora*, 28–31.
12. Hirsch, *Making the Second Ghetto*, 16–17; Wilkerson, *The Warmth of Other Suns*, 11.
13. Hirsch, *Making the Second Ghetto*, 3–4.
14. Satter, *Family Properties*, 39–41.
15. Grossman, *Land of Hope*, 178–180; Tuttle, *Race Riot*; Wilkerson, *The Warmth of Other Suns*, 272–273.
16. Grossman, *Land of Hope*, 118; Hirsch, *Making the Second Ghetto*, 45.
17. Hirsch, *Making the Second Ghetto*, 40–99; Lemann, *The Promised Land*, 71–74; Satter, *Family Properties*, 39.
18. Lemann, *The Promised Land*, 81.
19. Wilkerson, *The Warmth of Other Suns*, 268.
20. Grossman, *Land of Hope*, 89–97.
21. For an account of how the members of one African American family came to call "upsouth" Chicago their home, see Ramsey, *Race Music*, 4–16, 78–95, 134–149.
22. Gregory, *The Southern Diaspora*, 123.
23. Grossman, *Land of Hope*, 94–95; Ramsey, *Race Music*, 53–56.
24. Duncan and Duncan, *The Negro Population of Chicago*, 23.
25. DeSantis, "Selling the American Dream."
26. Lemann, *The Promised Land*, 64.
27. Baldwin, *Chicago's New Negroes*, 25.
28. William Everett Samuels, quoted in Spivey, *Union and the Black Musician*, 39.
29. Favors, quoted in Beauchamp, *Art Ensemble of Chicago*, 28.
30. Travis, *An Autobiography of Black Chicago*, 39–40.
31. Iain Anderson, *This Is Our Music*, 129; Baldwin, *Chicago's New Negroes*, 25; Kenney, *Chicago Jazz*, 162.
32. Hirsch, *Making the Second Ghetto*, 5.
33. Lewis, *A Power Stronger Than Itself*, 16; Radano, *New Musical Figurations*, 37–38.
34. Martin "Sparx" Alexander, telephone interview by author.
35. George Favors, Rosetta Rimmer, and Velena Daniels, interview by author.

36. Grossman, *Land of Hope*, 148–149.

37. Malba Allen, interview by author; Baldwin, *Chicago's New Negroes*, 168; Jerma A. Jackson, *Singing in My Soul*, 34; Edwin Walker, e-mail message to author.

38. Malba Allen, e-mail message to author; Litweiler, "There Won't Be Any More Music," 23; Rusch and Ryan, "Malachi Favors," 6. Later in life, Malachi Favors claimed that his birth year was 1937, not 1927, causing his would-be biographers a great deal of confusion. Lewis, *A Power Stronger Than Itself*, 530 n. 17.

39. Mal. 1:1, 3:1.

40. Beauchamp, *Art Ensemble of Chicago*, 27; Boyer, *How Sweet the Sound*, 20–21.

41. Costen, *In Spirit and in Truth*, 157–158.

42. Jerma A. Jackson, *Singing in My Soul*, 16.

43. Boyer, *How Sweet the Sound*, 22.

44. Favors, quoted in Beauchamp, *Art Ensemble of Chicago*, 27.

45. Baldwin, *Chicago's New Negroes*, 168; George Favors, Rosetta Rimmer, and Velena Daniels, interview by author.

46. Boyer, *How Sweet the Sound*, 24.

47. Beauchamp, *Art Ensemble of Chicago*, 27; Jerma A. Jackson, *Singing in My Soul*, 29–30, 77–102; Wald, *Shout, Sister, Shout!*, 17.

48. Darden, *People Get Ready!*, 140–141; Young, *Woke Me Up This Morning*, 223–224.

49. Favors, quoted in Beauchamp, *Art Ensemble of Chicago*, 27.

50. Young, *Woke Me Up This Morning*, 11–12.

51. Favors, quoted in Beauchamp, *Art Ensemble of Chicago*, 27.

52. Favors, quoted in Lewis, *A Power Stronger Than Itself*, 8.

53. Malba Allen, interview by author; Favors, interview by Peter Rosenbloom.

54. Favors, quoted in Aaron Cohen, "Malachi Favors Maghostut," 5.

55. Favors, interview by Peter Rosenbloom.

56. Favors, interview by Peter Rosenbloom.

57. Favors, interview by Peter Rosenbloom.

58. Jung, "A Fireside Chat with Malachi Favors"; Lewis, *A Power Stronger Than Itself*, 15.

59. Favors, quoted in Jung, "A Fireside Chat with Malachi Favors."

60. Favors, interview by Peter Rosenbloom.

61. Favors, interview by Peter Rosenbloom.

62. Favors, interview by Peter Rosenbloom.

63. Favors, quoted in Beauchamp, *Art Ensemble of Chicago*, 28.

64. Favors, interview by Peter Rosenbloom.

65. Favors, interview by Peter Rosenbloom; Young, *Woke Me Up This Morning*, 223.

66. Malba Allen, interview by author; George Favors, Rosetta Rimmer, and Velena Daniels, interview by author.

67. Favors, quoted in Rusch and Ryan, "Malachi Favors," 6.

68. Favors, interview by Peter Rosenbloom.

69. Favors, interview by Peter Rosenbloom; Rusch and Ryan, "Malachi Favors," 8.

70. Rusch and Ryan, "Malachi Favors," 6.

71. Favors, interview by Peter Rosenbloom.

72. Rusch and Ryan, "Malachi Favors," 6.

73. Favors, interview by Peter Rosenbloom.

74. Malba Allen, interview by author.

75. George Favors, Rosetta Rimmer, and Velena Daniels, interview by author.

76. Malba Allen, interview by author.

77. George Favors, Rosetta Rimmer, and Velena Daniels, interview by author.

78. Favors, quoted in Bowie and Favors, radio interview by Ted Panken.

79. Malba Allen, interview by author.

80. Büttner, Campbell, and Pruter, "The Parrot and Blue Lake Labels."

81. Campbell, Büttner, and Pruter, "The King Kolax Discography"; Porter, *John Coltrane*, 56.

82. Campbell, Büttner, and Pruter, "The King Kolax Discography."

83. Hill, *So in Love*; Lyles, "Andrew Hill Discography."

84. Fleming, *Stand By*.

85. Campbell, Pruter, and Büttner, "The King Fleming Discography"; Letman, "The Most," 16.

86. Beauchamp, *Art Ensemble of Chicago*, 27; Favors, interview by Peter Rosenbloom.

87. Thulani Davis, e-mail message to author; Lewis, *A Power Stronger Than Itself*, 62.

88. Lewis, *A Power Stronger Than Itself*, 62.

89. Beauchamp, *Art Ensemble of Chicago*, 70.

90. Thulani Davis, e-mail message to author.

91. Beauchamp, *Art Ensemble of Chicago*, 70; Jarman, telephone interview by author, 20 February 2015.

92. Jarman, *Black Case*, 109.

93. Duncan and Duncan, *The Negro Population of Chicago*, 279; Hirsch, *Making the Second Ghetto*, 3.

94. Lewis, *A Power Stronger Than Itself*, 62.

95. Jarman, quoted in Lewis, *A Power Stronger Than Itself*, 62.

96. "Army to Review Lake View and Waller Cadets," N2.

97. "Du Sable High R.O.T.C. Cadets Honor Winners," S5; "Honor R.O.T.C. Cadets at Two S. Side Schools," S3; Rusch, "Joseph Jarman," 3.

98. Beauchamp, *Art Ensemble of Chicago*, 70.

99. Jarman, quoted in Rusch, "Joseph Jarman," 4.

100. Lewis, *A Power Stronger Than Itself*, 62.

101. Jarman, interview by John Litweiler.

102. Jarman, interview by John Litweiler.

103. Jarman, interview by John Litweiler.

104. Lewis, *A Power Stronger Than Itself*, 64.

105. Beauchamp, *Art Ensemble of Chicago*, 70.

106. Lewis, *A Power Stronger Than Itself*, 64.

107. Jarman, quoted in Beauchamp, *Art Ensemble of Chicago*, 70.

108. Reich, "Saluting a Chicago Teacher Who Turned Out Jazz Stars," AE3.

109. Reich, "Saluting a Chicago Teacher Who Turned Out Jazz Stars," AE1.

110. Travis, *An Autobiography of Black Chicago*, 80.

111. Jarman, quoted in Beauchamp, *Art Ensemble of Chicago*, 70.

112. Jarman, quoted in Rusch, "Joseph Jarman," 3.

113. Figi, liner notes for Joseph Jarman, *Song For*.

114. Jarman, interview by John Litweiler.

115. Jarman, quoted in Lewis, *A Power Stronger Than Itself*, 65.

116. Lewis, *A Power Stronger Than Itself*, 65.

117. Jarman, interview by author, 11 November 2005.

118. Beauchamp, *Art Ensemble of Chicago*, 70.

119. Jarman, interview by John Litweiler.

120. Lewis, *A Power Stronger Than Itself*, 65.

121. Jarman, quoted in Beauchamp, *Art Ensemble of Chicago*, 71.

122. Jarman, quoted in Beauchamp, *Art Ensemble of Chicago*, 70.

123. Beauchamp, *Art Ensemble of Chicago*, 71.

124. Lewis, *A Power Stronger Than Itself*, 66.

125. Jarman, interview by John Litweiler.

126. Beauchamp, *Art Ensemble of Chicago*, 71.

127. Jarman, interview by John Litweiler.

128. Jarman, telephone interview by author, 10 May 2006.

129. Jarman, interview by John Litweiler.

130. Jarman, quoted in Beauchamp, *Art Ensemble of Chicago*, 71.

131. Jarman, *Black Case*, 5.

132. Jarman, interview by John Litweiler.

133. Jarman, *Black Case*.

134. Jarman, *Black Case*, 5.

135. Jarman, quoted in Beauchamp, *Art Ensemble of Chicago*, 71.

136. Thulani Davis, e-mail message to author; Jarman, interview by author, 19 August 2007.

137. Jarman, interview by author, 11 November 2005.

138. Jarman, telephone interview by author, 20 February 2015.

139. Jarman, interview by author, 19 August 2007. The book Jarman received may have been Bhargava, *The Teachings of the Buddha*.

140. Jarman, telephone interview by author, 10 May 2006.

141. Lewis, *A Power Stronger Than Itself*, 66.

142. Jarman, interview by John Litweiler.

143. Jarman, interview by John Litweiler.

144. Jarman, interview by John Litweiler.

145. Jarman, quoted in Lewis, *A Power Stronger Than Itself*, 66.

146. Figi, "Art Ensemble of Chicago," 44; Jarman, interview by John Litweiler.

147. Mitchell, telephone interview by author, 28 February 2015.

148. Hirsch, *Making the Second Ghetto*, 3–5.

149. Lewis, *A Power Stronger Than Itself*, 16, 62.

150. Kelley, "Dig They Freedom," 21; Lewis, *A Power Stronger Than Itself*, 63.

151. Mitchell, quoted in Figi, "Art Ensemble of Chicago," 44.

152. Mitchell, telephone interview by author, 28 February 2015.

153. Mitchell, interview by author, 4 December 2014.

154. Mitchell, quoted in McGraw-Beauchamp, "Roscoe Mitchell," 20.

155. Jung, "A Fireside Chat with Roscoe Mitchell."

156. Mitchell, quoted in Mitchell and Myers, radio interview by Ted Panken.

157. Bowie, "A.A.C.M.," 24; Figi, "Art Ensemble of Chicago," 44; Mitchell and Myers, radio interview by Ted Panken.

158. Lewis, *A Power Stronger Than Itself*, 63.

159. Mitchell, quoted in Mitchell and Myers, radio interview by Ted Panken.

160. Lewis, *A Power Stronger Than Itself*, 62.

161. Jung, "A Fireside Chat with Roscoe Mitchell."

162. Lewis, *A Power Stronger Than Itself*, 64.

163. Mitchell, radio interview by Ted Panken.

164. Bowie, "A.A.C.M.," 24; Lewis, *A Power Stronger Than Itself*, 64.

165. Lewis, *A Power Stronger Than Itself*, 18; Mitchell, telephone interview by author, 28 February 2015.

166. Mitchell, radio interview by Ted Panken.

167. Mitchell, radio interview by Ted Panken.

168. Gold-Molina, "Roscoe Mitchell."

169. Figi, "Art Ensemble of Chicago," 44; Lewis, *A Power Stronger Than Itself*, 65.

170. Mitchell, radio interview by Ted Panken.

171. Lewis, *A Power Stronger Than Itself*, 65.

172. Mitchell, radio interview by Ted Panken.

173. Mitchell, quoted in Mitchell and Myers, radio interview by Ted Panken.

174. Francis Davis, "Roscoe Mitchell," 28; Lewis, *A Power Stronger Than Itself*, 65.

175. Cromwell, "Jazz Mecca," 174.

176. Mitchell, quoted in Bill Smith, "Roscoe Mitchell," 3.

177. Mitchell, quoted in Bill Smith, "Roscoe Mitchell," 3.

178. Figi, "Art Ensemble of Chicago," 44.

179. Mitchell, radio interview by Ted Panken.

180. Mitchell and Myers, radio interview by Ted Panken.

181. Mitchell, quoted in Cromwell, "Jazz Mecca," 173.

182. Mitchell, quoted in Cromwell, "Jazz Mecca," 173–174.

183. Mitchell, quoted in Francis Davis, "Roscoe Mitchell," 28, 30.

184. Mitchell, quoted in Cromwell, "Jazz Mecca," 174.

185. Robert Palmer, "Art Ensemble of Chicago Takes Jazz to the Stage," 29.

186. Lewis, *A Power Stronger Than Itself*, 66–67.

187. Pierrepont, "Richard Wang," 9.

188. Jarman, interview by John Litweiler; Lewis, *A Power Stronger Than Itself*, 66.

189. Lewis, *A Power Stronger Than Itself*, 66; Pierrepont, "Richard Wang," 9–10.

190. Jarman, interview by John Litweiler.

191. Jarman, interview by John Litweiler.

192. ". . . Joseph et Henry Threadgill étaient parmi les plus assidus . . ." Pierrepont, "Richard Wang," 9.

193. Francis Davis, "Roscoe Mitchell," 30.

194. Jarman, quoted in Figi, "Art Ensemble of Chicago," 45.

195. Favors, interview by Peter Rosenbloom; Lewis, *A Power Stronger Than Itself*, 67.

196. Lewis, *A Power Stronger Than Itself*, 67; Terry Martin, "Blowing Out in Chicago," 21; Pierrepont, "Richard Wang," 10.

197. Bill Smith, "Roscoe Mitchell," 3. In addition to Mitchell and Jarman, the other group members were saxophonist Henry Threadgill, pianist Louis Hall, bassist Walter Chapel, and drummer Drahseer Khalid, then known as Richard Smith.

198. Jarman, quoted in Aaron Cohen, "Joseph Jarman," 33. The recording mentioned by Jarman is Ornette Coleman, *The Shape of Jazz to Come*.

199. Mitchell, quoted in Cromwell, "Jazz Mecca," 174.

200. Mitchell, quoted in Bill Smith, "Roscoe Mitchell," 4.

201. Mitchell, quoted in Lewis, *A Power Stronger Than Itself*, 64.

202. Lewis, *A Power Stronger Than Itself*, 61, 83.

203. Radano, *New Musical Figurations*, 79.

204. Eddie Harris, radio interview by Ted Panken.

205. Lewis, *A Power Stronger Than Itself*, 62.

206. Lewis, *A Power Stronger Than Itself*, 67; Terry Martin, "Blowing Out in Chicago," 21.

207. Cromwell, "Jazz Mecca," 175–176; Lewis, *A Power Stronger Than Itself*, 67–68.

208. Lewis, *A Power Stronger Than Itself*, 75.

209. Jarman, quoted in Lewis, *A Power Stronger Than Itself*, 68.

210. Lewis, *A Power Stronger Than Itself*, 68.

211. Muhal Richard Abrams, quoted in Townley, "Muhal Richard Abrams," 34.

212. Lewis, *A Power Stronger Than Itself*, 69–70.

213. Lewis, *A Power Stronger Than Itself*, 58–60, 62; Schillinger, *The Schillinger System of Musical Composition*.

214. Paul F. Berliner, *Thinking in Jazz*, 167.

215. Lewis, *A Power Stronger Than Itself*, 82.

216. Lewis, *A Power Stronger Than Itself*, 69, 135.

217. Mitchell, quoted in Francis Davis, "Roscoe Mitchell," 30.

218. Bill Smith, "Roscoe Mitchell," 8.

219. Lewis, *A Power Stronger Than Itself*, 86; Radano, *New Musical Figurations*, 80.

220. Lewis, *A Power Stronger Than Itself*, 85–87; Radano, *New Musical Figurations*, 80.

221. Favors, interview by Peter Rosenbloom; Lewis, *A Power Stronger Than Itself*, 87.

222. Radano, *New Musical Figurations*, 79–80.

223. Lewis, *A Power Stronger Than Itself*, 1; Radano, *New Musical Figurations*, 78.

224. Philip Kelan Cohran, telephone interview by author; Szwed, *Space Is the Place*, 176, 179.

225. Lewis, *A Power Stronger Than Itself*, 25; Radano, *New Musical Figurations*, 83.

226. Lewis, *A Power Stronger Than Itself*, 97.

227. Lewis, *A Power Stronger Than Itself*, 97–98.

228. Lewis, *A Power Stronger Than Itself*, 98–101.

229. Lewis, *A Power Stronger Than Itself*, 101–103.

230. Gene Dinwiddie, quoted in Lewis, *A Power Stronger Than Itself*, 71.

231. Eugene Easton, quoted in Lewis, *A Power Stronger Than Itself*, 102.

232. Lewis, *A Power Stronger Than Itself*, 106–111.

233. Lewis, *A Power Stronger Than Itself*, 111–114.

234. For a history of the Jazz Composers Guild, see Piekut, *Experimentalism Otherwise*, 102–139.

235. Absher, *The Black Musician and the White City*, 44.

236. Absher, *The Black Musician and the White City*, 141.

237. Absher, *The Black Musician and the White City*, 138.

238. Muhal Richard Abrams, quoted in Lewis, *A Power Stronger Than Itself*, 114.

239. Lewis, *A Power Stronger Than Itself*, 115.

240. Lewis, *A Power Stronger Than Itself*, 116.

Chapter 2

1. Epigraph: Jarman, quoted in Cromwell, "Jazz Mecca," 194.

2. Lewis, *A Power Stronger Than Itself*, 118–119.

3. Abrams and Chaney, "Creative Musicians Present Artistic Heritage Ensemble," 14; Abrams and Chaney, "Creative Musicians Sponsor Artists Concert Showcase," 14; Lewis, *A Power Stronger Than Itself*, 119.

4. Abrams and Chaney, "Creative Musicians Sponsor Artists Concert Showcase," 14.

5. Lewis, *A Power Stronger Than Itself*, 118.

6. Abrams and Chaney, "Creative Musicians Sponsor Artists Concert Showcase," 14.

7. Abrams and Chaney, "Creative Musicians Sponsor Artists Concert Showcase," 14.

8. Lewis, *A Power Stronger Than Itself*, 108–109.

9. Lewis, *A Power Stronger Than Itself*, 101–103.

10. Fred Anderson, interview by author.

11. Lewis, *A Power Stronger Than Itself*, 117–118.

12. Lewis, *A Power Stronger Than Itself*, 118.

13. Elaine Cohen, "Fred Anderson," 19; Radano, *New Musical Figurations*, 82–83.

14. Fred Anderson, interview by author.

15. Jarman, quoted in Jung, "A Fireside Chat with Joseph Jarman," 2002.

16. Friedman and Birnbaum, "Fred Anderson," 21.

17. Lewis, *A Power Stronger Than Itself*, 118–119.

18. Terry Martin, liner notes for Roscoe Mitchell, *Before There Was Sound*; Bill Smith, "Roscoe Mitchell," 3.

19. Alvin Fielder, telephone interview by author, 11 March 2006; Terry Martin, liner notes for Roscoe Mitchell, *Before There Was Sound*.

20. Alvin Fielder, telephone interview by author, 11 March 2006.

21. Litweiler, "Chicago's AACM," 45.

22. Alvin Fielder, telephone interview by author, 11 March 2006.

23. Alvin Fielder, telephone interview by author, 11 March 2006.

24. Favors, interview by Peter Rosenbloom; Alvin Fielder, telephone interview by author, 11 October 2006.

25. Alvin Fielder, telephone interview by author, 11 March 2006.

26. Favors, interview by Peter Rosenbloom.

27. Favors, quoted in Cromwell, "Jazz Mecca," 189.

28. Terry Martin, liner notes for Roscoe Mitchell, *Before There Was Sound*. The

Berry-Favors-Fielder-Mitchell quartet made two recordings in 1965. Almost five decades later, the recordings were released as Mitchell, *Before There Was Sound.*

29. Alvin Fielder, telephone interview by author, 11 March 2006.

30. Mitchell, quoted in Terry Martin, liner notes for Roscoe Mitchell, *Before There Was Sound.*

31. Mitchell, quoted in Favors, liner notes for Art Ensemble of Chicago, *Tribute to Lester.*

32. Bowie, "A.A.C.M.," 25.

33. Lewis, *A Power Stronger Than Itself,* 135.

34. Beauchamp, *Art Ensemble of Chicago,* 35.

35. Stokes, *The Jazz Scene,* 136.

36. Bowie, quoted in Coppens and Lagerwerff, "Lester Bowie," 12.

37. Stokes, *The Jazz Scene,* 136.

38. Bowie, "A.A.C.M.," 25; Lewis, *A Power Stronger Than Itself,* 136.

39. Lewis, *A Power Stronger Than Itself,* 135.

40. Bowie, quoted in Stokes, *The Jazz Scene,* 136.

41. Rusch, "Lester Bowie," 3.

42. Coppens and Lagerwerff, "Lester Bowie," 14.

43. Lewis, *A Power Stronger Than Itself,* 135.

44. Looker, *"Point from Which Creation Begins,"* 6.

45. Besecker, "Lester Bowie," 5; Looker, *"Point from Which Creation Begins,"* 7.

46. Bowie, quoted in Glasgo, "Lester Redux," 2.

47. Bowie, quoted in Rendle and Zabor, "Lester Bowie," 67.

48. Rendle and Zabor, "Lester Bowie," 67.

49. Rendle and Zabor, "Lester Bowie," 67.

50. Jung, "A Fireside Chat with Lester Bowie."

51. Lewis, *A Power Stronger Than Itself,* 136; Rusch, "Lester Bowie," 3–4.

52. Bowie, quoted in Beauchamp, *Art Ensemble of Chicago,* 36.

53. Bowie, quoted in Figi, "Art Ensemble of Chicago," 45.

54. Rendle and Zabor, "Lester Bowie," 67.

55. Bowie, quoted in Rendle and Zabor, "Lester Bowie," 68.

56. Lewis, *A Power Stronger Than Itself,* 136.

57. Beauchamp, *Art Ensemble of Chicago,* 37.

58. Bowie, quoted in Beauchamp, *Art Ensemble of Chicago,* 36.

59. Bowie, quoted in Beauchamp, *Art Ensemble of Chicago,* 37.

60. Rendle and Zabor, "Lester Bowie," 67.

61. Bowie, quoted in Beauchamp, *Art Ensemble of Chicago,* 36.

62. Bowie, quoted in Lewis, *A Power Stronger Than Itself,* 136.

63. Lewis, *A Power Stronger Than Itself,* 136–137.

64. Bowie, quoted in Beauchamp, *Art Ensemble of Chicago,* 38.

65. Lewis, *A Power Stronger Than Itself,* 137.

66. Beauchamp, *Art Ensemble of Chicago,* 38.

67. Bowie, quoted in Beauchamp, *Art Ensemble of Chicago,* 38.

68. Lewis, *A Power Stronger Than Itself,* 137.

69. Bowie, quoted in Rendle and Zabor, "Lester Bowie," 67.

70. Bowie, quoted in Beauchamp, *Art Ensemble of Chicago*, 38.

71. Corbett, "Fanfare for a Warrior," 23; Looker, *"Point from Which Creation Begins,"* 10.

72. Bowie, quoted in Beauchamp, *Art Ensemble of Chicago*, 39.

73. Rusch, "Lester Bowie," 4.

74. Beauchamp, *Art Ensemble of Chicago*, 38–39; Looker, *"Point from Which Creation Begins,"* 10.

75. Bowie, quoted in Beauchamp, *Art Ensemble of Chicago*, 39.

76. Beauchamp, *Art Ensemble of Chicago*, 39.

77. Bowie, quoted in Rendle and Zabor, "Lester Bowie," 67.

78. Bowie, quoted in Beauchamp, *Art Ensemble of Chicago*, 39.

79. Bowie, quoted in Beauchamp, *Art Ensemble of Chicago*, 39.

80. Rendle and Zabor, "Lester Bowie," 67.

81. Bowie, "A.A.C.M.," 25; Coppens and Lagerwerff, "Lester Bowie," 13.

82. Lewis, *A Power Stronger Than Itself*, 138.

83. Pareles, "A Family of Gospel Singers," C21.

84. Wilmer, *As Serious as Your Life*, 121.

85. Pareles, "A Family of Gospel Singers," C21.

86. Bass and McClure, "Don't Mess Up a Good Thing"/"Baby, What You Want Me to Do"; Bass and McClure, "You'll Miss Me (When I'm Gone)"/"Don't Jump."

87. Bass, "Rescue Me"/"Soul of the Man"; "R&B Spotlights," 16.

88. Sachs, "A Long Road Back," FTR41.

89. Pareles, "A Family of Gospel Singers," C21.

90. Bowie, quoted in Beauchamp, *Art Ensemble of Chicago*, 40.

91. "Boss!," 28; "Fontella Bass Says," 28.

92. Beauchamp, *Art Ensemble of Chicago*, 40; Ratliff, "Lester Bowie Is Dead at 58," B15.

93. Bowie, quoted in Beauchamp, *Art Ensemble of Chicago*, 40.

94. Bowie, quoted in Bowie and Favors, radio interview by Ted Panken.

95. Bowie, quoted in Stokes, *The Jazz Scene*, 137.

96. Thurman Barker, radio interview by Ted Panken; Bowie and Favors, radio interview by Ted Panken.

97. Bowie, quoted in Beauchamp, *Art Ensemble of Chicago*, 40.

98. Bowie, quoted in Figi, "Art Ensemble of Chicago," 46.

99. Cromwell, "Jazz Mecca," 189.

100. Favors, liner notes for Art Ensemble of Chicago, *Tribute to Lester*.

101. Bowie, quoted in Beauchamp, *Art Ensemble of Chicago*, 40.

102. Bowie, quoted in Lewis, *A Power Stronger Than Itself*, 138.

103. Favors, interview by Peter Rosenbloom.

104. Lyon, "Tower Ticker," 30.

105. Favors, interview by Peter Rosenbloom.

106. Favors, interview by Peter Rosenbloom.

107. Hill, *So in Love*.

108. Favors, interview by Peter Rosenbloom.

109. Blumenthal, "A Kaleidoscope of Sound," N1.

110. Braxton, *Tri-Axium Writings*, 1:428.

111. Braxton, *Tri-Axium Writings*, 1:420; Jost, *Free Jazz,* 170.

112. Mitchell, *Sound.*

113. Mitchell, quoted in Terry Martin, "Blowing Out in Chicago," 21.

114. Alvin Fielder, telephone interview by author, 11 October 2006.

115. Silverstein, "Recording History," 58.

116. Mathieu, "*Sound,*" 34.

117. Litweiler, "Roscoe Mitchell, The Happening, Chicago," 38.

118. Terry Martin, "The Chicago Avant-Garde," 17.

119. Alvin Fielder, telephone interview by author, 11 March 2006; Terry Martin, "The Chicago Avant-Garde," 17.

120. Litweiler, "Three to Europe," 21.

121. Mitchell, quoted in Cromwell, "Jazz Mecca," 192.

122. Favors, quoted in Cromwell, "Jazz Mecca," 190.

123. Bowie, quoted in Coppens and Lagerwerff, "Lester Bowie," 13.

124. Beauchamp, *Art Ensemble of Chicago*, 28; Lewis, *A Power Stronger Than Itself,* 68.

125. Nessa, liner notes for Art Ensemble [of Chicago], *1967/68.*

126. Beauchamp, *Art Ensemble of Chicago*, 59; Rout, "AACM," 133.

127. Mitchell, telephone interview by author, 18 October 2006.

128. [Gravenites], "Whole Lotta Soul"/"Drunken Boat."

129. Mitchell, telephone interview by author, 18 October 2006.

130. Beauchamp, *Art Ensemble of Chicago*, 25.

131. Levi, "Lester Speaks Out," 25.

132. Wolkin and Keenom, *Michael Bloomfield*, 142.

133. Favors, quoted in Cromwell, "Jazz Mecca," 190.

134. Terry Martin, "Roscoe Mitchell, Ida Noyes Hall, University of Chicago," 29.

135. Michaels, "How I Was a Fly on the Wall in the Creation of the Greatest Song in the History of Rock and Roll," 53; Rusch and Ryan, "Malachi Favors," 12.

136. Litweiler, "Roscoe Mitchell, Cobb Hall, University of Chicago," 30; Litweiler, "Three to Europe," 20–21.

137. Favors, quoted in Rusch and Ryan, "Malachi Favors," 12.

138. Bowie, quoted in Figi, "Art Ensemble of Chicago," 46.

139. Litweiler, "Three to Europe," 21; Terry Martin, liner notes for Art Ensemble [of Chicago], *1967/68.*

140. Mitchell, quoted in Cromwell, "Jazz Mecca," 192–193.

141. Mitchell, quoted in Hicks, "Roscoe Mitchell," 26.

142. Litweiler, "Roscoe Mitchell, Cobb Hall, University of Chicago," 29–31.

143. Mitchell, quoted in Hicks, "Roscoe Mitchell," 26.

144. Silverstein, "Recording History," 58.

145. Bowie, *Numbers 1 & 2*; Mitchell, *Congliptious.* Another recording from 1967 was not released until several years later: Mitchell, *Old/Quartet.*

146. Litweiler, "Roscoe Mitchell, Cobb Hall, University of Chicago," 30.

147. Beauchamp, *Art Ensemble of Chicago*, 25.

148. Lewis, *A Power Stronger Than Itself*, 189.

149. Looker, *"Point from Which Creation Begins,"* 17.

150. Silverstein, "Recording History," 57–58.

151. Bowie and Favors, radio interview by Ted Panken.

152. Looker, *"Point from Which Creation Begins,"* 17, 31.

153. Collins and Crawford, "Power to the People!," 14–15; Kellie Jones, "Black West," 46.

154. Donaldson, "The Rise, Fall and Legacy of the *Wall of Respect* Movement," 22.

155. Lewis, *A Power Stronger Than Itself*, 165–166.

156. Radano, *New Musical Figurations*, 94.

157. Lewis, *A Power Stronger Than Itself*, 475; Moye, e-mail message to author, 10 March 2015.

158. Neal, "The Black Arts Movement," 29.

159. For an account by one of OBAC's cofounders, see Donaldson, "The Rise, Fall and Legacy of the *Wall of Respect* Movement."

160. Lewis, *A Power Stronger Than Itself*, 189.

161. Henry Threadgill, quoted in Tate, "Gone Fishing," 165.

162. Lewis, *A Power Stronger Than Itself*, 177–179.

163. Bowie, quoted in Lewis, *A Power Stronger Than Itself*, 179.

164. Jarman, quoted in Kostakis and Lange, "An Interview with Joseph Jarman," 94.

165. Kelley, "Dig They Freedom," 22; Lewis, *A Power Stronger Than Itself*, 59.

166. Bowie, *Numbers 1 & 2*; Abrams, *Levels and Degrees of Light*.

167. Lewis, *A Power Stronger Than Itself*, 165.

168. Litweiler, "Altoists and Other Chicagoans," 29; Rusch and Ryan, "Malachi Favors," 14.

169. Litweiler, *The Freedom Principle*, 180.

170. Quinn, "Joseph Jarman, Abraham Lincoln Center, Chicago," 27–28.

171. Terry Martin, "The Chicago Avant-Garde," 15.

172. John Litweiler, interview by author.

173. Lewis, *A Power Stronger Than Itself*, 128.

174. Douglas Mitchell, interview by author.

175. Jarman, concert flyer for performance at the Harper Theater, Chicago.

176. Rusch, "Joseph Jarman," 5.

177. Kim, "John Cage in Separate Togetherness with Jazz," 76.

178. Lewis, *A Power Stronger Than Itself*, 129; Douglas Mitchell, interview by author.

179. Kim, "John Cage in Separate Togetherness with Jazz," 79–80; Douglas Mitchell, interview by author.

180. Walmsley, "An Interesting Workout in Jazz Sounds," 39.

181. Welding, "Joseph Jarman-John Cage, Harper Theater, Chicago," 35.

182. Rusch, "Joseph Jarman," 4.

183. Jarman, quoted in Lewis, *A Power Stronger Than Itself*, 129. See also Cage, *Silence*.

184. Kim, "John Cage in Separate Togetherness with Jazz," 64.

185. Jarman, quoted in Rusch, "Joseph Jarman," 4.

186. Jarman, quoted in Pfleiderer, "Das Art Ensemble of Chicago in Paris, Sommer 1969," 97.

187. Jarman, scrapbook.

188. Jarman, résumé.

189. Lewis, *A Power Stronger Than Itself*, 82, 143.

190. Jarman, quoted in Lewis, *A Power Stronger Than Itself*, 143.

191. Terry Martin, "The Chicago Avant-Garde," 14; Quinn, "Joseph Jarman, Abraham Lincoln Center, Chicago," 27.

192. Jarman, *Song For.*

193. Mitchell, *Sound.*

194. Jarman, *Black Case*, 95–97.

195. Jarman, *Black Case*, 95.

196. Jarman, *Black Case*, 97.

197. Quinn, "Joseph Jarman, Abraham Lincoln Center, Chicago," 27–28.

198. Beauchamp, *Art Ensemble of Chicago*, 59; Figi, liner notes for Joseph Jarman, *Song For.*

199. Jarman, interview by John Litweiler.

200. Jarman, "New York," 14.

201. Litweiler, "The Chicago Scene," 37.

202. Litweiler, "Joseph Jarman, Hyde Park Art Center, Chicago," 36; Jordan Sandke, telephone interview by author.

203. Jarman, résumé; Jarman, scrapbook.

204. Jarman, quoted in Lewis, *A Power Stronger Than Itself*, 152.

205. Lewis, *A Power Stronger Than Itself*, 152.

206. Jarman, quoted in Lewis, *A Power Stronger Than Itself*, 152.

207. Jarman, quoted in Lewis, *A Power Stronger Than Itself*, 152.

208. Lewis, *A Power Stronger Than Itself*, 144.

209. Lewis, *A Power Stronger Than Itself*, 187.

210. Jarman, liner notes for Joseph Jarman, *As If It Were the Seasons.*

211. Jarman, *As If It Were the Seasons.*

212. Jarman, scrapbook.

213. Larayne Black, interview by author.

214. Evans-Wentz, *The Tibetan Book of the Dead*; Jarman, concert flyer for performance at the Francis W. Parker School, Chicago.

215. Jarman, concert flyer for performance at the Francis W. Parker School, Chicago.

216. Litweiler, "Three to Europe," 20.

217. Jarman, quoted in Beauchamp, *Art Ensemble of Chicago*, 73.

218. Lewis, *A Power Stronger Than Itself*, 204–205.

219. Jarman, quoted in Beauchamp, *Art Ensemble of Chicago*, 73.

220. Jarman, quoted in Cromwell, "Jazz Mecca," 194–195.

Chapter 3

1. Epigraph: Bowie, quoted in Beauchamp, *Art Ensemble of Chicago*, 47.

2. Favors, quoted in Bowie and Favors, radio interview by Ted Panken.

3. Favors, quoted in Beauchamp, *Art Ensemble of Chicago*, 28.

4. Bowie, quoted in Bowie and Favors, radio interview by Ted Panken.

5. Bowie, quoted in Bowie and Favors, radio interview by Ted Panken.

6. Bowie, quoted in Beauchamp, *Art Ensemble of Chicago*, 46; Lewis, *A Power Stronger Than Itself*, 140.

7. Blake, *Le Tumulte Noir*, 63; Jeffrey H. Jackson, *Making Jazz French*, 18.

8. Drott, *Music and the Elusive Revolution*, 112.

9. The pioneering history of African American writers in France is Fabre, *From Harlem to Paris*.

10. Gillett, "Jazz and the Evolution of Black American Cosmopolitanism in Interwar Paris," 486–487.

11. Bowie, quoted in Levi, "Lester Speaks Out," 25.

12. Bowie and Favors, radio interview by Ted Panken.

13. Drott, *Music and the Elusive Revolution*, 118.

14. Jarman, *Song For*.

15. Lewis, *A Power Stronger Than Itself*, 217.

16. Jacques Bisceglia, interview by author.

17. Lewis, *A Power Stronger Than Itself*, 218.

18. ". . . féderation libre des musiciens . . ." Sklower, *Free Jazz, la Catastrophe Féconde*, 190.

19. Cotro, *Chants Libres*, 78.

20. Warne, "Bringing Counterculture to France," 314.

21. Lewis, *A Power Stronger Than Itself*, 218.

22. Delcloo, "Letter to the AACM."

23. Anthony Braxton, quoted in Lewis, *A Power Stronger Than Itself*, 219.

24. Lewis, *A Power Stronger Than Itself*, 219.

25. Anthony Braxton, quoted in Lock, *Forces in Motion*, 55.

26. Jarman, quoted in Beauchamp, *Art Ensemble of Chicago*, 73.

27. Anthony Braxton, quoted in Lock, *Forces in Motion*, 55.

28. Bowie, quoted in Rendle and Zabor, "Lester Bowie," 68.

29. Mitchell, quoted in Glasgo, "Lester Redux," 2.

30. Bass, "Rescue Me"/"Soul of the Man."

31. Newsome, "It's After the End of the World! Don't You Know That Yet?," 262.

32. Bowie, quoted in Beauchamp, *Art Ensemble of Chicago*, 45.

33. Bowie, quoted in Rendle and Zabor, "Lester Bowie," 68.

34. Litweiler, "Three to Europe," 20.

35. Jarman, quoted in Beauchamp, *Art Ensemble of Chicago*, 73.

36. Rendle and Zabor, "Lester Bowie," 68.

37. Favors, quoted in Beauchamp, *Art Ensemble of Chicago*, 28.

38. Bowie, quoted in Beauchamp, *Art Ensemble of Chicago*, 41.

39. Art Ensemble [of Chicago], concert poster for performance at the Blue Gargoyle, Chicago; Cooley, "Goodbye, Joseph Jarman!," 3.

40. Litweiler, "Three to Europe," 22.

41. Bowie, quoted in Choice, "Jazz Notes," B18.

42. Birnbaum, "Art Ensemble of Chicago," 16.

43. Litweiler, "Three to Europe," 22.

44. Beauchamp, *Art Ensemble of Chicago*, 73.

45. Beauchamp, *Art Ensemble of Chicago*, 25; Moye, e-mail message to author, 22 October 2005.

46. Newsome, "It's After the End of the World! Don't You Know That Yet?," 262–263.

47. Favors, quoted in Beauchamp, *Art Ensemble of Chicago*, 28.

48. Jacques Bisceglia, interview by author.

49. Mitchell, quoted in Mitchell and Myers, radio interview by Ted Panken.

50. Jarman, quoted in Beauchamp, *Art Ensemble of Chicago*, 73.

51. Jarman, interview by John Litweiler. See also Ginsberg, *Howl and Other Poems*.

52. Jarman, interview by John Litweiler.

53. Favors, quoted in Beauchamp, *Art Ensemble of Chicago*, 29.

54. Jacques Bisceglia, interview by author.

55. Drott, *Music and the Elusive Revolution*, 118.

56. "Merde mon vieux, les seules révolutionnaires que j'ai vus à Paris, je les ai rencontrés dans une cave de jazz, au Chat qui Pêche!" Stokely Carmichael, quoted in Joans, "Black Power et New Thing," 19.

57. Drott, *Music and the Elusive Revolution*, 112.

58. Beauchamp, *Art Ensemble of Chicago*, 29.

59. Lewis, *A Power Stronger Than Itself*, 233.

60. Favors, quoted in Beauchamp, *Art Ensemble of Chicago*, 29.

61. Delanoë, *Le Raspail Vert*, 34.

62. Looker, *"Point from Which Creation Begins,"* 200.

63. See Delanoë, *Le Raspail Vert*, 137–155.

64. Lewis, *A Power Stronger Than Itself*, 226, 233.

65. Caux, "Le délire et la rigueur de 'l'Art Ensemble' de Chicago," 8.

66. ". . . quatre membres prestigieux de l'AACM . . ." Caux, "Le délire et la rigueur de 'l'Art Ensemble' de Chicago," 8.

67. Caux, "Alan Silva à Paris," 9; "Flashes," 12.

68. ". . . musique aux multiples facettes dont le feeling est si différent de celui de New-York." Caux, "Le délire et la rigueur de 'l'Art Ensemble' de Chicago," 8.

69. Lewis, *A Power Stronger Than Itself*, 222.

70. "Quand se produit le quartet de Chicago, la scène de ce curieux théâtre de 140 places se trouve presque entièrement envahie par une multitude d'instruments; xylophones, basson, sarrussophone, saxophones divers, clarinettes, banjo, cymbales, gongs, cloches, grosse caisse, balafon, crécelles, etc . . . Le premier soir, les auditeurs furent assez surpris de voir Joseph Jarman, torse nu, le visage peint, passer lentement dans leurs rangs en marmonnant un poème pendant que le bassiste Malachi Favors, qui portait un masque d'épouvante, hurlait des imprécations à Lester Bowie et que Roscoe Mitchell actionnait des trompes d'auto . . . De toute évidence, le spectacle fait partie intégrante de leur expression: ils prennent véritablement possession de l'espace d'une salle qui, dès lors, semble avoir été spécialment conçue pour eux." Caux, "Le délire et la rigueur de 'l'Art Ensemble' de Chicago," 8.

71. ". . . les nouveaux rapports entre le visuel et l'auditif . . ."; ". . . une musique d'une impeccable précision formelle"; "Le langage de la New Thing que nous connaissons est

parfaitement assimilé et sert de tremplin pour d'autres audaces"; ". . . la discrétion et la retenue . . ."; ". . . d'un humour dévastateur et souvent grinçant"; ". . . une musique grave et profonde . . ."; ". . . un ambigu et violent psychodrame Black-Power." Caux, "Le délire et la rigueur de 'l'Art Ensemble' de Chicago," 8.

72. Mitchell, telephone interview by author, 18 October 2006.

73. "Les quatre hommes ne dissocient pas éthique et esthétique, art et idéologie"; ". . . leur souveraine individualité . . ." Hofstein, "Chronique du jazz," 84.

74. "Tous quatre sont noirs, jeunes, originaires de Chicago et membres de l'AACM"; ". . . l'AACM est un organisme de lutte qui regroupe les jeunes musiciens et adapte les principes du Black Power à l'univers musical: [ne] plus d'intermédiares blancs; le jazz doit être totalement l'affaire des Noirs. La musique des Chicagoans 69 est à l'image de leurs idées: violente et révolutionnaire." Adler, "L'été torride du Lucernaire," 30.

75. Caux, "L'été au Lucernaire," 15.

76. Lewis, *A Power Stronger Than Itself*, 224–225.

77. ". . . ces autels de torture et de sacrifice . . ."; "Parler des musiciens de Chicago, c'est toujours employer les mêmes expressions: *black music, black power, agression, happening politique et musical. Le critique se sent dépassé car, musicalement, l'explosion paralyse les mots; seules les oreilles bourdonnantes ou agacées peuvent témoigner.*" Alessandrini, "Jazz on the Grass," 9.

78. Anthony Braxton, quoted in Lewis, *A Power Stronger Than Itself*, 235.

79. Nettelbeck, *Dancing with de Beauvoir*, 100–101; Vihlen, "Sounding French," 168.

80. Brett A. Berliner, *Ambivalent Desire*, 111–116.

81. Jeffrey H. Jackson, *Making Jazz French*, 26–27.

82. Brett A. Berliner, *Ambivalent Desire*, 7, 13.

83. Nettelbeck, *Dancing with de Beauvoir*, 100.

84. Gendron, *Between Montmartre and the Mudd Club*, 106.

85. Stovall, *Paris Noir*, 70.

86. Jeffrey H. Jackson, *Making Jazz French*, 29.

87. Blake, *Le Tumulte Noir*, 69.

88. Blake, *Le Tumulte Noir*, 23. See also Agawu, *Representing African Music*, 55–70.

89. ". . . une musique de libération . . ." Jamin, "Au-delà du Vieux Carré," 286.

90. Stovall, *Paris Noir*, 31. See also Blake, *Le Tumulte Noir*, 91–101.

91. Stovall, *Paris Noir*, 33.

92. ". . . le jazz était une musique de 'Nègre,' c'est-à-dire d'un être d'origine inconnue . . . d'un ailleurs désincarné, d'un monde exotique . . ." Denis-Constant Martin, "De l'excursion à Harlem au débat sur les 'Noirs,'" 262.

93. Denis-Constant Martin, "De l'excursion à Harlem au débat sur les 'Noirs,'" 270–271.

94. Drott, *Music and the Elusive Revolution*, 127.

95. Stovall, *Paris Noir*, 135.

96. Vihlen, "Sounding French," 168–169.

97. Stovall, *Paris Noir*, 251–252.

98. Ross, *May '68 and Its Afterlives*, 8.

99. Ross, *May '68 and Its Afterlives*, 80.

100. Ross, *May '68 and Its Afterlives*, 3–4.

101. Ross, *May '68 and Its Afterlives*, 13–14.

102. Alex Dutilh, interview by author.

103. "Dans le context précis de mai 68, le free-jazz apparaît . . . à la fois comme le symbole de la révolte politique contre le système, et comme une contestation culturelle, se trouvant ainsi en phase avec l'une des caractéristiques essentielles de l'esprit soixante-huitard." Tournès, *New Orleans sur Seine*, 395.

104. Willener, *The Action-Image of Society*.

105. Drott, *Music and the Elusive Revolution*, 139–140; Tournès, *New Orleans sur Seine*, 456.

106. Drott, *Music and the Elusive Revolution*, 112, 118–119; Tournès, *New Orleans sur Seine*, 388–389.

107. Lehman, "I Love You with an Asterisk," 41.

108. Carles and Comolli, *Free Jazz/Black Power*. For more on *Free Jazz/Black Power*, see Drott, *Music and the Elusive Revolution*, 131–135; Lane, *Jazz and Machine-Age Imperialism*, 195–199; and Lewis, *A Power Stronger Than Itself*, 235–238.

109. Carmichael and Hamilton, *Black Power*, 47.

110. Fabre, *From Harlem to Paris*, 274.

111. Lehman, "I Love You with an Asterisk," 41; Tournès, *New Orleans sur Seine*, 396.

112. Stovall, *Paris Noir*, 33. See also Lehman, "I Love You with an Asterisk," 42.

113. Lehman, "I Love You with an Asterisk," 40.

114. "Que signifie pour vous la tradition, le blues, par exemple?" "Nous jouons le blues, nous jouons le jazz, le rock, la musique espagnole, gitane, africaine, la musique classique, la musique européenne contemporaine, vaudou . . . tout se que vous voudrez . . . parce que, finalement, c'est 'la musique' que nous jouons: nous créons des sons, un point c'est tout." Jarman, quoted in Gras, Caux, and Bernard, "A.A.C.M. Chicago," 18.

115. Drott, *Music and the Elusive Revolution*, 116.

116. "Aux U.S.A., êtes-vous en relation avec des organisations politiques telles que, par exemple, les Black-Panthers?" "Nous sommes en contact avec toutes les organisations noires." "Nous n'avons d'affiliation avec aucune association politique, cela est étranger aux desseins de l'AACM. Bien sûr, nous avons des relations, des amities dans ces mouvements, mais tout cela demeure sur un plan strictement personnel. Nous entendons maintenir intacts les concepts de l'AACM dont les objectifs expliquent, d'ailleurs, notre position politique et sociale. Ce qui nous intéresse avant tout est de transmettre autour de nous la musique et la puissance de cette musique. La musique est une réponse à ces problèmes; c'est-à-dire que lorsque les gens l'entendent, ils peuvent percevoir un echo de ces problèmes. Grâce à la musique, ils peuvent devenir à leur tour plus actifs et plus responsables." Bowie and Jarman, quoted in Gras, Caux, and Bernard, "A.A.C.M. Chicago," 17.

117. Jarman, quoted in Beauchamp, *Art Ensemble of Chicago*, 73–74.

118. Lewis, *A Power Stronger Than Itself*, 246.

119. Favors, quoted in Beauchamp, *Art Ensemble of Chicago*, 28.

120. Mitchell, quoted in Mitchell and Myers, radio interview by Ted Panken.

121. Jacques Bisceglia, interview by author.

122. Beauchamp, *Art Ensemble of Chicago*, 74.

123. Jacques Michelou, telephone interview by author.

124. Jarman, quoted in Beauchamp, *Art Ensemble of Chicago*, 74.

125. Beauchamp, *Art Ensemble of Chicago*, 74.

126. Beauchamp, *Art Ensemble of Chicago*, 74.

127. Bowie, quoted in Beauchamp, *Art Ensemble of Chicago*, 41–42.

128. Hennessey, "Art Ensemble of Chicago," 10.

129. Jarman, quoted in Beauchamp, *Art Ensemble of Chicago*, 74.

130. Lewis, *A Power Stronger Than Itself*, 224.

131. Lewis, *A Power Stronger Than Itself*, 225; Litweiler, "Three to Europe," 20.

132. Moye, quoted in Tate, "Gone Fishing," 166.

133. Bowie, quoted in Figi, "Art Ensemble of Chicago," 47.

134. Art Ensemble [of Chicago], concert poster for performance at the Blue Gargoyle, Chicago.

135. Lewis, *A Power Stronger Than Itself*, 219. See also Cromwell, "Jazz Mecca," 197–198.

136. Jarman, quoted in Beauchamp, *Art Ensemble of Chicago*, 74. For the first usages of "Art Ensemble of Chicago" in *Jazz Magazine* and *Jazz Hot*, respectively, see Carles, "O. C. et la centrifugeuse," 15; and Postif, "Discomania," 10.

137. Moye, quoted in Tate, "Gone Fishing," 166.

138. Lewis, *A Power Stronger Than Itself*, 227, 255.

139. Bowie, quoted in Figi, "Art Ensemble of Chicago," 47.

140. Moye, e-mail message to author, 22 October 2005; Newsome, "It's After the End of the World! Don't You Know That Yet?," 264.

141. Mitchell, quoted in Cromwell, "Jazz Mecca," 195.

142. Bowie, quoted in Beauchamp, *Art Ensemble of Chicago*, 47.

Chapter 4

1. Epigraph: ". . . dans les chants que nous chantons l'amour, c'est la vie." Jarman, liner notes for Art Ensemble of Chicago, *A Jackson in Your House*.

2. Art Ensemble of Chicago, *A Jackson in Your House*.

3. Art Ensemble of Chicago, *The Spiritual*; Art Ensemble of Chicago, *Tutankhamun*.

4. "They give us some money and we go get a house." Mitchell, quoted in Cromwell, "Jazz Mecca," 196.

5. ". . . Byg . . . fait un gros effort sur le jazz moderne . . ." "Une nouvelle collection," 9.

6. "Les cloisonnements entre les différentes tendances de la musique actuelle . . ." Jean Georgakarakos, quoted in Koechlin, "'Pas de ça chez nous!,'" 37.

7. Pierrepont, "'A Brain for the Seine,'" 2 n. 9. See also Pierrepont, *La Nuée, l'AACM*.

8. "BYG à l'avant garde," 16–17.

9. Art Ensemble of Chicago, *Message to Our Folks*; Art Ensemble of Chicago, *Reese and the Smooth Ones*.

10. Schwartz and Fitzgerald, "BYG Records Listing."

11. Art Ensemble of Chicago, *People in Sorrow*.

12. Jarman, liner notes for Art Ensemble of Chicago, *A Jackson in Your House*.

13. Mitchell, e-mail message to author, 15 September 2007.

14. Monson, *Saying Something*, 128. For more on intermusicality, see Klein, *Intertextuality in Western Art Music*; and Monson, *Saying Something*, 97–132.

15. Jarman, telephone interview by author, 10 December 2008.

16. Jost, *Free Jazz*, 178.

17. Jost, *Free Jazz*, 179.

18. Monson, *Saying Something*, 188.

19. "... entrée fracassante de la New-Thing à Paris ..." Caux, "Le délire et la rigueur de 'l'Art Ensemble' de Chicago," 8.

20. Mitchell, e-mail message to author, 15 September 2007.

21. "... violente et révolutionnaire." Adler, "L'été torride du Lucernaire," 30.

22. Lewis, "*Gittin' to Know Y'All*," 19.

23. "... humour aussi sérieux que celui de la vie. . . . [ç]a sonne comme du bon vieux jazz, parce qu'ici on est bien comme on l'était là-bas." Jarman, liner notes for Art Ensemble of Chicago, *A Jackson in Your House*.

24. Braxton, *Tri-Axium Writings*, 3:297–298.

25. "Ce flot sonore, torrentiel et d'une grande violence, suppose un engagement physique, nerveux et spirituel total." Bernard, "The Art Ensemble of Chicago," 1.

26. Ross, *May '68 and Its Afterlives*, 80–81.

27. Alex Dutilh, interview by author.

28. For an analysis of text-music relationships and politics in "Get in Line," see Jost, *Sozialgeschichte des Jazz in den USA*, 193.

29. Jarman, quoted in Litweiler, "There Won't Be Any More Music," 23.

30. Bowie, quoted in Coppens and Lagerwerff, "Lester Bowie," 14.

31. Mitchell, interview by author, 18 November 2010.

32. Beauchamp, *Art Ensemble of Chicago*, 37–38; Jarman, interview by author, 11 November 2005; Lewis, *A Power Stronger Than Itself*, 136–137.

33. Here, Jarman adopts a typical cadence-calling inflection in which the initial consonants of both "left" and "right" shift to an "h" sound, while the vowel in "right" takes on a diphthong character, threatening to obliterate the final consonant. The result is a cadence that sounds less like "left, right" and more like "het, hoit" or "het, ho."

34. "Short subjects" is a term used by the AACM composer Mwata Bowden to describe miniature, episodic improvisations lasting a few seconds or less.

35. Lewis, "Singing Omar's Song," 76.

36. "En marche dans le flot intense du monde militaire qui nous encercle." Jarman, liner notes for Art Ensemble of Chicago, *A Jackson in Your House*.

37. Lewis, "Singing Omar's Song," 76.

38. Jarman, interview by author, 11 November 2005. For another account of this incident, see Myers, *Why Jazz Happened*, 186.

39. Jarman, quoted in Figi, "Art Ensemble of Chicago," 44.

40. Lewis, *A Power Stronger Than Itself*, 65.

41. Lewis, "Singing Omar's Song," 76.

42. Huron, *Sweet Anticipation*, 323.

43. Sutton-Smith, *The Ambiguity of Play*, 147–148.

44. Sutton-Smith, *The Ambiguity of Play*, 212.

45. hooks, *Yearning*, 22.

46. hooks, *Yearning*, 20.

47. Rosenstone, "'The Times They Are A-Changin,'" 135–136.

48. Nielsen, *Black Chant*, 244.

49. Jarman, *Black Case*, 93.

50. See the discussion of "energy-sound" approaches to saxophone playing in Shepp, "A View from the Inside," 41; and also Willener, *The Action-Image of Society*, 238–239.

51. Bowie, quoted in Coppens and Lagerwerff, "Lester Bowie," 14.

52. Cotro, *Chants Libres*, 63; Trombert, "Soirée de soutien au Black Panthers Party," 9.

53. hooks, *Yearning*, 28.

54. hooks, *Yearning*, 29.

55. Jost, *Free Jazz*, 178.

56. Jarman, *Black Case*, 93.

57. Baker, "Roscoe Mitchell," 19–20.

58. "Nous jouons. . . . tout se que vous voudrez . . . parce que, finalement, c'est 'la musique' que nous jouons . . ." Jarman, quoted in Gras, Caux, and Bernard, "A.A.C.M. Chicago," 18.

59. ". . . dans l'attente passionnée d'une réponse . . ." Jarman, liner notes for Art Ensemble of Chicago, *A Jackson in Your House*.

60. For an analysis of the composed melodies in "Erika" and "Song for Charles," see Pfleiderer, "Das Art Ensemble of Chicago in Paris, Sommer 1969," 118–119.

61. Jarman, *Black Case*, 75.

62. Jarman, interview by author, 19 August 2007.

63. Art Ensemble [of Chicago], *1967/68*; Jarman, interview by author, 19 August 2007.

64. Nielsen, *Black Chant*, 241.

65. Litweiler, *The Freedom Principle*, 179–180.

66. Jarman, *Black Case*, 95.

67. Jarman, *Black Case*, 52.

68. Jordan Sandke, telephone interview by author.

69. Jarman, *Black Case*, 52.

70. LeRoi Jones, *Black Music*, iii.

71. Jarman, *Black Case*, 52.

72. Jarman, *Black Case*, 52.

73. Jarman, interview by author, 19 August 2007.

74. Jarman, *Black Case*, 52.

75. Mitchell, telephone interview by author, 18 October 2006.

76. Mitchell, quoted in Baker, "Roscoe Mitchell," 20.

77. For a poetic analysis of Mitchell's text, see Nielsen, *Black Chant*, 247–248.

78. Nielsen, *Black Chant*, 248.

79. Nielsen, *Black Chant*, 247.

Chapter 5

1. Epigraph: Mitchell, telephone interview by author, 18 October 2006.

2. Art Ensemble of Chicago, *A Jackson in Your House*; Art Ensemble of Chicago,

Message to Our Folks; Art Ensemble of Chicago, *People in Sorrow*; Art Ensemble of Chicago, *Reese and the Smooth Ones*; Art Ensemble of Chicago, *The Spiritual*; Art Ensemble of Chicago, *Tutankhamun*.

3. Art Ensemble of Chicago, *Eda Wobu*.

4. Shepp, *Blasé*; Shepp, *Live at the Panafrican Festival*; Shepp, *Poem for Malcolm*; Shepp, *Yasmina, a Black Woman*; Shepp and Beau, *Black Gipsy*; Shepp and Jones, *Archie Shepp & Philly Joe Jones*.

5. Sunny Murray, *Big Chief*; Sunny Murray, *An Even Break (Never Give a Sucker)*; Sunny Murray, *Hommage to Africa*; Sunny Murray, *Sunshine*.

6. Braxton, *B-X0 NO-47A*; Braxton, Jenkins, and Smith, *Silence*.

7. Janssens and de Craen, *Art Ensemble of Chicago Discography*.

8. Lyons, *Other Afternoons*; Moncur, *New Africa*; Sunny Murray, *An Even Break (Never Give a Sucker)*; Sunny Murray, *Hommage to Africa*; Sunny Murray, *Sunshine*; Redman, *Tarik*; Shepp, *Blasé*; Shepp, *Poem for Malcolm*; Shepp, *Yasmina, a Black Woman*; Silva, *Luna Surface*.

9. Delcloo and Jones, *Africanasia*; Panou, "Je suis un sauvage"/"Le moral nécessaire."

10. Janssens and de Craen, *Art Ensemble of Chicago Discography*; Jarman and Braxton, *Together Alone*.

11. Jarman, résumé.

12. Lewis, *A Power Stronger Than Itself*, 234.

13. Fontaine, interview by Philippe Katerine.

14. For more on the French *chanson* after May 1968, see Drott, *Music and the Elusive Revolution*, 70–110.

15. Fontaine, *Comme à la radio*; Szyfmanowicz, "Brigitte Fontaine, Areski, Art Ensemble of Chicago," 6.

16. Art Ensemble of Chicago, concert poster for series at La Pagode, Paris; "Jazz à Drancy," 9.

17. "Cette école de poly-musiciens, qui nous a délégué quelques-uns de ses représentants les plus estimables, a été la révélation musicale de l'an dernier." "Concert et disque de jazz," 5.

18. Dumetz, "Brigitte et l'Art Ensemble," 13; Koechlin, "Brigitte et quatre Noirs," 47.

19. "Etrange et belle jungle . . ." Koechlin, "Brigitte et quatre Noirs," 47.

20. "Brigitte Fontaine est assez folle pour établir la jonction avec les sorciers de Chicago." Koechlin, "Brigitte et quatre Noirs," 47. The LP alluded to by Koechlin is Fontaine, *Brigitte Fontaine est . . . folle*.

21. Janssens and de Craen, *Art Ensemble of Chicago Discography*.

22. "Festival 'Actuel,'" 24–25.

23. Albert-Levin and Summers, "Sous le chapiteau," 16; Sklower, *Free Jazz, la Catastrophe Féconde*, 197.

24. Drott, *Music and the Elusive Revolution*, 113; Koechlin, "'Pas de ça chez nous!,'" 36.

25. Albert-Levin and Summers, "Sous le chapiteau," 17; Caux, "L'Europe, le 'free jazz' et la 'pop music,'" 2.

26. Wilmer, *As Serious as Your Life*, 251.

27. ". . . d'abolir les cloisonnements qui . . . délimitent plus ou moins arbitrairement

la pop music, le free jazz et la musique contemporaine . . ." Caux, "L'Europe, le 'free jazz' et la 'pop music,'" 2.

28. Alessandrini, "Les folles nuits d'Amougies," 48.

29. Caux, "L'Europe, le 'free jazz' et la 'pop music,'" 3.

30. Albert-Levin and Summers, "Sous le chapiteau," 16.

31. Wilmer, *As Serious as Your Life*, 251.

32. Alessandrini, "Les folles nuits d'Amougies," 49; Sklower, *Free Jazz, la Catastrophe Féconde*, 198.

33. Alessandrini, "Les folles nuits d'Amougies," 54.

34. Albert-Levin and Summers, "Sous le chapiteau," 17.

35. Brown, "Cold Sweat—Part I"/"Cold Sweat—Part II."

36. ". . . et it y eut alors, comme jamais peut-être sur une scène parisienne, la participation du public. Du public aux provocateurs, des provocateurs au public, la révolte courut: la mise en scène se construisit de manière à dépasser le niveau de l'échange . . ." Alessandrini, "Freepop," 29–30.

37. "Joseph Jarman . . . empoigna le micro à la James Brown et commença à hurler d'une voix rauque une parodie, les paroles interchangeables d'une semblant de chanson (have you seen my baby, I love you, etc.). . . .—À la façon des super-stars jetant aux fans les objets touchés par leurs divines mains, les uns après les autres ('do you want it, do you really want it?') il jeta tous ses vêtements au public et apparut tout nu." Albert-Levin and Summers, "Sous le chapiteau," 17.

38. Favors, quoted in Litweiler, "There Won't Be Any More Music," 23.

39. Favors, quoted in Beauchamp, *Art Ensemble of Chicago*, 30.

40. For the first Art Ensemble feature story to appear in a French publication, see Gras, Caux, and Bernard, "A.A.C.M. Chicago."

41. Jarman, "Gens en peine," 14.

42. Dumas and Pierrepont, "Roscoe Mitchell," 82.

43. Lewis, "*Gittin' to Know Y'All*," 2.

44. Goddet, "Lester Bowie," 28.

45. Janssens and de Craen, *Art Ensemble of Chicago Discography*.

46. Bowie, *Gittin' to Know Y'All*.

47. Lewis, "*Gittin' to Know Y'All*," 3–7. The definitive study of European free jazz is Heffley, *Northern Sun, Southern Moon*.

48. Lewis, "*Gittin' to Know Y'All*," 12–18.

49. Mitchell, radio interview by Ted Panken.

50. "From Gritty Soul, to Some Hard Jazz," A5.

51. Litweiler, "Three to Europe," 21.

52. Beauchamp, *Art Ensemble of Chicago*, 29.

53. Cromwell, "Jazz Mecca," 198–199.

54. Wilmer, "Art Ensemble of Chicago, Vieux-Colombier, Paris, France," 26.

55. Moye, quoted in Rusch, "Don Moye," 15.

56. Moye, e-mail message to author, 3 March 2015; Moye, résumé.

57. Beauchamp, *Art Ensemble of Chicago*, 53; Jung, "A Fireside Chat with Famoudou Don Moye"; Milkowski, "The Art Ensemble of Chicago's Famoudou Don Moye," 90.

58. Moye, e-mail message to author, 3 March 2015.

59. Geerken, "Vom 'Accidental Shooting' zum 'Lohnhobeln'"; Günther, "Wie ich zum Trommeln kam, ist ziemlich uninteressant"; Lewis, *A Power Stronger Than Itself*, 245.

60. Moye, quoted in Beauchamp, *Art Ensemble of Chicago*, 53.

61. Moye, e-mail message to author, 3 March 2015.

62. Moye, quoted in Beauchamp, *Art Ensemble of Chicago*, 53.

63. Moye, quoted in Lewis, *A Power Stronger Than Itself*, 245.

64. Moye, e-mail message to author, 3 March 2015.

65. Moye, résumé.

66. Moye, quoted in Mattingly, "Famoudou Don Moye," 15.

67. Mattingly, "Famoudou Don Moye," 15.

68. Jung, "A Fireside Chat with Famoudou Don Moye"; Lewis, *A Power Stronger Than Itself*, 245; Moye, telephone interview by author, 5 March 2015.

69. Lewis, "The AACM in Paris," 114; Moye, e-mail message to author, 3 March 2015; Moye, résumé.

70. Moye, quoted in Mattingly, "Famoudou Don Moye," 15.

71. Moye, quoted in Lewis, *A Power Stronger Than Itself*, 245.

72. Moye, quoted in Mattingly, "Famoudou Don Moye," 15.

73. Moye, résumé.

74. Jung, "A Fireside Chat with Famoudou Don Moye"; Lewis, *A Power Stronger Than Itself*, 246.

75. Beauchamp, *Art Ensemble of Chicago*, 59; Szwed, *Space Is the Place*, 244.

76. Lewis, *A Power Stronger Than Itself*, 246.

77. Beauchamp, *Art Ensemble of Chicago*, 59; Litweiler, "There Won't Be Any More Music," 26; Moye, telephone interview by author, 5 March 2015.

78. Looker, *"Point from Which Creation Begins,"* 160.

79. Beauchamp, *Art Ensemble of Chicago*, 59; Gold-Molina, "Roscoe Mitchell"; Lewis, *A Power Stronger Than Itself*, 144.

80. Moye, telephone interview by author, 5 March 2015.

81. Moye, quoted in Mattingly, "Famoudou Don Moye," 15–16.

82. Moye, quoted in Beauchamp, *Art Ensemble of Chicago*, 54.

83. Moye, résumé.

84. Moye, e-mail message to author, 6 May 2009.

85. Beauchamp, *Art Ensemble of Chicago*, 54.

86. Moye, quoted in Rusch, "Don Moye," 14.

87. Moye, quoted in Beauchamp, *Art Ensemble of Chicago*, 54.

88. Moye, résumé; Moye, telephone interview by author, 5 March 2015.

89. Lewis, *A Power Stronger Than Itself*, 247.

90. Moye, quoted in Jung, "A Fireside Chat with Famoudou Don Moye."

91. Moye, telephone interview by author, 5 March 2015.

92. Mattingly, "Famoudou Don Moye," 16.

93. Moye, quoted in Beauchamp, *Art Ensemble of Chicago*, 55.

94. Moye, quoted in Beauchamp, *Art Ensemble of Chicago*, 59.

95. Moye, quoted in Beauchamp, *Art Ensemble of Chicago*, 59.

96. Beauchamp, *Art Ensemble of Chicago*, 60.

97. Favors, quoted in Cromwell, "Jazz Mecca," 198.

98. Moye, quoted in Milkowski, "The Art Ensemble of Chicago's Famoudou Don Moye," 94.

99. Janssens and de Craen, *Art Ensemble of Chicago Discography*; Moye, telephone interview by author, 5 March 2015.

100. Moye, liner notes for Art Ensemble of Chicago, *Tribute to Lester*.

101. Moye, quoted in Jung, "A Fireside Chat with Famoudou Don Moye."

102. Moye, quoted in Mattingly, "Famoudou Don Moye," 16.

103. Moye, quoted in Mattingly, "Famoudou Don Moye," 16.

104. Art Ensemble of Chicago, *Chi-Congo*.

105. The title "Chi-Congo" may have been proposed by Favors, who was playing in Andrew Hill's trio when the pianist composed an unrelated piece with a similar title, "Chiconga." See Hill, *So in Love*.

106. Art Ensemble of Chicago, *Les Stances à Sophie*; Mizrahi, *Les Stances à Sophie*.

107. Mizrahi, *Les Stances à Sophie*.

108. "Soirée à la Mutualité au profit des 'Black Panthers,'" 33.

109. Drott, *Music and the Elusive Revolution*, 140.

110. Moye, quoted in Lewis, *A Power Stronger Than Itself*, 241.

111. Bowie, quoted in Beauchamp, *Art Ensemble of Chicago*, 42.

112. Bowie, quoted in Beauchamp, *Art Ensemble of Chicago*, 42.

113. Beauchamp, *Art Ensemble of Chicago*, 42; Janssens and de Craen, *Art Ensemble of Chicago Discography*.

114. Stokes, "Lester Bowie," 13.

115. Beauchamp, *Art Ensemble of Chicago*, 37.

116. Bowie, quoted in Bowie and Favors, radio interview by Ted Panken.

117. Bowie, quoted in Rendle and Zabor, "Lester Bowie," 69.

118. Bowie, quoted in Beauchamp, *Art Ensemble of Chicago*, 43.

119. Janssens and de Craen, *Art Ensemble of Chicago Discography*; Newsome, "It's After the End of the World! Don't You Know That Yet?," 269.

120. Beauchamp, *Art Ensemble of Chicago*, 43; Dumas and Pierrepont, "Roscoe Mitchell," 82.

121. Moye, quoted in Jung, "A Fireside Chat with Famoudou Don Moye."

122. Lewis, *A Power Stronger Than Itself*, 254.

123. Lewis, *A Power Stronger Than Itself*, 326.

124. "18th Annual International Jazz Critics Poll," 18–20.

125. "Les musiciens furent retenus 24 h par la police française et interrogés en présence d'inspecteurs qui étaient au courant de tous leurs déplacements et activités. Le prétexte de cette détention arbitraire était le suivant: leurs camions étant immatriculés en tourisme, les musiciens ne s'étaient pas acquittés des taxes nécessaires sur les instruments. On leur infligea une amende de deux millions (AF); une partie étant payée immédiatement, un camion de matériel était retenu comme caution. Ils furent alors soumis au chantage suivant: payer l'amende et quitter le territoire français dans les 8 jours; payer l'amende et de nombreuses taxes durant tout leur séjour; troisième possibilité, intenter un procès fort coûteux qu'ils perdraient inévitablement. Les termes de ce chantage montrent bien que le motif de cette arrestation est politique et raciste. Les policiers leur

ont reproché ouvertement de politiser leur musique et, entre autres choses, d'avoir joué au profit du Black Panthers Party." "Lettre de Caen," 16.

126. Moye, quoted in Beauchamp, *Art Ensemble of Chicago*, 60.

127. Beauchamp, *Art Ensemble of Chicago*, 60.

128. Janssens and de Craen, *Art Ensemble of Chicago Discography*.

129. Dumas and Pierrepont, "Roscoe Mitchell," 82.

130. Saba, liner notes for Art Ensemble of Chicago, *Reunion*.

131. Bowie, quoted in Beauchamp, *Art Ensemble of Chicago*, 43.

Chapter 6

1. Epigraph: Bowie, quoted in Moye and Jackson, "Art Ensemble of Chicago Biographies," 1.

2. Kunle Mwanga, telephone interview by author.

3. Tate, "Gone Fishing," 166.

4. Rasul Siddik, interview by author.

5. Jarman, interview by John Litweiler.

6. Art Ensemble of Chicago, publicity brochure.

7. Prior to 1966, when the Chicago union was integrated, the musicians' building belonged to the black-only Local 208. See Absher, *The Black Musician and the White City*, 123, 144; and Malcolm, *The Musicians Building*.

8. Litweiler, "The Art Ensemble of Chicago," 22.

9. Jarman, résumé.

10. Rasul Siddik, interview by author.

11. Beauchamp, *Art Ensemble of Chicago*, 60.

12. Art Ensemble of Chicago, publicity brochure.

13. Looker, *"Point from Which Creation Begins,"* 194.

14. Looker, *"Point from Which Creation Begins,"* 31.

15. Looker, *"Point from Which Creation Begins,"* 17; Charles "Bobo" Shaw, interview by author.

16. John Litweiler, interview by author.

17. Looker, *"Point from Which Creation Begins,"* 31.

18. Looker, *"Point from Which Creation Begins,"* 31.

19. Looker, *"Point from Which Creation Begins,"* 56–62.

20. Art Ensemble of Chicago, *The Alternate Express*; Art Ensemble of Chicago, *Ancient to the Future*; Art Ensemble of Chicago, *Naked*; Art Ensemble of Chicago, *Urban Bushmen*.

21. Looker, *"Point from Which Creation Begins,"* 131–132, 189–190.

22. Moye, quoted in Beauchamp, *Art Ensemble of Chicago*, 60.

23. Looker, *"Point from Which Creation Begins,"* 180. For more on the 1968 four-day concert, see Tate, "Gone Fishing," 165.

24. Moye, quoted in Beauchamp, *Art Ensemble of Chicago*, 60.

25. Looker, *"Point from Which Creation Begins,"* 25, 114.

26. Beauchamp, *Art Ensemble of Chicago*, 60–61.

27. Looker, *"Point from Which Creation Begins,"* 194.

28. Bowie, quoted in Looker, *"Point from Which Creation Begins,"* 194.

29. Looker, *"Point from Which Creation Begins,"* 194–195. This album was recorded in 1971 and commercially released five years later: Oliver Lake, *NTU: Point from Which Creation Begins.*

30. Looker, *"Point from Which Creation Begins,"* 197.

31. Looker, *"Point from Which Creation Begins,"* 197–208.

32. Art Ensemble of Chicago, concert poster for performance at Ida Noyes Hall, Chicago.

33. Litweiler, "There Won't Be Any More Music," 37.

34. Kunle Mwanga, telephone interview by author.

35. Art Ensemble of Chicago, concert flyer for performances at Alice's Revisited, Chicago.

36. Bowie, quoted in Bowie and Favors, radio interview by Ted Panken.

37. Drott, *Music and the Elusive Revolution,* 117.

38. Figi, "Art Ensemble of Chicago," 49; Litweiler, "There Won't Be Any More Music," 37.

39. Moye, e-mail message to author, 22 October 2005.

40. Moye, quoted in Beauchamp, *Art Ensemble of Chicago,* 62.

41. Birnbaum, "Art Ensemble of Chicago," 17.

42. Bowie, quoted in Rusch, "Lester Bowie," 6.

43. Mitchell, "'Nonaah' and the Composition/Improvisation Connection."

44. Lewis, "Singing Omar's Song," 75; Rusch, "Lester Bowie," 14.

45. Janssens and de Craen, *Art Ensemble of Chicago Discography*; Jarman and Braxton, *Together Alone.*

46. John Litweiler, interview by author.

47. Rusch, "Lester Bowie," 14.

48. Mitchell, quoted in Gross, "Roscoe Mitchell Interview."

49. Moye, quoted in Mattingly, "Famoudou Don Moye," 48, 56.

50. "L'Art Ensemble est comme un gâteau confectionné à partir de cinq ingredients: supprimez l'un de ces ingredients et le gâteau n'existe plus. Lorsqu'on observe l'Art Ensemble avec un certain recul, c'est de cela qu'il s'agit, bien plus que de tel ou tel individu dont on parviendrait à isoler la personnalité. . . . [N]ous avons développé, une sorte de fidélité interne, une prise de conscience de notre interdépendance. Toutes les experiences que nous avons vécues ensemble, nos experiences émotionnelles, positives ou dramatiques, toutes les situations dans lesquelles nous sommes trouvés ensemble ou séparément, tout ceci nous a rapproché les uns des autres au point que nous ne formons plus aujourd'hui qu'un seul cerveau." Jarman, quoted in Goddet and Dutilh, "L'art, ensemble," 26.

51. Moye, quoted in Gans, "Art Ensemble of Chicago," 37.

52. Lewis, *A Power Stronger Than Itself,* 227, 255.

53. Lewis, *A Power Stronger Than Itself,* 227; Lewis, "Experimental Music in Black and White," 100.

54. Lewis, *A Power Stronger Than Itself,* 117, 545 n. 71; Moye, interview by author, 20 October 2009.

55. Moye, e-mail message to author, 7 July 2005; Moye, e-mail message to author, 22 October 2005; Moye, telephone interview by author, 4 February 2006. For a poetic description of the "upside up and downside down" baobab tree, see Joans, *Afrodisia*, 64.

56. Jarman, quoted in Wilmer, "Rainy Day in the Windy City," 24.

57. Moye, quoted in Beauchamp, *Art Ensemble of Chicago*, 62.

58. Art Ensemble of Chicago, *Live at Mandel Hall*; Moye, interview by author, 19 January 2007.

59. Rand, "Art Ensemble of Chicago, University of Wisconsin, Madison, Wis.," 38; Spitzer, "Art Ensemble of Chicago," 29.

60. Favors, quoted in Beauchamp, *Art Ensemble of Chicago*, 30; Favors, interview by Peter Rosenbloom.

61. Steve Smith, liner notes for Art Ensemble of Chicago, *Bap-tizum*.

62. Cuscuna, liner notes for Art Ensemble of Chicago, *Bap-tizum*.

63. Art Ensemble of Chicago, *Bap-tizum*.

64. Ertegun, *"What'd I Say,"* 232–233.

65. Choice, "Newport and All That Jazz," A22.

66. Carles, "Six voix dans la ville," 38.

67. "Jazz Grants," 46.

68. Iain Anderson, *This Is Our Music*, 169; Lewis, *A Power Stronger Than Itself*, 332.

69. Art Ensemble of Chicago, *Fanfare for the Warriors*.

70. Mitchell, "'Nonaah': From Solo to Full Orchestra."

71. Jarman, *Black Case*, 46.

72. Jarman, *Black Case*, 46.

73. Carles and Soutif, "L'Art Ensemble de Chicago au-delà du Jazz," 14.

74. "Concerts," January 1974, 42; "Concerts," February 1974, 9; "Concerts," March 1974, 10.

75. "Informations," 11.

76. Janssens and de Craen, *Art Ensemble of Chicago Discography*.

77. Lewis, *A Power Stronger Than Itself*, 302.

78. "En fait, nous préférons enregistrer pendant un concert plutôt que dans un studio." Jarman, quoted in Carles, "Six voix dans la ville," 39.

79. Art Ensemble of Chicago, *Kabalaba*.

80. Janssens and de Craen, *Art Ensemble of Chicago Discography*.

81. Bowie, quoted in Beauchamp, *Art Ensemble of Chicago*, 47. Emphasis in the original.

82. Moye, quoted in Beauchamp, *Art Ensemble of Chicago*, 62.

83. Green, "Lester Bowie, Don Moye," 18.

84. Moye, e-mail message to author, 22 October 2005.

85. Moye, e-mail message to author, 22 October 2005.

86. Favors, *Natural & Spiritual*; Jarman, *Sunbound Volume One*; Moye, *Sun Percussion Volume One*.

87. Art Ensemble of Chicago, *Kabalaba*.

88. Levi, "Lester Speaks Out," 25.

89. Jarman, *Black Case*.

90. Hennessey, "Art Ensemble of Chicago," 11.

91. Beauchamp, *Art Ensemble of Chicago*, 61.

92. Lewis, *A Power Stronger Than Itself*, 133, 279.

93. Beauchamp, *Art Ensemble of Chicago*, 61; Lewis, *A Power Stronger Than Itself*, 439.

94. Moye, e-mail message to author, 22 October 2005; Rusch, "Lester Bowie," 5.

95. Mitchell, quoted in Anthony Coleman, "Roscoe Mitchell," 71.

96. Art Ensemble of Chicago, *The Complete Live in Japan*; Art Ensemble of Chicago, *Live from the Jazz Showcase*; Art Ensemble of Chicago, *The Third Decade*.

97. Kunle Mwanga, telephone interview by author.

98. Lewis, *A Power Stronger Than Itself*, 326.

99. Kunle Mwanga, telephone interview by author.

100. Kunle Mwanga, telephone interview by author.

101. Radano, *New Musical Figurations*, 183–184.

102. Kunle Mwanga, telephone interview by author.

103. Kunle Mwanga, telephone interview by author.

104. Lewis, *A Power Stronger Than Itself*, 329.

105. Lewis, *A Power Stronger Than Itself*, 106.

106. Albin, "Art Ensemble of Chicago, Five Spot, New York City," 34.

107. Kunle Mwanga, telephone interview by author.

108. Beauchamp, *Art Ensemble of Chicago*, 62.

109. Litweiler, "There Won't Be Any More Music," 37.

110. Moye, e-mail message to author, 10 March 2015.

111. Moye, quoted in Beauchamp, *Art Ensemble of Chicago*, 66.

112. Beauchamp, *Art Ensemble of Chicago*, 66.

113. Favors, quoted in Jung, "A Fireside Chat with Malachi Favors."

114. Moye, quoted in Beauchamp, *Art Ensemble of Chicago*, 65–66.

115. Kunle Mwanga, telephone interview by author.

116. Mitchell, *Nonaah*.

117. [Denis-Constant Martin], "Les exces de Moers," 13.

118. Chadbourne, "Art Ensemble of Chicago," 36; Janssens and de Craen, *Art Ensemble of Chicago Discography*.

119. Jarman, quoted in Hentoff, "'Great Black Music' from Chicago's Art Ensemble," 25.

120. Kostakis and Lange, "An Interview with Joseph Jarman," 99.

121. Safane, "Lester Bowie's Sho' Nuff Orchestra," 37.

122. Bowie, quoted in Bowie and Favors, radio interview by Ted Panken.

123. Mitchell, telephone interview by author, 18 October 2006.

124. McAdams and Reynolds, "A Tribute to David Wessel (1942–2014)," 434.

125. Mitchell, telephone interview by author, 18 October 2006.

126. Mitchell, quoted in Bill Smith, "Roscoe Mitchell," 4.

127. "Jazz on Campus," 35.

128. Dallinger, "Roscoe Mitchell named Darius Milhaud Chair in Composition at Mills College."

129. Mitchell, telephone interview by author, 18 October 2006.

130. Lewis, *A Power Stronger Than Itself*, 399–400.

131. Francis Davis, "Roscoe Mitchell," 28; Mitchell, telephone interview by author, 18 October 2006.

132. Jaribu Shahid, telephone interview by author.

133. Mitchell, radio interview by Ted Panken; Robert Palmer, "New Sounds from Roscoe Mitchell," C15.

134. Mitchell, résumé.

135. Looker, *"Point from Which Creation Begins,"* 221–222.

136. Lewis, *A Power Stronger Than Itself*, 333–334.

137. Saba, liner notes for Art Ensemble of Chicago, *Reunion*; Wilmer, *As Serious as Your Life*, 121.

138. Pareles, "A Family of Gospel Singers," C21.

139. Cotensin, "From the Roots to the Source," 10; Quénum, "Jazz à Vienne," 14.

140. Tepperman, *"Rope-A-Dope,"* 12.

141. Beauchamp, *Art Ensemble of Chicago*, 64; Janssens and de Craen, *Art Ensemble of Chicago Discography*.

142. David Bowie, *Black Tie White Noise*; Flexingburgstein, "Open Letter to a Great Pretender," 24.

143. Such, *Avant-Garde Jazz Musicians*, 84.

144. Bowie, quoted in Bennett, "The Brass Fantasies of Lester Bowie," 44.

145. Weiss, "Lester Leaps In," 8.

146. Bowie, quoted in Bennett, "The Brass Fantasies of Lester Bowie," 44.

147. Bowie, *The Odyssey of Funk & Popular Music*; Bowie, *When the Spirit Returns*.

148. Bowie, quoted in Jung, "A Fireside Chat with Lester Bowie."

149. Bourget, "Action poétique à Chicago," 31; Mandel, "Joseph Jarman, University of Chicago," 33.

150. Jarman, résumé.

151. Jarman and Moye, *Egwu-Anwu*.

152. Jarman, résumé.

153. Choice, "Sweet Jams for Jazz Fair," E14.

154. Pareles, "Multimedia Jazzman from Chicago," C6; Rockwell, "Joseph Jarman's Multimedia 'Liberation Suite,'" C16.

155. Shipp, "Their Muse is Malcolm X," H1, H22.

156. Jarman's aikido teacher was Fumio Toyoda, founder of the Chicago-based Aikido Association of America. Sweet, "Joseph Jarman."

157. Jarman, interview by author, 11 November 2005; Litweiler, liner notes for Joseph Jarman, *LifeTime Visions for the Magnificent Human*.

158. Jarman, quoted in Jung, "A Fireside Chat with Joseph Jarman," 2002.

159. Beauchamp, *Art Ensemble of Chicago*, 61; Moye, e-mail message to author, 10 March 2015.

160. Beauchamp, *Art Ensemble of Chicago*, 62; Kern, "Don Moye Quartett," 27.

161. Lewis, *A Power Stronger Than Itself*, 334.

162. Beauchamp, *Art Ensemble of Chicago*, 62.

163. Beauchamp, *Art Ensemble of Chicago*, 64; Detro, "The Leaders," 18.

164. Later, Moye joined two other Bowie-led bands, From the Root to the Source and the New York Organ Ensemble. Moye, e-mail message to author, 12 March 2015.

165. Beauchamp, *Art Ensemble of Chicago*, 56.

166. Milkowski, "The Art Ensemble of Chicago's Famoudou Don Moye," 94.

167. Mattingly, "Famoudou Don Moye," 48.

168. Moye, quoted in Mattingly, "Famoudou Don Moye," 16.

169. Moye, quoted in Henderson, "Don Moye," 24.

170. Moye, *Sun Percussion Volume One*; Moye and Williamson, *Afrikan Song*.

171. Favors, interview by Peter Rosenbloom; Henderson, "Don Moye," 24.

172. Moye, résumé; Rusch, "Don Moye," 15.

173. Moye, quoted in Milkowski, "The Art Ensemble of Chicago's Famoudou Don Moye," 96.

174. "Nach diesem Konzert kam ein kleiner Mann auf die Musiker zu und be-glückwünschte sie zu ihrer Musik: es war der beste westafrikanishe (natürlich schwarze) Trommler Famoudou Konaté, der Mann, den Moye schon immer so sehr verehrt hatte, dass er seinen Vornamen annahm: Famoudou. Eine wunderbare Begegnung!" Hauff, "Auf Westafrika-Tournee," 35.

175. Moye, quoted in Milkowski, "The Art Ensemble of Chicago's Famoudou Don Moye," 96.

176. Melis, *The New Village on the Left*; Schiano et al., *Uncaged*.

177. Moye, e-mail message to author, 29 May 2014; Moye, e-mail message to author, 10 March 2015.

178. George Favors, Rosetta Rimmer, and Velena Daniels, interview by author; Moye, e-mail message to author, 10 March 2015.

179. Lewis, *A Power Stronger Than Itself*, 488.

180. Kahil El'Zabar, quoted in Aaron Cohen, "Art Ensemble Bassist Malachi Favors Maghostut Dies," 26.

181. Janssens and de Craen, *Art Ensemble of Chicago Discography*; Lewis, *A Power Stronger Than Itself*, 318.

182. Mitchell, *L-R-G / The Maze / S II Examples*.

183. Moye, e-mail message to author, 10 March 2015. Over the years, Favors spelled his adopted name in various ways: Maghostus, Maghostut, Magistus, Magostus, Magoustous, Meghismus, Megistus, Moghostut.

184. Ratliff, "Malachi Favors, 76, Jazz Bassist with Art Ensemble of Chicago," B8. For more on Favors's studies of Egyptology and African history, see Radano, *New Musical Figurations*, 99; and Solothurnmann, "What's Really Happening," 32.

185. Mackey, *Djbot Baghostus's Run*, 184.

186. Malba Allen, interview by author; Favors, *Natural & Spiritual*; Reich, "When Jazz Fest Stops, Notes Go Underground," B3.

187. Abrams, *Sightsong*; Fred Anderson, *Black Horn Long Gone*; Janssens and de Craen, *Art Ensemble of Chicago Discography*.

188. El'Zabar, *The Ritual*.

189. Wadada Leo Smith, *Golden Quartet*.

190. Favors, interview by Peter Rosenbloom.

Chapter 7

1. Epigraph: Moye, quoted in Mattingly, "Famoudou Don Moye," 56.

2. Lewis, "Singing Omar's Song," 90.

3. Art Ensemble of Chicago, *Live at Mandel Hall*.

4. Lewis, "Singing Omar's Song," 75.

5. Favors, quoted in Bowie and Favors, radio interview by Ted Panken.

6. Bowie, quoted in Bowie and Favors, radio interview by Ted Panken.

7. Moye, interview by author, 19 January 2007.

8. Muhal Richard Abrams, quoted in Litweiler, "Chicago's Richard Abrams," 26.

9. Lewis, "Singing Omar's Song," 75.

10. Moye, interview by author, 19 January 2007.

11. Michaelsen, "Analyzing Musical Interaction in Jazz Improvisations of the 1960s," 59–61; Sawyer, *Group Creativity*, 173–176.

12. Mitchell, quoted in Baker, "Roscoe Mitchell," 19.

13. "In fact Leo Smith and I were talking about opposition in Chicago." Anthony Braxton, quoted in Lock, *Forces in Motion*, 203. See also Braxton, *Composition Notes*; and [Wadada] Leo Smith, *notes (8 pieces) source a new world music*.

14. For more on contingency and emergence in improvised performance, see Sawyer, *Group Creativity*, 86–93.

15. Lewis, "Singing Omar's Song," 76.

16. Mitchell, e-mail message to author, 14 January 2007.

17. For a discussion of circular compositions in jazz, see Waters, *The Studio Recordings of the Miles Davis Quintet, 1965–68*, 74–76.

18. George E. Lewis, e-mail message to author.

19. Moye, interview by author, 19 January 2007.

20. Moye, interview by author, 19 January 2007.

21. Lewis, "Singing Omar's Song," 75.

22. Moye, quoted in Blumenthal, "A Kaleidoscope of Sound," N1.

23. Favors was famous for refusing to use a pickup or amplifier on his bass. Litweiler, "The Art Ensemble of Chicago," 21–22; Mattingly, "Famoudou Don Moye," 58.

24. Moye, interview by author, 19 January 2007.

25. Moye, interview by author, 19 January 2007.

26. The suddenness of this textural change may be the result of repairs or edits to the master tape recording. Moye, interview by author, 19 January 2007.

27. Braxton, *Composition Notes*, 4:137–138, 150–151; George E. Lewis, e-mail message to author; Nyman, *Experimental Music*, 144, 148–149.

28. Moye, interview by author, 6 September 2007.

29. Mitchell, e-mail message to author, 14 January 2007.

30. Corbett, "Fanfare for a Warrior," 24.

31. Bowie, quoted in Livingston, "Lester Bowie," 9.

32. Moye, interview by author, 19 January 2007.

33. Moye, interview by author, 19 January 2007. The album referred to by Moye is Miles Davis, *Sketches of Spain*.

34. Moye, interview by author, 19 January 2007.

35. Moye, interview by author, 19 January 2007.

36. Litweiler, liner notes for Roscoe Mitchell, *L-R-G / The Maze / S II Examples*.

37. Mitchell, quoted in Baker, "Roscoe Mitchell," 19–20.

38. For an examination of "instrumental roles" in jazz performance practice, see Monson, *Saying Something*, 26–72.

39. Nicholas Cook, "Making Music Together, or Improvisation and Its Others"; Schutz, "Making Music Together."

40. Mitchell, quoted in Baker, "Roscoe Mitchell," 19.

41. Lewis, "Singing Omar's Song," 76.

42. Moye, interview by author, 19 January 2007.

43. Mitchell, quoted in Cromwell, "Jazz Mecca," 192.

44. Mitchell, quoted in Lewis, *A Power Stronger Than Itself*, 145.

45. Moye, quoted in Mattingly, "Famoudou Don Moye," 56.

46. Jarman, quoted in Beauchamp, *Art Ensemble of Chicago*, 75.

47. Lewis, "Singing Omar's Song," 76; Jost, *Free Jazz*, 166.

48. Moye, interview by author, 19 January 2007.

49. Moye, interview by author, 19 January 2007.

50. Art Ensemble of Chicago, *People in Sorrow*.

51. Moye, interview by author, 19 January 2007.

52. Moye, interview by author, 19 January 2007.

53. Beauchamp, *Art Ensemble of Chicago*, 63–65.

54. Bowie, quoted in Beauchamp, *Art Ensemble of Chicago*, 43.

55. Bowie, quoted in Beauchamp, *Art Ensemble of Chicago*, 47.

Chapter 8

1. Epigraph: Jarman, quoted in Solothurnmann, "What's Really Happening," 30.

2. Kunle Mwanga, telephone interview by author.

3. Figi, "Art Ensemble of Chicago," 48.

4. Kunle Mwanga, telephone interview by author.

5. "Potpourri," 11.

6. Marty Khan, telephone interview by author.

7. Saba, liner notes for Art Ensemble of Chicago, *Reunion*.

8. Bowie, quoted in Bowie and Favors, radio interview by Ted Panken.

9. Bowie, quoted in Bowie and Favors, radio interview by Ted Panken.

10. Bowie, quoted in Beauchamp, *Art Ensemble of Chicago*, 41.

11. Bowie, quoted in Rendle and Zabor, "Lester Bowie," 64.

12. Jarman, *Black Case*, 45.

13. Litweiler, "The Art Ensemble of Chicago," 21.

14. Bowie, quoted in Rendle and Zabor, "Lester Bowie," 64.

15. Litweiler, "The Art Ensemble of Chicago," 21.

16. Veal, *Fela*, 155–157.

17. Bowie, quoted in Bowie and Favors, radio interview by Ted Panken.

18. Bowie, quoted in Bowie and Favors, radio interview by Ted Panken.

19. Bowie, quoted in Litweiler, "The Art Ensemble of Chicago," 21.

20. Kuti, *Fear Not for Man*; Kuti, *No Agreement*; Kuti, *Shuffering and Shmiling*; Kuti, *Sorrow Tears and Blood*; Kuti, *Stalemate*.

21. Bowie, quoted in Besecker, "Lester Bowie," 5.

22. Saba, liner notes for Art Ensemble of Chicago, *Reunion*; Veal, *Fela*, 158.

23. Janssens and de Craen, *Art Ensemble of Chicago Discography*.

24. Saba, liner notes for Art Ensemble of Chicago, *Reunion*.

25. Marty Khan, telephone interview by author.

26. Beauchamp, *Art Ensemble of Chicago*, 63; Lewis, *A Power Stronger Than Itself*, 334.

27. Marty Khan, telephone interview by author.

28. Art Ensemble of Chicago, *Fanfare for the Warriors*; Art Ensemble of Chicago, *Live at Mandel Hall*.

29. Marty Khan, telephone interview by author.

30. Thomas Stöwsand, telephone interview by author.

31. Thomas Stöwsand, telephone interview by author.

32. Art Ensemble of Chicago, *People in Sorrow*; Eicher, "The Free Matrix," 223.

33. Marty Khan, telephone interview by author.

34. Art Ensemble of Chicago, *Nice Guys*; Janssens and de Craen, *Art Ensemble of Chicago Discography*.

35. Bragg, "A Change in Perspective," 13.

36. Richard Cook, *Blue Note Records*, 203–204.

37. Steve Lake, "Introduction," 1.

38. Farber et al., "The Engineers," 324.

39. Art Ensemble of Chicago, *Full Force*; Art Ensemble of Chicago, *Nice Guys*; Art Ensemble of Chicago, *The Third Decade*; Art Ensemble of Chicago, *Urban Bushmen*.

40. Martin Wieland, e-mail message to author.

41. Solothurnmann, "*Nice Guys, Full Force*," 49.

42. Moye, quoted in Rusch, "Don Moye," 18.

43. Favors, interview by Peter Rosenbloom.

44. "C'est une maison honnête, on ne peut pas en dire autant de Byg et Atlantic. Nous avons confiance en Manfred Eicher et Thomas Stöwsand." Moye, quoted in Carles, "De l'AACM à ECM," 52.

45. Hentoff, "'Great Black Music' from Chicago's Art Ensemble," 25.

46. Robert Palmer, "The Pop Life," C12.

47. Shoemaker, "Page One."

48. "28th Annual International Jazz Critics Poll," 17; "29th Annual International Jazz Critics Poll," 19; "30th Annual International Jazz Critics Poll," 18.

49. "44th Annual Readers Poll," 21; "45th Annual Readers Poll," 16.

50. "29th Annual International Jazz Critics Poll," 19.

51. Thomas Stöwsand, telephone interview by author.

52. Moye, e-mail message to author, 15 March 2015.

53. Moye, quoted in Beauchamp, *Art Ensemble of Chicago*, 63.

54. Thomas Stöwsand, telephone interview by author.

55. Moye, e-mail message to author, 27 May 2007.

56. Beauchamp, *Art Ensemble of Chicago*, 63.

57. Moye, e-mail message to author, 27 May 2007.

58. Jarman, liner notes for Art Ensemble of Chicago, *Urban Bushmen*.

59. "International Briefs," 64; Kopp, "Art Ensemble of Chicago Tours," 62; Moye, interview by author, 6 September 2007.

60. George Favors, Rosetta Rimmer, and Velena Daniels, interview by author.

61. Janssens and de Craen, *Art Ensemble of Chicago Discography*.

62. Beauchamp, *Art Ensemble of Chicago*, 63.

63. Mitchell, curriculum vitae.

64. Bowie, quoted in Choice, "Jazz Notes," B18.

65. Marty Khan, telephone interview by author.

66. Marty Khan, telephone interview by author.

67. Rusch, "Lester Bowie," 14.

68. Moye, quoted in Beauchamp, *Art Ensemble of Chicago*, 62.

69. Marty Khan, telephone interview by author.

70. Marty Khan, telephone interview by author.

71. Giddins, "Bird Is the Word," 66; Marty Khan, telephone interview by author.

72. Marty Khan, telephone interview by author.

73. "For the Record," 102.

74. Beauchamp, *Art Ensemble of Chicago*, 63–64.

75. Harrington, "D.C. Curators," WE19; West, "Art Ensemble," D9.

76. Marty Khan, telephone interview by author.

77. Harrington, "D.C. Curators," WE19; Marty Khan, telephone interview by author.

78. "For the Record," 102; Marty Khan, telephone interview by author.

79. Marty Khan, telephone interview by author.

80. Marty Khan, telephone interview by author.

81. Marty Khan, telephone interview by author.

82. Art Ensemble of Chicago, *Bap-tizum*.

83. Marty Khan, telephone interview by author.

84. Marty Khan, telephone interview by author.

85. Art Ensemble of Chicago, concert poster for performance at the Kool Jazz Festival, Los Angeles; Art Ensemble of Chicago, concert poster for performance at the Wadsworth Theater, Los Angeles.

86. Marty Khan, telephone interview by author.

87. Art Ensemble of Chicago, *Live from the Jazz Showcase*; Tucker, "Narrative, Extra-musical Form, and the Metamodernism of the Art Ensemble of Chicago," 29.

88. Bowie, quoted in Don Palmer, "About Time," 51.

89. Favors, liner notes for Art Ensemble of Chicago, *Tribute to Lester*.

90. Bowie, quoted in Don Palmer, "About Time," 51.

91. Lewis, *A Power Stronger Than Itself*, 98–103, 110–111.

92. Don Palmer, "About Time," 51.

93. Bowie, quoted in Green, "Lester Bowie, Don Moye," 17.

94. Bowie, quoted in Green, "Lester Bowie, Don Moye," 17.

95. Moye, quoted in Green, "Lester Bowie, Don Moye," 17.

96. Wolf, *Story Jazz*, 133.

97. Favors and Bowie, quoted in Zabor, "The Art Ensemble," 40.

98. Favors, interview by Peter Rosenbloom.

99. Favors, quoted in Wolf, *Story Jazz*, 133.

100. Jarman, quoted in Johnson, "Don't Call Jarman a 'Jazz Musician,'" 12.

101. Bowie, quoted in Besecker, "Lester Bowie," 5.

102. Berry, "Declamations on Great Black Music," 50–53; Richter, *Zu einer Ästhetik des Jazz*, 115–121.

103. Mitchell, quoted in Pierrepont, "Roscoe Mitchell," 8.

104. Mitchell, quoted in Gold-Molina, "Roscoe Mitchell."

105. Mitchell, quoted in Gold-Molina, "Roscoe Mitchell."

106. Mitchell, quoted in Gold-Molina, "Roscoe Mitchell."

107. Mitchell, quoted in Lewis, "Singing Omar's Song," 81.

108. Jarman, quoted in Rusch, "Joseph Jarman," 4.

109. Jarman, quoted in Kostakis and Lange, "An Interview with Joseph Jarman," 98.

110. Jarman, quoted in Solothurnmann, "What's Really Happening," 30.

111. Favors, interview by Peter Rosenbloom.

112. Jarman, quoted in Mandel, *Future Jazz*, 38.

113. Moye, e-mail message to author, 27 May 2007; Rendle and Zabor, "Lester Bowie," 70.

114. Bowie, quoted in Solothurnmann, "What's Really Happening," 29.

115. Townley, "Lester . . . Who?," 11.

116. Jarman, quoted in Beauchamp, *Art Ensemble of Chicago*, 74–75.

117. Bowie, quoted in Levi, "Lester Speaks Out," 25.

118. Bowie, quoted in Rendle and Zabor, "Lester Bowie," 69.

119. Porter, *What Is This Thing Called Jazz?*, 289.

120. Tate, "Gone Fishing," 165–166.

121. Lewis, *A Power Stronger Than Itself*, 333–334.

122. Pareles, "Five Hot Trumpets," C27.

123. Joyce, "Herald the Trumpeters," F11; Litweiler, "The Art Ensemble of Chicago," 21.

124. Marsalis, *Wynton Marsalis*; Porter, *What Is This Thing Called Jazz?*, 290–292.

125. Pareles, "Five Hot Trumpets," C27; Rendle and Zabor, "Lester Bowie," 66.

126. Bowie, quoted in Livingston, "Lester Bowie," 10.

127. Marsalis and Stewart, *Sweet Swing Blues on the Road*, 141; Porter, *What Is This Thing Called Jazz?*, 304–311.

128. Bowie, quoted in Bouchard, "Blindfold Test," 41.

129. Bowie, quoted in Whitehead, "Jazz Rebels," 18.

130. Bowie, quoted in Whitehead, "Jazz Rebels," 19.

131. Watrous, "Lester Bowie, Sweet Basil," C19.

132. Burns, *Jazz*.

133. Ward, *Jazz*, 490.

134. Burns, *Jazz*; DeVeaux, "Struggling with *Jazz*," 365.

135. Burns, *Jazz*; Lock, *Forces in Motion*, 55.

136. Burns, *Jazz*.

137. Bowie, quoted in Green, "Lester Bowie, Don Moye," 21.

138. Marty Khan, telephone interview by author.

139. Mitchell, curriculum vitae.

140. DeVeaux, *Jazz in America*, 21–25; Taylor, "Finding a New Audience for Jazz," 11.

141. Mitchell, quoted in Aaron Cohen, "Art Ensemble of Chicago," 64.

142. "30th Annual International Jazz Critics Poll," 19; "41st Annual International Jazz Critics Poll," 29; "43rd Annual International Jazz Critics Poll," 28.

143. "28th Annual International Jazz Critics Poll," 17; "29th Annual International Jazz Critics Poll," 19; "30th Annual International Jazz Critics Poll," 18; "33rd Annual International Jazz Critics Poll," 21; Aaron Cohen, "Art Ensemble of Chicago," 62–65; "47th Annual International Jazz Critics Poll," 54.

144. Solomon, "Lincoln Center's Culture Gap," 28.

145. "Traditionalisten in dem Sinne, dass Rebellion die eigentliche Tradition des Jazz ist." Bowie, quoted in Broecking, *Der Marsalis-Faktor*, 153.

146. "Hingegen ist die Revolution eine Sache für junge Leute: das wäre eher Wyntons Job . . ." Bowie, quoted in Broecking, *Der Marsalis-Faktor*, 153.

147. Bowie, quoted in Whitehead, "Jazz Rebels," 18.

148. Whitehead, "Jazz Rebels," 19–20.

149. Bouchard, "Blindfold Test," 41; Glasgo, "Lester Redux," 1; "Jazz on Campus," 35; Sweet, *Music Universe, Music Mind*, 76–81; Tate, "Gone Fishing," 166.

150. Marsalis and Stewart, *Sweet Swing Blues on the Road*, 145; Albert Murray, *Stomping the Blues*, 87.

151. Mitchell, quoted in Baker, "Roscoe Mitchell," 18.

152. Mitchell, quoted in Baker, "Roscoe Mitchell," 19.

153. Mitchell, quoted in Gonzalez, "Mastering the Fine Art of Improvisation," 85.

Chapter 9

1. Epigraph: Jarman, quoted in Gans, "Art Ensemble of Chicago," 35.

2. Art Ensemble of Chicago, *Live from the Jazz Showcase*.

3. Richard Wang, e-mail message to author.

4. Moye, interview by author, 6 September 2007.

5. Art Ensemble of Chicago, *Among the People*; Art Ensemble of Chicago, *Baptizum*; Art Ensemble of Chicago, *Urban Bushmen*.

6. Art Ensemble of Chicago, *The Complete Live in Japan*; Art Ensemble of Chicago, *Naked*; Art Ensemble of Chicago, *The Third Decade*.

7. Jarman, liner notes for Art Ensemble of Chicago, *Urban Bushmen*.

8. Moye, quoted in Beauchamp, *Art Ensemble of Chicago*, 51.

9. Art Ensemble of Chicago, *Live at Mandel Hall*.

10. Moye, interview by author, 19 January 2007.

11. Art Ensemble of Chicago, *A Jackson in Your House*.

12. For more on performers' onstage personas, movements, and gestures, see Nicholas Cook, *Beyond the Score*, 288–307.

13. Moye, interview by author, 6 September 2007.

14. Moye, quoted in Mattingly, "Famoudou Don Moye," 56.

15. Jarman, quoted in Mandel, *Future Jazz*, 39.

16. Lewis, *A Power Stronger Than Itself*, 108.

17. Bowie, quoted in Levi, "Lester Speaks Out," 25.

18. Jost, *Free Jazz*, 178; Litweiler, *The Freedom Principle*, 176.

19. Mitchell, quoted in Alvin Fielder, telephone interview by author, 11 March 2006.

20. Bowie, quoted in Rendle and Zabor, "Lester Bowie," 69.

21. Mitchell, quoted in Gross, "Roscoe Mitchell Interview."

22. Levi, "Lester Speaks Out," 25; Mandel, *Future Jazz*, 39.

23. Art Ensemble of Chicago, *Naked*.

24. Rollins, *Plus 4*.

25. Nielsen, *Black Chant*, 240.

26. Beauchamp, *Art Ensemble of Chicago*, 74–75.

27. Jarman, quoted in Beauchamp, *Art Ensemble of Chicago*, 74.

28. Jarman, quoted in Solothurnmann, "What's Really Happening," 30–31.

29. Moye, interview by author, 6 September 2007.

30. Favors, advertisement in concert program for the AACM 25th Anniversary Festival, Chicago.

31. Moye, interview by author, 6 September 2007.

32. Art Ensemble of Chicago, *Urban Bushmen*.

33. Moye, interview by author, 6 September 2007.

34. Moye, interview by author, 6 September 2007.

35. Moye, e-mail message to author, 16 March 2015.

36. Moye, interview by author, 6 September 2007.

37. For a survey of the research on composite rhythms, emergent rhythms, and resultant rhythms in various African musics, see Agawu, *Representing African Music*, 71–96.

38. Beauchamp, *Art Ensemble of Chicago*, 54; Moye, interview by author, 6 September 2007.

39. Moye, interview by author, 6 September 2007.

40. Jarman, quoted in Beauchamp, *Art Ensemble of Chicago*, 75.

41. Jarman, quoted in Beauchamp, *Art Ensemble of Chicago*, 75.

42. George Favors, Rosetta Rimmer, and Velena Daniels, interview by author.

43. Favors, quoted in Beauchamp, *Art Ensemble of Chicago*, 27.

44. Favors, quoted in Beauchamp, *Art Ensemble of Chicago*, 27.

45. Bowie first recorded "New York Is Full of Lonely People" under the alternate title "Sardegna Amore": Bowie, *The 5th Power*.

46. Moye, interview by author, 6 September 2007. The two halves of *Live from the Jazz Showcase* may even come from two different sets. Richard Wang, e-mail message to author.

47. Art Ensemble of Chicago, *Live at Mandel Hall*.

48. Moye, interview by author, 6 September 2007.

49. Art Ensemble of Chicago, *A Jackson in Your House*.

50. Monson, *Saying Something*, 127.

51. Zabor, *The Bear Comes Home*, 39.

52. Zabor, *The Bear Comes Home*, 40.

53. Marty Khan, telephone interview by author.

54. Moye, interview by author, 6 September 2007.

55. John Litweiler, interview by author; *Loving v. Virginia*, 388 U.S. 1 (1967).

56. Marty Khan, telephone interview by author.

57. Art Ensemble of Chicago, *Live at Mandel Hall*; Moye, interview by author, 19 January 2007.

58. Moye, interview by author, 6 September 2007.

59. Ayler, *Bells*; Moye, interview by author, 6 September 2007.

60. Jarman, telephone interview by author, 10 December 2008.

61. Art Ensemble of Chicago, concert recording.

62. Art Ensemble of Chicago, *Among the People*.

63. Kevin Beauchamp, interview by author.

64. Jarman, *Black Case*, 46–47.

65. Jarman, *Black Case*, 47.

66. Moye, quoted in Rusch, "Don Moye," 18.

Conclusion

1. Epigraph: Jarman, *Black Case*, 9.

2. Art Ensemble of Chicago, *The Third Decade*.

3. Mitchell, *Sound*.

4. Kevin Beauchamp, interview by author; Don Palmer, "About Time," 50.

5. Beauchamp, *Art Ensemble of Chicago*, 64.

6. Mitchell, curriculum vitae.

7. Art Ensemble of Chicago, *Live in Japan*.

8. Beauchamp, *Art Ensemble of Chicago*, 64–65.

9. Art Ensemble of Chicago, *Ancient to the Future*; Art Ensemble of Chicago, *Dreaming of the Masters Suite*; Art Ensemble of Chicago, *Thelonious Sphere Monk*.

10. Shipp, "Their Muse Is Malcolm X," H22.

11. Beauchamp, *Art Ensemble of Chicago*, 65; Hofstein, "Soirs de Paris," 14.

12. Art Ensemble of Chicago, *Live at the 6th Tokyo Music Joy '90*.

13. Art Ensemble of Chicago, *America-South Africa*; Art Ensemble of Chicago, *Art Ensemble of Soweto*.

14. Mitchell, quoted in Cromwell, "Jazz Mecca," 196.

15. Marty Khan, telephone interview by author; Jaribu Shahid, telephone interview by author.

16. Moye, quoted in Tate, "Gone Fishing," 166.

17. Nessa, liner notes for Art Ensemble [of Chicago], *1967/68*.

18. Beauchamp, *Art Ensemble of Chicago*, 65.

19. Art Ensemble of Chicago, *Fundamental Destiny*; Art Ensemble of Chicago, *Salutes the Chicago Blues Tradition*; Art Ensemble of Chicago, *Swim—A Musical Adventure*.

20. Jung, "A Fireside Chat with Joseph Jarman," 2000.

21. Litweiler, liner notes for Joseph Jarman, *LifeTime Visions for the Magnificent Human*.

22. Jarman, quoted in Jung, "A Fireside Chat with Joseph Jarman," 2002.

23. Moye, quoted in Jung, "A Fireside Chat with the Art Ensemble of Chicago."

24. Reich, "A Man and His Music," AE14.

25. Saba, liner notes for Art Ensemble of Chicago, *Reunion*.

26. Reich, "A Man and His Music," AE14.

27. Lewis, *A Power Stronger Than Itself*, 481.

28. Tate, "Gone Fishing," 165.

29. Saba, liner notes for Art Ensemble of Chicago, *Reunion*.

30. Jung, "A Fireside Chat with the Art Ensemble of Chicago."

31. Murph, "Don't Call It a Comeback," 29.

32. Art Ensemble of Chicago, *Tribute to Lester*.

33. Mitchell, quoted in Jung, "A Fireside Chat with the Art Ensemble of Chicago."

34. Jung, "A Fireside Chat with Joseph Jarman," 2002.

35. Jarman, quoted in Mandel, "Resurrected Spirit," 58.

36. Art Ensemble of Chicago, *The Meeting*; Art Ensemble of Chicago, *Reunion*; Art Ensemble of Chicago, *Sirius Calling*.

37. Jung, "A Fireside Chat with the Art Ensemble of Chicago"; Mitchell, curriculum vitae.

38. Lewis, *A Power Stronger Than Itself*, 488.

39. Ratliff, "Malachi Favors, 76, Jazz Bassist with Art Ensemble of Chicago," B8.

40. Lewis, *A Power Stronger Than Itself*, 488.

41. Douglas Ewart, quoted in Reich, "Favors' Spirit Will Live On Through Music," AE7.

42. Mitchell, *Song for My Sister*.

43. Mitchell, telephone interview by author, 18 October 2006; Jaribu Shahid, telephone interview by author.

44. Art Ensemble of Chicago, *Non-Cognitive Aspects of the City*.

45. Kevin Beauchamp, interview by author; Rasul Siddik, interview by author.

46. Thulani Davis, e-mail message to author; Moye, e-mail message to author, 29 May 2014; Moye, e-mail message to author, 10 March 2015.

47. Art Ensemble of Chicago, *Full Force*.

48. Moye, interview by author, 19 January 2007.

49. Art Ensemble of Chicago, *A Jackson in Your House*; Art Ensemble of Chicago, *Live at Mandel Hall*; Art Ensemble of Chicago, *Live from the Jazz Showcase*.

50. Elaine Cohen, "Joseph Jarman in Concert," 23; Figi, "Art Ensemble of Chicago," 43–44; Hentoff, "'Great Black Music' from Chicago's Art Ensemble," 26.

51. Bowie, quoted in Beauchamp, *Art Ensemble of Chicago*, 49.

52. Moye, quoted in Tate, "Gone Fishing," 166.

53. Favors, quoted in Beauchamp, *Art Ensemble of Chicago*, 30.

References

"18th Annual International Jazz Critics Poll." *Down Beat* 37, no. 16 (20 August 1970): 13–20.

"28th Annual International Jazz Critics Poll." *Down Beat* 47, no. 8 (August 1980): 16–20.

"29th Annual International Jazz Critics Poll." *Down Beat* 48, no. 8 (August 1981): 18–22.

"30th Annual International Jazz Critics Poll." *Down Beat* 49, no. 8 (August 1982): 18–21.

"33rd Annual International Jazz Critics Poll." *Down Beat* 52, no. 8 (August 1985): 20–22.

"41st Annual International Jazz Critics Poll." *Down Beat* 60, no. 8 (August 1993): 26–29.

"43rd Annual International Jazz Critics Poll." *Down Beat* 62, no. 8 (August 1995): 22–33.

"44th Annual Readers Poll." *Down Beat* 46, no. 18 (December 1979): 20–24.

"45th Annual Readers Poll." *Down Beat* 47, no. 12 (December 1980): 16–19.

"47th Annual International Jazz Critics Poll." *Down Beat* 66, no. 8 (August 1999): 23–57.

Abrams, Richard L., and Ken Chaney. "Creative Musicians Present Artistic Heritage Ensemble." *Chicago Defender*, 11 September 1965: 14.

Abrams, Richard L., and Ken Chaney. "Creative Musicians Sponsor Artists Concert Showcase." *Chicago Defender*, 7 August 1965: 14.

Absher, Amy. *The Black Musician and the White City: Race and Music in Chicago, 1900–1967*. Ann Arbor: University of Michigan Press, 2014.

Adler, Philippe. "L'été torride du Lucernaire." *L'Express*, no. 944 (11–17 August 1969): 30.

Agawu, V. Kofi. *Representing African Music: Postcolonial Notes, Queries, Positions*. New York: Routledge, 2003.

Albert-Levin, Marc, and Barbara A. Summers. "Sous le chapiteau: Perplexes." *Le Monde*, 12 November 1969: 16–18.

Albin, Scott. "Art Ensemble of Chicago, Five Spot, New York City." *Down Beat* 42, no. 20 (4 December 1975): 34.

Alessandrini, Paul. "Les folles nuits d'Amougies." *Rock & Folk*, no. 35 (December 1969): 46–57.

Alessandrini, Paul. "Freepop." *Jazz Magazine*, no. 173 (December 1969): 26–31.

Alessandrini, Paul. "Jazz on the Grass." *Jazz Magazine*, no. 169–170 (September 1969): 9.

Alexander, Martin "Sparx." Telephone interview by author. Chicago, 9 March 2006.

Allen, Malba. E-mail message to author. 12 December 2006.

Allen, Malba. Interview by author. Chicago, 19 February 2006.

Anderson, Fred. Interview by author. Chicago, 5 August 2009.

Anderson, Iain. *This Is Our Music: Free Jazz, the Sixties, and American Culture*. Philadelphia: University of Pennsylvania Press, 2007.

"Army to Review Lake View and Waller Cadets: Hold Inspections Today and Tomorrow." *Chicago Tribune*, 22 May 1952: N2.

Art Ensemble of Chicago. Concert flyer for performances at Alice's Revisited, Chicago. 1971. Jazz Institute of Chicago, Jamil Figi Papers, Box 1, Folder 3. Special Collections Research Center, University of Chicago Library.

Art Ensemble of Chicago. Concert poster for performance at Ida Noyes Hall, Chicago. 1971. Association for the Advancement of Creative Musicians Publicity Materials, Box 1, Folder 1. Chicago History Museum.

Art Ensemble [of Chicago]. Concert poster for performance at the Blue Gargoyle, Chicago. 1969. Association for the Advancement of Creative Musicians Publicity Materials, Box 1, Folder 1. Chicago History Museum.

Art Ensemble of Chicago. Concert poster for performance at the Kool Jazz Festival, Los Angeles. 1982. Don Moye/Art Ensemble of Chicago Papers, Box 2. Vivian G. Harsh Research Collection of Afro-American History and Literature, Chicago Public Library.

Art Ensemble of Chicago. Concert poster for performance at the Wadsworth Theater, Los Angeles. 1990. Don Moye/Art Ensemble of Chicago Papers, Box 1. Vivian G. Harsh Research Collection of Afro-American History and Literature, Chicago Public Library.

Art Ensemble of Chicago. Concert poster for series at La Pagode, Paris. 1970. Association for the Advancement of Creative Musicians Publicity Materials, Box 1, Folder 2. Chicago History Museum.

Art Ensemble of Chicago. Publicity brochure. 1971. Archives of the Art Ensemble of Chicago.

Baker, Paul. "Roscoe Mitchell: The Next Step." *Coda*, no. 228 (October–November 1989): 18–21.

Baldwin, Davarian L. *Chicago's New Negroes: Modernity, the Great Migration, & Black Urban Life*. Chapel Hill: University of North Carolina Press, 2007.

Barker, Thurman. Radio interview by Ted Panken. WKCR-FM, New York, 18 November 1985. http://www.jazzhouse.org/library/?read=panken13

Beauchamp, Kevin. Interview by author. St. Louis, MO, 5 December 2014.

Beauchamp, Lincoln T. Jr. *Art Ensemble of Chicago: Great Black Music, Ancient to the Future.* Chicago: Art Ensemble of Chicago Publishing, 1998.

Bennett, Bill. "The Brass Fantasies of Lester Bowie." *JazzTimes* 27, no. 8 (October 1997): 42–44.

Berliner, Brett A. *Ambivalent Desire: The Exotic Black Other in Jazz-Age France.* Amherst: University of Massachusetts Press, 2002.

Berliner, Paul F. *Thinking in Jazz: The Infinite Art of Improvisation.* Chicago: University of Chicago Press, 1994.

Bernard, Marc. "The Art Ensemble of Chicago: Free Jazz." *Noroit,* no. 141 (October 1969): 1, 3.

Berry, Jason. "Declamations on Great Black Music." *Lenox Avenue,* no. 3 (1997): 42–54.

Besecker, Bill. "Lester Bowie: A Brass Fantasy." *Coda,* no. 244 (July–August 1992): 4–5.

Bhargava, Krishna Dayal. *The Teachings of the Buddha: A Brief Review of the Life and Teachings of Gautama Buddha.* Calcutta: A. Mukherjee, 1956.

Birnbaum, Larry. "Art Ensemble of Chicago: 15 Years of Great Black Music." *Down Beat* 46, no. 9 (3 May 1979): 15–17, 39–40, 42.

Bisceglia, Jacques. Interview by author. Paris, 28 July 2006.

Black, Larayne. Interview by author. Chicago, 18 February 2006.

Blake, Jody. *Le Tumulte Noir: Modernist Art and Popular Entertainment in Jazz-Age Paris, 1900–1930.* University Park: Pennsylvania State University Press, 1999.

Blumenthal, Bob. "A Kaleidoscope of Sound: Listening to the Big Picture with the Art Ensemble of Chicago." *Boston Globe,* 13 June 1999: N1.

Bone, Robert, and Richard A. Courage. *The Muse in Bronzeville: African American Creative Expression in Chicago, 1932–1950.* New Brunswick, NJ: Rutgers University Press, 2011.

"Boss! 'Things Go Better with Coke.'" *Chicago Defender,* 22 February 1966: 28.

Bouchard, Fred. "Blindfold Test: Lester Bowie." *Down Beat* 51, no. 9 (September 1984): 41.

Bourget, Jean-Loup. "Action poétique à Chicago." *Jazz Magazine,* no. 254 (May 1977): 31.

Bowie, Lester. "A.A.C.M." *Jazz Hot,* no. 256 (December 1969): 24–25.

Bowie, Lester, and Malachi Favors. Radio interview by Ted Panken. WKCR-FM, New York, 22 November 1994. http://www.jazzhouse.org/nlib/index.php3?read=panken8

Boyer, Horace Clarence. *How Sweet the Sound: The Golden Age of Gospel.* Washington, DC: Elliot & Clark Publishing, 1995.

Bragg, Aaron. "A Change in Perspective: ECM Records Revives Jazz Classics—For the Artists, Not the Beancounters." *The Local Planet* 3, no. 28 (17 July 2002): 13.

Braxton, Anthony. *Composition Notes.* Vol. 4, *Book D.* Lebanon, NH: Frog Peak Music, 1988.

Braxton, Anthony. *Tri-Axium Writings.* Vol. 1, *Writings One.* Lebanon, NH: Frog Peak Music, 1985.

Braxton, Anthony. *Tri-Axium Writings.* Vol. 3, *Writings Three.* Lebanon, NH: Frog Peak Music, 1985.

Broecking, Christian. *Der Marsalis-Faktor: Gespräche über afroamerikanische Kultur in den neunziger Jahren.* Waakirchen: Oreos, 1995.

Burns, Ken. *Jazz.* Washington, DC: PBS, 2001. DVD.

Büttner, Armin, Robert Campbell, and Robert Pruter. "The Parrot and Blue Lake Labels." 2011. https://archive.today/7MLb

"BYG à l'avant garde: Une date dans l'histoire de la nouvelle musique—Paris août 1969." *Jazz Hot,* no. 253 (September 1969): 16–17.

Cage, John. *Silence: Lectures and Writings.* Middletown, CT: Wesleyan University Press, 1961.

Calloway, Earl. "Yusef Lateef Set: The Brown Shoe." *Chicago Defender,* 2 September 1972: 19.

Campbell, Robert L., Armin Büttner, and Robert Pruter. "The King Kolax Discography." 2012. https://archive.today/DQRO

Campbell, Robert L., Robert Pruter, and Armin Büttner. "The King Fleming Discography." 2011. https://archive.today/Q3YC

Carles, Philippe. "De l'AACM à ECM: L'Art Ensemble." *Jazz Magazine,* no. 320 (July–August 1983): 52–53.

Carles, Philippe. "O. C. et la centrifugeuse." *Jazz Magazine,* no. 171 (October 1969): 15.

Carles, Philippe. "Six voix dans la ville." *Jazz Magazine,* no. 215 (September 1973): 36–47.

Carles, Philippe, and Jean-Louis Comolli. *Free Jazz/Black Power.* Paris: Éditions Champ Libre, 1971.

Carles, Philippe, and Daniel Soutif. "L'Art Ensemble de Chicago au-delà du Jazz." *Jazz Magazine,* no. 220 (March 1974): 12–16.

Carmichael, Stokely, and Charles V. Hamilton. *Black Power: The Politics of Liberation in America.* New York: Random House, 1967.

Caux, Daniel. "Alan Silva à Paris." *Jazz Hot,* no. 249 (April 1969): 9.

Caux, Daniel. "Le délire et la rigueur de 'l'Art Ensemble' de Chicago." *Jazz Hot,* no. 252 (July–August 1969): 8.

Caux, Daniel. "L'été au Lucernaire." *Jazz Hot,* no. 253 (September 1969): 15.

Caux, Daniel. "L'Europe, le 'free jazz' et la 'pop music.'" *Chroniques de l'Art Vivant,* no. 6 (December 1969): 2–7.

Chadbourne, Eugene. "Art Ensemble of Chicago." *Coda,* no. 147 (May 1976): 36.

Choice, Harriet. "Jazz Notes." *Chicago Tribune,* 16 May 1969: B18.

Choice, Harriet. "Newport and All That Jazz." *Chicago Tribune,* 7 July 1973: A22.

Choice, Harriet. "Sweet Jams for Jazz Fair." *Chicago Tribune,* 24 January 1982: E14.

Cohen, Aaron. "Art Ensemble Bassist Malachi Favors Maghostut Dies." *Down Beat* 71, no. 4 (April 2004): 26.

Cohen, Aaron. "Art Ensemble of Chicago." *Down Beat* 65, no. 8 (August 1998): 62–65.

Cohen, Aaron. "Joseph Jarman." *Coda,* no. 259 (January–February 1995): 32–34.

Cohen, Aaron. "Malachi Favors Maghostut: Natural & Spiritual." *Coda,* no. 256 (July–August 1994): 4–6.

Cohen, Elaine. "Fred Anderson." *Coda,* no. 197 (August 1984): 18–20.

Cohen, Elaine. "Joseph Jarman in Concert: Koncepts Cultural Gallery, Oakland, California, June 30, 1985." *Coda,* no. 204 (October 1985): 23.

Cohran, Philip Kelan. Telephone interview by author. Chicago, 30 August 2006.

Coleman, Anthony. "Roscoe Mitchell." *BOMB*, no. 91 (Spring 2005): 68–73.

Collins, Lisa Gail, and Margo Natalie Crawford. "Power to the People! The Art of Black Power." In *New Thoughts on the Black Arts Movement*, edited by Lisa Gail Collins and Margo Natalie Crawford, 1–19. New Brunswick, NJ: Rutgers University Press, 2006.

"Concert et disque de jazz: Art Ensemble of Chicago." *Le Nouvel Observateur*, no. 274 (9 February 1970): 5.

"Concerts." *Jazz Magazine*, no. 218 (January 1974): 42.

"Concerts." *Jazz Magazine*, no. 219 (February 1974): 9.

"Concerts." *Jazz Magazine*, no. 220 (March 1974): 10.

Cook, Nicholas. *Beyond the Score: Music as Performance*. New York: Oxford University Press, 2014.

Cook, Nicholas. "Making Music Together, or Improvisation and Its Others." *The Source* 1, no. 1 (2004): 5–25.

Cook, Richard. *Blue Note Records: The Biography*. London: Secker & Warburg, 2001.

Cooley, Rob. "Goodbye, Joseph Jarman!" *The Chicago Maroon* 77, no. 67 (23 May 1969): 3.

Coppens, George, and Frits Lagerwerff. "Lester Bowie." *Coda*, no. 164–165 (January–February 1979): 12–15.

Corbett, John. "Fanfare for a Warrior: Remembering Lester Bowie." *Down Beat* 67, no. 3 (March 2000): 22–27.

Costen, Melva Wilson. *In Spirit and in Truth: The Music of African American Worship*. Louisville, KY: Westminster John Knox Press, 2004.

Cotensin, Patrice. "From the Roots to the Source." *Jazz Magazine*, no. 284 (March 1980): 10.

Cotro, Vincent. *Chants Libres: Le free jazz en France, 1960–1975*. Paris: Éditions Outre Mesure, 1999.

Crawford, Margo Natalie. "Black Light on the *Wall of Respect*: The Chicago Black Arts Movement." In *New Thoughts on the Black Arts Movement*, edited by Lisa Gail Collins and Margo Natalie Crawford, 23–42. New Brunswick, NJ: Rutgers University Press, 2006.

Cromwell, Arthur Carrall. "Jazz Mecca: An Ethnographic Study of Chicago's South Side Jazz Community." PhD diss., Ohio University, 1998.

Cuscuna, Michael. Liner notes for Art Ensemble of Chicago, *Bap-tizum*. Atlantic SD 1639, 1973, 33⅓ rpm.

Dallinger, Deborah. "Roscoe Mitchell named Darius Milhaud Chair in Composition at Mills College." 2007. http://www.mills.edu/news/2007/newsarticle07032007roscoe _mitchell_milhaud_chair.php

Darden, Robert. *People Get Ready! A New History of Black Gospel Music*. New York: Continuum, 2004.

Davis, Francis. "Roscoe Mitchell: The Art Ensemble's Sage Saxist Brings Order Out of Improvisatory Chaos." *Musician*, no. 62 (December 1983): 26, 28, 30, 32, 34.

Davis, Thulani. E-mail message to author. 18 February 2015.

Delanoë, Nelcya. *Le Raspail Vert: L'American Center à Paris 1934–1994—Une histoire des avant-gardes franco-américaines*. Paris: Éditions Seghers, 1994.

Delcloo, Claude. "Letter to the AACM." *New Regime* 1, no. 1 (16 December 1968).

DeSantis, Alan Douglas. "Selling the American Dream: The *Chicago Defender* and the Great Migration of 1915–1919." PhD diss., Indiana University, 1993.

Detro, John. "The Leaders." *JazzTimes* 19, no. 5 (May 1989): 18–19.

DeVeaux, Scott. *Jazz in America: Who's Listening?* National Endowment for the Arts Research Division Report, no. 31. Carson, CA: Seven Locks Press, 1995.

DeVeaux, Scott. "Struggling with *Jazz*." *Current Musicology*, no. 71–73 (Spring 2001–Spring 2002): 353–374.

Donaldson, Jeff. "The Rise, Fall and Legacy of the *Wall of Respect* Movement." *International Review of African-American Art* 15, no. 1 (1998): 22–26.

Drott, Eric. *Music and the Elusive Revolution: Cultural Politics and Political Culture in France, 1968–1981.* Berkeley: University of California Press, 2011.

Dumas, Anne, and Alexandre Pierrepont. "Roscoe Mitchell: L'art, ensemble et seul." *Jazz Magazine*, no. 490 (March 1999): 80–83.

Dumetz, Gabriel. "Brigitte et l'Art Ensemble." *Jazz Magazine*, no. 177 (April 1970): 13.

Duncan, Otis Dudley, and Beverly Duncan. *The Negro Population of Chicago: A Study of Residential Succession.* Chicago: University of Chicago Press, 1957.

"Du Sable High R.O.T.C. Cadets Honor Winners: Students Get Medals at Inspection." *Chicago Tribune*, 21 June 1953: S5.

Dutilh, Alex. Interview by author. Paris, 25 July 2006.

Eicher, Manfred. "The Free Matrix." In *Horizons Touched: The Music of ECM*, edited by Steve Lake and Paul Griffiths, 217–224. London: Granta Books, 2007.

Elsdon, Peter. *Keith Jarrett's* The Köln Concert. New York: Oxford University Press, 2013.

Ertegun, Ahmet. *"What'd I Say": The Atlantic Story—50 Years of Music.* Compiled and edited by C. Perry Richardson. New York: Welcome Rain Publishers, 2001.

Evans-Wentz, Walter Yeeling. *The Tibetan Book of the Dead, or The After-Death Experiences on the Bardo Plane, according to Lāma Kazi Dawa-Samdup's English Rendering.* New York: Oxford University Press, 1960.

Fabre, Michel. *From Harlem to Paris: Black American Writers in France, 1840–1980.* Urbana: University of Illinois Press, 1991.

Farber, James, Peter Laenger, Jan Erik Kongshaug, Stefano Amerio, and Gérard de Haro. "The Engineers." In *Horizons Touched: The Music of ECM*, edited by Steve Lake and Paul Griffiths, 319–327. London: Granta Books, 2007.

Favors, George, Rosetta Rimmer, and Velena Daniels. Interview by author. Chicago, 3 September 2006.

Favors, Malachi. Advertisement in concert program for the AACM 25th Anniversary Festival, Chicago. 1990. Chicago Jazz Archive, R. Howard Courtney Collection, Box 3, Folder 3. Special Collections Research Center, University of Chicago Library.

Favors, Malachi. Interview by Peter Rosenbloom. Chicago, 16 December 2002.

Favors, Malachi. Liner notes for Art Ensemble of Chicago, *Tribute to Lester*. ECM 1808, 2003, compact disc.

"Festival 'Actuel.'" *Jazz Hot*, no. 254 (October 1969): 24–25.

Fielder, Alvin. Telephone interview by author. Jackson, MS, 11 March 2006.

Fielder, Alvin. Telephone interview by author. Jackson, MS, 11 October 2006.

Figi, J[amil] B. "Art Ensemble of Chicago." *SunDance*, November–December 1972: 43–50.

Figi, J[amil] B. Liner notes for Joseph Jarman, *Song For*. Delmark DS-410, 1967, 33⅓ rpm.

"Flashes." *Jazz Hot*, no. 250 (May 1969): 12.

Flexingburgstein, Dave. "Open Letter to a Great Pretender." *Coda*, no. 288 (November–December 1999): 22–24.

Fontaine, Brigitte. Interview by Philippe Katerine. 2003. http://katerine.free.fr/katint 10.php

"Fontella Bass Says." *Chicago Defender*, 21 September 1968: 28.

"For the Record." *Billboard* 92, no. 46 (15 November 1980): 102.

Friedman, Sharon, and Larry Birnbaum. "Fred Anderson: AACM's Biggest Secret." *Down Beat* 46, no. 5 (8 March 1979): 20–21, 46.

"From Gritty Soul, to Some Hard Jazz." *Chicago Defender*, 26 April 1975: A5.

Gans, Charles. "Art Ensemble of Chicago: Nice Guys Finish First." *Jazz Forum*, no. 68 (June 1980): 33–37.

Geerken, Hartmut. "Vom 'Accidental Shooting' zum 'Lohnhobeln.'" 2016. http://daten -messie.blogspot.com/2016/01/vom-accidental-shooting-zum-lohnhobeln.html

Gendron, Bernard. *Between Montmartre and the Mudd Club: Popular Music and the Avant-Garde*. Chicago: University of Chicago Press, 2002.

Giddins, Gary. "Bird Is the Word." *New York Magazine* 13, no. 26 (30 June 1980): 66.

Gillett, Rachel. "Jazz and the Evolution of Black American Cosmopolitanism in Interwar Paris." *Journal of World History* 21, no. 3 (September 2010): 471–496.

Ginsberg, Allen. *Howl and Other Poems*. San Francisco: City Lights Books, 1956.

Glasgo, Don. "Lester Redux: Moving the Music Forward." *Jazzlines*, no. 16 (February 1993): 1–4.

Goddet, Laurent. "Lester Bowie: *Gittin' to Know Y'All*." *Jazz Hot*, no. 274 (July–August 1971): 28.

Goddet, Laurent, and Alex Dutilh. "L'art, ensemble." *Jazz Hot*, no. 356–357 (December 1978–January 1979): 23–29.

Gold-Molina, Jack. "Roscoe Mitchell: In Search of the Super Musician." 2004. http://www .allaboutjazz.com/roscoe-mitchell-in-search-of-the-super-musician-roscoe-mitchell -by-jack-gold-molina.php

Gonzalez, Fernando. "Mastering the Fine Art of Improvisation." *Boston Globe*, 22 March 1991: 85.

Gras, Philippe, Daniel Caux, and Marc Bernard. "A.A.C.M. Chicago." *Jazz Hot*, no. 254 (October 1969): 16–19.

Green, John. "Lester Bowie, Don Moye: Two Spirited Forces behind the Art Ensemble of Chicago." *Be-Bop and Beyond*, no. 2 (January–February 1984): 16–21.

Gregory, James N. *The Southern Diaspora: How the Great Migrations of Black and White Southerners Transformed America*. Chapel Hill: University of North Carolina Press, 2005.

Gross, Jason. "Roscoe Mitchell Interview." *Perfect Sound Forever* (May 1998). http://www .furious.com/perfect/roscoemitchell.html

Grossman, James R. *Land of Hope: Chicago, Black Southerners, and the Great Migration.* Chicago: University of Chicago Press, 1989.

Günther, Egon. "Wie ich zum Trommeln kam, ist ziemlich uninteressant." *Jungle World* 33, no. 14 (August 2008). http://jungle-world.com/artikel/2008/33/22444.html

Harrington, Richard. "D.C. Curators: Showy Types." *Washington Post*, 7 October 1988: WE19.

Harris, Eddie. Radio interview by Ted Panken. WKCR-FM, New York, 29 June 1994. http://www.jazzhouse.org/library/?read=panken15

Hauff, Sigrid. "Auf Westafrika-Tournee: Moye — Tchicai — Geerken." *Jazz Podium* 34, no. 8 (August 1985): 34–35.

Heffley, Mike. *Northern Sun, Southern Moon: Europe's Reinvention of Jazz.* New Haven, CT: Yale University Press, 2005.

Henderson, Bill. "Don Moye: Sun Drummer." *Black Music and Jazz Review* 2, no. 5 (August 1979): 24–25.

Hennessey, Mike. "Art Ensemble of Chicago." *Jazz Journal International*, no. 44 (December 1991): 10–11.

Hentoff, Nat. "'Great Black Music' from Chicago's Art Ensemble." *Chronicle of Books & Arts*, 9 July 1979: 24–26.

Hicks, Robert. "Roscoe Mitchell: An Interesting Breakfast Conversation." *Coda*, no. 242 (March–April 1992): 23–26.

Higgins, Dick. "Intermedia." *The Something Else Newsletter* 1, no. 1 (February 1966): 1–3.

Hirsch, Arnold R. *Making the Second Ghetto: Race & Housing in Chicago, 1940–1960.* Cambridge: Cambridge University Press, 1983.

Hofstein, Francis. "Chronique du jazz." *Présence Africaine* 71, no. 3 (1969): 81–84.

Hofstein, Francis. "Soirs de Paris: Echos et extraits du cinquième Festival de Jazz de Paris." *Jazz Magazine*, no. 335 (January 1985): 14.

"Honor R.O.T.C. Cadets at Two S. Side Schools: Civic, Veteran Groups Reward Efficiency." *Chicago Tribune*, 28 February 1954: S3.

hooks, bell. *Yearning: Race, Gender, and Cultural Politics.* Boston: South End Press, 1990.

Huron, David. *Sweet Anticipation: Music and the Psychology of Expectation.* Cambridge, MA: MIT Press, 2006.

"Informations." *Jazz Magazine*, no. 220 (March 1974): 11.

"International Briefs." *Billboard* 92, no. 27 (5 July 1980): 64.

Jackson, Jeffrey H. *Making Jazz French: Music and Modern Life in Interwar Paris.* Durham, NC: Duke University Press, 2003.

Jackson, Jerma A. *Singing in My Soul: Black Gospel Music in a Secular Age.* Chapel Hill: University of North Carolina Press, 2004.

Jamin, Jean. "Au-delà du Vieux Carré: Idées du jazz en France." *L'Homme*, no. 158–159 (2001): 285–300.

Janssens, Eddy, and Hugo de Craen. *Art Ensemble of Chicago Discography: Unit & Members.* Brussels: New Think, 1983.

Jarman, Joseph. *Black Case: Volume I & II, Return from Exile.* Chicago: Art Ensemble of Chicago Publishing, 1977.

Jarman, Joseph. Concert flyer for performance at the Harper Theater, Chicago. 1965. Jazz

Institute of Chicago, Jamil Figi Papers, Box 1, Folder 2. Special Collections Research Center, University of Chicago Library.

Jarman, Joseph. Concert program for performance at the Francis W. Parker School, Chicago. 1968. Jazz Institute of Chicago, Jamil Figi Papers, Box 1, Folder 3. Special Collections Research Center, University of Chicago Library.

Jarman, Joseph. "Gens en peine: L'Art Ensemble de Chicago vous offre cette musique pour Noël." *Le Monde*, 24 December 1969: 14.

Jarman, Joseph. Interview by author. New York, 11 November 2005.

Jarman, Joseph. Interview by author. Brooklyn, NY, 19 August 2007.

Jarman, Joseph. Interview by John Litweiler. Chicago, 4 November 1981. Jazz Institute of Chicago, Oral Histories, Box 6, Items 7–12. Special Collections Research Center, University of Chicago Library.

Jarman, Joseph. Liner notes for Art Ensemble of Chicago, *A Jackson in Your House*. BYG/Actuel 529302, 1969, 33⅓ rpm.

Jarman, Joseph. Liner notes for Art Ensemble of Chicago, *Urban Bushmen*. ECM 1211/12, 1982, 33⅓ rpm.

Jarman, Joseph. Liner notes for Joseph Jarman, *As If It Were the Seasons*. Delmark DS-417, 1968, 33⅓ rpm.

Jarman, Joseph. "New York." *CHANGE*, no. 2 (Spring–Summer 1966): 14.

Jarman, Joseph. Résumé. 1978. Archives of the Art Ensemble of Chicago.

Jarman, Joseph. Scrapbook of concert flyers, photographs, and press clippings. 2006. Collection of Joseph Jarman.

Jarman, Joseph. Telephone interview by author. Brooklyn, NY, 10 May 2006.

Jarman, Joseph. Telephone interview by author. Montclair, NJ, 10 December 2008.

Jarman, Joseph. Telephone interview by author. Englewood, NJ, 20 February 2015.

"Jazz à Drancy." *Jazz Hot*, no. 259 (March 1970): 9.

"Jazz Grants." *Down Beat* 40, no. 17 (25 October 1973): 46.

"Jazz on Campus." *Down Beat* 40, no. 15 (13 September 1973): 35.

Joans, Ted. *Afrodisia*. London: Marion Boyars, 1970.

Joans, Ted. "Black Power et New Thing." *Jazz Magazine*, no. 150 (January 1968): 19.

Johnson, Martin. "Don't Call Jarman a 'Jazz Musician.'" *The City Sun*, 29 May–4 June 1985: 11–12.

Jones, Kellie. "Black West: Thoughts on Art in Los Angeles." In *New Thoughts on the Black Arts Movement*, edited by Lisa Gail Collins and Margo Natalie Crawford, 43–74. New Brunswick, NJ: Rutgers University Press, 2006.

Jones, LeRoi [Amiri Baraka]. *Black Music*. New York: W. Morrow, 1967.

Jost, Ekkehard. *Free Jazz*. Graz: Universal Edition, 1974. Reprint, New York: Da Capo Press, 1994.

Jost, Ekkehard. *Sozialgeschichte des Jazz in den USA*. Frankfurt am Main: Fischer Taschenbuch, 1982.

Joyce, Mike. "Herald the Trumpeters." *Washington Post*, 2 May 1982: F11.

Jung, Fred. "A Fireside Chat with Famoudou Don Moye." 2000. http://www.jazzweekly.com/interviews/moye.htm

Jung, Fred. "A Fireside Chat with Joseph Jarman." 2000. http://www.jazzweekly.com/interviews/jarman.htm

Jung, Fred. "A Fireside Chat with Joseph Jarman." 2002. http://www.jazzweekly.com
/interviews/jjarman.htm

Jung, Fred. "A Fireside Chat with Lester Bowie." 1999. http://www.jazzweekly.com
/interviews/bowie.htm

Jung, Fred. "A Fireside Chat with Malachi Favors." 1999. http://www.jazzweekly.com
/interviews/favors.htm

Jung, Fred. "A Fireside Chat with Roscoe Mitchell." 2000. http://www.jazzweekly.com
/interviews/mitchell.htm

Jung, Fred. "A Fireside Chat with the Art Ensemble of Chicago." 2003. http://www
.jazzweekly.com/interviews/aec.htm

Kelley, Robin D. G. "Dig They Freedom: Meditations on History and the Black Avant-
Garde." *Lenox Avenue*, no. 3 (1997): 13–27.

Kenney, William Howland. *Chicago Jazz: A Cultural History, 1904–1930*. New York:
Oxford University Press, 1993.

Kern, Roman. "Don Moye Quartett." *Jazz Podium* 31, no. 3 (March 1982): 27.

Khan, Marty. Telephone interview by author. Tucson, AZ, 17 October 2006.

Kim, Rebecca Y. "John Cage in Separate Togetherness with Jazz." *Contemporary Music
Review* 31, no. 1 (February 2012): 63–89.

Klein, Michael L. *Intertextuality in Western Art Music*. Bloomington: Indiana University
Press, 2005.

Koechlin, Philippe. "Brigitte et quatre Noirs." *Le Nouvel Observateur*, no. 275 (16 February 1970): 47.

Koechlin, Philippe. "'Pas de ça chez nous!' Les hippies français auront tout de même leur
festival . . . en Belgique." *Le Nouvel Observateur*, no. 258 (20 October 1969): 36–37.

Kopp, George. "Art Ensemble of Chicago Tours." *Billboard* 92, no. 38 (20 September
1980): 62.

Kostakis, Peter, and Art Lange. "An Interview with Joseph Jarman." *Brilliant Corners: A
Magazine of the Arts*, no. 8 (Winter 1978): 92–115.

Lake, Steve. "Introduction." In *Horizons Touched: The Music of ECM*, edited by Steve
Lake and Paul Griffiths, 1–4. London: Granta Books, 2007.

Lane, Jeremy F. *Jazz and Machine-Age Imperialism: Music, "Race," and Intellectuals in
France, 1918–1945*. Ann Arbor: University of Michigan Press, 2013.

Lehman, Stephen. "I Love You with an Asterisk: African-American Experimental Music
and the French Jazz Press, 1970–1980." *Critical Studies in Improvisation* 1, no. 2
(May 2005): 38–53.

Lemann, Nicholas. *The Promised Land: The Great Migration and How It Changed America*. New York: Alfred A. Knopf, 1991.

Letman, Sloan T. III. "The Most." *Chicago Defender*, 20 June 1964: 16.

"Lettre de Caen: Des ennuis pour l'Art Ensemble of Chicago." *Jazz Magazine*, no. 187
(March 1971): 16.

Levi, Titus. "Lester Speaks Out." *Option*, no. 1 (March–April 1985): 24–25.

Lewis, George E. "The AACM in Paris." *Black Renaissance Noire* 5, no. 3 (Spring–
Summer 2004): 105–121.

Lewis, George E. E-mail message to author. 10 January 2007.

Lewis, George E. "Experimental Music in Black and White: The AACM in New York, 1970–1985." *Current Musicology*, no. 71–73 (Spring 2001–Spring 2002): 100–157.

Lewis, George E. "*Gittin' To Know Y'All*: Improvised Music, Interculturalism, and the Racial Imagination." *Critical Studies in Improvisation* 1, no. 1 (December 2004): 1–33.

Lewis, George E. *A Power Stronger Than Itself: The AACM and American Experimental Music*. Chicago: University of Chicago Press, 2008.

Lewis, George E. "Singing Omar's Song: A (Re)construction of Great Black Music." *Lenox Avenue*, no. 4 (1998): 69–92.

Litweiler, John [B.]. "Altoists and Other Chicagoans." *Coda* 7, no. 12 (February–March 1967): 28–29.

Litweiler, John [B.]. "The Art Ensemble of Chicago: Adventures in the Urban Bush." *Down Beat* 49, no. 6 (June 1982): 19–22, 60.

Litweiler, John [B.]. "Chicago's AACM." *Sounds & Fury* 2, no. 3 (June 1966): 45.

Litweiler, John [B.]. "The Chicago Scene." *Coda* 8, no. 1 (April–May 1967): 36–38.

Litweiler, John [B.]. "Chicago's Richard Abrams: A Man with an Idea." *Down Beat* 34, no. 20 (5 October 1967): 23, 26, 41.

Litweiler, John [B.]. *The Freedom Principle: Jazz after 1958*. New York: W. Morrow, 1984.

Litweiler, John [B.]. Interview by author. Chicago, 21 February 2006.

Litweiler, John [B.]. "Joseph Jarman, Hyde Park Art Center, Chicago." *Down Beat* 36, no. 2 (23 January 1969): 35–36.

Litweiler, John [B.]. Liner notes for Joseph Jarman, *LifeTime Visions for the Magnificent Human*. Bopbuda Music 7786 3 14024 2 4, 2000, compact disc.

Litweiler, John B. Liner notes for Roscoe Mitchell, *L-R-G / The Maze / S II Examples*. Nessa N-14/15, 1978, 33⅓ rpm.

Litweiler, John [B.]. "Roscoe Mitchell, Cobb Hall, University of Chicago." *Down Beat* 35, no. 15 (25 July 1968): 29–32.

Litweiler, John [B.]. "Roscoe Mitchell, The Happening, Chicago." *Down Beat* 33, no. 25 (15 December 1966): 38.

Litweiler, John B. "There Won't Be Any More Music." In *Down Beat Music '71: 16th Annual Yearbook*, 23–26, 37. Chicago: Maher Publications, 1971.

Litweiler, John B. "Three to Europe." *Jazz Monthly*, no. 177 (November 1969): 20–22.

Livingston, Tim. "Lester Bowie: Interview." *Cadence* 27, no. 1 (January 2001): 5–10.

Lock, Graham. *Forces in Motion: Anthony Braxton and the Meta-Reality of Creative Music*. London: Quartet Books, 1988.

Looker, Benjamin. "*Point from Which Creation Begins": The Black Artists' Group of St. Louis*. St. Louis: Missouri Historical Society Press, 2004.

Lyles, Ronald. "Andrew Hill Discography." 2011. http://www.jazzdiscography.com/Artists /Hill/hill-disc.htm

Lyon, Herb. "Tower Ticker." *Chicago Tribune*, 29 April 1959: 30.

Mackey, Nathaniel. *Djbot Baghostus's Run*. Los Angeles: Sun & Moon Press, 1993.

Magee, Jeffrey. *The Uncrowned King of Swing: Fletcher Henderson and Big Band Jazz*. New York: Oxford University Press, 2005.

Malcolm, Dino. *The Musicians Building*. Chicago: Community Film Workshop, 1987. Videocassette (VHS).

Mandel, Howard. *Future Jazz*. New York: Oxford University Press, 1999.

Mandel, Howard. "Joseph Jarman, University of Chicago." *Down Beat* 44, no. 6 (24 March 1977): 33.

Mandel, Howard. "Resurrected Spirit: The Art Ensemble of Chicago Reunites with Joseph Jarman and Pays Tribute to Lester Bowie." *Down Beat* 70, no. 10 (October 2003): 56–61.

Marsalis, Wynton, and Frank Stewart. *Sweet Swing Blues on the Road*. New York: W. W. Norton, 1994.

Martin, Denis-Constant. "De l'excursion à Harlem au débat sur les 'Noirs': Les terrains absents de la jazzologie française." *L'Homme*, no. 158–159 (2001): 261–278.

[Martin, Denis-Constant]. "Les exces de Moers." *Jazz Magazine*, no. 256 (July–August 1977): 10–15.

Martin, Terry. "Blowing Out in Chicago: Roscoe Mitchell." *Down Beat* 34, no. 7 (6 April 1967): 20–21, 47–49.

Martin, Terry. "The Chicago Avant-Garde." *Jazz Monthly*, no. 157 (March 1968): 12–18.

Martin, Terry. Liner notes for Art Ensemble [of Chicago], *1967/68*. Nessa NCD-2500, 1993, compact disc.

Martin, Terry. Liner notes for Roscoe Mitchell, *Before There Was Sound*. Nessa NCD-34, 2011, compact disc.

Martin, Terry. "Roscoe Mitchell, Ida Noyes Hall, University of Chicago." *Down Beat* 34, no. 18 (7 September 1967): 28–29.

Mathieu, Bill. "*Sound*." *Down Beat* 34, no. 12 (15 June 1967): 34–35.

Mattingly, Rick. "Famoudou Don Moye: Drawing on Tradition." *Modern Drummer* 5, no. 2 (April 1981): 14–16, 48, 56, 58–59, 76–77.

McAdams, Stephen, and Roger Reynolds. "A Tribute to David Wessel (1942–2014): Consulting Editor for *Music Perception*, 1983–2008." *Music Perception* 32, no. 4 (April 2015): 434–436.

McGraw-Beauchamp, L. [Lincoln T. Beauchamp Jr.]. "Roscoe Mitchell." *Jazz Masters Journal*, 1991: 19–24.

Michaels, Mike. "How I Was a Fly on the Wall in the Creation of the Greatest Song in the History of Rock and Roll." *The University of Chicago Magazine* 104, no. 6 (July–August 2012): 52–53.

Michaelsen, Garrett. "Analyzing Musical Interaction in Jazz Improvisations of the 1960s." PhD diss., Indiana University, 2013.

Michelou, Jacques. Telephone interview by author. Paris, 17 October 2006.

Milkowski, Bill. "The Art Ensemble of Chicago's Famoudou Don Moye: Multi-Directional Drummer for All Seasons." *Modern Drummer* 31, no. 5 (May 2007): 86–91, 93–94, 96.

Mitchell, Douglas. Interview by author. Chicago, 19 February 2006.

Mitchell, Roscoe. Curriculum vitae. 2003. http://www.akamu.net/mitchell/cv.htm

Mitchell, Roscoe. E-mail message to author. 14 January 2007.

Mitchell, Roscoe. E-mail message to author. 15 September 2007.

Mitchell, Roscoe. Interview by author. Chicago, 18 November 2010.

Mitchell, Roscoe. Interview by author. St. Louis, MO, 4 December 2014.

Mitchell, Roscoe. "'Nonaah' and the Composition/Improvisation Connection." Lecture presented at the University of Chicago, 18 November 2010.

Mitchell, Roscoe. "'Nonaah': From Solo to Full Orchestra." Lecture presented at Washington University in St. Louis, 5 December 2014.

Mitchell, Roscoe. "People in Sorrow." Score. 1988. Archives of the Art Ensemble of Chicago.

Mitchell, Roscoe. Radio interview by Ted Panken. WKCR-FM, New York, 5 December 1995. http://www.jazzhouse.org/nlib/index.php3?read=panken10

Mitchell, Roscoe. Résumé. 1998. Archives of the Art Ensemble of Chicago.

Mitchell, Roscoe. Telephone interview by author. Fitchburg, WI, 18 October 2006.

Mitchell, Roscoe. Telephone interview by author. Oakland, CA, 28 February 2015.

Mitchell, Roscoe, and Amina Claudine Myers. Radio interview by Ted Panken. WKCR-FM, New York, 13 June 1995. http://www.jazzhouse.org/nlib/index.php3?read=panken9

Mizrahi, Moshé. *Les Stances à Sophie*. Paris: Les Films de la Licorne, 1971.

Monson, Ingrid T. *Saying Something: Jazz Improvisation and Interaction*. Chicago: University of Chicago Press, 1996.

Moye, Don. E-mail message to author. 7 July 2005.

Moye, Don. E-mail message to author. 22 October 2005.

Moye, Don. E-mail message to author. 27 May 2007.

Moye, Don. E-mail message to author. 6 May 2009.

Moye, Don. E-mail message to author. 29 May 2014.

Moye, Don. E-mail message to author. 3 March 2015.

Moye, Don. E-mail message to author. 10 March 2015.

Moye, Don. E-mail message to author. 12 March 2015.

Moye, Don. E-mail message to author. 15 March 2015.

Moye, Don. E-mail message to author. 16 March 2015.

Moye, Don. Interview by author. Chicago, 19 January 2007.

Moye, Don. Interview by author. Chicago, 6 September 2007.

Moye, Don. Interview by author. Chicago, 20 October 2009.

Moye, Don. Liner notes for Art Ensemble of Chicago, *Tribute to Lester*. ECM 1808, 2003, compact disc.

Moye, Don. Résumé. 1978. Archives of the Art Ensemble of Chicago.

Moye, Don. Telephone interview by author. Chicago, 4 February 2006.

Moye, Don. Telephone interview by author. Marseille, 5 March 2015.

Moye, Don, and John Shenoy Jackson. "Art Ensemble of Chicago Biographies." 1984. Archives of the Art Ensemble of Chicago.

Murph, John. "Don't Call It a Comeback: Art Ensemble of Chicago Reemerges with Two New CDs." *JazzTimes* 33, no. 9 (November 2003): 28–29.

Murray, Albert. *Stomping the Blues*. New York: Da Capo Press, 2000.

Mwanga, Kunle. Telephone interview by author. Middletown, CT, 14 October 2006.

Myers, Marc. *Why Jazz Happened*. Berkeley: University of California Press, 2013.

Neal, Larry. "The Black Arts Movement." *The Drama Review* 12, no. 4 (Summer 1968): 29–39.

Nessa, Chuck. Liner notes for Art Ensemble [of Chicago], *1967/68*. Nessa NCD-2500, 1993, compact disc.

Nettelbeck, Colin. *Dancing with de Beauvoir: Jazz and the French*. Carlton, Victoria: Melbourne University Press, 2004.

Newsome, Thomas Aldridge. "It's After the End of the World! Don't You Know That Yet? Black Creative Musicians in Chicago (1946–1976)." PhD diss., University of North Carolina at Chapel Hill, 2001.

Nielsen, Aldon Lynn. *Black Chant: Languages of African-American Postmodernism*. New York: Cambridge University Press, 1997.

"Une nouvelle collection: Archives of Jazz." *Jazz Hot*, no. 252 (July–August 1969): 9.

Nyman, Michael. *Experimental Music: Cage and Beyond*. Cambridge: Cambridge University Press, 1999.

Palmer, Don. "About Time." *Jazziz* 15, no. 11 (November 1998): 48–53.

Palmer, Robert. "Art Ensemble of Chicago Takes Jazz to the Stage." *Rolling Stone*, no. 303 (1 November 1979): 9, 29–30.

Palmer, Robert. "New Sounds from Roscoe Mitchell." *New York Times*, 4 December 1981: C15.

Palmer, Robert. "The Pop Life." *New York Times*, 30 November 1979: C12.

Pareles, Jon. "A Family of Gospel Singers." *New York Times*, 13 January 1989: C21.

Pareles, Jon. "Five Hot Trumpets." *New York Times*, 26 August 1982: C27.

Pareles, Jon. "Multimedia Jazzman from Chicago." *New York Times*, 13 August 1982: C6.

Pfleiderer, Martin. "Das Art Ensemble of Chicago in Paris, Sommer 1969: Annäherungen an den Improvisationsstil eines Musikerkollektivs." *Jazzforschung*, no. 29 (1997): 87–157.

Piekut, Benjamin. *Experimentalism Otherwise: The New York Avant-Garde and Its Limits*. Berkeley: University of California Press, 2011.

Pierrepont, Alexandre. "'A Brain for the Seine': Paris et l'Europe, de 1969 à 1974." Unpublished manuscript. 29 January 2006.

Pierrepont, Alexandre. *La Nuée, l'AACM: Un jeu de société musicale*. Paris: Éditions Parenthèses, 2015.

Pierrepont, Alexandre. "Richard Wang." *Improjazz*, no. 112 (February 2005): 8–11.

Pierrepont, Alexandre. "Roscoe Mitchell." *Improjazz*, no. 94 (April 2003): 8–10.

Porter, Eric. *What Is This Thing Called Jazz? African American Musicians as Artists, Critics, and Activists*. Berkeley: University of California Press, 2002.

Porter, Lewis. *John Coltrane: His Life and Music*. Ann Arbor: University of Michigan Press, 1997.

Postif, François. "Discomania." *Jazz Hot*, no. 256 (December 1969): 37.

"Potpourri." *Down Beat* 41, no. 21 (19 December 1974): 11.

Quénum, Thierry. "Jazz à Vienne." *Jazz Magazine*, no. 451 (September 1995): 14.

Quinn, Bill. "Joseph Jarman, Abraham Lincoln Center, Chicago." *Down Beat* 34, no. 5 (9 March 1967): 27–28.

"R&B Spotlights." *Billboard* 71, no. 36 (4 September 1965): 16.

Radano, Ronald M. *New Musical Figurations: Anthony Braxton's Cultural Critique*. Chicago: University of Chicago Press, 1993.

Ramsey, Guthrie P. Jr. *Race Music: Black Cultures from Bebop to Hip-Hop.* Berkeley: University of California Press, 2003.

Rand, Richard. "Art Ensemble of Chicago, University of Wisconsin, Madison, Wis." *Down Beat* 39, no. 15 (14 September 1972): 38.

Ratliff, Ben. "Lester Bowie Is Dead at 58: Innovative Jazz Trumpeter." *New York Times*, 11 November 1999: B15.

Ratliff, Ben. "Malachi Favors, 76, Jazz Bassist with Art Ensemble of Chicago." *New York Times*, 9 February 2004: B8.

Reich, Howard. "Favors' Spirit Will Live On Through Music: Bassist's Funeral Draws Musicians Singing Praises." *Chicago Tribune*, 8 February 2004: AE7.

Reich, Howard. "A Man and His Music: Artists Pay Tribute to Lester Bowie but Can't Replace His Impact." *Chicago Tribune*, 16 January 2000: AE14.

Reich, Howard. "Saluting a Chicago Teacher Who Turned Out Jazz Stars." *Chicago Tribune*, 21 August 2013: AE1, AE3.

Reich, Howard. "When Jazz Fest Stops, Notes Go Underground." *Chicago Tribune*, 4 September 1981: B3.

Rendle, Phillippa, and Rafi Zabor. "Lester Bowie: Roots, Research, & the Carnival Chef." *Musician*, no. 44 (June 1982): 64–71.

Richter, Stephan. *Zu einer Ästhetik des Jazz.* Frankfurt am Main: Peter Lang, 1995.

Rockwell, John. "Joseph Jarman's Multimedia 'Liberation Suite.'" *New York Times*, 16 August 1982: C16.

Rosenstone, Robert A. "'The Times They Are A-Changin'": The Music of Protest." *Annals of the American Academy of Political and Social Science*, no. 382 (March 1969): 131–144.

Ross, Kristin. *May '68 and Its Afterlives.* Chicago: University of Chicago Press, 2002.

Rout, Leslie B. Jr. "AACM: New Music (!) New Ideas (?)." *Journal of Popular Culture* 1, no. 2 (Fall 1967): 128–140.

Rusch, Bob. "Don Moye." *Cadence* 5, no. 10 (October 1979): 14–18.

Rusch, Bob. "Joseph Jarman." *Cadence* 5, no. 5 (May 1979): 3–6.

Rusch, Bob. "Lester Bowie." *Cadence* 5, no. 12 (December 1979): 3–6, 14.

Rusch, Bob, and Hillary J. Ryan. "Malachi Favors." *Cadence* 17, no. 3 (March 1991): 5–14.

Saba, Isio. Liner notes for Art Ensemble of Chicago, *Reunion.* Il Manifesto CD 122, 2003, compact disc.

Sachs, Lloyd. "A Long Road Back: Return to Gospel Rescued Bass' Career." *Chicago Sun-Times*, 8 March 1995: FTR41, FTR44.

Safane, Clifford Jay. "Lester Bowie's Sho' Nuff Orchestra." *Down Beat* 46, no. 9 (3 May 1979): 37.

Sandke, Jordan. Telephone interview by author. Chicago, 7 March 2006.

Satter, Beryl. *Family Properties: Race, Real Estate, and the Exploitation of Black Urban America.* New York: Metropolitan Books, 2009.

Sawyer, R. Keith. *Group Creativity: Music, Theater, Collaboration.* Mahwah, NJ: Lawrence Erlbaum Associates, 2003.

Schillinger, Joseph. *The Schillinger System of Musical Composition.* Edited by Lyle Dowling and Arnold Shaw. 2 vols. New York: Carl Fischer, 1946.

Schutz, Alfred. "Making Music Together: A Study in Social Relationship." In *Collected Papers II: Studies in Social Theory*, edited by Arvid Brodersen, 159–178. The Hague: Martinus Nijhoff, 1964.

Schwartz, Jeff, and Michael Fitzgerald. "BYG Records Listing." 2002. http://www.jazz discography.com/Labels/byg.htm

Shahid, Jaribu. Telephone interview by author. Long Beach, NY, 23 October 2006.

Shaw, Charles "Bobo." Interview by author. St. Louis, MO, 1 March 2014.

Shepp, Archie. "A View from the Inside." In *Down Beat Music '66: 11th Annual Yearbook*, 39–42, 44. Chicago: Maher Publications, 1966.

Shipp, E. R. "Their Muse Is Malcolm X." *New York Times*, 4 December 1988: H1, H22–23.

Shoemaker, Bill. "Page One." *Point of Departure*, no. 46 (March 2014). http://www .pointofdeparture.org/archives/PoD-46/PoD46PageOne.html

Siddik, Rasul. Interview by author. Paris, 3 August 2006.

Silverstein, Steve. "Recording History: The AACM and the Chicago Avant-Garde Jazz Scene of the Mid-Sixties." *Tape Op*, no. 11 (November–December 1998): 56–59.

Sklower, Jedediah. *Free Jazz, la Catastrophe Féconde: Une histoire du monde éclaté du jazz en France (1960–1982)*. Paris: L'Harmattan, 2006.

Smith, Bill. "Roscoe Mitchell." *Coda*, no. 141 (September 1975): 2–10.

Smith, Steve. Liner notes for Art Ensemble of Chicago, *Bap-tizum*. Koch Jazz KOC-CD-8500, 1998, compact disc.

Smith, [Wadada] Leo. *notes (8 pieces) source a new world music: creative music*. Self-published, 1973.

"Soirée à la Mutualité au profit des 'Black Panthers.'" *Jazz Hot*, no. 264 (September 1970): 33.

Solis, Gabriel. *Thelonious Monk Quartet with John Coltrane at Carnegie Hall*. New York: Oxford University Press, 2014.

Solomon, Deborah. "Lincoln Center's Culture Gap." *New York Times Magazine*, 5 October 2003: 24–30.

Solothurnmann, Jürg. "*Nice Guys, Full Force.*" *Jazz Forum*, no. 68 (June 1980): 49–50.

Solothurnmann, Jürg. "What's Really Happening: Insights and Views of the Art Ensemble of Chicago." *Jazz Forum*, no. 49 (May 1977): 28–33.

Spitzer, David D. "Art Ensemble of Chicago." *Different Drummer* 1, no. 12 (October 1974): 26–29.

Spivey, Donald. *Union and the Black Musician*. Lanham, MD: University Press of America, 1984.

Steinbeck, Paul. "Analyzing the Music of the Art Ensemble of Chicago." *Dutch Journal of Music Theory* 13, no. 1 (February 2008): 56–68.

Steinbeck, Paul. "'Area by Area the Machine Unfolds': The Improvisational Performance Practice of the Art Ensemble of Chicago." *Journal of the Society for American Music* 2, no. 3 (August 2008): 397–427.

Steinbeck, Paul. "The Art Ensemble of Chicago's 'Get in Line': Politics, Theatre, and Play." *Twentieth-Century Music* 10, no. 1 (March 2013): 3–23.

Steinbeck, Paul. "Intermusicality, Humor, and Cultural Critique in the Art Ensemble of Chicago's 'A Jackson in Your House.'" *Jazz Perspectives* 5, no. 2 (August 2011): 135–154.

Stokes, W. Royal. *The Jazz Scene: An Informal History from New Orleans to 1990.* New York: Oxford University Press, 1991.

Stokes, W. Royal. "Lester Bowie: The Realities of Jazz." *JazzTimes* 15, no. 7 (July 1985): 12–13.

Stovall, Tyler. *Paris Noir: African Americans in the City of Light.* New York: Houghton Mifflin, 1996.

Stöwsand, Thomas. Telephone interview by author. Vienna, 18 July 2006.

Such, David G. *Avant-Garde Jazz Musicians: Performing "Out There."* Iowa City: University of Iowa Press, 1993.

Sutton-Smith, Brian. *The Ambiguity of Play.* Cambridge, MA: Harvard University Press, 1997.

Sweet, [Robert E.]. "Joseph Jarman: All the Voices Are There Again." 2004. http://www.onefinalnote.com/features/2004/jarman

Sweet, Robert E. *Music Universe, Music Mind: Revisiting the Creative Music Studio, Woodstock, New York.* Ann Arbor, MI: Arborville Publishing, 1996.

Szwed, John F. *Space Is the Place: The Lives and Times of Sun Ra.* New York: Da Capo Press, 1998.

Szyfmanowicz, R. "Brigitte Fontaine, Areski, Art Ensemble of Chicago: *Comme à la radio.*" *Jazz Hot*, no. 264 (September 1970): 38–39.

Tate, Greg. "Gone Fishing: Remembrances of Lester Bowie." *Village Voice*, 14 December 1999: 165–166.

Taylor, Kate. "Finding a New Audience for Jazz." *New York Sun*, 15 October 2007: 11.

Tepperman, Barry. "*Rope-A-Dope.*" *Coda*, no. 153 (January–February 1977): 12.

Tournès, Ludovic. *New Orleans sur Seine: Histoire du jazz en France.* Paris: Librarie Arthème Fayard, 1999.

Townley, Ray. "Lester . . . Who?" *Down Beat* 41, no. 2 (31 January 1974): 11–12.

Townley, Ray. "Muhal Richard Abrams." *Down Beat* 41, no. 14 (15 August 1974): 34.

Travis, Dempsey J. *An Autobiography of Black Chicago.* Chicago: Urban Research Institute, 1981.

Trombert, Thierry. "Soirée de soutien au Black Panthers Party: Mutualité le 2–11–70." *Jazz Hot*, no. 267 (December 1970): 9.

Tucker, Bruce. "Narrative, Extramusical Form, and the Metamodernism of the Art Ensemble of Chicago." *Lenox Avenue*, no. 3 (1997): 29–41.

Tuttle, William M. Jr. *Race Riot: Chicago in the Red Summer of 1919.* New York: Atheneum, 1970.

Veal, Michael E. *Fela: The Life and Times of an African Musical Icon.* Philadelphia: Temple University Press, 2000.

Vihlen, Elizabeth. "Sounding French: Jazz in Postwar France." PhD diss., State University of New York at Stony Brook, 2000.

Wald, Gayle F. *Shout, Sister, Shout! The Untold Story of Rock-and-Roll Trailblazer Sister Rosetta Tharpe.* Boston: Beacon Press, 2007.

Walker, Edwin. E-mail message to author. 11 February 2015.

Walmsley, Buck. "An Interesting Workout in Jazz Sounds." *Chicago Daily News*, 29 November 1965: 39.

Wang, Richard. E-mail message to author. 14 April 2008.

Ward, Geoffrey C. *Jazz: A History of America's Music.* New York: Alfred A. Knopf, 2000.

Warne, Chris. "Bringing Counterculture to France: *Actuel* Magazine and the Legacy of May '68." *Modern & Contemporary France* 15, no. 3 (August 2007): 309–324.

Waters, Keith. *The Studio Recordings of the Miles Davis Quintet, 1965–68.* New York: Oxford University Press, 2011.

Watrous, Peter. "Lester Bowie, Sweet Basil." *New York Times*, 12 May 1994: C19.

Weiss, Jason. "Lester Leaps In." *Jazz Forum*, no. 90 (May 1984): 8.

Welding, Pete. "Joseph Jarman–John Cage, Harper Theater, Chicago." *Down Beat* 33, no. 1 (13 January 1966): 35–36.

West, Hollie I. "Art Ensemble." *Washington Post*, 6 October 1978: D9.

Whitehead, Kevin. "Jazz Rebels: Lester Bowie & Greg Osby." *Down Beat* 60, no. 8 (August 1993): 16–20.

Wieland, Martin. E-mail message to author. 23 October 2006.

Wilkerson, Isabel. *The Warmth of Other Suns: The Epic Story of America's Great Migration.* New York: Random House, 2010.

Willener, Alfred. *The Action-Image of Society: On Cultural Politicization.* Translated by A. M. Sheridan Smith. London: Tavistock Publications, 1970.

Wilmer, Valerie. "Art Ensemble of Chicago, Vieux-Colombier, Paris, France." *Down Beat* 37, no. 12 (25 June 1970): 26.

Wilmer, Valerie. *As Serious as Your Life: The Story of the New Jazz.* London: Serpent's Tail, 1992.

Wilmer, Valerie. "Rainy Day in the Windy City." *Melody Maker*, 23 September 1972: 24.

Wolf, Robert. *Story Jazz: A History of Chicago Jazz Styles.* Lansing, IA: Free River Press, 1995.

Wolkin, Jan Mark, and Bill Keenom. *Michael Bloomfield: If You Love These Blues.* San Francisco: Miller Freeman Books, 2000.

Young, Alan. *Woke Me Up This Morning: Black Gospel Singers and the Gospel Life.* Jackson: University Press of Mississippi, 1997.

Zabor, Rafi. "The Art Ensemble." *Musician*, no. 17 (March–April 1979): 39–44.

Zabor, Rafi. *The Bear Comes Home.* New York: W. W. Norton, 1997.

Recordings

Abrams, Muhal Richard. *Levels and Degrees of Light.* Delmark DS-413, 1968, 33⅓ rpm.

Abrams, Muhal Richard. *Sightsong.* Black Saint BSR 0003, 1976, 33⅓ rpm.

Anderson, Fred. *Black Horn Long Gone.* Southport S-SSD 0128, 2010, compact disc.

Art Ensemble [of Chicago]. *1967/68.* Nessa NCD-2500, 1993, compact disc.

Art Ensemble of Chicago. *The Alternate Express.* DIW 832, 1989, compact disc.

Art Ensemble of Chicago. *America-South Africa.* DIW 848, 1991, compact disc.

Art Ensemble of Chicago. *Among the People.* Praxis CM 103, 1981, 33⅓ rpm.

Art Ensemble of Chicago. *Ancient to the Future: Dreaming of the Masters Series Vol. 1.* DIW 804, 1987, compact disc.

Art Ensemble of Chicago. *Art Ensemble of Chicago with Fontella Bass.* America 30 AM 6117, 1971, 33⅓ rpm.

Art Ensemble of Chicago. *Art Ensemble of Soweto.* DIW 837, 1990, compact disc.

Art Ensemble of Chicago. *Bap-tizum.* Atlantic SD 1639, 1973, 33⅓ rpm.

Art Ensemble of Chicago. *Bap-tizum.* Koch Jazz KOC-CD-8500, 1998, compact disc.

Art Ensemble of Chicago. *Certain Blacks.* America 30 AM 6098, 1970, 33⅓ rpm.

Art Ensemble of Chicago. *Chi-Congo.* Decca 258054, 1972, 33⅓ rpm.

Art Ensemble of Chicago. *Coming Home Jamaica.* Atlantic 83149–2, 1998, compact disc.

Art Ensemble of Chicago. *The Complete Live in Japan.* DIW 815/816, 1988, compact disc.

Art Ensemble of Chicago. Concert recording. Recorded in Athens, GA, 30 April 1979, compact disc. Collection of Jonathan Piper.

Art Ensemble of Chicago. *Dreaming of the Masters Suite.* DIW 854, 1991, compact disc.

Art Ensemble of Chicago. *Eda Wobu.* JMY 1008–2, 1991, compact disc.

Art Ensemble of Chicago. *Fanfare for the Warriors.* Atlantic SD 1651, 1974, 33⅓ rpm.

Art Ensemble of Chicago. *Full Force.* ECM 1167, 1980, 33⅓ rpm.

Art Ensemble of Chicago. *Fundamental Destiny.* AECO 008, 2007, compact disc.

Art Ensemble of Chicago. *Go Home.* Galloway 600 502, 1970, 33⅓ rpm.

Art Ensemble of Chicago. *A Jackson in Your House.* BYG/Actuel 529302, 1969, 33⅓ rpm.

Art Ensemble of Chicago. *Kabalaba.* AECO 004, 1978, 33⅓ rpm.

Art Ensemble of Chicago. *Live.* BYG YX-2040/41, 1975, 33⅓ rpm.

Art Ensemble of Chicago. *Live at Earshot Jazz Festival.* Milo WJM 01, 2006, compact disc.

Art Ensemble of Chicago. *Live at Mandel Hall.* Delmark DS-432/433, 1974, 33⅓ rpm.

Art Ensemble of Chicago. *Live at the 6th Tokyo Music Joy '90.* DIW 842, 1990, compact disc.

Art Ensemble of Chicago. *Live from the Jazz Showcase.* Chicago: University of Illinois, 1982. Videocassette (VHS).

Art Ensemble of Chicago. *Live in Berlin.* West Wind 2051, 1993, compact disc.

Art Ensemble of Chicago. *Live in Japan.* DIW 8005, 1985, 33⅓ rpm.

Art Ensemble of Chicago. *The Meeting.* Pi Recordings PI07, 2003, compact disc.

Art Ensemble of Chicago. *Message to Our Folks.* BYG/Actuel 529328, 1969, 33⅓ rpm.

Art Ensemble of Chicago. *Naked.* DIW 8011, 1986, 33⅓ rpm.

Art Ensemble of Chicago. *Nice Guys.* ECM 1126, 1979, 33⅓ rpm.

Art Ensemble of Chicago. *Non-Cognitive Aspects of the City—Live at Iridium.* Pi Recordings PI20, 2006, compact disc.

Art Ensemble of Chicago. *Peace Be Unto You.* AECO 0013LE, 2008, compact disc.

Art Ensemble of Chicago. *People in Sorrow.* Pathé 2C 062–10523, 1969, 33⅓ rpm.

Art Ensemble of Chicago. *Phase One.* America 30 AM 6116, 1971, 33⅓ rpm.

Art Ensemble of Chicago. *Reese and the Smooth Ones.* BYG/Actuel 529329, 1969, 33⅓ rpm.

Art Ensemble of Chicago. *Reunion.* Il Manifesto CD 122, 2003, compact disc.

Art Ensemble of Chicago. *Salutes the Chicago Blues Tradition.* AECO 012, 1993, compact disc.

Art Ensemble of Chicago. *Sirius Calling.* Pi Recordings PI11, 2004, compact disc.

Art Ensemble of Chicago. *The Spiritual.* Freedom FLP 40108, 1972, 33⅓ rpm.

Art Ensemble of Chicago. *Les Stances à Sophie.* Pathé 2C 062–11365, 1970, 33⅓ rpm.

Art Ensemble of Chicago. *Swim—A Musical Adventure.* West Long Branch, N.J.: Kultur, 2001. DVD.

Art Ensemble of Chicago. *Thelonious Sphere Monk: Dreaming of the Masters Vol. 2.* DIW 846, 1991, compact disc.

Art Ensemble of Chicago. *The Third Decade.* ECM 1273, 1985, compact disc.

Art Ensemble of Chicago. *Tribute to Lester.* ECM 1808, 2003, compact disc.

Art Ensemble of Chicago. *Tutankhamun.* Freedom FLP 40122, 1974, 33⅓ rpm.

Art Ensemble of Chicago. *Urban Bushmen.* ECM 1211/12, 1982, 33⅓ rpm.

Art Ensemble of Chicago. *Urban Magic.* Musica Jazz MJCD 1150, 2003, compact disc.

Ayler, Albert. *Bells.* ESP Disk 1010, 1965, 33⅓ rpm.

Bass, Fontella. "Rescue Me"/"Soul of the Man." Checker 1120, 1965, 7" single.

Bass, Fontella, and Bobby McClure. "Don't Mess Up a Good Thing"/"Baby, What You Want Me to Do." Checker 1097, 1965, 7" single.

Bass, Fontella, and Bobby McClure. "You'll Miss Me (When I'm Gone)"/"Don't Jump." Checker 1111, 1965, 7" single.

Bowie, David. *Black Tie White Noise.* Virgin 7243 8 40987 2 8, 1993, compact disc.

Bowie, Lester. *The 5th Power.* Black Saint BSR 0020, 1978, 33⅓ rpm.

Bowie, Lester. *Gittin' to Know Y'All.* MPS 15269, 1970, 33⅓ rpm.

Bowie, Lester. *Numbers 1 & 2.* Nessa N-1, 1967, 33⅓ rpm.

Bowie, Lester. *The Odyssey of Funk & Popular Music.* Atlantic 83159–2, 1998, compact disc.

Bowie, Lester. *Serious Fun.* DIW 834, 1989, compact disc.

Bowie, Lester. *When the Spirit Returns.* Warner 8573–83471–2, 2000, compact disc.

Braxton, Anthony. *B-X0 NO-47A.* BYG/Actuel 529315, 1969, 33⅓ rpm.

Braxton, Anthony, Leroy Jenkins, and Leo Smith. *Silence.* Freedom FLP 40123, 1974, 33⅓ rpm.

Brown, James. "Cold Sweat—Part 1"/"Cold Sweat—Part 2." King 45–6110, 1967, 7" single.

Coleman, Ornette. *The Shape of Jazz to Come.* Atlantic 1317, 1959, 33⅓ rpm.

Davis, Miles. *Sketches of Spain.* Columbia CS 8271, 1960, 33⅓ rpm.

Delcloo, Claude, and Arthur Jones. *Africanasia.* BYG/Actuel 529306, 1969, 33⅓ rpm.

El'Zabar, Kahil. *The Ritual.* Sound Aspects SAS 011, 1986, 33⅓ rpm.

Favors, Malachi. *Natural & Spiritual.* AECO 003, 1978, 33⅓ rpm.

Fleming, King. *Stand By.* Argo LPS 4019, 1962, 33⅓ rpm.

Fontaine, Brigitte. *Brigitte Fontaine est . . . folle.* Saravah SH 10001, 1968, 33⅓ rpm.

Fontaine, Brigitte. *Comme à la radio.* Saravah SH 10006, 1970, 33⅓ rpm.

Geerken, Hartmut, and the Art Ensemble of Chicago. *Zero Sun No Point.* Leo CD LR 329/330, 2001, compact disc.

[Gravenites,] Nick "The Greek." "Whole Lotta Soul"/"Drunken Boat." Out of Sight 45–1, 1965, 7" single.

Hill, Andrew. *So in Love.* Warwick W 2002, 1959, 33⅓ rpm.

Jarman, Joseph. *As If It Were the Seasons.* Delmark DS-417, 1968, 33⅓ rpm.

Jarman, Joseph. *LifeTime Visions for the Magnificent Human*. Bopbuda Music 7786 3 14024 2 4, 2000, compact disc.

Jarman, Joseph. *Song For*. Delmark DS-410, 1967, 33⅓ rpm.

Jarman, Joseph. *Sunbound Volume One*. AECO 002, 1978, 33⅓ rpm.

Jarman, Joseph, and Anthony Braxton. *Together Alone*. Delmark DS-428, 1974, 33⅓ rpm.

Jarman, Joseph, and Don Moye. *Egwu-Anwu*. India Navigation IN 1033, 1978, 33⅓ rpm.

Kuti, Fela. *Fear Not for Man*. Afrodisia DWAPS 2035, 1977, 33⅓ rpm.

Kuti, Fela. *No Agreement*. Afrodisia DWAPS 2039, 1977, 33⅓ rpm.

Kuti, Fela. *Shuffering and Shmiling*. Coconut PMLP 1005, 1978, 33⅓ rpm.

Kuti, Fela. *Sorrow Tears and Blood*. Kalakuta KK 001, 1977, 33⅓ rpm.

Kuti, Fela. *Stalemate*. Afrodisia DWAPS 2033, 1977, 33⅓ rpm.

Lake, Oliver. *NTU: Point from Which Creation Begins*. Arista AL 1024, 1976, 33⅓ rpm.

Lyons, Jimmy. *Other Afternoons*. BYG/Actuel 529309, 1970, 33⅓ rpm.

Marsalis, Wynton. *Wynton Marsalis*. Columbia FC 37574, 1982, 33⅓ rpm.

Melis, Marcello. *The New Village on the Left*. Black Saint BSR 0012, 1977, 33⅓ rpm.

Mitchell, Roscoe. *Before There Was Sound*. Nessa NCD-34, 2011, compact disc.

Mitchell, Roscoe. *Congliptious*. Nessa N-2, 1968, 33⅓ rpm.

Mitchell, Roscoe. *L-R-G / The Maze / S II Examples*. Nessa N-14/15, 1978, 33⅓ rpm.

Mitchell, Roscoe. *Nonaah*. Nessa N-9/10, 1977, 33⅓ rpm.

Mitchell, Roscoe. *Old/Quartet*. Nessa N-5, 1975, 33⅓ rpm.

Mitchell, Roscoe. *Song for My Sister*. Pi Recordings PI03, 2002, compact disc.

Mitchell, Roscoe. *Sound*. Delmark DS-408, 1966, 33⅓ rpm.

Moncur, Grachan III. *New Africa*. BYG/Actuel 529321, 1969, 33⅓ rpm.

Moye, Don. *Sun Percussion Volume One*. AECO 001, 1975, 33⅓ rpm.

Moye, Don, and Enoch Williamson. *Afrikan Song*. AECO 3009, 1996, compact disc.

Murray, Sunny. *Big Chief*. Pathé 2C 062–10096, 1969, 33⅓ rpm.

Murray, Sunny. *An Even Break (Never Give a Sucker)*. BYG/Actuel 529332, 1970, 33⅓ rpm.

Murray, Sunny. *Hommage to Africa*. BYG/Actuel 529303, 1970, 33⅓ rpm.

Murray, Sunny. *Sunshine*. BYG/Actuel 529348, 1969, 33⅓ rpm.

Panou, Alfred. "Je suis un sauvage"/"Le moral nécessaire." Saravah SH 40014, 1970, 7" single.

Redman, Dewey. *Tarik*. BYG/Actuel 529334, 1970, 33⅓ rpm.

Rollins, Sonny. *Plus 4*. Prestige PRLP 7038, 1956, 33⅓ rpm.

Schiano, Mario, Don Moye, Marcello Melis, and Giancarlo Schiaffini. *Uncaged*. Splasc(H) CD H 357–2, 1991, compact disc.

Shepp, Archie. *Blasé*. BYG/Actuel 529318, 1969, 33⅓ rpm.

Shepp, Archie. *Live at the Panafrican Festival*. BYG/Actuel 529351, 1971, 33⅓ rpm.

Shepp, Archie. *Poem for Malcolm*. BYG/Actuel 529311, 1969, 33⅓ rpm.

Shepp, Archie. *Yasmina, a Black Woman*. BYG/Actuel 529304, 1969, 33⅓ rpm.

Shepp, Archie, and Chicago Beau. *Black Gipsy*. America 30 AM 6099, 1970, 33⅓ rpm.

Shepp, Archie, and Philly Joe Jones. *Archie Shepp & Philly Joe Jones*. America 30 AM 6102, 1970, 33⅓ rpm.

Silva, Alan. *Luna Surface*. BYG/Actuel 529312, 1969, 33⅓ rpm.

Smith, Wadada Leo. *Golden Quartet*. Tzadik TZ 7604, 2000, compact disc.

Index